ISBN 978-1-331-18906-0
PIBN 10156051

Forgotten Books is a registered trademark of FB &c Ltd.
Copyright © 2015 FB &c Ltd.
FB &c Ltd, Dalton House, 60 Windsor Avenue, London, SW19 2RR.
Company number 08720141. Registered in England and Wales.

For support please visit www.forgottenbooks.com

English
Français
Deutsche
Italiano
Español
Português

www.forgottenbooks.com

Mythology Photography **Fiction**
Fishing Christianity **Art** Cooking
Essays Buddhism Freemasonry
Medicine **Biology** Music **Ancient
Egypt** Evolution Carpentry Physics
Dance Geology **Mathematics** Fitness
Shakespeare **Folklore** Yoga Marketing
Confidence Immortality Biographies
Poetry **Psychology** Witchcraft
Electronics Chemistry History **Law**
Accounting **Philosophy** Anthropology
Alchemy Drama Quantum Mechanics
Atheism Sexual Health **Ancient History**
Entrepreneurship Languages Sport
Paleontology Needlework Islam
Metaphysics Investment Archaeology
Parenting Statistics Criminology
Motivational

THE

EARLY SCOTTISH CHURCH:

THE

ECCLESIASTICAL HISTORY OF SCOTLAND,

FROM

THE FIRST TO THE TWELFTH CENTURY.

BY THE

REV. THOMAS M‘LAUCHLAN, M.A., F.S.A.S.,

EDINBURGH.

EDINBURGH:

T. & T. CLARK, 38 GEORGE STREET.

LONDON : HAMILTON, ADAMS, & CO.   DUBLIN : JOHN ROBERTSON & CO.

MDCCCLXV.

PREFACE.

THIS volume is the result of an effort to fill up a blank in the Ecclesiastical History of Scotland. Monograms exist on periods and persons introduced throughout it; and also brief sketches of the period, in works on Scottish Church History, preparatory to the history of more recent and more prominent events, but no work exists whose sole object is to present the reader with a consecutive and connected view of the period embraced. This was to be regretted, considering the importance of the events recorded, and their influence upon the future state of the Church in Scotland. Inferences, not borne out by historical facts, were drawn from assumptions regarding the early Church, by parties of various, and even of contending views, and antiquity was cited in support of conclusions which in reality derived no aid from its testimony. The author has endeavoured to collect his facts from the most trustworthy sources, linking them in a continuous narrative. Although these sources are few, yet, when the straggling rays are gathered together, it is wonderful how much light they afford. Impartiality has been earnestly studied throughout, the writer having but one object in view, the discovery of truth in questions of national interest.

In pursuing the history of the Scottish Church, it was impossible to exclude a reference to the civil history of the country during the same period. It will be found, in consequence, that a sketch of the civil history of Scotland, brief, but it is hoped sufficiently comprehensive, accompanies that of the Church; while some questions are discussed connected with topography and the names of persons and tribes, which may add interest to the volume in the eyes of a growing class of readers.

The sources whence information has been sought in preparing this work, will be found on referring to the work itself. They come down to the most recent contributions made by writers of authority. The references might be more extensive, for there are few works on the subject which have not been consulted with some care; but the works cited are those whose authority stands highest on the various points discussed.

EDINBURGH, *Oct.* 1864.

CONTENTS.

CHAPTER IX.

CHAPTER X.

CHAPTER XI.

CHAPTER XII.

CHAPTER XIII.

CHAPTER XIV.

CHAPTER XV.

CHAPTER XVI.

CHAPTER XVII.

CHAPTER XVIII.

CHAPTER XIX.

THE EARLY SCOTTISH CHURCH.

CHAPTER I.

THE ROMAN POWER IN SCOTLAND.

Julius Cæsar landed in Britain about half a century before Christ. It has been said that he was induced to make his descent upon a country so distant from the great centre of the Roman empire, and separated from the rest of Europe by a wide and stormy strait, by the hope of obtaining pearls. If this be true, we are in-- debted to a motive apparently very inadequate for the establishment of Roman power and influence in our country, with all the consequences that resulted to the interests of civil, social, and religious progress. But were the motives inquired into which primarily actuated many of those great discoverers, of whose names the world is proud, it might be proved that they were of an order no higher than that which actuated the mighty Cæsar in his expedition against Britain. From the days of Cæsar Britain may be said to be known to history. Not that previous ages had no knowledge of its existence, for so early as about 320 B.C., in a treatise "De mundo," usually ascribed to Aristotle, although its authenticity is perhaps justly doubted, Britain and Ireland both appear under the respective names of Albion and Ierne. Little was known however beyond their mere existence. Herodotus, who wrote B.C. 440 years, says, "I have nothing certain to

relate concerning the western bounds of Europe. . . .
I know as little of the islands called *Cassiterides*, from
the tin which is thence imported among us." But Cæsar
was in Britain himself, and from him for the first time
we have authentic details of its condition. It is true he
was, in the case of the Britons, no conqueror. He found
the men of South Britain well nigh as indomitable as
Agricola did those of the north. Cæsar's history is a
record of battles won, but no record of a territory conquered. He had to retire foiled from his enterprise, and it
was ninety years afterwards ere Rome, under her Emperor Claudius, with his generals, Plautius, Vespasian,
and Titus, possessed permanently any portion of Britain;
nor were these possessions acquired until thirty pitched
battles had been fought with the native tribes. So famous
were their victories over those tribes held to be by the
conquerors, that the British General Caractacus was carried prisoner to Rome, and exposed in chains to the public
gaze, as a wonderful trophy of Roman courage and Roman
generalship. Nor is this surprising if we can give credence
to such statements as come down to us respecting those
battles, where we are told that in that fought with
Boadicea 70,000 of the Britons fell; and in that gained
by Suetonius in A.D. 61, the same tribes suffered a loss
of 80,000 men. Rome gradually extended northwards,
and the empire in Britain may be said to have reached
its farthest limits under Agricola in A.D. 81, during the
reign of the emperor Domitian, when Agricola fortified the
line between the Forth and Clyde, and was recalled out
of jealousy by the emperor, who appointed Lucullus to
succeed him. With the withdrawal of Agricola the Roman
empire in Britain again contracted, and the region between
the Tyne and the Forth was left to the possession of the
native tribes, its limit to the north being marked by the
wall of Hadrian.

About A.D. 144, the emperor Antoninus Pius sent Lollius Urbicus into Britain. Capitolinus in his life of Antonine tells us that by his generals he carried on many wars; and that by Lollius Urbicus he conquered the Britons, removing the northern barbarians by a turf wall. This is the wall erected between the Forth and the Clyde, almost in the line of the forts erected by Agricola sixty years before, consisting of a deep ditch, a breast-work of turf, and a Roman military road, the whole defended by a series of forts at regular intervals. By the Romans it was named the wall of Antonine in honour of the reigning emperor; but it presented a very inefficient obstacle to the restless and enterprising tribes beyond, who, in a short time after its erection, penetrated into every quarter of the neighbouring Roman territory.

Dio, quoted by Xiphilin, tells us (L. 72, c. 8) that "Commodus, who reigned about A.D. 180, had some wars with the barbarians . . . . But the British war was by far the greatest. Forasmuch as when the nations of this island had passed over the wall which ran between themselves and the Roman camp, and wasted many parts, the Roman commander, and the soldiers which he had with him being slain, Commodus, affrighted, sent against them Ulpius Marcellus, who affected the barbarians in Britain with the greatest and most grievous losses."

Lucius Septimius Severus became emperor in A.D. 193. Dio tells us (L. 76, c. 13) that in the beginning of his reign, not much more than half of Britain was in the hands of the Romans, and that Severus, wishing to reduce it all, entered Caledonia. "He felled forests, demolished high places, filled marshes with heaps of earth, and joined rivers by bridges." There are felled forests, demolished forts, heaps of earth, and bridges as ancient as the Roman period still existing in the north of Scotland, which may have been the work of Severus. But Severus failed to take permanent possession of the country. The incursion was apparently a raid, inflicting, it may be, no little damage on the native tribes, but bringing neither glory nor territory to the Roman empire. He satisfied himself with uniting the Tyne and the Solway anew by a wall, erected in the line of that of Hadrian, and fixing there the limit of Roman Britain. In his different conflicts with the Caledonians, Severus lost 50,000 men. He died at York A.D. 211.

For nearly a century after this little is heard of the Romans in Britain. They held possession of the territory up to the wall of Severus ; but although occasional memorials of their existence are to be found to the north, there is no evidence of any permanent occupation. Galgacus, the Caledonian general, is reported by Tacitus to have said, in his famous address to his troops previous to the battle of Mons Grampius : " We are the noblest people in all Britain, and situated in the very heart of it," and hitherto the Romans had found ample verification of the boast.

Constantius Chlorus, the father of Constantine the Great, was Emperor in Britain about A.D. 306. He had previously been governor under Diocletian, and extended no little favour to British Christians during the fierce persecution under the government of that emperor ; may not the conversion of Constantine be traced in some measure to the influence of a father who seems to have been himself almost a Christian ? Constantius obtained victories over the Scots and Picts, and was succeeded as emperor by his son, Constantine, who reduced those ancient and inveterate enemies to so low a state that they could give him no trouble, and his reign in Britain was one of outward peace and progress.

In the year 367 the Emperor Valentinian sent Theodosius into Britain. Ammianus Marcellinus relates, in (Lib. xxvii.) his History, that this able general found it necessary, from the number and power of the enemies of Rome in the north of Britain, to use policy for their reduction. He accordingly published a general amnesty to all who would lay down their arms, and thus brought some of them to submission. All the information we receive from Roman authors of the state of the inhabitants of Scotland at this period, indicates a numerous, brave, and energetic people. Even Agricola could say that it were no disgrace to him, were he to fall in battle, to fall among so brave a people. By a remarkable combination of skill and bravery, Theodosius again extended the Roman territory to the Forth and Clyde, and in honour of his master, Valentinian, he called the territory north of the wall of Severus by the name of Valentia. The poet Claudian calls this general, whose son afterwards became emperor, *Debellator Britanni Littoris*, "conqueror of the coasts of Britain," and of his victories it is he says :—

> " Maduerunt Saxone fuso
> Orcades, incaluit Pictorum sanguine Thule,
> Scotorum cumulos flevit glacialis Ierne."
> " The Orkney Isles were soaked
> With Saxon blood, Thule was warmed with that of the Picts,
> Icy Hibernia wept the heaps of her slain Scots."

The victories of Theodosius must have deeply impressed the minds of the Roman people ; none of their generals ever received a more marked ovation than he on his return to the imperial city. He restored the northern wall about A.D. 370.

Maximus, who usurped imperial dignity in Britain about A.D. 380, obtained some victories over the Scots and Picts, as we learn from Prosper of Aquitaine ; but passing over to France, as Bede relates, with the flower of the British youth, he laid South Britain open to the incursions of those enemies. To this draining

away of the men capable of bearing arms, to fight the
battles of imperial Rome, may in all probability be
traced the gradual weakening of the power of the native
Britons, and not to the influence either of luxury or of
cowardice, as has too often been alleged. Britain often
afforded the men by means of whom aspiring generals
strove to open their way towards the imperial purple.

After the death of Maximus at Aquileia, several
governors, among others Stilicho, ruled Britain under
the Roman emperors : the last being Constantine, who,
though a common soldier, was chosen emperor by his com-
rades. He was slain in Gaul about A.D. 409, and with
him, Bede tells us, closed the Roman dominion in Britain.
This happened about one year after the sacking of Rome
by Alaric and his warlike Goths. From this period the
Britons were left to their own resources. The Romans
advised them to reconstruct their wall ; which they did,
building it as formerly of turf ; but so feebly was it
defended that the Scots and Picts pulled them down
from their defences with hooks. Bede calls these Scots
and Picts transmarine nations, adding that he calls them
so, not because they dwelt out of Britain, but because
they were separated from the southern part of it by interjacent arms of the sea. These crossed the firths of Forth
and Clyde, broke down the wall, and as Bede informs us,
trampled down the Britons like ripe corn ; it was then
the latter sent their loud cry for help to Rome. Three
times did they detail their calamities, without correspond-
ing results ; "The groans of the Britons" they say, in
their last letter (Bede's Eccl. Hist., chap. xiii.) "are sent
to Etius," and this is one of those touching groans: "The
barbarians urge us toward the sea, and the sea pushes us
back to the barbarians ; betwixt them we have two kinds
of death before us,—either to have our throats cut, or to
be drowned." But the hands of the Romans were full of

their conflict with Attila and his Huns, and they could not aid their ancient subjects; famine succeeded the devastations of the Scots and Picts, and, pressed on every side, it is said that the Britons were compelled, in A.D. 449, to entreat the aid of the Saxons. Thus did the Roman dominion in Britain extend over a period of 499 years, closing with the third letter of the despairing Britons to Etius in A.D. 423.

In Scotland the Roman power became established under Agricola in A.D. 81; but it fluctuated for a long series of years, the province of Valentia being held, though not subdued, until the reign of Antonine, about A.D. 140. It was lost again, notwithstanding the energy and generalship of Severus, who was content to build his wall between the Tyne and Solway about A.D. 208. Theodosius again took firm possession of Valentia about A.D. 370, and it was then held for a period of about 50 years. Thus no part of Scotland was held so long or so uniformly as the English provinces. The tribes to the north were numerous and turbulent, and frequently broke into the Roman territory, notwithstanding Roman power and Roman precautions. At the same time, the imperial generals retaliated with severity and success; they, too, passed beyond the wall with their legions, and carried devastation into the territories of their restless foes. Agricola planted his camps far amidst the wilds of the present Highlands, and Severus found his way beyond the Spey, while his fleet circumnavigated the whole island. Still Rome had little to boast of her victories; and finally the Caledonians could rejoice in deliverance from their oppressors, and in the enjoyment of their national liberty.

At the same time, the occupation of the greater part of the island for 500 years, by a people like the Romans, must have wrought mighty changes; changes so great, indeed, that we can hardly form an adequate conception of them, though such remains as have been found of the Roman period show to how high a state of outward prosperity the people had attained. The civilization of Rome had been transferred to Britain, and seemed to have found a congenial soil. Cities were built, and adorned with the richest products of Roman art ; municipal government was organized ; Roman law was introduced and justice dispensed accordingly; money was coined and circulated, of which there is abundant evidence ; the art of war, including fortification and the training and arranging of troops after the Roman method, was introduced ; the Britons received a more general knowledge of letters, and were brought into contact with the literature of Rome (not that they were totally ignorant of literature before, for Cæsar tells us that the Gauls used the Greek letters, and that they sent their youth to Britain to be educated) ; roads were made, extending from Kent to the Moray Firth, levelled and paved for the use of chariots, at an immense expense of labour and money ; agriculture flourished, so much so that we learn from Zosimus (Lib. iii. p. 43, Ed. Bas.) that in the reign of Julian, 800 pinnaces were built in order to supply Germany with corn from Britain. But above all, Christianity travelled to Britain, and throughout Britain, as shall again be shown, in the footsteps of the Roman legions : the extension of the Roman power there, as elsewhere, being made subordinate to a great end. By means of it, and under the shelter of its eagles, the Christian faith spread over the then known world ; at times, no doubt, sorely persecuted and hardly used, but deriving from that very persecution much of its purity and its strength, and finally becoming co-extensive with the Roman empire. When that end was reached, the power raised for the purpose, like the scaffolding for the erection of a temple, was suffered to fall to pieces, and the retreating Roman legions left principles behind them of which they were in a large measure ignorant, but whose power was in reality infinitely greater and more lasting than their own.

To the Romans mainly does Britain owe the beginnings of her civilization. The 500 years of Roman occupancy were the most important in her early history. The Saxons brought nothing with them but the raw material; material as raw, at least, as it was in the case of the early Britons. They came to Britain in every sense to get, and not to give. For the Romans laid the foundation of our future progress as a nation, and to them we owe an amount of obligation which is due to none but themselves.

CHAPTER II.

THE NATIVE INHABITANTS DURING THE ROMAN OCCUPATION.

THE earliest notices we have of the native population of Scotland are from Tacitus. Julius Agricola was his uncle, and he wrote from his relation, the historian himself having never been in Britain. The war under Agricola, in Scotland, continued for six years, during which period he penetrated into the heart of the country, and must have come into contact with a large number of the natives. Tacitus calls the country Caledonia, and from him we first hear of the name (Tac. Vit. Agric., c. 26); the word, altogether unknown among the modern inhabitants, except as a Latin one, appearing to be an adaptation of a British name to the Roman tongue.[1] Dio, as already quoted, tells us of the forests felled by Severus ; and from other sources we gather that much of Scotland was at the time a forest. A dense thicket is in Welsh "celyd," in the plural number "celyddon ;" and "Celyddon" is to this day the British term for Caledonia, as preserved among the Cumbri of Wales. In Gaelic the synonyme of "Celyddon" is "Coilltean," and an author of no common ingenuity (Grant on the "Origin and Descent of the Gael,") suggests that the Gaelic "Coille" is the source of the Latin name. Many things, however, point rather to the British word, and

---

[1] The Romans being more immediately in contact with the southern Britons, would naturally derive from them their names of the surrounding localities, with their tribes. In addition to those in Britain, there can be little doubt that "Hibernia" is a mere adaptation of the British Ywerddon, pronounced Iwerthon.

none more distinctly than the fact that there are remains of the word existing in the topography of the country. The town of Dunkeld, said to have been once the capital of ancient Caledonia, is called, in the language of the native Highlander, "Dunchaillein," pronounced precisely as a Briton would pronounce his "Din Chelyddon," *the city of the forests.* In the heart of ancient Caledonia stands the celebrated mountain Schiehallion, the " hallion " pronounced as the "chaillein," in Dunkeld. Whatever the words are, they are identical in the language of the native, and, if "celyddon" be their origin, the one becomes the city, and the other the mountain of the forests, or of Caledonia.[1]

Tacitus uses no word for the inhabitants of Scotland but that applied to those of England—Britones; they are both equally Britons. All Agricola's battles in Scotland are with Britons, and in one case alone does he give us the name of a separate tribe, when he says that Agricola, at the close of his sixth campaign, led his troops into winter quarters among the Horestii. This is all we learn of the country from our earliest Roman authority ; the country itself is Caledonia, the people are Britons, and one tribe are called Horestii. Ptolemy, who wrote his Geography in A.D. 120, makes no mention of the Horestii. Tacitus might have misrepresented the meaning of his uncle, and might have mistaken a place for a people, for the Horestii may be represented by the modern Forres ; and certainly no part of Scotland could afford better winter quarters for a Roman army than the province of Moray, in which the town of Forres lies. This idea is confirmed by the statement, that from his quarters among the Horestii Agricola sailed with the Roman fleet to circumnavigate the island (Vit. Agric., c. 28). From

[1] Ritson points out cases in which the word " Caledonia " is associated with *silva* and *nemus*, both in Greece and in Britain.—Ritson's Cal., p. 8.

no point is it more likely that he would have set out than from some of the ports in the Moray Firth, the mouth of the Findhorn, or Burghead affording him most suitable points of departure.

The state of the country at the time of Agricola is indicated by several of the statements of Tacitus ; for instance, there were large cities beyond the Forth, and Agricola, we are told (Vit. Agric., c. 26, 27), fearing the movements of the more distant nations, explored those cities with his fleet. This could not mean cities which be himself had erected, and which were still in his hands, such as Victoria, on the Tay, the predecessor of modern Perth ; for Agricola, who was the first Roman that ever invaded Scotland, had only been six years in the country, and it is impossible to conceive that in that period cities had arisen, and "amplas civitates," *great cities*, as we learn from his biographer (Vit. Agric., c. 28), more especially among a hostile and warlike population. The necessary inference from the statement of Tacitus is, that among the natives of Caledonia in A.D. 81, there were large cities, indicating a certain measure of wealth and social organization, and that these cities lay upon the coast beyond the Forth, and could be explored by the Roman fleet. We learn also from the same writer (Vit. Agric., c. 28), that the people were well trained and armed for war ; in the battle-field they formed themselves into battalions ; the soldiers were armed with huge swords and short targets ; they carried darts which they hurled in showers on the enemy ; they had chariots and cavalry which careered through the field, filling the air with shouts. Such were the impressions conveyed to the mind of the Roman historian—impressions very different from those generally entertained in modern times.

The next writer from whom we derive any knowledge of early Scotland is Ptolemy, who composed his work on

Geography about A.D. 120, or sixty years after the period of Tacitus. The interval must have afforded to both the Greeks and Romans much information regarding the state of Britain. There was constant intercourse maintained, and facilities for ascertaining the condition of the people must have increased. Ptolemy's conceptions regarding the form of Scotland were not accurate in one point, for he made the country bend to the east at the firths of Clyde and Forth ; but otherwise he had a pretty correct idea of its shape. With him Caledonia is a forest,

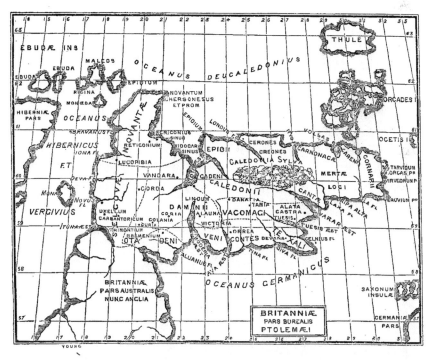

Caledonia silva; but for the first time we find the *Caledonii* or Caledonians as a people. The extent of their territory shows that he understood them to be the most powerful of the native tribes, while their position assigns to them the very heart of the country. To account for the different tribes whom he places along the coasts surrounding the great central nation of the Cale-

donians, is now utterly hopeless. It is questionable how
far the geographer himself had reliable information, and
if he had how far he could make use of it. If a Greek
were even now to visit the Scottish highlands, and hearing from the mouth of a native the names of the different clans in the Gaelic tongue, were he to write them
down in Greek, it is doubtful how far the Celt would
again recognise his own utterances when spoken from a
book; and besides, as if to show how little reliance can
be placed upon the nomenclature of Ptolemy, tribes
appear in his Geography for the first time of which
no trace can be discovered in the pages of any other
writer; they appear for a moment, and as suddenly
disappear with the Geography of Ptolemy.

Our next authority of any value is Dio Cassius, who
wrote his "Historia Romana" about A.D. 230, and was
thus the contemporary of Origen. The sources of information respecting Britain among Roman writers must
by his time have largely increased; one hundred and
fifty years had passed since the days of Agricola and
Tacitus, and the intercourse between Rome and her island
province had been all the time unbroken. In Dio's time
the Caledonians still exist. From him we learn (L. 75, c.
5) that "when the Caledonians prepared to defend
the Meatæ, and Severus was intent on the border war,
Verrius Lupus was obliged to purchase a peace from the
Meatæ at a great price." He calls the country Caledonia, and the inhabitants Caledonians, but he introduces
for the first time a people whom he calls the Meatæ. Of
these Ptolemy knew nothing; their name does not
appear at all in his map, nor are they mentioned by any
other author. The nearest approach to the name on
Ptolemy's map is that of the Mertæ,[1] who are placed

---

[1] Richard of Cirencester mentions the Meatæ; but as his compilation is of no
authority, being in fact the work of Dr. Bertram, the professed editor in last
century, no reference is made to it in these pages.

north of the present Sutherland. It has been repeatedly urged that the Meatæ were the inhabitants of that more level portion of Scotland which lay near the Roman wall, and that the origin of the word is the Gaelic " Magh," identical with the British " Maes," *a plain.* This may be true, but the name could not thus have been a distinctive one, and these Meatæ would just have been a portion of the Caledonians distinguished by the physical character of the country they occupied. The lowlands of Scotland are to this day called in Gaelic " Machair," and there is nothing improbable in the inhabitants of the " Machair," or as a Briton would call it, " Maesdir," *the plain country,* being latinized " Meatæ ;" this, however, gives us no new people ; the inhabitants of the country are still called Caledonii.

Thus, in A.D. 120, the Britones of Scotland became Caledonii, and continued to be so named by Roman authors in A.D. 230. There is nothing in this to indicate any change in the people, but simply that as the Romans were becoming better informed, they were, like the natives, able to distinguish between the rest of the inhabitants of Britain and the inhabitants of the "Celyddon," or forests. It is extremely doubtful whether the Romans, in any of the instances adduced, gave the real name by which the people described themselves ; or at any rate, in so far as they made use of native names, they would, as already said, adopt those of the Britons with whom they were most familiar, and who at that time extended at least as far as the Roman wall. Of the language of a Gaelic-speaking race to the north and west they could have little opportunity of knowing anything, and could therefore have little knowledge of their native names.

Dio relates an anecdote (L. 76) which indicates a low state of morality among the Caledonian tribes. Severus

had made stringent laws against adultery, and persons
guilty of this crime were severely punished. Upon
which the wife of Argentocoxus, a Caledonian, said to
Julia Augusta, the empress, who taunted her with the
gross laxity of her countrymen, that "they had open
intercourse with the best men," &c.; indicating an entire
disregard for the marriage relation. It is somewhat
difficult to believe this story, suggestive as it is of a state
of barbarism not consistent with much else that we learn
of the condition of the early Caledonians; but Dio
gives it, from which it appears that it was believed at
Rome. Dio calls the Caledonian lady a Britoness, thus
using the term Briton and Caledonian indiscriminately.

Up to the period of Dio Cassius, then, about A.D. 230,
we hear but of one great people in Scotland, the Caledonii, with the apparently subordinate tribes of the
Horestii and Meatæ, and those named by Ptolemy.
These all receive from Roman writers the generic appellation of Britons. The subordinate tribes named are
supposed by some writers to be the people afterwards
named Picts. However this may be, it is worthy
of remark, that in A.D. 81 we learn from Tacitus of
the existence of only two Scottish tribes the Caledonii and the Horestii, if the latter be a tribe; and in
A.D. 230 there are still the two as related by Dio, the
Caledonii and the Mcatæ:[1] there is no mention as
yet among Roman writers of either Scots or Picts. The
older Irish historians maintained that the Scots came to
Scotland from Ireland before the Christian era. We
have not the slightest evidence of this from Roman
authors; on the contrary, the name does not appear

---

[1] When the light of history first breaks in distinctly upon Scotland, *two* nations,
the Scots and Picts, still occupy the country. Should this be lost sight of in
studying our earlier History?

in connection with either Scotland or Ireland down to the
end of the third century.

In A.D. 296 we have the first mention of Picts by
Roman authors. Eumenius, the orator, in his oration
in praise of Constantius Chlorus, for his victory over the
usurper Alectus, says : *Ad hoc natio etiam tunc rudis, et
soli Britanni Pictis modo et Hibernis assueta hostibus
adhuc seminudis, facile Romanis armis, signisque cesse-
runt.* 'Besides, the nation was rude at that time, and
the Britons, accustomed only to the Picts and Irish,
half-naked enemies, readily submitted to the Roman
arms and ensigns.' About A.D. 309 the same orator, in
a panegyric on Constantius, pronounced before his son
Constantine, the emperor, says of Constantius : "That
he did not deign to acquire the woods and marshes of
the Caledonians and other Picts (Caledonum, aliorumque
Pictorum), nor even Ireland, near at hand, nor farthest
Thule." From this writer it would appear that the
Britons had had conflicts with the Picts previous to the
coming of Julius Cæsar to Britain ; for the orator contrasts Constantius with that emperor ; it would appear,
also, that the Picts were semi-nude, a description very
applicable to the modern Highlander in his native dress.
The chief inference, however, from Eumenius is, that a
portion of the inhabitants of Britain were called Picts in
his day.

Ammianus Marcellinus, the historian, flourished from
about A.D. 350 to A.D. 380, and from him we learn, that
in the tenth consulate of Constantius, and the third of
Julian, that is, about A.D. 363, the Scots and Picts broke
the peace, and harassed the country near the Roman
boundary. Onward from this time till the middle of
the ninth century, we have the Picts filling up a large
portion of our Scottish history, and occupying a large
portion of our Scottish territory. They then disappear ;

B

they appear suddenly about the year 296, and they disappear as suddenly in 843, the tradition being that the whole race was extirpated by the Scottish king, Kenneth; a strange history, affording, if true, the only instance known of a whole people suddenly extirpated, leaving hardly a trace of their past existence.   Fordun's words are : *Sic quidem, non solum reges et duces gentis illius deleti sunt, verum etiam stirps, et genus, adeo cum idiomatis sui lingua defecisse legitur.*   ' So that not only were the kings and chiefs of that nation destroyed, but we read that the very race itself, with its language, utterly perished.'

[1] Scotichron, Lib. iv. c. 4.

CHAPTER III.

THERE is a remarkable difference of view in the discussions that have taken place regarding the Picts among writers on early Scottish history, and a vast amount of learning has been brought into requisition without apparently settling much. A reference to the pages of Ritson and Pinkerton will put the student in possession of most of what has been said on the subject, from which he may, by a comparison of contending opinions, come to some conclusion of his own more or less satisfactory. Taking a few of the leading and incontrovertible facts of the case, it appears that early Roman writers considered the name as derived from *pictus* 'painted.' Claudian, who wrote about A.D. 400, very soon after the name appears, says—

—— " Nec falso nomine Pictos."

" Not named Picts (or painted), without cause."

He also relates of them, that—

—— " ferroque notatas
Perlegit exanimes Picto moriente, figuras."
" He discovers lifeless figures traced with iron,
Upon the dying Pict."

Ritson calls this a conceit of the poet, on what ground it is difficult to say, unless as a conceit of the critic ; for Cæsar tells us that all the Britons painted themselves with woad, which produced a blue colour, and gave them

a more horrible aspect. Nothing is more probable, than
that this is the origin of the name, for there is not a fragment of evidence to prove that there ever was a people in
Scotland called Picts by themselves, or by the other natives
of the island.   There is not an approach to the name in
the native language of the Gael of either Ireland or Scotland; although the Welsh speak of Gwyddyl Ffichti, or the
Pictish Gael, indicating that in their estimation the Picts
were Gael, and borrowing probably the distinctive Ffichti
from the Latin.   Among the Irish annalists we find
reference to a people called Cruithne,[1] occupying a portion
of Ulster, and forming a powerful kingdom in Scotland,
who are generally understood to have been the Roman
Picti. The name Cruithne, said, in the Chronicle appended
to Innes' Critical Essay, to be derived from Cruithne their
first king, is not now known among the Scottish Celts.
It is to be found, however, in their topography : upon the
banks of Loch Torridon, in Wester Ross, is a place called,
in Gaelic, Airidh nan Cruithneach, or the pasture-ground
of the Cruithne ; upon the banks of the Spean in Lochaber
is Cruithneachan, a name formed of " Cruithneach," and
the common topographical Celtic affix " an ;" in the Tay
above Dunkeld, there is an island called Innis nan Cruithneach.   This name, then, was known among the Gael both
of Scotland and Ireland.   In the Irish annals it is inter-
changed apparently with that of Piccardich, which is said
to be applied to the Southern Picts, so that there is reason
to believe that the Roman name of Picts is applied in
them to the Cruithne ; the Picts being, however, simply

---

[1] Mr. Robertson (*Scot. under her early Kings*, II: App. I.) suggests that this
word means *painted,* but there is no authority for such an interpretation.
The word "cruinn" in both British and Gaelic means *round,* used sometimes
in the sense of *handsome,* from the British root " crw," *a curve.* " Cruinne"
also means *the earth,* from which it appears that the Celt believed the earth
to be globular. The word "cruithneachd" in Gaelic means *wheat,* and it has
been argued that the Cruithne were agriculturists as distinguished from the
Scots who were hunters and shepherds.

the painted people of the Romans, the name originating probably in the fact that they continued to paint after the other Britons had ceased from the practice under the influence of Roman civilization.

Alongside of the Picts, in the pages of Ammianus Marcellinus, about the year 360, appear the Scots. This is about 143 years before what is usually called the Dalriadic settlement, or the settlement of the Irish Scots in Argyllshire. The name Scot, like that of Pict, is, in its present form, purely a Roman one, and this may in some measure account for other names given to the Scottish tribes.[1] It is entirely unknown by either the Irish or Scottish Celt, except in so far as he has received it from without ; it has no place in his own language— an important consideration in discussing its historical import, as it shews that its value historically is much less than is usually imagined. The name appears to be a corruption of Scyth, the c being pronounced hard, and appears to have originated in the common idea among the Romans, that these people had passed over from Scythia, their usual name for all Northern Europe. Gildas, who wrote about the year 550, says, that the Scots and Picts crossed the Scythian[2] valley into the Roman Province, meaning obviously the great valley which crosses the kingdom between the Firths of Forth and Clyde ; he uses "Scythicum" manifestly as synonymous with "Scoticum." In the case of "Iona," Dr. Reeves has shewn (Vit. Col. App.) how the name has assumed its present form ; beginning with the ancient Celtic Hy, which, when

[1] It has been already said, that the Romans adopted their names of persons and places in Britain from the native Britons, with whom they were in constant communication. The British name for a Scot is Y-sgut, the same name which is applied to a Scythian; but in this case the Briton seems to have been debtor to the Roman.

[2] Ritson says it should be Tethicum, from Tethys, the Irish sea. It is easy to deal in this manner with any ancient authority. "Vallis" is never applied to the sea.

used in Latin in connection with *insula* 'an island,' became an adjective, the word assumed the form of Iova· inaccurate transcribers mistook the *v* for an *n*, and the word settled into Iona, which in due time became the name of the island, with numerous fictions clustering around its history. Thus do words grow. Porphyry in his argument against Christianity, written about A.D. 267, uses "Scyth-icæ" for "Scotticæ" gentes, *Scythic* for *Scottish* nations. Ritson says that only some copies have this peculiarity; if so, the process of change is manifest. (Ann. of the Caled. II. 1). If the Latin "Scythus," however, be objected to, the root of "Scot" may be found in the Greek "Σχυθος." The Greeks had no word for Scot, but called all northerns Σχυθοι. Nennius was quite of the opinion that the Scot was simply the Scythian, for he tells us (Hist. chap. 8), "that the Scythians, that is the Scots, in the 4th century after the creation, obtained Ireland." Ritson, who strenu-ously opposed the idea of the Scots being Scythians, more as an antagonist of Pinkerton than aught else, says, "that the remark of Reinerius Rinectius 'that the name Scythian survives in that of Scot,' is a false and absurd conceit," without affording the slightest proof of the charge. The Scots were not Scythians in the sense in which Pinkerton strove to make them so, but there is little doubt that the name "Scot" is a mere adaptation of that of Scythian to a people whom the Romans found inhabiting a northern country. The name is altogether a Roman one, is entirely unknown to the people so called, and except on the theory stated, cannot be accounted for in any plausible way. The attempts to derive it from *Scuit* and other Celtic words equally intelligible, are as unworthy of respect as the ancient story of the descent of the Scots from Scota, a daughter of one of the Egyptian Pharaohs. It may be well here to observe that "Scots" is not the name by which the inhabitants of Ireland first appear in history ; in the passage already quoted from Eumenius, they are called Hiberni. Nor does it appear that the term Scots is first of all applied to the people of Ireland. Bede (Lib. 1, c. 3), as already cited, says most distinctly, in referring to the ancient accounts of the inroads of the Scots and Picts upon the Britons, that "though called transmarine nations, it is not because they inhabited a different island, but because they were separated from the Britons by interjacent arms of the sea." This points distinctly to the Firths of Forth and Clyde, and shews that Bede believed the Scots to have inhabited Britain long before A.D. 503, the period of the Dalriadic immigration, although he afterwards relates the occurrence of that immigration. But for the fact of their existence in Scotland at this early period, we have abundant evidence from Roman authors ; so much, indeed, that it does not admit of dispute. That Ireland is said by Claudian to "mourn her slaughtered Scots" is true, nor is it deniable that the term "Scots" was at an early period applied to the inhabitants of Ireland ; yet every reliable testimony that can be gathered from ancient writers on the subject goes to shew, that so early as A.D. 360, the Picts inhabited the east and north of Scotland, while a people called then for the first time Scots, inhabited the west ; and that these peoples were in close and lasting alliance against the Romans and the Provincial Britons. It is hardly necessary to discuss the statement advanced by some writers that, at that period, the Scots and Picts both made their appearance in Scotland for the first time ; the Picts from Scandinavia, or elsewhere, the Scots from Ireland. If it be true, what had become of the Caledonians, the ancient antagonists of Agricola and Severus ? Had they perished, like the Picts in after ages ? or, though capable of resisting the Roman arms with success, were they overwhelmed by this irruption of Barbarians from the north and west? This theory, although maintained by so able a scholar as Ritson, is altogether untenable in the face of arguments drawn from such considerations as these. Were there no other argument, indeed, such mighty changes among their near neighbours could not have taken place without the knowledge of the Romans; and if they knew of them, it is impossible to conceive that we should be left entirely without notice of them in the pages of their contemporary historians.

The conclusion is irresistible, that the ancient Caledonians, as the Romans became better acquainted with their social state, resolve themselves into Picts and Scots, as the Picts resolve themselves soon after into Dicaledones and Vecturiones; not that they were altogether different nations, but distinguished by the country they occupied, their peculiar dialect, and the colour of their dress. The Dicaledones were, from the name, manifestly a part of the Caledonians, although said to be a section of the Picts, and the Picts and Scots are so uniformly associated in early history, that, while there may have been subordinate differences between them, so as to account for the difference of name, as between the inhabitants of different counties of Scotland now, they were originally the same people. Bede (Hist. c. 12) says, that these two nations are separated from the Britons by two arms of the sea, the one running in far and broad from the Eastern, the other from the Western ocean. Further, he mentions two cities, one on each of those arms, without distinguishing them as belonging to one or other of the nations. The one, he says, lay in the eastern firth, the other on the western;

the former, called Giudi, supposed to be Inchkeith,[1] the other Alcluith, supposed to be the modern Dunbarton or Dunbriton, called in Gaelic to this day Dun Bhreatuin, or the city of the Britons. He speaks of those cities as if they appertained to either nation.

But let us here take a look into the contents of a volume which has hitherto been very little studied, but which is likely to shed some light upon the discussion now on hand—the modern topography of Scotland. This topography exhibits many curious phenomena—phenomena which shed a steady and unerring light upon the past history of the nation, although often in danger of being misapplied. The topography of England presents us with the footprints of the Briton, the Roman, the Teuton, as distinctly as if formed yesterday, and in like manner, Scotland presents us with the footprints of the Briton, the Gael, the Roman, and the Norseman, each as clear and distinct as if the people had but just moved away ; and the depth of these indicates with almost historical accuracy the extent of the sway which each people exercised in the land. The Romans left few of their footprints, because their sway was short and unsteady. The topography of the west and south-west, bears testimony to the power and long occupancy of the Gael. In the north and south-east, we learn of the dominion of the Northman, and over great sections of the country we see unmistakeable marks of the existence and long-continued sway of the Briton. The Teutonic topography being the more recent, indeed coming very much within the Historic

---

[1] The Gaelic name of Inchkeith is Innis Ché, the latter word easily changable into Giudi. The same word Cé appears in Dalché, the modern Dalkeith. Have we any memorial here of Cé, the ancient Pictish prince, one of the seven sons of Cruithne, of whom Mr. Robertson, in his recent most valuable History of Scotland under her early kings, says we have no relic; or does the name rather appear in Beinu Ché, Benachie, in Aberdeenshire. The British " Giudi " comes very near the Gaelic " Fiu," the name for Fife. Did Bede mistake a town for a province ?

period, may be put aside, as not indicating to any extent
the state of the Scottish population at the period under
review ; nor need we advert to that of the Roman ; but
let us look for a little at the rest of our Scottish topography, and see what is to be learned from it respecting
the ancient inhabitants. South of the Forth, and onwards to the Tweed, British words are found in considerable numbers. Such streams as Blackadder, Whiteadder,
Leader, contain distinctly the British *dwfr* or *dur*,
'water.' The modern " Yester " in East Lothian, is in old
charters called *Ystrad*, which is just the British word for
'strath,' the Gaelic 'valley.' Near the coast is Aberlady
anciently Aberlessic (Joc. Life of Kentigern), containing the
British 'Aber.' Inland is Tranent or 'Trenant,' a common
name in Wales ; " the town on the stream." Then there
are Traquair, and Traprain, both having the British
'Tre,' the equivalent for the Gaelic 'Baile,' or the
Saxon 'Town.' In West Lothian is Abercorn, anciently
Abercurnig. Inland are the Calders, deriving their name
from a stream, Calder being one of the commonest
British names for a stream, ranging from Lancashire to
the Moray Firth, having the British *dwfr* in its formation. In all this region the British names appear alongside of a few Gaelic ones, such as Drem, Garvald in the
east, and Strathbrock in the west, overborne by a multi-
tude of those derived from Teutonic sources. Still the
British element is clear and unmistakeable. On crossing
the Forth British names still appear ; nowhere more
clearly than in the name of the Ochil hills, where the
British *uchel*, 'high,' cannot be mistaken. In Fife,
although its topography is almost purely Gaelic, we find
several 'Abers,' as Aberdour, Abercrombie, with numerous 'Pits' and 'Pittens,' as Pittenweem, Pittencrief,
&c., indicating the existence of a British population. In
Perth and Forfar the British names are still more numerous,

but not extending west beyond the east end of Loch Earn.
There is a Gowrie, the name identical with the Gowery of
Montgomery. We have Lanrick, identical with the Welsh
Llanerch. Trinafour, of Perthshire, is synonymous with
the Balfour of Fife, having the British 'Tre.' The Tay
is the Taw in Wales. Comrie is derived from the British
Cwm, 'a hollow,' which enters into the formation of
many words in our Scottish topography. The 'Pits'
and 'Pittens' of Forfarshire are numerous. As we
travel northwards these British names multiply. We
have 'Pens,' and 'Abers,' and 'Pits' in abundance, on
through Kincardine and Aberdeenshires. There is a
Lbanbryde in Morayshire, just what a Welshman would
call St. Bridget's Church. The Dee of Aberdeenshire is
synonymous with the Dee of Cheshire and of Wales. In
Nairn and Inverness-shires British words are numerous.
There are several Calders among the streams, and 'Abers'
applied to places at their mouths. The 'Pits' are frequent along the valley of the Spey. To the south of
Loch Ness, in the valley of Stratherrick, two 'Tres'
appear, apparently much out of place, amidst a mass of
pure Gaelic names on every hand. The farthest west
'Aber' is Aberchalder, on Loch Oich, in the line of the
Caledonian Canal. To the north, British names cannot be
so clearly traced beyond the Moray Firth, where a Norse
nomenclature occupies the same relation to the Gaelic
names that the British do to the south. There are few
names that can with any confidence be called British to
the north of the Moray Firth. Returning to the south,
British names appear across the whole kingdom. The
name Ochiltree, the British *Uchel Tre,* or 'high town,'
in Ayrshire, is unquestionable, while in such names
as Ecclefechan, *the little church*, and others in the
same neighbourhood, the British element is equally
distinct, a fact in no way surprising in what was

the territory of the Strathclyde Britons. British names, then, appear in the south-west, in Galloway, Ayr, Dumfries, &c., amidst an overwhelming mass of Gaelic names. In the south-east, Berwick, Roxburgh, and the Lothians, they appear amidst an equal number of Teutonic names. They crop out among the Gaelic names of Fife, and the Gaelic and Scandinavian names of Aberdeen, Moray, and the Eastern Highlands. But beyond the Dorsum Britanniæ, or great mountain range that divides Scotland, from the Caledonian valley to the valley of the Clyde, there is not a trace to be discovered of a British nomenclature; not one 'Aber,' or 'Pit,' or 'Com,' or 'Tre,' or 'Lan,' but a purely Gaelic topography, mixed with one of Scandinavian extraction. The only approach to a British word is in the stream called Neant, which flows from the south into Loch Etive, and which does resemble the British *nant*, 'a stream.'[1] The statement can be verified by an ample induction of facts, that throughout the whole of the south of Scotland, and along the east coast as far as the Moray Firth, and inwards as far as the west end of Loch Oich, and the summit level of the kingdom terminating at Dunbarton, there are numerous British names in every district; while to the west of those boundaries, on the

---

[1] It has been maintained that the word "Aber" is not peculiar to the British language; but it has been the misfortune of Scottish topography that it has been so little studied hitherto by parties versant with the different dialects of the Celtic tongue. Much has been done by students of the language from without, but mingled with much that strikes a native Scot as untenable and absurd. Gaelic knows none of the topographic forms quoted above as peculiar to the Briton. It has been urged that the British "Pen" is the Gaelic "Ben," and that thus a British word pervades the topography of all Scotland; but the British "Pen," *a head*, is not the Gaelic "Beinn." *a hill*, but the Gaelic "Ceann," *a head*. It is sufficiently well known that the *p* of the Briton interchanges with the Gaelic *c* hard or *k*, whence, the British "Pwy," *who*, is the Gaelic "Co," "Plant," *children*, is "Clann," "Pimp," *five*, is "Cuig." This principle runs through the texture of both languages, and at once excludes "Beinn" from being the representative of the British "Pen." There is a British word "Cwn," which more probably represents the Gaelic "Beinn" or "Ben."

other hand, there is not one, and there are, apparently, very few to the north. A careful survey does not present one unmistakeable British term in the whole topography of the county of Argyll. These facts are significant. They indicate one of two things—either that the one race overpowered the other in the east, and superinduced a new nomenclature over the old throughout the country,—that we have in fact two successive strata of Celtic names, the Gaelic underlying the British, which is by no means impossible ; or, what is more likely, that the Pictish people were a people lying midway between the Gael and the Cymri—more Gaelic than the Cymri, and more Cymric than the Gael. This is precisely the character of the old Pictish topography ; it is a mixture of Gaelic and Cymric ; and if the language of the people was like their topography, it too was a language neither Gaelic nor Cymric, but occupying a middle space between them, indicating the identity of the races at some distant period, although they afterwards became rivals for the possession of the land. This theory would account for the tradition referred to by Bede, that the Picts were a foreign race, who came in as aggressors and settled in Scotland : it will account also for the fact that the Pictish language is given as a distinct one in Bede's enumeration of the languages of Britain. The topography of the Pictish territory is so peculiar, and so marked in its difference from that of the ancient Scottish territory to the west, that there must be some reason for it, and that suggested is the only one that seems to accord with the conditions of the case. The west of Scotland must have been early occupied by a purely Gaelic race. The Pictish aggression seems to have spent its strength ere it reached it ; and while in the one quarter the races may have anew amalgamated, in the other there was no mingling. Excluding the more recent Norse, there is not a remnant of a word in Argyleshire to show that there ever was any language spoken there but pure Gaelic ; nor does its topography give any evidence of an Irish origin. Lorn (Latharn) is indeed said to be a name derived from Loarn mòr, the son of Erc. This will be credible when it is shown that the same word in Caithness pronounced "Latheron" in English, but in Gaelic "Lorn" (Latharn) is shown to be derived from the same source. It is needless to point to the Irish Larne as being the same word as both the Scottish Lorns.

About the Roman period, then, so far as can be gathered from existing evidence, the west of Scotland, from the Clyde to Loch Linnhe, was inhabited by a people whom the Romans called Scots, whom both history and topography shew to have spoken the Gælic language ; the south-west, including Galloway, Ayr, Kirkcudbright, and Dumfries, was inhabited by a Pictish population, whom topography distinctly identifies with the Picts of the North. From Cumberland to Dunbarton there existed a more purely British population, called afterwards the Strathclyde Britons ; to the east, occupying the Lothians, Berwick, and Roxburgh shires, was also a British race, but to a large extent Romanized as the consequence of a more decided Roman occupation ; while to the east and north was another section of the Pictish people, speaking a Gallocymbric tongue, the Gaelic element largely predominating beyond the Moray Frith. These are precisely the facts which topography brings to light, and they are in perfect accordance with any historical testimony of value we possess. They are in accordance also with the theory of a British wave of population following the Gaelic and pressing it west and north, mingling with it along the borders ; while this wave was followed by the Roman, and that again by the Teutonic, whether the earlier Frisians, or the later Saxons, Danes, and Normans. The Scottish conquest, as it is called, in the 9th century, gave complete predominance in large sections of the country to the Gaelic language, no difficult matter where the difference was merely dialectic, and where, no doubt, the Gaelic had made much progress for a long time previously as the language of the Church. It was the language of Iona, and as such would be held sacred over the Pictish territory. The Book of Deer shews that the language of ecclesiastics in Aberdeenshire in the 11th century was the Gaelic.

CHAPTER IV.

FROM the inhabitants of Scotland, and their condition during the period of the Roman occupation, we are led to view the entrance among them of the Christian faith, —that faith by whose influence more than by any other, the future progress of the country was governed, and its present condition attained. At the time of Julius Cæsar the religion of the Britons was what is usually called Druidism. This system appears to have had more or less in common with the heathenism of the rest of Europe. It had its priests divided into classes, one of those being the bards or poets, whose power over the Celtic races continued to a recent period. It had its mysteries and its sacrifices, the latter being said at times to consist of human victims. Druidism is said to have acknowledged a Supreme Being, whose name was synonymous with the Eastern Baal,[1] and if so, was visibly represented by the sun, and such remnants of the ancient worship as are still traceable in the language of the people, would indicate its having been a species of sun-worship. To this day the four leading points of the compass bear, in the terms which designate them among the Gael, marks of this.

[1] Origen, as quoted by Usher, De Brit. Eccl. Prim., p. 2, says that the name applied by them to the Deity was Andraste or Andate, the Goddess of Victory, very likely the Eastern Ashtoreth or Astarte, while Dio Cassius states that they worshipped Apollo and Diana. Gildas informs us that they held errors in common with other heathen nations, and had more magic arts than even the Egyptians; besides that they gave divine honours to mountains and hills, and rivers. He also states that some of the lineaments of these superstitions were traceable in his day both within and without the deserted walls.

The east is *ear*, like the Latin *oriens*, from the Gælic *eiridh*, ' to rise ;' the west is *iar*, ' after,' used also as a preposition ; the south is *deas*, and the north *tuath ;* and it is in the use of the two last terms that the reverence for the solar luminary chiefly appears. *Deas*, ' the south,' is in all circumstances *right ;* it is the *right* hand, which is easily intelligible, from the relation of that hand to the south when the face looks eastward ; and it is expressive of whatever is otherwise *right*. *Deas* also means complete, trim, ready ; whatever is *deas*, or southerly, is just as it should be. *Tuath*, ' north,' is the very opposite. *Tuathaisd* is a ' stupid fellow ;' *Tuathail* is ' wrong ' in every sense : south and north, then, as expressed in the words *deiseal* and *tuathail* are, in the Gælic language, the representatives of right and wrong. Thus everything that is to move prosperously among many of the Celts, must move sunwise : a boat going to sea must turn sunwise ; a man or woman immediately after marriage, must make a turn sunwise. In many parts of the Scottish Highlands there are spots round which the dead are borne sunwise in their progress towards the place of sepulture : all these being relics, not of a Christian but of a Pagan age, and an age in which the sun was an object of worship. There are relics of fire-worship too ; certain days are named from fire-lighting. *Beallteine*, or ' the first day of summer,' and *saimhtheine*, ' the first day of winter,'—the former supposed to mean the fire of Baal or Bel, the latter closing the saimhré, or summer period of the year, and bringing in the geamhré, or winter period, are sufficient evidence of this. There are places in Scotland where within the memory of living men the *teine eigin*, or ' forced fire,' was lighted once every year by the rubbing of two pieces of wood together, while every fire in the neighbourhood was extinguished in order that they might be lighted anew from this sacred

source. These relics of an extinct superstition are in
some measure indications of its character. Druidism
would seem to have had more in common with the religion of Zoroaster and the Magi than with any other.

It has been maintained that Druidism never existed
in Scotland, and this view is at present held by not a
few of the students of our national antiquities. The
opponents of the view have been in the habit of maintaining that the frequent occurrence of the word *draonaich*
in our topography is sufficient evidence of the truth of
their own conclusion. It has been said that Iona was a
seat of the Druids previous to the coming of Columba;
and the existence of a spot in the island called *cladh nan
Draoineach,* usually translated "the 'Druids' burying
place," is cited in proof of it; but there is no general
agreement among Celtic scholars that *draonaich* means
Druids. Mr. Grant, in his ingenious work on the "Origin
and descent of the Gael," maintains (p. 174) that it
means 'agriculturists,' and cites numerous instances of
its being so applied. Nor have we any very high authority for the opposite interpretation. This we know, however, from Adomnan (Vit. Col. Reeves, p. 73) that
there were *magi* (Heathen priests) in the palace of
Brude, near Inverness, and that the remnants of the
popular faith referred to above and still existing, indicate a religion having much in common with what we
know of that of the rest of Britain. It is not improbable,
however, that the religion of Roman Britain felt the influence of Pagan Rome, and it may not be easy to discover how far the religious views of our Pagan ancestors,
as they have come down to us, received an impression
from that quarter. The relics that have come to us,
fossilized amidst our forms of speech, are perhaps those
that have reached us least moulded by any such influence.

There is a Gaelic MS., still existing, from which the following quotation is made in the report furnished to the Highland Society of Scotland on Ossian's Poems :—*Luid iaromh Colum Cille ?fecht ann gu ri Cruithnech eadhon gu Bruidi mac Milcoin agus do dunadh dorus in dunaigh ?fris, agus do foscuil fo choir glais iarnuidhi an baile tre urnaidhthi Colum cille. Tainic iar sin mac in righ eadhon Maelcu agus a drui do friththagra fri Colum cille tre geintlighecht.*[1] 'Columba went once of a time to the king of the Cruithne (Picts) viz., to Brude son of Milcoin, and the door of the dun (castle) was shut against him, and the iron locks of the town were opened readily through the prayers of Columba. Then Maelcu the king's son came with his Druid to resist Columba through Paganism.' This MS. is of the 12th or 13th century, if not earlier, and from it we gather that the belief was then that there were Druids in Scotland, that they were priests in attendance in the royal palace, and that they strenuously resisted Columba. Upon the whole there is reason to believe that Scotland had her magi, who practised certain magical arts called by succeeding Christian writers *Geintlighecht,* or Paganism, and that these were of the order of Druids, as described by Cæsar in his Gallic war (Book vi. 13), although there might be national distinctions between those of Gaul and those of different parts of Britain.

There is one feature about this ancient superstition which is worthy of being recorded with approval ; it was free of intolerance : there is no record of any British missionary ever having been a martyr. It has

---

[1] The family name Mailchon, which was the name of both King Brude's father and son, seems to have been *Mialchoin,* the genitive of *Mialchu,* 'a greyhound.' The name of the grandson, Maelcu or Mialchu, is in the nominative case.

been well said that there were numerous confessors, but no martyrs. The Paganism of civilized Rome had its thousands of victims among the early Christians ; the Paganism of uncivilized Britain had not so much as one ; and it would be well if the same could be said of some of the forms of Christianity which succeeded. There is indeed, as will be seen in the sequel, one martyrdom recorded in the early Scottish Church : Donnan perished in Eigg by the hands of the natives, to whom he had gone to preach the Gospel ; but, from such records of the event as we have, he would seem to have perished as a victim to the cupidity of a native chieftainess, and not to the intolerance of the native superstition.

As already said, early Christianity in Scotland would appear to have followed the footsteps of the Roman legions. The Scottish province was not held so long nor so firmly as the English provinces, but during the 400 years of Roman sway, broken as it was, opportunity was afforded for sowing the seeds of mighty changes. The Romans in the beginning of the 5th century retired from the field, but seed had been sown which was destined to yield abundant fruit long after Rome had ceased to govern the world. Little did the legionaries imagine what the real work was in which they were engaged. As in many similar cases in the history of the world, the sword had made way for the cross, and, as has been said before, principles were left behind them by the retreating Roman soldiers, the value and the power of which they themselves little understood. No doubt during the latter part of their occupation, under the government of Constantine, all Roman Britain was avowedly Christian ; but the instances must have been many in which the Christian faith was assumed out of deference to the emperor, and not from personal conviction.

Tiberius Cæsar, under whose government our Lord

was crucified at Jerusalem, was himself no enemy to the Christian faith ; nay he would have fostered it in the face of an unwilling senate. Tertullian tells us (Apol. c. 5) that Tiberius had declared to the senate that he had received abundant evidence from Syria of Christ's having there revealed the truth of His divinity, and recommended the senate to acknowledge it. The senate refused, but Cæsar retained his opinion, and threatened to punish the accusers of the Christians. From this it may be gathered that Tiberius was in no respect hostile to the spread of the Gospel. Eusebius (Euseb. Chron.) tells us that the object of Tiberius was to have Jesus admitted among the number of the gods of Rome (inter cetera sacra), but that the senate resisted. There is reason, then, to conclude that the opportunities were ample for the spread of the Gospel, at the very outset, over the whole Roman empire ; and it does look like a wise and long designed purpose of Divine providence, that at that period an empire should exist, having reached its widest extent, wielding over its subjects its most unlimited power, and embracing within its grasp the chief portions of the three great continents of the ancient world ; while there was at the same time seated upon the throne of that empire a man more disposed to foster than to extinguish the tender spark of an infant Christianity. Until the days of Nero there was not much to interfere with the progress of this divine faith throughout the empire, and his persecution, horrible as it was, seems to have been felt chiefly by the Christians of Rome itself.

Theodoret, who wrote in Greek about the year 420, tells us (Relig. Hist. c. ix.) "that our fishermen and publicans, and our stitcher (*sutor*, meaning the apostle Paul) carried the Gospel to all nations who lived under the Roman government;" and among others he mentions "Britons, Cimmerians, and Germans (Britannos, Cimmerios, et Ger-

manos) so that all nations received the laws of the Crucified One." There may be a good deal here of the de
clamatory style of the early ecclesiastical writers, but it
shews that the impression existed at an early period,
that the Gospel was preached in Britain by the Apostles.

The traditions respecting this first preaching of the
Gospel in Britain have been various (Ussher, Ed. 1639 pp.
5, 20). It was said to have been preached by the
apostle James so early as A.D. 41.[1] Maximus says that
"returning from the west, St. James visited France,
Britain, and the towns of Venetia, where he preached;
and returned to Jerusalem, having to consult the blessed
Virgin and Peter concerning very important matters.
Richard of Cirencester, in his "Speculum Historiale"
(Book viii. c. 7) says, that the apostles visiting various
regions by the Divine purpose, James was cast upon the
Irish coast, and boldly preached the Word of God; where
it is said that he chose seven disciples, viz., Torquatus,
Secundus, Indalecius, Tisephon, Euphrasius, Cecilius,
Isichius, by whose aid he extirpated the tares, and committed to the dry and barren earth the seed of God's
Word; and when his end drew near he journeyed with
them to Jerusalem, and then suffered martyrdom. It is
so well known that James suffered death at the hands of
Herod Agrippa before the dispersion of the apostles, that
it is needless to attempt otherwise the confutation of
this statement. It is just one of those legends with
which the early Church swarmed, and which did more
permanent injury than any immediate good to the interests of the Christian faith.

Nicephorus Callistus (quoted by Ussher, p. 7) says that
Simon Zelotes preached in Britain. That he was crucified there and buried, is also related by several early
writers. In the Roman Breviary and Martyrologium
(Ussher) he is said to have suffered martyrdom in Persia.

[1] Max. Chron., written about A.D. 621.

Eusebius, as quoted by Simeon Metaphrastes, relates that Simon Peter preached the Gospel in Britain, spending twenty-three years in the west between Rome and Britain (Ussher, p. 7) and other western states. Simeon himself adds that having preached and converted many in Britain, he founded churches, and ordained bishops, presbyters, and deacons, returning to Rome in the twelfth year of the Emperor Nero. For these statements there is no evidence of the slightest value : it cannot be shewn that Peter ever was in Rome, much less that he ever reached France or Britain. This is another of those legends which began to abound in the Church about the beginning of the sixth century, and which were in themselves indications of her declension from the simplicity of primitive times.

St. Paul, too, is said to have preached in Britain. Jerome says that he preached "from sea to sea" (Comm. in Amos cap. 5). Others of the Fathers maintain that this included Britain ; and Theodoret (on Psal. cxvi.) says that the words of the apostle in 2d Tim. iv. 16, 17, where he says, that by me "all the Gentiles might hear," include "the islands which lie in the sea." Nicephorus (Ussher, p. 9) says, that encircling the habitable globe like a heavenly bird, and thirty years being thus spent in preaching the Gospel, he finished his course by martyrdom under Nero. It is further said that he ordained Aristobolus, who is spoken of in the epistle to the Romans, ch. xiv. ver. 10, a bishop in Britain. In the Greek Martyrologies (15 Mar.) it is stated that he, one of the seventy disciples, was ordained by Paul in the region of the Britons, having followed him there preaching the Gospel. That they were a fierce and cruel people ; that after much harsh usage he converted many of them to Christ ; and that he died after founding churches and ordaining presbyters and deacons. Stillingfleet and

others, including Cardinal Baronius, adopt the statement
that Paul preached in Britain ; Stillingfleet only, however,
acquiescing in the probability of the fact. It is evident
enough that Paul proposed visiting Spain (Rom. xv. 24,
28) and if so he might have intended extending his visit
to Britain, but we have no evidence of any value to shew
that he ever extended his travels to the westward of
Rome. Scripture is perfectly silent on the subject, so are
the early Fathers, and the testimony of mediæval ecclesiastics, who were ever dealing in similar legends, and
pawning them on the world for truth, can be held to be
of no value in a question of the kind. It is not impossible that Paul may have preached in Britain, but there
is nothing to prove it, and the probability is strong on
the other side.

A story was got up in the middle ages that the Gospel
was preached in Britain by Joseph of Arimathea. It
originated in Glastonbury Abbey, and is told for the first
time by William of Malmesbury, who died about A.D.
1143. There were two ways in which the friends of
such institutions as that of Glastonbury sought to add to
their fame, and to increase their revenue. One of these
was by securing relics of the most distinguished saints.
We find a monk of Durham stealing the relics of St.
Cuthbert from Lindisfarne ; and the contest between Ireland and Scotland for the relics of Columba is sufficiently
well known. The other method was by tracing the
foundation of the establishment to some one of the more
distinguished of the early saints. This system arose in
the middle ages, and was unknown in the early history
of the Church ; and its rise was rendered perfectly possible at the period when it first appeared, by the general
ignorance of the people and the superstition which appears to have pervaded all classes.

In his second epistle to Timothy (2 Tim. iv. 21) the

apostle Paul sends to his young disciple the greetings of Eubulus, and with them those of Pudens, Linus, and Claudia. This Claudia is said by some writers to have been a native of Britain. Martial is cited in evidence of this (Lib. xi. Epig. 54, quoted by Ussher). She was the wife of Pudens, and the poet sings of their nuptials. Dempster says that Pudens was a Roman centurion, banished afterwards into Scotland for his Christianity, where he preached earnestly the faith. He founds this statement upon a couple of lines of Martial. But it is clear enough that the Claudia whose beauty Martial extols, by command of Trajan, could not be the Claudia whose greetings the apostle 'Paul sends to Timothy, (Ussher, p. 11) and that the legend is without any basis of historical truth. The story of Pudentiana is another similar legend. She is said to have been the daughter of Pudens a Christian, to whose house Peter came about A.D. 44 in Rome. The household received the faith, and Timotheus, one of the sons, was sent as a missionary to Britain, when Lucius, the British king, received the Gospel at his hands. Pudentiana, one of the daughters of Pudens, has been a popular saint in Britain, and is so to this day among those who adhere to the Roman Catholic faith. It is said that Peter received his chair at Rome from Pudens; and that it still exists in that city. A period of revolution afforded too strong a temptation to the French soldiery to test the truth of this legend, when its utter baselessness was made clear to the whole world. The story of Pudentiana rests on no firmer basis than the chair of St. Peter. It is by no means improbable that early missionaries were sent from Rome to preach the Gospel in France and Britain, but there is nothing to shew that Timotheus was one of them.

CHAPTER V

THERE can be no doubt then that the Christian faith found its way at an early period into Britain. The communication between the island province and Rome was almost as easy as now, and must have been frequent. Troops were passing to and fro, as the exigencies of the government required; and a government in the neighbourhood of foes so restless as the Caledonians, could not be held safe without a constant supply. Britons were sent as legionaries to fight the battles of Rome abroad; foreigners would have been necessarily sent to maintain Roman authority in Britain. There were thus for the British people two points of contact with the views and principles prevalent at Rome and throughout the empire. The British troops abroad were one : they mingled with men from every portion of the empire, and learned from them what was said and believed. These returning home, either wounded or on the proclamation of peace, would carry with them the knowledge of what they had seen and heard. The other point of contact was to be found in Britain itself, where the people were brought into communication with the stream of supply from Rome and elsewhere, to fill the ranks of the Roman army. Among those so visiting Britain some would have been Christians, indeed we have reason to know that some were ; and thus would have introduced the Christian faith. Tacitus tells us in his Annals (Book xiii. 32), that " Pomponia Grœcina, a noble lady, and the wife of Plautius, who returned from Britain to obtain a triumph, was accused of foreign superstition, and left to be judged by her husband." The husband, we are told, pronounced her innocent. The " foreign superstition" in this passage is supposed to be Christianity, and taking the historian as his own interpreter, the inference is correct, for elsewhere (Ann. xv. 44) he calls the Christian faith (*exitiabilis superstitio*), a ' horrid superstition,' making use of the very term " superstition" applied in the present case. It has been said that this charge against the wife of Plautius could not be true, else how could her husband declare her innocent. But may not he too have been favourable to the Christian faith, and would not his judgment necessarily have been biassed by affection for his wife, especially as he must have learned from his acquaintance with it in her case, that it was everything but a " horrid superstition?" It has been said too that her excessive grief, as related by Tacitus, for the death of a friend, was hardly consistent with her belief in the Gospel and its promises. Christians are not without their sources of grief like other men. Jacob could dread the going down of his grey hairs with sorrow to the grave, and we know not whether Pomponia had any warrant for indulging the hopes of a Christian in connection with her friend's decease. This incident is related by the historian as having occurred in A.D. 56, so that there is this evidence for the existence of Christianity in Britain in the middle of the first century. As Claudius, who was the first Roman emperor who really possessed Britain, did not come to the island till the year 44, we could hardly look for earlier tidings of the existence of Christianity than those afforded by Tacitus twelve years later ; and as the history of Tacitus had reference chiefly to Scottish affairs, Pomponia is probably the first Christian who we have any reason to believe was in Scotland.

Whether the Gospel was received previously by the Southern Britons we know not. Tertullian tells us that all Christians were called to be soldiers of the living God from their baptism. (Ad Mart. iii.) So that we may believe there were missionaries ready to devote themselves to the work of spreading the Gospel in any portion, however distant or savage, of the known world. That some of those may have found their way to Britain, is quite consistent with what we know of those early believers. Yet previous to A.D. 44, the Britons would not have been in the most favourable circumstances for receiving any importation from Rome. They would have a most painful recollection of the visit of Julius Cæsar to their country, nor would any emissaries from among the people who had sent him forth, have had much reason to expect a welcome among them. They had indeed had much pleasant and profitable communication with the east. The tin of Cornwall had found its way long before to the Levant, and the bond of connection between Britain and the East would thus have been drawn close and firm. A messenger from Syria would have been more readily received than one from Rome. This is held by some to account for the oriental character of early British Christianity, partaking, as it did, more of what characterised the Eastern than the Western Church ; the missionaries who conveyed it may have come from the East. Neander says (Gen. Ch. Hist., vol. i., 117), "that the peculiarity of the British Church is evidence against its origin from Rome ; for in many ritual matters (of human device, and therefore not such as two independent bodies were likely to adopt from their own study of the Sacred Scriptures) it departed from the usage of the Romish Church, and agreed much more nearly with the Churches of Asia Minor." Yet it cannot be forgotten, that so early as the middle of the first century the Eastern and Western Churches had not assumed their distinctive peculiarities. At that time the Church bore throughout the impress it had received in the East. The faith itself had travelled from the East, and it retained its original form throughout the Roman Empire for a much longer period than half a century. The East, indeed, continued very long to influence the development of the Church, as may be seen from the growth of the eremitical system which, originating in the habits of certain non-Christian Eastern sects, soon entered the Church of Christ, travelled westwards, and acquired finally all the dimensions of the great monastic system of Rome; and the great German historian had really no warrant for the inference he drew with respect to the early British Church. British Christianity retained the early form of the Christian Church; it was Rome departed from it, and assumed one which became distinctive of itself. But, however the Gospel was conveyed thither, Christianity was introduced into Britain by the middle of the first century, confined very probably to the Roman army, but extending along with it as far as the Roman possessions.

The Roman historians of that period were heathens, and knew little, while probably they cared less about the spread of Christianity. This places us at a serious disadvantage in elucidating the early history of the Church. The Christians were themselves otherwise engaged than in chronicling the progress of their faith—they were striving to ensure it; and heathen writers would rather have ignored its existence altogether, such being the policy which they almost universally pursued. The scanty testimony to be gathered from Christian writers presents us with the following facts :—Tertullian writing about A.D. 200, or about 150 years after the Romans really possessed any part of Britain, says, in a famous passage, (Adv. Ind., c. 7), " That the several races of the Geti, the extensive territories of the Moors, all the bounds of Spain, the different nations of the Gauls, and those localities of the Britons hitherto inaccessible to the Romans, had become subject to Christ ; together with the territories of the Sarmatians, Dacians, Germans, and Scythians, and many distant nations, and provinces, and islands, which we do not know and cannot enumerate. The name of Christ has reached all those places, and now reigns there." Further he says that "the kingdom and name of Christ have extended to places which defied the arms of Rome."

Origen (4 Hom. on Ezek.) who wrote about A.D. 230, says—"When did Britain, previous to the coming of Christ, agree to worship the one God ? When the Moors ? When the whole world ? Now, however, through the Church, all men call upon the God of Israel." The evidence of these writers is thoroughly trustworthy : they were themselves cotemporaries of the events to which they refer : they were subjects of the Roman Empire, with all parts of which there was speedy and frequent communication, and however there may be allowance made for an exaggerated style of description, neither of them could venture, in the face of well-known facts, to make statements altogether at variance with truth. We may then safely conclude, that Christianity prevailed extensively in Britain even beyond the Roman Province, so early as A.D. 200.

In writing on the subject of the early Scottish Church, it is hardly necessary to advert at length to the story of Bede and others regarding the conversion of King Lucius, said to have taken place about A.D. 156. Bede (Hist. Eccl. c. 4) relates the story briefly. He tells us that "In the year of our Lord's incarnation, 156, Marcus Antoninus Pius, the fourteenth from Augustus, was made emperor together with his brother, Aurelius Commodus. In their time, whilst Eleutherus, a holy man, presided over the Roman Church, Lucius, King of the Britons, sent a letter to him, entreating that, by his command, he might be made a Christian. He soon obtained his pious request, and the Britons preserved the faith which they had received uncorrupted and entire, in peace and tranquillity, until the time of the Emperor Diocletian." This is Bede's first statement regarding the conversion of the Britons. There is no real difficulty in regard to the title here given to Lucius. It was not necessary to his being king that he should reign over the whole Britons, or even a considerable portion of them. Every magnate was a king among the Celtic nations, the title being extended to their generals. Were he, then, but a chief of some sept among the natives, Lucius would be called a king of the Britons, and so called in perfect accordance with the custom of the people whom he governed. Nor is there any difficulty in the apparently Latin name of the British king. The Welsh writers call him Llewrwg, of which Lucius may be the Latin equivalent ; or he may have been, like Ambrosius Aurelius, who led the Britons for so long a time in their wars with the invading Saxons, a naturalised Roman (Bede, Hist. Eccl., c. xvi). Nor is there any real difficulty in the fact that he is called a king of the Britons at the time that Britain was a Roman Province. For we know that it was no uncommon thing for the Romans to suffer native kings to govern in subjection to their own supreme authority. The Herods so reigned in Judea. A British king, Cogidunns, was suffered to retain his kingly power in reward of his devotion to Roman interests ; and we know from the authority of early writers (Josc. Life of Kentigern), that the kings of the Strathclyde Britons continued to enjoy their dignity and power at the very time that Valentia, in which much of their territory was included, was a Roman province. Thus there is nothing incredible in a British king seeking instruction in the Christian faith about A.D. 156. But there are other difficulties in the statement of Bede. The two emperors of whom he speaks never reigned at the same time. Eleutherus became Bishop of Rome in A.D. 176. Antonine became emperor in A.D. 161. These dates cannot be made to harmonise with the story of King Lucius, even with the change of date made in Bede's Chronicle, where A.D. 156 is made A.D. 167. The time does not agree with that of Eleutherus' episcopate. These errors may, however, be accounted for in the case of a writer relating an event nearly 600 years after its occurrence, and with very scanty materials in the form of trustworthy documents to which to refer. But it is needful, in making use of all Bede's statements, to remember the peculiar bias with which he and the writers of his own and a subsequent age wrote. He was a devoted adherent of the Roman See, as was the whole Anglo-Saxon Church after the days of Augustine, and loses no opportunity of promoting its interests, as may be seen from the accounts he gives of the controversy with the Scottish Church on the subject of Easter and the tonsure. The ancient British Church was strenuously anti-Roman, as will appear from subsequent events, and Bede would have willingly caught at any statement, however indifferent the authority for it, were it but a floating popular tradition, which could in any way connect the early British Church with Rome. The great matter was to show the justness of the claims which Rome put forth to universal su premacy in the Christian Church ; and the story of King Lucius, told with marked and somewhat suspicious brevity, was too favourable to his object not to be laid hold of. Ussher believes the story (Prim., chap. iv.), and that there may have been some foundation for it in the early conversion of a British king is quite true ; but the details as to the letter to the Roman bishop are entirely at variance with what we know of the position of the Bishop of Rome in the Church generally, and more especially in the British Church, then and long afterwards. It is remarkable that Gildas, a British writer of the fifth century, makes no mention of the conversion of King Lucius.

The great persecution under Diocletian took place about A.D. 293. Bede says, " It was carried on incessantly for ten years, with burning of churches, outlawing of innocent persons, and the slaughter of martyrs. At length it reached Britain, and many persons, with the constancy of martyrs, died in the confession of the faith." At that time St. Alban perished, whom Dempster holds to have been a Scotsman ; and the name does give some likelihood to the statement, although in the absence of any farther evidence it is not one to be maintained. Many remarkable things are told of his death; he was the first British martyr, and perished as a victim not of British, but of Roman intolerance. With him suffered Aaron and Julius, citizens of Chester (Bede, Hist. Eccl., chap. vii.); and others are said to have perished besides. The names given by Bede, it may be well to remark, are more Roman than British in their form ; Albanus and Julius are very like Roman appellatives, while there is nothing in that of Aaron to show that it belonged to a Briton. The likelihood is that these men were Christian Romans, put to death for their adherence to the new faith. Indeed, it is not to be thought that the Roman government would concern itself much with the religion of its British subjects, while that of native Romans would be watched with the closest scrutiny. The persecution under Diocletian was the first which reached the extremities of the empire, and even it, with all its violence, and with all the determination of its promoters to extirpate the Christians, was largely modified in Britain by the favour of Constantius Chlorus, (See Eus. Hist. c. viii. 13 ; Sosom. Hist. Ecc. B. i. c. 6), who then governed there under the emperor. Bede calls him a man of "extraordinary meekness and courtesy." He was, as already stated, father of Constantine, the first Christian emperor, and there is reason to think that Constantine first learned to judge favourably of Christians in the house of his father ; the seed was probably sown there which afterwards germinated in the conversion of the son. How little do we know at what time principles sown early in the heart may come to exhibit their existence and their power !

During all this period it is impossible to separate the Scottish province of Valentia from the rest of Roman Britain. We may believe that in so far as it was subject to Rome, it shared a common fate with the other provinces, and that Christianity was equally favoured or equally persecuted in both. Southern Scotland was at the time a part of Britain, and nothing more, and is spoken of under the name common to the whole. We have no reason to doubt that the persecution which visited England extended to Scotland, and that it, too, had its early martyrs, although we have no record of their names. This persecution would in Britain, as elsewhere, have contributed to the spread of the faith; Christians would have perished, but many would have fled for their lives. Beyond the wall of Antonine to the north, lay an extensive region inaccessible either to the power or persecutions of Rome ; and thither many of the oppressed Christians would flee, betaking themselves for security to the kind offices of the neighbouring heathen ; nor would they have been received the less readily or cordially because of their being fugitives from Rome. These fugitives would carry with them the faith for which they suffered, and would strive to repay their hosts by communicating to them the knowledge of its saving truths.   Besides this mode, by which the knowledge of Divine truth would be carried beyond the limits of the Roman empire, prisoners would be taken by the hostile tribes of the north ; some of these would be Christians, and, like the Jewish slave girl in Syria, would teach their masters of the Christian's God.   Then, besides, missionaries, inspired by a dauntless courage and love for the truth would boldly venture across the Roman boundary, and, as in all ages of the living Christian Church, would have braved every danger on behalf of the souls of men.

Under Constantius, who began his reign in A.D. 305, and his son, Constantine, who succeeded him, persecution ceased, and under the latter the Roman empire became nominally Christian.   With external peace came, as is common in the history of the Church, internal dissension, and Constantine was constrained, in A.D. 314, to call a council to meet at Arles, a city of Gaul—the first council of the Christian Church called by a civil governor.   One of the resolutions of the council brings to light the condition of the empire with respect to the Christian faith at the time, for it decerns that all women married to unbelievers should be suspended for a time from Christian privileges ; showing plainly that at the time a proportion of the population had not as yet forsaken the religion of their heathen ancestors.   It was probably the same in Britain, and yet in the beginning of the 4th century Roman Britain was largely Christian, while Christianity had extended its influence in some measure to the region beyond the wall.

CHAPTER VI.

IT is necessary here to consider the tradition which has existed in the Scottish Church itself with respect to the early planting of Christianity in Scotland. The story, as told by Fordun, is, that in the reign of Donald I., King of the Scots, whom he makes contemporary with the Emperor Severus, who died at York in 210, ambassadors were sent by the Scottish king to Pope Victor I., asking for religious instructors (Scotochronicon, B. II., c. 40), (see also Boece's Hist., B. v.) ; that these were sent, and that the king and his subjects received instruction, and were baptised. The Aberdeen Breviary gives the names of the missionaries sent, Mark and Denys, but upon what authority does not appear ; and Dempster, upon autho rity which has no real existence (App. on Hist. Scot., B. i. c. 6)—a pretended quotation from Fordun, tells us that the messenger of the Pope was Paschasius, a Sicilian. The event took place, according to Fordun, in A.D. 203 ; but the chronology of this statement has been often shown to be erroneous. Pope Victor, as he is called—although the term Pope in the 2d century had a very different sig- nification from the same title in after ages—died in A.D. 196, so that King Donald could not have received his missionaries from him in A.D. 203. Besides, putting aside the fact that the name Scot was then unknown, although the people afterwards called Scots were at the period inhabitants of North Britain, the relation of the independent tribes beyond the Firths to Rome in the age of Severus, was such as to preclude the possibility of such an embassy. The whole reign of Severus was in North Britain a period of incessant warfare between the Romans and the neighbouring tribes. This very King Donald, if such a king ever existed, must have been contending for that very existence with the Roman power. How, then, are we to believe in a peaceful embassy from him to Rome, and that at a time when even during peace such Christian ambassadors were not likely to receive favour from the Roman government? Such an embassy in the reign of Severus may justly be said to have been impossible.

This legend has been made to serve the purposes of various sections of the Christian Church (Grub's Eccl. Hist., vol. i. p. 5); but there are two ways in which its origin may be very naturally accounted for. It may have arisen during the controversy between the Scottish and English Churches after the period of Malcolm III., on the subject of supremacy. It is easily seen that it would be natural for the Scottish Church, in maintaining its independence, to attempt to prove that it did not receive the Gospel at first through the medium of England, but had received it directly from the same source. This was a point of the most urgent consequence to the Scots in the discussion, and we can readily imagine how the most trivial story floating like a grain of dust in the atmosphere of popular tradition, would be laid hold of and magnified into this great history of a special embassy from Rome. This would place the Scottish Church fairly abreast of that of England, notwithstanding the well-known mission of Augustine.

There is another way, however, of accounting for the adoption of the legend. We have already shown how, with regard to the British king Lucius, Bede relates a

history of which we have no notice whatsoever from
Gildas, a British historian, who lived much nearer the
period of the event, and who would necessarily take espe-
cial interest in what so nearly concerned the honour of
his own nation. But Gildas belonged to the ancient
British Church—Bede to that of Rome. Hence the readiness of the latter, as already shown, to adopt the story,
whatever the authority for it might have been, if it
showed that Britain had been christianized from Rome.
The resemblance of the story of King Lucius and King
Donald is too close to have escaped the observation of
our historical writers (Goodall's Prelim. Diss. to Keith's
Hist.) ; it is but changing the names and the story remains the same. In both instances the historians are
wrong in their chronology, from the defective authority
on which their statements were made : and have we not
reason to believe that both stories originated in the same
cause, that cause being the desire of mediæval ecclesiastical writers to maintain the doctrine of Papal supremacy ? We read nothing of Pope Victor or King
Donald in Adomnan, and this story is not related by
Bede ; we find it first in Fordun, and in it we see, probably, one of those pious frauds, not invented by him,
which were at the time considered justifiable when
applied to a good purpose. Such is, on the face of it,
the story of King Donald and Pope Victor ; it is historically untrue, and the support it affords to any cause
is of not the slightest value whatsoever.

It was about A.D. 423 that the Romans finally retired
from Britain, their last act being to assist the native
Britons in building the ancient wall as a defence against
the Scots and Picts beyond. It is of this last wall, built
chiefly by Britons, and hence probably called Grim's
dyke from some chief who governed during its erection,
that the remains now exist, traceable along the valley

which traverses the country between the Forth and the Clyde. The state of the population does not indicate the reign of the Gospel of peace at the time, on either side of this rampart.

From this time, in tracing the progress of Christianity, we must deal entirely with the labours of native missionaries; the Romans had retired, but the Gospel of God's grace remained in the land. The first of those missionaries of whom we have any authentic information, if authentic much of it may be called, was Ninian, usually called St. Ninian, or St. Ringan, commemorated in the mediæval church on 16th Sept., as well as in the several Kilninians, or Ninian's churches, scattered widely over Scotland. Our chief authorities for the events of his life are Bede, who gives a brief notice of him in his history (Bede, Hist. Eccl. B. iii. ch. 4), and Ailred or Ethelred, Abbot of Rievaux in Yorkshire, who wrote a life of the saint at the request of the canons of Whitehorn Cathedral, in Galloway, where Ninian is said to have been the first bishop (Vit. Nin., Pink. Edition). Bede's notice is as follows,—He says that Columba came to preach to the northern Picts; " for the southern Picts who dwell on this side of those mountains, had long before, as is reported, forsaken the errors of idolatry and embraced the truth, by the preaching of Ninias, a most reverend bishop and holy man of the British nation, who had been regularly instructed at Rome in the faith and mysteries of the truth; whose episcopal see, named after St. Martin the bishop, and famous for a stately church (wherein he and many other saints rest in the body) is still in existence among the English nation.[1] The place belongs to the province of the Bernicians, and is generally called the White House, because he there built a church of stone,

---

[1] Whithorn was in Bede's time in Bernicia, an English province.

which is not usual among the Britons." This is all Bede relates of him, and was probably gathered from Pecthelm, the bishop of Whithorn in Bede's time, with whom he seems to have had personal intercourse (Bede, Hist. Eccles. B. v., c. 18), although Pecthelm himself, being a Saxon, could not have the means of knowing much of the British missionary, who lived 300 years before, from the animosity subsisting between the two nations ; and also from the fact that during the greater portion of the time between the age of Ninian and that of Pecthelm the church at Whithorn was vacant, and there were no successive pastors to preserve documents, or to transmit authentic traditions. Bede was, however, well acquainted with the state of the Scottish Church, as appears from the notices he affords of it ; the Scottish missions still existed in Northumbria, and any information he gives may be held as generally authentic.

Ailred, the other biographer of Ninian, wrote in A.D. 1150, or about 400 years after Bede, and 700 years after the death of Ninian. This is sufficient to make us cautious as to how far we are to receive his testimony. He is himself indebted to Bede, whose brief notices he expands with a remarkable exuberance of diction, and singular declamatory power ; but he tells us also that he had a book, "Barbario Scriptus," *written in a barbarous language*, probably either British or Gaelic, in which all that Bede said was more fully detailed. No copy of this earlier life is known to exist, and we are ignorant both of its age and of its author.

Ninian, according to Bede and Ailred, was a Briton, a native of the Roman province, where he was born about A.D. 360, or about 200 years before the time of Columba. His parents were Christians, and early devoted him to the Christian ministry. Ailred says of him (Vit. Nin.

Pink. Ed., p. 4) " He was characterized by deep devotion in the church, and warm affection among his associates ; moderate in eating, sparing of his words, assiduous in study, courteous in manner, abstaining from jests, and ever subjecting his flesh to the spirit ; devoting himself to much searching of the Holy Scriptures, so much so that he discovered that among his people its real sense was not thoroughly understood." Upon this, we are told, he journeyed to Rome in search of the truth. The first portion of Ailred's description is extremely beautiful, and is an admirable sketch of the character of a true missionary of Christ ; nor do we doubt that such were the men who first preached the cross among barbarous nations,— men whose character commended the truth which their preaching taught ; men of warm zeal, deep humility, and dauntless courage—courage fed by their love to Christ and their love to the souls of men ; such men were in every true sense the successors of the apostles. But in this account of Ailred's, there are two statements which cannot fail to strike the observant reader. The first is the statement respecting British Christians, that they did not apprehend the real sense of Scripture, or in other words, that there were doctrines in the early British Church which would not have been held orthodox by an ecclesiastical writer of the 12th century. The Romish party was ever jealous of that Church, and it is pretty clear that this statement of Ailred's is an exhibition of this jealousy ; or at the very least it may be taken as clear evidence of the fact that the early British Church held doctrines which were not held orthodox in Ailred's time at Rome. The other statement is, that Ninian journeyed to Rome to obtain correct views of the truth ; both Bede and Ailred relate this fact, and it may be true. Rome was at the time the capital of that empire, of which Britain formed a part ; all Roman citizens or subjects must have looked up to it as the seat of every living influence that permeated and acted upon the empire, while Christians must have looked to it with peculiar interest, as the scene of many testimonies and many martyrdoms, and the residence of many faithful Christian men. It is easy enough to see that there was much in the age of Ninian to attract men like him to Rome; but the manifest desire indicated by Bede, and subsequent writers down to the time of Ailred, and after it, to hold Rome up as the one source of everything good to the Church, has something suspicious in it. It looks extremely like as if the same cause were in operation here as in the case of the stories of King Lucius and King Donald. Would it not be an additional argument in favour of the universal supremacy of the Roman see, if it could be shewn that, from the very earliest ages of the Christian Church, men looked to Rome as the one source of all true knowledge, and to the Bishop of Rome as the one head of the true Church? We cannot but regret that Ailred did not specify what the precise views were which Ninian, by searching the Scriptures, had learned to condemn; but we shall find as we proceed, that this instance is not singular, and that the mediæval writers feel themselves constrained pretty generally to testify against what they call the false doctrine of the early British Church.

The statement of Ailred (Vit. Nin., cap. ii.) is, that coming to Rome the blessed youth wept over the relics of the apostles, and gave himself over to their care; then going to the Pope (presul summæ sedis) he was most graciously acknowledged and received as a son. He was thereupon handed over to the teachers of the truth, to be instructed in the discipline of the faith, and the sound interpretation of Scripture. By this he largely profited; for he came to understand that he and his countrymen held many views contrary to sound doctrine. Then like a bee he sucks in instruction, both for his own edification and that of many others, and finally, so chaste was he in body, so prudent in mind, so wise in counsel, so circumspect in word and deed, that all men spoke of him, and he enjoyed the highest favour of the supreme pontiff himself. After many years spent in Rome, the Roman pontiff, hearing that in the western parts of Britain, while some had not received the Christian faith at all, others had received it either from heretics or from men unlearned in the divine law, consecrated Ninian to the episcopal office, and sent him as the first apostle to the people of his own nation, giving him his benediction. Such is the substance of Ailred's statement ; it agrees with Bede's, of which it is a manifest amplification throughout ; but Bede, however, does not say that Ninian was consecrated a bishop by the Pope, although he tells us distinctly ʃthat he was a bishop ; nor does Bede, in his notice of him, refer to the errors held by British Christians in Ninian's time. He speaks of him simply as a missionary. Yet there is good reason to believe that there was some difference between the Church at Rome and that in Britain in the days of Ninian, although Bede's story would go to shew that there was none ; for he tells us that Ninian was instructed at Rome, and afterwards taught his countrymen what he learned ; and if there was, it was in all likelihood chiefly connected with the very doctrine which it is Ailred's object to establish,—the doctrine of the supremacy of the Romish see. The controversy regarding Easter and the tonsure had hardly emerged, but Rome was towards the close of the 4th century muttering its claims to govern the whole Church. The Arian heresy had no doubt broken out in the early part of the century ; views were propounded by its supporters, subversive of the faith of the Church in the divinity of our Lord, and reducing Him to the level of a mere creature; and we have evidence to shew that these views reached Britain, and were adopted by some professing Christians (Gild. Works, sec. 12; Bede, B. i., c. 8).

The Council of Nice assembled in A.D. 325, summoned not by the Pope but by the Emperor Constantine. "This prince thought it equitable that questions of superior importance, and such as intimately concerned the interests of Christianity in general, should be examined and decided in assemblies that represented the whole body of the Christian Church" (Mosh. Eccl. Hist., cent. iv). At the council of Nice, the views of Arius and his supporters were condemned, and the true doctrine regarding the person of Christ declared. We do not learn that Arianism was extensively adopted in Britain; nay, many of the writers of this age testify that the British churches were adherents to the Nicene doctrine. Stillingfleet (Ant. of Brit. Churches, c. 175) quotes Athanasius, Jerome, and Chrysostom in evidence of this, who all mention those churches as "agreeing with other churches in the true faith." At the same time it is true that three British bishops were present at the council of Ariminum, A.D. 354, where Constantius had summoned the western bishops to meet, and where the Nicene creed was virtually disowned; a fact which can be made to consist with the former only on the assumption that, like many others, the British bishops did not really agree in the finding of the council, or if they did, that their doctrine was not received generally by their own countrymen.

Nor could it be the errors of Pelagius to which Bede and Ailred refer as having been held by the British Church. It was about A.D. 381 that Pelagianism first made its appearance in the Church, and though its author was a

Briton its promulgation did not take place in Britain, but at Rome. This was about the time that Ninian would have had his views directed towards his future work, and it was then that he came to be convinced, not that a grievous defection was taking place, but that his country-men had held, apparently since their conversion to Christianity, certain views which, in the estimation of Ailred, were opposed to the orthodox faith. Thus it was neither Arianism nor Pelagianism with which the British Churches were chargeable ; nor could it have been laxity of morals, for the very writers who condemn those doctrines testify to the admirable character, the zeal, and the success of the men who sprung up from amidst those churches. Still, writers in the interest of Rome, in a later age, lose no opportunity of blackening the British Churches in so far as their orthodoxy is concerned ; there is manifestly a standing grudge. We shall find, as we proceed, besides such charges of unsoundness in the faith as we are dealing with, that they are charged with a want of missionary spirit, proved by the absence of effort towards the conversion of the heathen Saxons, at the very moment that they were the victims of those men's cruelty, and had to save their lives by fleeing to caves and forests from their pursuit. But the real truth is, that the defection was not in Britain but in Rome. From Rome error travelled in the train of Augustine and others to Britain, where it entered into the early Saxon Church, while the British Churches long withstood its influence. Above all, the latter denied that they had received the Gospel through the Roman See, and refused to submit to its claims of supremacy ; *Hinc illæ lacrymæ.* This is the only sub-stantial charge that can be brought against the early British Churches ; it may have been a grievous one in the eyes of a Monk of Jarrow in the 8th century, or a Cistercian Monk of Rievaux in the 12th ; but it will not be held as

a charge involving any loss of credit by those who have
in after ages joined them in throwing off the incubus of
similar claims.   It can never be safely or justly forgotten,
that most of what we know of those early churches is from
men who, while disposed to extol every thing in them which
accorded with their own peculiar views, held views diame-
trically opposite to theirs on some impoitant questions,
and who, so far as these questions are concerned, cannot
be received as altogether trustworthy witnesses; but
from their very censures we can gather somewhat of the
character of the views on such questions which were
held by those early Christians.

It is of consequence to note that in the early accounts
which we have of the state of the Church, the final appeal
in all doctrinal questions is to the Holy Scriptures.   There
is not a word said of mere papal authority, or the authority of the Church; the error of the Britons, even according to Bede and Ailred, was in their interpretation of
Scripture.   Ninian went to Rome to learn the truth, and
he was set to read the Scriptures.   It was remarked by
Polydore Vergil respecting Gildas, that he quoted no
book, in his long letter on the state of the Britons, but
the Bible; and certainly his quotations from it shew, on
the part of the British historian, a very thorough acquaintance with the word of God.   The idea seems completely
to pervade the minds of the men who relate to us the
events of this period, that the people possessed the Scriptures; their error was in what these historians hold to have
been the misinterpretation of them; but they never once
suggest that a remedy for such misinterpretation was to be
found in withholding the book from them altogether.   It
may be said that the fact of the Scriptures being in Latin,
was a security against a promiscuous acquaintance with
them, and the use of them among the people; but that
afforded no security in the time of Ninian, when the Latin

language was spoken extensively over the whole Roman Province. It is worthy of notice that, while Gildas quotes the Scriptures in Latin, it is not the Latin of the Vulgate, or the ordinary Bible of the Roman Church, but a translation largely differing in the forms of expression, although usually identical in point of meaning. At this period of the Church, then, the Bible was very generally disseminated, and men used such translations of the sacred text as commended themselves most to their own judgment. The withholding of the Bible from the people, and excluding every translation but one from use, even among the ministers of the Church, belonged to the ecclesiastical legislation of a later and more corrupt age, an age when the light of truth came to be an object of fear to the governors of the Church, and when ecclesiastical power came to be based not on the intelligence, but on the ignorance of the people.

But to return to Ninian. He was sent from Rome destined as the first apostle of his own people, according to Ailred. Bede does not say whether he was sent or returned to Britain of his own accord ; the legend grew in the hands of Ailred, but so grew as to become more favourable to the claims of the Roman See ; at all events, both writers concur in relating his return to Britain. On his way he visited the famous Martin of Tours, usually called St. Martin, the originator of the monastic system in Western Europe, who is commemorated in the Roman Calendar on the 25th November, usually called Martinmas. Whether owing to the visit of Ninian or otherwise, this ecclesiastic became famous in the Celtic churches, a fact which, in Scotland, the numerous Kilmartins scattered all over the kingdom amply testify. According to Ailred Ninian derived much edification from his intercourse with this saint. Ailred's account is—" Returning from the city, the man of God, filled with the Spirit, and touched

with the desire of seeing him (St. Martin), turned aside to
the city of Tours ; who can tell with what joy, what devotion, what affection he was received. For through the
grace of the prophetic light, the qualities of this new
priest (pontifex) were not concealed from him. He knew,
by revelation of God, that he was sanctified by the Spirit
and was to profit many unto salvation. The doves are
joined in the tabernacle of God, one to the other, and as
two cherubims expanding their wings, they touch each
other mutually, and borne on the wings of their graces,
they depart to God ; and standing and laying these wings
again aside, they become calmed at once." Mosheim in
speaking of the arrogance of the clergy even in this age,
says (Eccl. Hist. Cent. v. chap. 2)—"The office of a presbyter was looked upon as of such a high and eminent
nature, that Martin, Bishop of Tours, was so audacious as
to maintain at a public entertainment, that the emperor
was inferior in dignity to one of that order." And he quotes
Sulpitius Severus, the biographer of Martin, as authority
for the fact. Ninian must have been impressed with the
ecclesiastical buildings at Tours, more so, it would appear,
than by those at Rome ; for he requested of Martin to supply him with masons (*cementarios*), adding, "that he was
instructed to imitate, as of the faith of the Roman Church,
the manner of building churches, as well as of celebrating
(*constituendis*) the ecclesiastical offices" (Vit. Nin. chap. 2).
The friends parted with embraces, kisses, and tears, and
Ninian continued his journey to his own country. Here
he was received by a great concourse of people, among
whom was joy, devotion, and praise of Christ ; the people held him as one of the prophets. He commenced by
tearing up what was ill planted, dispersing what was
improperly gathered together, and pulling down what
was ill built ; "upon which, after much else, he showed
the duty of the faithful, teaching by his word and ex-

ample, and confirming by miracles" (Vit. Nin., c. 2). According to Ailred's statement Ninian was the first apostle to his countrymen, and yet his countrymen received him as Christians. Ailred manifestly represents him as an emissary from Rome, sent to bring the faith and practice of his countrymen into accordance with those of the Roman Church, which they could not have previously been. It was not to convert them, for they had been converted ; what else then could his apostolic mission mean ? The Britons had received the Gospel previously, but here was their first emissary from Rome in the fourth century, and hence he is called their first apostle. It may be true that this biography by the Abbot of Rievaux is not trustworthy evidence with regard to the facts of Ninian's life and mission. In many respects it certainly is not, being a mere piece of wordy declamation ; and yet it is well to know, in looking back to those early times, what the character of the medium is through which they must be viewed. And the more we study this the more will we see that the early Church was very different from what the mediæval writers strive to make it. The lives of the saints in which they abound, cannot be received as history without close and constant inquiry. On this subject Pinkerton says (Vit. ant. Sanct., p. 111), that "as gold is gathered from dross, so from their trifles fruits may be gathered by him who seeks to illustrate the history, geography, and manners of the middle ages . . for if we allow that the miracles are most absurd, it does not at all follow that what refers to history, geography, and morals, is of no authority." To this, however, it must be added, that in all their statements the circumstances and bias of the writers must be taken into account ; for instance, the life of Ninian was undertaken by Ailred at the request of the canons of Whithorn, of

E

which church Ninian was the founder, and this fact could not but have a certain influence on his biographer; and the need for caution in receiving his testimony will appear the more clearly when we remember that he was a monk of the twelfth century.

On his return to Britain Ninian erected a church at Whithorn, in Galloway, employing the builders sent from Tours to aid him in this great undertaking. The church was called Candida Casa, or White House, in all likelihood from the whiteness of the walls, and was built about the year 400, or twenty-three years before the final withdrawal of the Romans from Britain. It was in fact built in a Roman province, and could not therefore be the first stone building erected in the country, as we have ample testimony to show that Roman Britain abounded in such buildings. Martin of Tours having died about the time the church was erected, it was dedicated to him, and became a memorial of the esteem cherished for him by Ninian.

"Then," says his biographer, "the candle being placed in its candlestick, it began to give forth its light with heavenly signs to those who were in the house of God (Vit. Nin., c. 4), and the flame of its graces radiating, those who were dark in their mind were enlightened by the bright and burning word of God, and the frigid were warmed." From this it would appear that Ninian, now established at Whithorn, became a zealous and faithful preacher of the Gospel, establishing at the same time a sound and scriptural discipline among his flock. If this be true, how interesting it is to contemplate the fact, that amidst the far-off wilds of Galloway, men of God maintained their faithful testimony for Christ at a period so remote that secular history has failed to afford us any tidings of it, encountering and overcoming danger, and bravely and fearlessly carrying the word of God amongst a people steeped in ignorance and barbarism.

CHAPTER VII.

THE MISSION OF NINIAN.

MUCH of Ailred's life of Ninian is taken up with an account of his miracles. These early writers thought it of more importance to convince their readers of the miraculous gifts of their heroes, than to inform them of the real facts of their lives, and yet these miracles are not destitute of interest, as showing the character of the belief existing in the mediæval Church, and the kind of instruction communicated by its teachers. Ninian's first miracle was healing the sickness and blindness of Tuduvallus, king of the Strathclyde Britons, thought to be the same with Totail, father of Rhydderch Hael, in Gaelic Ruaraidh Fial, afterwards king of the same Britons, and the generous friend of St. Kentigern. The Roman government, as has already been observed, was manifestly such as to admit, although in rare cases, of the existence of local kings or governors of the native races ; and the Cumbrian kingdom of Strathclyde was one of those in which such an arrangement was permitted. Dunbarton,[1] the ancient Alcluith, or Rock of Clyde, and Dunbritton, or Castle of the Britons, the capital, was beyond the Roman wall, but the territories of those Britons extended far within it. Tuduvallus had been the bitter enemy of the missionary, but his miraculous healing, and the restoration of his sight, had the effect of converting him into his truest and firmest friend.—(Vit. Nin., chap. iv.)

---

1 In Gaelic Dun Bhreatuin is the name to this day. The word "Breatuineach," or Briton, is still retained in ordinary Gaelic names. The surname Galbraith is in Gaelic, Mac a Bhreatunaich, or the son of the Briton.

On one occasion a presbyter was accused of licentious-
ness, but was miraculously relieved from the charge by
the saint ; for when the child with whose parentage the
presbyter was charged was a few days old, he was
brought to Ninian for baptism ; and the missionary having commanded it, the child proclaimed aloud the inno-
cence of the presbyter and the name of its guilty parent.
"Oh rem stupendam!" says the writer, " et omni admira-
tione dignam! Oh miram Dei clementiam! Oh ineffa-
bilem fidei Christianæ virtutem."—(Vit. Nin., c. 6.)

On another occasion the saint made the garden which
supplied himself and his brethren with vegetables, to furnish, at a moment's notice, a bountiful supply of onions,
upon which his biographer remarks, "A wonderful thing,
and credible only by such as believe that nothing is impossible to the faithful." (Vit. Nin., c. 7.)

At another time he visited his herds, which he kept
for the benefit of strangers and the poor, in order to give
them his episcopal benediction. He blessed them and
drew with his staff a circle around them, within which
they would be safe for the night. Meantime, in the silence
of night, thieves arrived and attempted to drive them
away ; but the divine power resisted them, nay more, a
bull attacked them, and gored their leader, his life and
his entrails rushing out at the same wound. The man
was brought to life by the saint, and all his followers
became humble penitents. The enraged bull left the
mark of his hoof in a stone, as if it had been wax, and to
this day the place is called *Farres last* (Vit. Nin., c. 8),
which is in Latin, *the bull's footmark.* The F in Farres
is obviously a misreading or misprint for T, as *Tarw* in
British and *Tarbh* in Gaelic means a bull ; the other word
may be the Welsh *Llast*, a receptacle. The place, if the
name now exists in the neighbourhood of Whithorn, would
in all probability be called Tarr's Last. In Gaelic the

word for " footprint" is *Lorg*, so that if that be the language the name would be *Lorg an tairbh.*

One day Ninian, along with a friend, was reading the Psalter in the open air. A shower began to fall, but so much were the good men favoured, that no drop fell upon them or on their books; Ninian allowed for a moment a forbidden thought (cogitatio illicita) to fill his mind, and in an instant, he and the pages of his volume became wetted by the falling rain. Having dismissed the intruding thought, they became again dry, in the very midst of the shower, as if under a cover.

One of Ninian's scholars fled on one occasion from fear of the rod, which the saint is described as using freely, and knowing the virtues of his master, he appropriated his pastoral staff. He sought the ship which was used as a means of conveyance to Scotia. It was a vessel made of twigs of such a size that three men could find room in it by sitting closely, and it was covered with hide which rendered it perfectly safe and water-tight. The youth, by mistake, went on board a vessel as yet uncovered with hide, which immediately slid into the sea, and he was in imminent danger. Having prayed, he placed the staff of the saint in one of the openings of the wicker; at once the water of the sea becomes tremblingly obedient, and ceases to flow into the ship; then a gentle wind rises, the staff becomes a sail, the staff becomes a helm, and finally the staff becomes an anchor; the people stand on the eastern shore filled with wonder. When landed, the youth plants the staff, and in answer to his prayer it becomes a tree, nay more, a limpid fountain wells up near the root, and both become memorials of the miraculous power of Ninian.

These are the miracles said to be wrought by the living Ninian; his biographer is no less minute in detailing those wrought by his relics, but of them it is unnecessary to give

any account here.   It has been said that these miracles are
related merely as moral lessons, and that in this aspect
there is much beauty in them.—(See Mr. Grub's Eccl.
Hist. vol. i., p. 19).   For instance, speaking of the miracle
of the shower it is said that "a parable such as this,
though in the dress of a miracle, may surely escape deri-
sion.   Allegorically construed, it is the vehicle of high
truth ; it speaks of that protection which encompasses the
just—of the tenure on which it depends—of the negli-
gence whereby it may be forfeited—of the need, common
to the strongest and the weakest, to watch and pray,
lest they enter into temptation."   This may be very true,
but the question arises, were these legends received as
mere allegories, charged with moral lessons ; nay more,
were they intended to be so received ?   Have we not
every reason to believe that they were related as facts,
that they were received as facts, and that they were calculated to nourish in the people who so received them,
the most unworthy and degrading superstition.   Bede
mentions none of them, they are only related by Ailred,
and from him they are manifestly transferred to the Aberdeen Breviary, where they form part of the commemorative service on the saint's day.—(Brev. Aberd., vol. i.,
fol. 107).

The real mission work of Ninian is dismissed by Ailred
in a few sentences, bearing a very inadequate proportion
to the account of his miracles.   The relation is as follows :
"Meantime the blessed man, grieved that the devil (Zabu-
lus) expelled from the world beyond the sea, should have
found a seat in a corner of this island, in the hearts of the
Picts, set himself as an able athlete to drive out his kingdom, taking for this end the shield of faith, the helmet
of salvation, the breastplate of love, and the sword of the
spirit, which is the word of God.   Fortified with such
arms, and the companionship of holy fathers, as if sur-

rounded with heavenly troops, he invaded the empire of
the strong man armed, about to deliver many captive
vessels from his dominion. Assailing, therefore, the
Southern Picts, who were hitherto steeped in heathen
error, and who worshipped in consequence dumb and deaf
idols, he preached Gospel truth, and the purity of the
Christian faith to them, God co-operating and confirming
his teaching with many signs. The blind saw, the lame
walked, the lepers were cleansed, the deaf heard, the dead
rose, the possessed by the devil were delivered. He
opened his mouth with the word of God, through the
grace of the Holy Spirit ; the faith is received, error is
put away, the temples are destroyed, churches are erected ;
men rush to the fountain of saving cleansing,[1] the rich and
poor alike, youths and virgins, old men and young, mothers
with their infants ; renouncing Satan, and all his works
and pomps, they are joined to the family of believers by
faith, and word, and sacraments. They give thanks to
the most merciful God, who had revealed his word in the
far distant isles, sending them a preacher of the truth,
the light of his salvation, and calling them a people who
were not a people, and her beloved who was not beloved,
and her who had not sought mercy, one that sought
mercy. Then the sacred Pontiff (Sacer Pontifex) began
to ordain presbyters, to consecrate bishops, and to dis-
pense the other dignities of the ecclesiastical grades, to
divide the whole territory into regular parishes (parochias).
His sons begotten in Christ being thereupon confirmed in
faith and good works, and all things being settled which
might conduce to the honour of God, and the salvation of
souls, taking farewell of his brethren, he returns to his
own church, where, having spent a life of much sanctity

---

[1] Wells seem to have been used at an early period for baptism, which, as has
been suggested, may be the origin of their being held sacred.

and glorified by miracles, he died at length in great peace." Such is Ailred's account of Ninian's great mission to the Southern Picts. Bede's is much more brief: "The Southern Picts who dwell on this side of those mountains had long before (the age of Columba), as is reported, forsaken the errors of idolatry, and embraced the truth, by the preaching of Ninias, a most reverend bishop, and holy man of the British nation, who had been regularly instructed at Rome in the faith and mysteries of the truth."

The main fact here is that Bede had gathered from report that the southern Picts had been converted by Ninian. This is positively all we know on reliable evidence; and from this fact we might infer that an important share in christianizing those Picts belonged to Ninian. Ailred's account is clearly an expansion of Bede's, and the Aberdeen breviary transcribes Ailred's. Bede says he was a bishop instructed at Rome, Ailred says that he was sent by the Roman pontiff as the first apostle of the southern Picts. Let us examine a little who those southern Picts were. It is a general impression among modern writers upon this subject that those Picts were the ancient inhabitants of the region between the Grampian hills and the wall of Antonine, and that they occupied the present county of Fife, with part of Forfar, Perth, and Stirling. Bede (Hist. Eccl. Book iii., c. 4) describes them as lying to the south of those steep and rugged mountains, which mark the southern limit of the northern Picts. This might be true without confining them to the region beyond the wall. Johannes Major (De Gestibus Scotor. Lib. ii., cap. 2), says that "many years after the overturn of the Pictish kingdom, the Scots held sacred the dwelling-place and body of Ninian. The Picts frequently possessed Lothian, and those parts beyond the Scottish sea (the Firth of

Forth), and the better and more fertile portion of what was north of it ; both because they occupied the island before the Scots, and because, by their number and strength, they were somewhat superior to the Scots, which is shewn by this, that they occupied territory obtained from the Britons, which marks greater prudence and superiority." Ralph Higden (Polychronicon, Lib. i., cap. 58), speaking of the territory of the southern Picts, says that it was traversed by the Roman wall as far as the Scottish sea, and "included Galloway and Lothian." In the life of Kentigern, the great apostle of the Strathclyde Britons, by Joceline of Furness, written in A.D. 1180, we read that the diocese of Kentigern was co-extensive with the Cumbrian kingdom, extending along the wall of Severus (a mistake for Antonine) which was built for purposes of defence against the incursions of the Picts, as far as the river Forth, dividing Scotland from England (Vit. Kentig. cap. v.). The labours of Kentigern, then, were confined within the wall of Antonine, and yet in another place Joceline tells us (cap. xxvii.) that "the Picts were first of all in a great measure converted by St. Ninian ; afterwards by Saint Kentigern and St. Columba, and that having lapsed into apostasy, they, as well as Scots, and many other people in Britain, were reclaimed by the preaching of St. Kentigern." This quotation shews very clearly that the Picts were not held by our older writers to have been confined to the region beyond the Forth, but to have extended southwards, embracing Galloway and the Lothians. It is not by any means clear, then, that Ninian's field of labour among the southern Picts was confined to the country beyond the wall ; the probability is, that the wall ran partly through a Pictish territory, which the Romans never were able thoroughly to subdue. It may be very true at the same time that Ninian did labour to the northward of the wall, but there is no reason to believe that he confined his labours to that portion of the Pictish territory. This region, then, must have been in a large measure Christian before the days of Ninian, Christianity having existed in the country for nearly 300 years. Even in Tertullian's day the Christian faith had passed the Roman wall ; its progress in a period of 200 years, during a large portion of which the Roman empire might be denominated Christian, could not be little. Ninian's reception at Whithorn, as Ailred states, was the reception of a Christian missionary by a Christian popu- lation ; nor have we reason to believe that the leaven of Christian truth had been less operative beyond the wall.

Ninian arrived among the southern Picts about 200 years after they had been brought into contact with the Christian faith ; and yet he is styled *primus apos- tolus suæ gentis,* 'the first apostle of his own people' (Vit. Nin., cap. 11). The very facility with which he succeeded in converting those people is remarkable ; he seems at once to have found it possible to set up a com- plete ecclesiastical organization. It is not conceivable that if there had been Christians among the Picts previ- ously, they would be entirely without a Christian min- istry. Ninian, however, proceeds to put things upon a new footing, and succeeds in a wonderfully short time in making the new arrangements. If this account be true it would indicate that Ninian was in reality an emissary from Rome, and that his mission was to conform the Pictish Church to the approved model there ; he is sent as the first bishop of that Church, just as Palladins was sent as first bishop to the Scots. Rome was undoubtedly now attempting to grasp the supremacy of the whole Christian Church for herself, and taking Ailred's or even Bede's statement to be true, Ninian came to Britain on a mission for attaining that end. If Ninian was in-

deed the first bishop of the southern Picts, they obtained
that bishop from Rome. It is thus clear that for the 300
previous years, however little else we know of the state
of the Christian Church among those Picts, we know that
they never possessed a bishop ; or the bishops they possessed were bishops of the apostolic and not of the Roman
type. It is not satisfactory to be led to this view of
our early missionary, and yet the evidence we possess
rather favours it, while that evidence is corroborated by
the fact of Ninian's intimacy with Martin of Tours, whose
disposition as described by Sulpitius Severus, has been
referred to already. But even should episcopacy have
reached Scotland in the fifth century from Rome, the
episcopacy of that period was very different from
the episcopacy of a later period or of modern times.
Ritson observes, with his usual causticity, that these men
were more like the methodist preachers of modern times
than those who, as bishops, profess to be their successors
now.

Ussher (Prim. p. 1059) states that there was in his
time a life of Ninian in Ireland, in which it was stated
that owing to the annoyance he received from his mother
and other relatives, he left Whithorn, and retired to
Ireland, when he received from the king a grant of a
place called Cluainconer, where he erected a monastery,
and died after many years spent there. There is not a
particle of historical evidence of any value for this statement, but it shews very distinctly how unreliable portions
of early Irish Church history are ; and it gives rise to a
question whether there has not been a tendency to appropriate British saints on the part of Irish writers. The
Irish calendar leaves Scotland in undisputed possession
of very few saints of the early Celtic Church, and yet
Scotland was neither later in being christianized, nor
were her establishments less famous than those of the

sister isle.   Ireland has much to boast of in her "Annals," but many of the statements in these and other early church documents, require a sifting which they have not yet received.

The churches in Scotland commemorative of Ninian are sufficiently numerous to shew how deep was the reverence for his name in the early Church.   Chalmers (Caled. i. 315; iii. 211) enumerates no fewer than twenty-four churches and chapels dedicated to him throughout Scotland, extending from the Shetland islands to the Mull of Galloway, and one additional in Kintyre has escaped his notice.

CHAPTER VIII.

THE Pelagian heresy made its appearance in the Church about the close of the fourth century. Such events do not usually take place without some preparatory process, and such a process was manifestly in progress in the early Church as led to the outbreak of this remarkable heresy. Its roots may be traced to the doctrines of the Gnostics and the writings of Origen, who had sown seed which could not but finally produce evil. Pelagius himself was a Briton (Bede's Eccl. Hist., Book i., cap. 10); his name is said to have been Morgan, a word composed of the two Welsh words, *mor*, 'the sea,' and *gan*, 'birth,' which, translated into Latin, a practice common in the Church, makes Pelagius. He was a man of unquestion able learning and talent, as his controversy with Augustine shews; and he is said to have written several works, including a "Commentary on the Epistles of Paul," and a part of a treatise on the power of nature and free will. The doctrine which has handed his name down with reproach to after ages had reference mainly to the person and work of the Holy Spirit. It is remarkable that no sooner were the doctrines of Arius, which had reference to the person and work of the Son, suppressed, and upon the whole effectually, than similar doctrines were broached regarding the person and work of the Divine Spirit. It would seem as if the tendency of opinion which would lead to the dishonouring of one person of the

Trinity is just as prone to touch the honour of another. The unity of the Divine Trinity may be discovered from the actings of its enemies, as well as from the faith and joy of believers. Thus the Arian controversy of the 4th century became the Pelagian controversy of the 5th. Bede tells us that the great friend and coadjutor of Pelagius was Julianus of Campania, whose anger was kindled by the loss of his bishopric, of which he had been deprived; he further informs us that Pelagius "spread far and near the infection of his perfidious doctrine." It does not appear that he himself taught it in Britain, but Agricola the son of Severianus, a Pelagian bishop, brought the heresy over; hereupon we learn that the Gallican prelates gathered a great synod, and after consultation, by unanimous consent, chose Germanus, bishop of Auxerre, and Lupus of Troyes to go to Britain, to confirm it in the faith. It has been generally held that the mission of Palladius to the Scots had some connection with the Pelagian controversy. Bede, however, says nothing of this; all we learn from him respecting the mission is, that in the 8th year of Theodosius the younger, or A.D. 431, Palladius was sent by Celestinus, the Roman pontiff, to the Scots that believed in Christ, to be their first bishop. He represents the Gallican bishops as earnest on the subject of the Pelagian heresy, the Roman pontiff as earnest on the subject of furnishing the Scots with a bishop. It was not for the conversion of the Scots, for they already believed in Christ, nor for the confirming of them, but more likely for the purpose of organizing them after the Roman model. If Palladius was in reality an emissary from Rome, this is the only inference that can be fairly deduced from the narrative of Bede; the Scots who believed in Christ, had obviously no bishop till now, and this event took place towards the middle of the 5th century.

Prosper, usually called of Aquitaine, in his Chronicon, written about the year 455, is the earliest authority existing regarding this mission; nor can he be much in error, as he writes within twenty years after the event. All he says is, that in the year 431, " Palladins, being ordained by Pope Celestine, is sent as first bishop to the Scots believing in Christ " (Mon. Hist. Britt., p. lxxvii.). Prosper was one of the most energetic opponents of the Pelagians, so much so that in one place he calls Pelagius *Coluber Britannus,* 'the British serpent' (*ibid.,* p. ci.), yet he does not in this notice connect Palladins' mission in any way with Pelagianism. He, no doubt, in his work " Contra Collatorem " (Mon. Hist. Brit., p. ci.), tells us that while Celestine " strove to retain the Roman Island (Britain) Catholic, he made the barbarous island (probably Ireland, though Scotland was often called an island by early writers) Christian." If the Scots believed in Christ already, as Prosper himself intimates in his first notice, this could only have reference to organization. If Prosper and Bede be correct, Palladius was pretty manifestly, like Ninian, an emissary of the Roman see, which was now resolutely setting itself to grasp the sceptre of universal dominion in the Christian Church. Bede quotes the very words of Prosper's chronicle, and these are expanded by Nennius, who gives us some insight into the mode of growth of early ecclesiastical history, and the changes it underwent in process of time. The latter tells us (Hist. Nenn., cap. 25) that when Patrick had been at Rome for many years, Palladins was sent "as first (primitus) bishop by the Roman Pope Celestine,[1] in order to *convert* the Scots to Christ; that God hindered him by means of severe storms; for no man can receive anything on earth unless it be given him from heaven.

---

[1] The *Roman* Pope, seeing that Papa or Pope was at the time a common name for ecclesiastics.

and that Palladins crossed from Ireland and came to Britain, where he died in the land of the Picts." The earliest period assigned to Nennius, or the writer who is known by that name, is A.D. 796, so that if that be the correct date, the legend had grown somewhat during the sixty one years since the death of Bede.

These two facts are very clear in Bede's narrative ; that Ninian was sent as first bishop to the southern Picts, and Palladins as first bishop to the Scots. In the chapter immediately preceding that in which he relates the mission of Palladins, he tells us that the "Scots and Picts are called foreign nations, not because they are seated out of Britain, but because they were remote from that part of it which was possessed by the Britons ; two inlets of the sea lying between them." . . . From this it is by no means clear that the mission of Palladins was to the Irish Scots alone. The statement of Nennius throws some light on the destination of the missionary, when he tells us (Nenn. Hist., c. l.), that "leaving Ireland (Hibernia) he removed to Britain," and so does that of Prosper, when he speaks of the "barbarous island" as opposed to the "Roman island" (Mon. Hist. Brit., ci.) ; and from these authorities it appears probable that the mission was in the first instance to Ireland, but the statement of Bede, and the course adopted by Palladius himself, render it quite as probable that his mission embraced the Scots, whether in Ireland or in the northern portion of Britain.

It has already been shewn that the first writer who mentions the Scots is Ammianus Marcellinus, about A.D. 360, when they appear as allies of the Picts. Innes (Civ. and Eccl. Hist., p. 25) holds that this agrees with the opinion maintained by some, that the Scots crossed from Ireland about 150 years before ; that they had had time to increase, and to become able and dangerous allies of the Picts in their wars with the Romans. But it

would agree equally well with the opinion that they had
been in Scotland for any length of time previously, seeing it merely implies the application of a name to this
people, which had never been applied to them before,
either in Scotland or in Ireland. The Scots were never
heard of under that name before A.D. 360, and then we
find the name, as has been already noticed, for the first
time in the pages of a Latin author; we have nothing in
fact to shew that such a nation as the Scots existed at all
before A.D. 360. We know, at least, that the name did
not exist; and at the time that the name appears, we
find, upon unquestionable authority, that the people to
whom it is applied, inhabit Scotland, and are the allies of
the Picts in their inroads upon the Roman province.
The name Scots is, beyond dispute, applied first of all, as
it appears in authentic history, to a people inhabiting
North Britain. It is not disputed that these people were
the same race with the native inhabitants of Ireland, and
that the latter in consequence had a right to the same
appellation; but as to the first appearance of the name,
the fact is as has been stated.

The name Scotia is of considerably more recent date
than that of Scoti or Scots; it is not the earlier name
of Ireland. In the quotation from Aristotle, which the
compilers of the "Monumenta Historica Brittannica"
admit as authentic, the earliest name of Ireland is Ierne,
and of Britain, Albion; and these are the latest names
too, for, among the native Irish, Ireland is Erin at this
day, and, to the native Scot, Scotland is only known as
Alba. The name Scotia does not appear at all before the
seventh century, and is first used by Isidore of Seville (*Ibid.*
Hist. Orig. Lib. ix., c. 2), who wrote about A.D. 600. He
applies it to Ireland, although there is manifestly considerable confusion in his ideas; he tells us, for instance, that
" the Scots derive their name in their own language from

F

their painted bodies," where he obviously mistakes them for the Picts, and where he gives a very sensible account of the origin of the name Pict. He afterwards tells us that " Scotia is the same with Ibernia, the nearest island to Britain," obviously indicating that Ibernia was an established and well-known name, which must be made use of to explain this more recent appellation of Scotia. The name appears next in the writings of the Geographer of Ravenna, who also flourished in the seventh century, and who speaks (Mon. Hist. Britt., p. xxvi.) of *Insula maxima, quæ dicitur Hibernia, quæ ut dictum est, et Scotia appellatur*, 'The largest island which is called Hibernia, and which, as is said, is also called Scotia;' meaning that it is well known by the name of Hibernia, and is said to be also called Scotia; that there is no certainty on this point; men say so; but that there is perfect certainty as to its ancient and usual name being Hibernia. Towards the close of the seventh century and onwards the name was in general use, as we find from the writings of Adomnan and others.

We find, then, the name Scots first appearing in the year 360, and used to designate the allies of the Picts in their incursions into the Roman province; and 240 years after we find the name Scotia for the first time coming into use, transferred manifestly from the people to the country which they inhabited. From this time the practice of writers using the term is various. Adomnan almost uniformly, if not altogether so, applies it to Ireland, his own native island. But not so other writers. Bede applies it sometimes to Scotland. He calls Hi or Iona "insula Scottorum," *an island of the Scots* (Eccl. Hist., B. iii. 17.); and tells of Ceallach, who had been appointed missionary to the Mercians, that he quitted his episcopate, adding (B. iii. c. 21), that he returned to Hi, which, he says, was among the Scots a chief monastery; and he relates of Colman (B. iii. 26), that he returned from England to Scotia to consult with his friends, adding (B. iv. 4), that he repaired to Hi. What is equally significant is, that generally throughout his history Bede applies the term Hibernia to Ireland. Isidore, and the Geographer of Ravenna, who lived on the continent, the one in Spain and the other in Italy, might have heard that the name Scotia was applied to Ireland, and Adomnan, with the usual nationality of his countrymen, and knowing Ireland to be the chief country of the Scots, might appropriate the name, newly originated, to his own country; but Bede follows a different practice, and while applying the term Scots indiscriminately to those of Ireland and Britain, distinguishing the latter by the term "Scoti septemptrionales," or northern Scots, he in like manner uses Scotia indiscriminately, sometimes applying it to modern Scotland, as in the case already quoted, and at other times to Ireland, as in describing Egfrid's invasion (Lib. iv., c. 26.) The only way in which the difficulties of this question can be met, is by the assumption which all the evidence referred to bears out, that the term Scotia was applied to the whole territory of the Scots, whether in Scotland or Ireland. It is so in the case of Bede, the most reliable of all our early historians; the people were Scots in both islands, and their territory became Scotia in consequence. For a time Ireland was Scotia major, and north-western Scotland Scotia minor; but in the long-run Scotia minor won the day, and carried off the prize, if it be considered one. This is the only satisfactory solution of the difficulties connected with the question regarding the locality of ancient Scotia. In modern times we find a nearly analogous case. The islands which compose this united kingdom are often denominated Britain; our Sovereign is called the Queen of Bri-

tain, and our Parliament is called the British Parliament;
in like manner, while Erin and Alba retained their distinctive denominations, the territory of the Scots in either
island was denominated Scotia from the seventh century
downwards.   Ussher devotes much time and space to con-
trovert this view, and some writers in modern Scotland
have agreed with him, maintaining that no country was
known as Scotia, but Ireland, until the beginning of the
tenth century.   If Adomnan and writers of the same
school alone be referred to as authorities, there may be
some ground for this conclusion, but in the face of the
authority of Bede, who was an entirely neutral party,
utterly indifferent, as he must have been, to national
claims involved, it is hard to see how it can be defended.
Gordon, in his " Intinerarium Septemptrionale," and Innes
in his " Civil and Ecclesiastical History," both agree in
the view now stated and defended—the latter, a Roman
Catholic priest, and one of the most learned, temperate,
profound, and judicious writers on the early history of
this or any other country, and most trustworthy, if sufficient allowance be made for the bias acquired from his
views on ecclesiastical polity.

It is not possible, then, from the notice given by Prosper and Bede, to say whether Palladius was deputed
to visit the Scots in Ireland or in Britain.   The statement of Nennius alone enables us to conclude that his
mission embraced chiefly Ireland, as he first directed his
course to that island.   All writers on the subject, however,
allow that the stay of Palladius in Ireland was brief.[1]
The island was probably at the time in a large measure
heathen, and whether impelled by persecution, or by
what he judged the want of success, he crossed to Scotland, and finally took up his residence in the land of the

---

[1] See Dr. Todd of Dublin's recent work on St. Patrick.

Picts (terra Pictorum), where he died, as is usually thought, at Fordoun, in the county of Kincardine, or Mearns. Colgan says (Vita Secunda Sancti Patricii, cap. xxiv., p. 13), that after a short time he died "in Campo Girgin, in a place called Fordun." This Campus Girgin is said to be a translation of Magh Ghirgin (*the Plain of Girgin*), the Gaelic name of which "the Mearns" is an abbreviation ; the same word on the west coast is Marbhairn (Morvern). Colgan seems to have been mistaken in his analysis of the name. But there is ample reason to believe that the facts of Palladins' death are as stated, there being to this day at Fordoun an annual fair, called Padie's fair (Innes' Civil and Eccles. Hist., p. 65), or Palladie's fair, commemorative of his name, while the church and a neighbouring well were both dedicated to him, and Innes farther mentions that his relics were preserved there till the Reformation. Irish annalists give a short period to Palladius' labours in Scotland. "Post parvum intervallum," says Colgan, *after a short interval* he died ; but Scotch writers give him a much longer period, during which he baptized and admitted Servanus and Ternan to the office of the ministry. Early Irish writers cannot, for several reasons, be held so trustworthy in historical questions relating to Scotland, or in which Scotland and Ireland have a mingled interest, as in those which relate to Ireland alone. This must be borne in mind in dealing with their evidence, nor need we wonder that that evidence should require sifting, on reaching us from an age in which such statements as are made regarding the miracles of Patrick and Columba were given to the world as facts.

Reference has already been made to the term "primus apostolus," as applied by Ailred to Ninian. The "pri mus episcopus," in the case of Palladins, has also given rise to much discussion. It cannot be maintained in this case, as it has been in another of a later date, which we shall meet with as we proceed, that the 'primus' here had reference to ecclesiastical rank, and referred to ecclesiastical Primacy as conferred on Palladius. The 'primus' here has been, without dispute, allowed to refer to priority of time; Palladius was the first Bishop of the Scots. Ninian was sent from Rome as first Bishop to the Picts about A.D. 400, and about thirty years after Palladius was sent from Rome as first Bishop to the Scots, and both laboured and died in what is now called Scotland. The mission of Palladius took place about 350 years after Christianity first entered Scotland, and yet he was the first Bishop of the Scots, no doubt, the Scots in Ireland, but the Scots who were settled in Scotland also.

Fordun's account of the Church in the intervening period, is remarkable, and has been much canvassed; yet coming from a monk of the Roman Catholic Church in the fourteenth century, it is entitled to an amount of weight which writers who depreciate Fordun's authority have denied to it. His words are, speaking of Palladius coming to Scotland—"Before whose coming the Scots had, as teachers of the faith (doctores fidei), and administrators of the sacraments, presbyters only, and monks, following the order (ritum) of the primitive church." (Scotochr. Lib. iii., c. 8). He also states that the Scots had been "long before believers in Christ." Innes (Civ. and Eccl. Hist., Book i., p. 58, &c.) takes Fordun to task for this statement, and ridicules his quoting as his authority Ralph Higden's Polychronicon, a work the author of which was his own cotemporary, and which in reality does not contain the passage quoted. Let that be as it may, Innes' reply to Fordun is at least as unsatisfactory as Fordun's authority. For Fordun's statement we have ample vouchers in the words of Prosper and Bede. If

Palladius was the "first bishop," there could have been none before him. But Innes says that "neither Fordun nor any of the Catholic writers that copied him, ever dreamed that those priests or doctors of the Scots had no episcopal ordination." (Civil and Eccl. Hist., p. 60). We do not know what Fordun dreamed; he does not tell us, but he gives us to know that so far as he could learn the Scots had only presbyters, or as Innes translates the word, priests and monks, previous to the coming of Palladius. Now they could not have had monks, for the monkish order was first introduced into Western Europe by Martin of Tours, who died very shortly before the mission of Palladius, so that from Fordun's statement we must conclude that the Scots, who believed in Christ, were ministered to by presbyters previous to the mission of Palladius. If, as Innes maintains, these had episcopal ordination, whence did they obtain it? The Picts had no bishop to confer it; the Britons were in similar circumstances, so far as any evidence goes to shew; and even were it otherwise, it is not very probable that Scottish Christians would have ventured within the Roman wall to obtain ordination for their ministers, at a time when there was chronic war between the nation, and the Roman government. There would, no doubt, have been Christian ministers, and Christian ordinances, but they would have been ministers after the Bible model, and not after that of Rome. Many mistakes m connection with Church history arise from misapprehension of the meaning of words, and no word has conveyed more erroneous ideas than that of episcopus or bishop. Presbyterians agree with Episcopalians in respecting the Episcopal order, they differ only in the meaning they attach to the term. It is remarkable how rarely writers, who maintain the existence of the episcopal order, as now constituted, in the early Church, go beyond the early fathers in citing their autho-

rities; how rarely they quote the Scriptures and apostolical practice as there exhibited. Ussher, Lloyd, Stillingfleet, Innes, are all equally characterized by this peculiarity,
and by entirely ignoring the fact that presbyterians do
not deny episcopacy, but maintain that in Scripture the
bishop and the presbyter are one, and that every presbyter is an "episcopus," or overseer of the flock of Christ.
That very different views on the subject of bishops
existed at an early period from those which exist now, is
sufficiently clear from what Ussher quotes from Joceline
in his life of St. Patrick (Eccl. Prim., p. 950), where he
says, "that under St. Patrick there were 350 famous,
holy bishops, filled with the Holy Ghost;" he says he
consecrated this number with his own hand. Nennius
also says, that "he founded 365 churches, ordained 365
bishops, and 3000 presbyters." Antonine and Vincentius
and other authors make the same statement; 365 bishops
and 3000 presbyters in Ireland is surely more like a pres
byterian than an episcopal organization. If these state
ments be true, and they are made on the authority of Roman
Catholic writers, who may surely be believed when writing what is opposed to their own system, the episcopacy
of St. Patrick's time was a very different institution from
the modern episcopacy of either Rome or England.
Neither Innes, nor any other writer who has followed
him, have touched Fordun's statement, that Scotland had
only presbyters previous to the mission of Palladius;
and if so, Palladius, like Ninian, must, from the evidence
we possess, have been an emissary of the Roman See,
whose object was to organize Christianity among the
Scots of Ireland and Scotland, in accordance with what
was then the Roman model. The civil power of Rome
being on the wane, the ecclesiastical power began to rise
on its ruins, and there may have been no little connection
between the two processes; the loss of one species of

power may have helped to impel an ambitious people, accustomed to universal dominion, to seek after the establishment of another.

It may be asked whether the See of Rome had really assumed such an attitude and reached to so high an ambition at so early a period. ˋ It is true indeed that the Rome of the fourth and fifth centuries was very different from the Rome of the twelfth and thirteenth. The power of the Roman See was not the growth of a day ; century after century of wise and persistent management secured for it that power, the possession of which led to its gradual and still progressive downfal. Rome differed much from itself at different periods of its history ; this is true, both with regard to its doctrine and organization, much as it may pretend to infallibility.

So early, however, as the age of Cyprian, Bishop of Carthage, who suffered martyrdom A.D. 260, the claims of Rome were beginning to be put forth and acknowledged ; not that the actual supremacy of the Roman See was established, for in his controversy with Stephen the Roman bishop, Cyprian shews not the least respect for his office, as one implying infallibility, or entitling its possessor to submission independent of the convictions of one's own mind ; but the state of the Church was undergoing a certain measure of change from primitive times. A late distinguished writer (Cunningham's Hist. Theol., vol. i., p. 168) has described its condition in the age of Cyprian in a few sentences, which may be quoted—" First, There is enough in the writings of Cyprian to prove that down even to the middle of the third century, the substantial identity of bishops and presbyters was maintained ; and the idea of the episcopate being by divine appointment a distinct, independent, higher office than the presbyterate was yet not generally received ; Secondly, There is enough to prove, that in Cyprian's time, and in a great measure through his exertions, an important distinction between bishops and presbyters, implying some superiority, not well defined, of the one over the other, became prevalent; and, Thirdly, That he has laid down, though very vaguely and obscurely, some principles which, when fully carried out and applied, lay a good foundation for maintaining, that there should be one visible head of the whole Church, and for vesting some kind or degree of primacy or supremacy in the Bishop of Rome."

Nearly a century after Cyprian, the Roman emperor had become Christian, and exercised without dispute the function of calling general councils of the Church; the councils of Nice, Sardis, and Rimini, were all called by the authority of the emperor. At this time steps were taken by the civil government to set limits to the power both of the bishops and the people. In depriving the latter of their privileges the ecclesiastical rulers willingly gave their aid, and by the close of the century "there remained no more than a shadow of the ancient government of the Church." (Mosh. Eccl. Hist. Cent. iv., cap. 2). In connection with this change, the Bishop of Rome, although by no means as yet a Pope, came to be " the first in rank, and to have a sort of pre-eminence over all other prelates."—-(Mosh. *ibid*).

In the fifth century in which the mission of Palladius took place, the ambition of Rome was stimulated by the rivalry of Constantinople. The removal of the seat of government to the east required some change in the arrangements of the Church; so, to suit the convenience of the court, Constantine set up the Bishop of Constantinople as, in a great measure, the rival of the Bishop of Rome. The emulation was keen and persistent, and was one of the means which conduced to the final establishment of Roman supremacy in the west. The barbarians of the north, while crushing the civil power in Rome, became, for political purposes, the slaves of the Church, and in the hands of such a man as Leo the Great, the power of the Roman See was largely increased, although still far short of what it became in the hands of a Hildebrand and similar men. There is nothing inconsistent then with what we know about the Rome of the fifth century in the assumption that she sent her emissaries to Britain ; nay, taking the condition of the Western Church generally, which had accommodated itself to her model, and the condition of the British Church, which our most trustworthy authorities shew had not, there is strong ground for the conclusion that these first bishops had been sent as missionaries in her interest, and were in all probability zealous, earnest men, who believed that in altering the organization of the British Church they were doing God acceptable service. It would appear that the mission of Palladins differed from that of Ninian in being unsuccessful. The after condition of the Scottish Church is corroborative of this conclusion.

CHAPTER IX.

THE mission of Patrick, the son of Calphurnius or Patrick Mac Alpin, as he is usually styled in the Scottish Highlands, although connected chiefly with the ecclesiastical history of Ireland, cannot be overlooked in any account of the early history of the church in Scotland. The place of Patrick's birth has been made a matter of much controversy; latterly some doubts have been thrown even on his existence, and some writers have been led to think that he is identical with Palladins. Both are said to have been Scots, and the year 431 is that held pretty generally to have been the date of the mission of both. "The legend of St. Patrick, in its present shape, is not older than the ninth century, and under the influence of an investigation into older authorities, he dissolves into three personages : Sen-Patricius, whose day in the calendar is the 24th August; Palladius, *qui est Patricius*, to whom the mission in 432 properly belongs, and who is said to have retired to Alban or Scotland, where he died among the Cruithne; and Patricius, whose day is the 27th March, and to whom alone a certain date can be assigned, for he died in the chronological period in the year 493,—and from the acts of these three saints the subsequent legend of the great apostle of Ireland was compiled, and an arbitrary chronology applied to it " (W. F. Skene, In. to Dean of Lismore's Book, p. 73). The confusion with reference to Patrick and Palladius seems to have arisen from viewing both as being sent by the Pope. There is no authority for this as respects Patrick.

The story of St. Patrick is variously related. In his own confession (Confessio Pat.) he says, "I Patrick, a sinner, the most rude, and the least of all the faithful, and the most contemptible with most people, had as my father, Calpurnius, formerly a deacon, the son of Potitus, a presbyter,[1] who lived in the village of Bonaven, belonging to Tabernia; for he had a cottage in the neighbourhood where I was captured. I was then about sixteen years old. But I was ignorant of the true God, and was led away into captivity to Ireland." Such is the account said to be given of the great Irish missionary by himself. There is very considerable reason to suppose that the document called the *Confessio Patricii* is authentic, although its authenticity has been questioned, and the probability is, that the real Patrick of Irish history was the son of Calpurnius, a deacon, and the grandson of Potitus, a priest, who lived at Bonaven, belonging to Tabernia. If this story had been the production of a later age, Calpurnius would not have been made the son of a father in holy orders; it must be older than the practice of celibacy among the clergy. It is not an easy matter to identify the locality given by the saint as the place of his birth. That it was in Britain is manifest from other passages in the confession. He tells us, for instance (c. 10), that he was "in Britain with his parents" on one occasion; and again, that "he was ready to go into Britain, yea, most willingly as to his own country and parents; and not only so, but to go even to Gaul to visit the brethren." Some writers have held that the Britain spoken of here was Armorica. The strong emphasis laid upon his going to Gaul in the last extract quoted, is sufficient to shew that Gaul must

---

[1] The word "Presbyter" is almost uniformly translated priest by one class of writers. Innes does so, and others besides.

have been at a much greater distance from Britain than could be implied in crossing the line from Armorica into France, while, if the Bretons were but fugitive colonists from the invading Saxons of the fifth century, the name of Britannia could not have existed at the period of Patrick's birth as applied to Brittany. Ussher (Prim., p. 819) agrees in the statement that Patrick was a native of Britain, and is disposed to fix the place of his birth at Kilpatrick on the Clyde. The name of this locality is not however of the slightest value as evidence on the question. There is a Kilpatrick in Dumfriesshire, and there are Kilpatricks in places which can have no possible connection with either the birth or the life of the saint. All that the name shews is, that the church in that locality was dedicated to him. Ussher quotes Probus in his life of the saint who gives us Patrick's own account of his birth, adding that the place was not far from the western sea (*haud procul a mare occidentali*). Joceline in his life of St. Patrick, writing in the twelfth century, adds that he was by nation a Briton, and that Tabernia is from "*Campus Tabernaculorum*," because the Romans pitched their tents there. He also tells us that his father lived (*secus oppidum Empthor*) near the town of Empthor, which some imagine to be Nemphlar in Renfrewshire. Fiach (Prim. Eccl., p. 819) calls the place of his birth Nempthur in the northern part of Britain. Joceline (Vit. Pat., cap. 11) says, "This place was in the valley of the Clyde, and was usually called by the people themselves *Dunbretan*, or *Mons Britonum*, 'the hill of the Britons.' Joceline thus makes his birth-place Dunbarton, which he makes identical with Nempthur. All these older authorities point to the north bank of the Clyde as the birth-place of the saint. And yet there is not much reliance to be placed on the evidence of men who write seven or eight hundred years after the event which they are narrating. Were we to be guided by the words of the saint himself, we would fix upon Banavie in Lochaber as the place of his birth. Bonaven of Tabernia, making allowance for the changes made in latinizing Celtic words, is far more like the translation of these words than of any other that have been suggested, and the place lies towards the western sea. Besides, Ussher notices that Sigibert (Prim. Eccl., p. 820) calls Patrick a Scot, which is much more in harmony with the fact of his being born in Lochaber than in the very heart of a British kingdom. Cardinal Baronius also calls him a Scot, though an Irish Scot (Bar. Ann. 431).

If St. Patrick was a Scot, and some authorities, if there are any that can be relied on, are in favour of this conclusion, we have an interesting view afforded us of the condition of the early Scottish Church.[1] Patrick M'Alpine (and the very name savours of Ben Nevis), or the son of Calpurnius, as latinized by himself, was the son of a deacon, who was himself the son of a presbyter, named Potitus. These names are held to savour of a Latin origin. But we have Emchadus and Virolecus inhabiting the valley of Glenurquhart, near Loch Ness, in the days of Columba (Vit. Col. Adomn. Lib. iii., c. 14), and why not Calpurnius and Potitus in the near neighbourhood in those of St. Patrick. Here then we have a succession of three generations holding office in the Scottish Church previous to the years from 372 to 376, when Patrick is said to have been born, although, if he commenced his mission in 432, the real period of his birth was more likely about 400. But speaking generally, these three generations of Christian office-bearers existed in the Scottish Church during the fourth century, or nearly a century before the

---

[1] We have not taken up the question regarding the claims of Wales to be held as the birth-place of St. Patrick, nor the story of his mother Conchessa, and of his being nephew to St. Martin of Tours. There is not a particle of trustworthy authority on any one of these questions.

mission of Palladius. This is in a measure corroborative of Fordun's statement, regarding the early condition of that Church, to which Innes and others have taken so much exception.

But we have been dealing with authorities most of them belonging to a period nearly 1000 years later than the age of St. Patrick himself. What do we learn from the earlier writers ? From himself we learn that he was a native of Britain as already observed, that he was taken prisoner at an early age by the Irish, that he spent several years in Ireland in menial service of the lowest kind, that he was converted to Christ, that he was miraculously delivered from bondage, that Christ commanded him to go to Ireland, and that he devoted himself to preaching the Gospel among the Irish, that he met with many trials, but had great success, for he tells us that "in Ireland they who never knew God, and worshipped idols and unclean things, have now become the people of God, and are called the sons of God. The sons of Scots and daughters of chieftains are seen to be monks and virgins of Christ. There was also one blessed Scottish virgin (Bridget) of noble race, most fair, and adult, whom I baptized." (These two last paragraphs do savour of a later era than the beginning of the fifth century.) At the same time we learn nothing in the "Confession" of his being at Rome at any time. He seems never to have gone beyond Britain. We learn nothing of his having ordained bishops or founded churches. He speaks like a true apostle of having baptized a convert, but relates nothing of what is detailed most fully regarding him by writers 1000 years after.[1]

[1] There is a remarkable difference between the "confession" and the "epistle about Coroticus" of St. Patrick. In the latter he is the full-blown churchman, an "episcopus," and one invested with a power and jurisdiction to which the other makes no reference. It is hardly possible to believe them to be the writing of the same man. They may be severally the work of the older and the later Patrick.

Prosper, of Aquitaine, who wrote during the currency of St. Patrick's mission, makes no reference whatsoever to him; he neither tells us that he was at Rome, nor that he was sent from Rome. He speaks of Palladius, but not of Patrick; and yet some are credulous enough to believe that he succeeded Palladius as an emissary from Rome, and was the second Bishop of the Scots. There is not so much as one shred of reliable evidence in proof of this. Gildas, our next oldest authority to Prosper, does not mention the name of Patrick; he makes no allusion either to him or his mission; nor does Bede; the name of Patrick never occurs in his whole history. It has been said that Bede's object was to give the history of the Anglo-Saxon Church, and that he might not have felt it incumbent on him to make any mention of such a work as St. Patrick's among the Celts. But he tells of Ninian, of Palladius, and of Columba; and why not of Patrick? He either knew nothing of him or he had some reason for making no reference to what he knew. Was it because he could not say honestly that Patrick was in Rome, and could not connect his name in any way with the support of Romish pretensions? Was it because Patrick had been building up what Augustine had been sent to destroy? Besides, in one of the oldest Irish MSS., the Book of Durrow, St. Patrick is styled a "presbyter" (Vit. Col. Reeves' Ed., p. 242 n.). Putting all these things together—that St. Patrick never was at Rome, that he was a mere presbyter, that he had dedicated himself to the Irish mission by command of Christ—we can see that Patrick held a different place from Ninian and Palladius, and may discover some reason why Bede in his history entirely ignores his existence.[1] From all that can be learned of him,

---

[1] Bede does enter him in his Martyrology as a Presbyter, which is at any rate a proof of his existence.

G

there never was a nobler Christian missionary than Patrick. He and Columba were men of a class, true representatives of the ministers of the ancient Scottish Church, and men who, while having much in common with the earnestness and zeal of Ninian and Palladius, were not, like them, engaged in fostering an organization which was to lead to the future enslavement of the Church. It is obvious that objection may be taken to what is said with reference to Bede, from the fact that he does refer to Columba, and devotes more space to his account of him than to that of Ninian or Palladius. Bede could not avoid referring to Columba; the early conversion of the Anglo-Saxons was so intimately connected with Columba and his successors, that to ignore him would have been to ignore history itself. Unless this be the true account of the matter, it is hard to say where it is to be found, and to deny the existence and mission of St. Patrick altogether, would be to treat the uniform tradition as well as the authentic history of the Irish Church, in a manner for which we have no warrant. Patrick was like Columba, a Presbyter; he went to Ireland from love to Christ, and love to the souls of men, as he tells us in his "Confession;" he might have had no great respect for certain ecclesiastical forms which came to be held in much esteem in the days of Bede, yet was he nevertheless a true missionary of Christ, who conveyed inestimable blessings to the Irish people. Strange that a people who owed Rome nothing in connection with their conversion to Christ, and who long struggled against her pretensions, should be now ranked among her most devoted adherents, and that they should associate this devotion to Rome with their devotion to St. Patrick, who owed nothing to Rome either. No people in Europe have more completely changed their position in reference to that taken up by their early Christian ancestors, than have the modern Irish.

Many of the legends told of St. Patrick are undeserving of the slightest credence, though the number of the lives of the saint said to have been written is very great. The tripartite life edited by Colgan is that most worthy of regard; but as the mission of St. Patrick pertains more to Irish than to Scottish history, it is not needful to enter here into its alleged details.[1] The Scottish form of these will be found detailed in the Aberdeen Breviary. The only additional fact regarding St. Patrick which it may be important to notice is, that Adomnan only adverts once either to his existence or his mission to Ireland, in his whole work on the life of Columba; a remarkable fact, if all related of him by more recent Irish hagiologists be true.

---

[1] Dr. Todd's volume on St. Patrick contains almost everything that can be collected regarding the early Irish missionary.

CHAPTER X

THE next names that appear among the early missionaries of Scotland after Ninian are Servanus and Ternan.
These men were the disciples of Palladius, having, in all
probability, been baptized and afterwards ordained by
him about the year 440. St. Serf is famous in the hagiology of Scotland, as connected with the ancient ecclesiastical institution at Loch Leven. The name of Ternan,
or Tighearnan, is less famous, but is commemorated at
Banchory-Ternan, in Kincardineshire, and has been con-
founded in other cases with that of Ernan, an Irish saint of
later date. Killearnan, of which there are several in
Scotland, is, when pronounced in Gaelic, Cille Thighear-
nan, and may be the Church of Ternan, as well as that of
Ernan. Ussher speaks of a life of Servanus existing in
his time, which was full of idle legends (Prim. 674), and
the story of St. Serf is variously related by our early
Scottish writers. Fordun (Scotochr. iii. 9) tells us
that Palladius made him his own coadjutor in teaching the people the "orthodox faith," where there is
distinct reference to the particular work which Palladius had assigned to him. In the life of Kentigern,
in the Glasgow Chartulary (Chart. Glas., p. 85), we read
that Servanus taught the Christian law to the clergy, it
being mentioned previously that his residence was at

Collenros (Culros).[1] The Breviary of Aberdeen (Brev. Aber., 1st July), seems to contain in full the legend of Servanus, and an epitome of it will present the reader with what was believed concerning him in the middle ages, the MS. from which it has been printed being written about the beginning of the sixteenth century. From this we learn that Servanus, who derived his origin from the nation of the Scots, lived according to the form and rites of the primitive Church (*sub ʸforma et ritu primitive ecclesie vixit*) until the coming of Palladius, who was sent by Pope Celestine to convert the nation of the Scots, and who found there the holy Servanus. There are two remarkable statements here, bearing out the views already presented with regard to those Roman missions; that the primitive Church in Scotland was, in respect of organization and rites, different from what it afterwards became, and that Palladius was sent to conform it to the Roman model. The authority here is that of the Roman Catholic Church itself in the sixteenth century, and it is vain for Innes or others to say that writers of the Roman Catholic party could never mean anything in such statements that could militate against the claims of their own Church: reasoning thus is begging the whole question. These men wrote what was known and believed at the time, and we give them the more credit, just because, judging from Innes, we might expect their bias to be the other way.

The legend in the Breviary tells us farther, that Servanns being thoroughly instructed, was raised by Palladius to the Episcopal dignity, among all the nation of the Scots, and made his own Suffragan. What truth is in this we know not; but the institution at Loch Leven,

[1] "Ros" means "Nemus," *a forest* as well as a *promontory*, hence "Muc Ros," or "Nemus porcorum." "Culros" means *the back of the forest*, as "Kinross" means *the end of the forest*.

which claimed St. Serf as its founder, was afterwards a Culdee establishment, and only yielded to Rome, after a severe struggle, in the twelfth century. The miracles attributed to this saint are numerous, and some of them are interesting as containing topographical allusions. On one occasion a poor man had killed his sow in order to provide refreshment for the saint and his followers ; but such was the merit of the saint, that although a large portion of the sow had been eaten, the generous host found it alive immediately after. The saint converted water into wine, and, giving it to a sick monk[1] to drink, he was restored to perfect health.

On one occasion he was sorely tempted with many questions by the devil in a cave at Dysart.[2] The devil, utterly unsuccessful in his assaults on the saint, entered into a certain miserable man, whom he rendered so voracious that no amount of food could satisfy him. The saint, however, placed his thumb in the mouth of the poor sufferer, when, the demon terrified and screaming horribly, fled away.

A thief stole a sheep belonging to the blessed Servanus. He killed and ate it forthwith ; but suspicion falling on him, he hastened into the presence of the saint, where he endeavoured to vindicate himself. He swore solemnly that he was innocent of the crime ; when, strange to say, the bleating of the eaten sheep was heard in the throat of the thief ; conscience-stricken he fell to the earth, and besought pardon of the saint.

In a place called Dunnyne (Dunning) the inhabitants were harassed by a dreadful dragon, which destroyed both men and cattle. The saint assailed the terrible

---

[1] This before monks existed.

[2] Dysart, in Fifeshire, where the cave still exists. This cave seems to have given its name to the place, the name being from *Diseart*, the adaptation in Gaelic of the Latin ' Desertum,' and applied to " a hermitage." These *disearts* were common in Scotland. The Church of Glenorchy derives its name of ' *Clachan an diseairt*," from this word.

beast alone, armed with the breast-plate of faith, and smiting him with the point of his staff, he slew him. In memory of this event the place is to this day called *Vallis draconis*, 'the Glen of the dragon.'[1]

The blind, the lame, the dumb, were all healed by him. The Breviary adds, that there was another Servanus, an Israelite, who, in the time of the blessed Adomnan, Abbot in the island of Petmook (Portmoak, near Loch Leven), performed many miracles. It is not improbable that there were two early missionaries of the name of Servanus; that St. Serf of Loch Leven was a different person from St. Serf of Culross; and that the Servanus of whom we are now treating was the disciple of Palladius, and, like his master's, that his mission was in some respects not a successful one. That is, if the legend of the medi-æval Church be true, which there is reason to doubt, from what we can gather from the life of his pupil, Ken-tigern. The impression produced by the perusal of the latter is, that Servanus preached and taught as a Christian missionary at Culross, according to the system of the ancient British Church. He may have been ordained by Palladins; but there was nothing in the state of the early Church in Fife to indicate an influence different from that which moulded it throughout the rest of Britain.

Of Ternan or Tighearnan, the Aberdeen Breviary (Brev. Aberdon., 12th June), says that he was a confessor and priest, and in the calendar makes him a bishop. He was by birth a Scot, born of noble parents, in the province which is called Myrma (probably the Mearns, or Kincardine) ; he was baptized and instructed by Palladius, who was admonished in doing so by divine revelation. If bap-tized in his infancy, this would make him considerably

---

[3] The name continues to adhere to this locality

the junior of Servanus, whom Palladins found a member of the primitive British Church when he arrived in Scotland in 431. Having heard of the fame of Pope Gregory, the youth paid a visit to Rome, earnestly thirsting after the instruction and counsel of so holy a man. Gregory having heard of it received him honourably, and after seven years raised him to the Episcopal office, and sent him to preach the Gospel to the unbelieving.

Gregory presented the saint with a bell which, however, he and his companions found so ponderous that, unable to carry it, they left it behind them at Rome. But morning after morning the bell was found lying beside the saint, borne on its journey by Divine power, until at length both reached their destination in Scotland.

A certain Convecturius, who was prince of the territory where Ternan resided, seeing the saint approach with a number of followers, said, " Hypocrite, what doest thou in my territory ?" The saint replied, " We seek thy salvation, that thou mayest know God, and serve Him alone." But Convecturius said, " Cease from those deceiving words." The saint, repulsed, drew off. The other, beginning to retire too, his foot adhered firmly to a stone, so that he could not move from the spot. The saint thereupon prayed, when the prince was released and baptized.

On another occasion Machar of Aberdeen sent to Ternan for the use of some seed grain. The saint, having none at his disposal, sent in stead some sacks of sand. Machar, moved by a faith similar to that of his brother, sowed the sand, and reaped an abundant harvest.

The anachronism in the above legend with regard to Pope Gregory is too glaring to escape immediate observation. If Ternan was baptized by Palladins in 440, he must have been 150 years old when Gregory the Great was elevated to the papal chair in 590. This anachronism stamps at once the character of the legend; and yet the existence of Ternan, and the fact of his being in Scotland, and perhaps baptized by Palladius, is as well-founded as any similar historical fact of the time. The portion of the legend referring to his visit to Rome is just one of those mis-statements which came at a later age to be connected with the history of such men in order to exalt Rome; and the anxiety to have them made and accepted, does but indicate the feeling existing among mediæval ecclesiastics, that they were necessary, because there was a weak point at the very foundation of the papal church in Scotland, which needed to be strengthened at whatever cost.

Some of our earlier writers distinguish Servanus and Ternan, the one as the first bishop of the Scots, and the other of the Picts (Fordun, Lib. iii., Boece. Fol. 128, Ed. Ferrer), and they are quoted as authorities by Innes (Civ. and Eccl. Hist., p. 157). The Aberdeen breviary makes Servanus suffragan to Palladius, as first bishop of the Scots, but does not make Ternan first bishop of the Picts. Other authorities, however, give this dignity to Ternan, and fix his episcopal seat at Abernethy, the Pictish capital. If this be true, it corroborates the view that these bishops of the fifth century were emis-saries from Rome. This is clearly Innes' idea, and he thinks he has made out in a way that cannot be gain-said, that Scotland derived her episcopacy from Rome. But if so, he has made out just as clearly, though he does not say so, in opposition to Lloyd and Stillingfleet, and writers of that school, that Scotland had no episcopacy until she derived it from Rome in the fifth century,— that in fact a non-episcopal church existed for upwards of 300 years in that country, previous to the coming of those emissaries of the Roman see; and further, he has

shewn that the idea prevalent with Protestant episcopalians, of an episcopate in Scotland distinct from that
transmitted from Rome, has not a fragment of evidence
to rest upon.   Innes has most thoroughly made out his
case as to the derivation of the early Scottish episcopate
from Rome, if such a thing had any existence, and he has
as thoroughly shewn that that episcopacy was an importation into Scotland at a period 300 years after the introduction of Christianity; but it is equally clear that so far
from the mission of Ninian and Palladius being successful in introducing the Romish system into Scotland, they
had no successors, and it was 700 years after ere Scotland
submitted to the jurisdiction of the Roman see.   No
doubt Rome herself was advancing during that period ;
and it would be as absurd to judge of the Rome of the
twelfth century by the Rome of the fifth, as it would be
to judge of the full-orbed moon by the crescent whose
streak of light is barely discernible in the sky.   But the
principles which led to the full development of the Rom
ish system were all at work as early as the days of Leo
the Great.   It is a curious inconsistency in writers holding the Protestant episcopal view to acquiesce in those
statements of Fordun and others, that Palladius and other
missionaries of the fifth century were the first bishops of
the people of Scotland, and yet at the same time to
maintain strenuously, as they do, that there must have
been bishops before them.   They must give up one or
other of those views, and if they give up the Romish
episcopate and fall back on the ancient British bishops,
they must be prepared to face first the question of their
existence, and secondly, that of the character of their episcopate, and whether that episcopate was one which either
Roman Catholic or Protestant episcopalians would feel
themselves at liberty to acknowledge.

It is not necessary to advert to the legend which

makes Servanus the first missionary to the Orkney islands. It has been well said that the state in which the Iona missionaries found the inhabitants of those islands is ample proof that there could have been no missionaries there before them. Yet this story is told by Fordun, Boece, Lesly, and a host of others, who also make Ternan archbishop of the Picts before such a thing as an archbishop was known in the Church at all.

The early chroniclers present us at this period with the life and mission of Kentigern, usually called St. Mungo, said to be the founder of the see of Glasgow, missionary to the Strathclyde Britons, whose day in the calendar is the 13th January. Kentigern was born about the year 514, or about forty years before Columba came to Iona. The chief sources of our information regarding him are two; a life, written at the suggestion of Herbert, Bishop of Glasgow from 1147 to 1164, contained in the chartulary of Glasgow: the name of the author is not given, nor does he give any information regarding his authority; and a life by Joceline, Abbot of Furness in Lancashire, written apparently at the suggestion of Joceline, who was Bishop of Glasgow from 1174 to 1179 (Chart. Glas. Int., p. xxv.). Joceline tells us in his biography that he derived his information from an ancient life of the saint, existing in the cathedral church of Glasgow, of which he states that it was written in a barbarous language (probably like that of Ninian, either Gaelic or British) and that on the face of it were statements adverse to sound doctrine, and opposed to the Catholic faith. In this we have another testimony to the fact, so generally detailed by mediæval writers, that the early Church differed in point of doctrine from the Roman Catholic Church of the middle ages. Joceline undertakes in his work to improve the style of his predecessor, and to improve his doctrine too. It cannot but be a source of regret that these ancient lives have perished ; we are glad to have such relics existing as those of Joceline and his predecessor under Bishop Herbert, mingled as they are with superstition and fable ; but their loss would be a small matter in comparison with that of the older and more authentic documents.   If these, however, were held to be heterodox, it is no wonder although they should have been lightly cared for and finally allowed to perish altogether by the churchmen of the middle ages.

Kentigern, " Cwn Tyern " in British, and " Ceann Tighearna " in Gaelic, although the name in this case is probably derived from the British, in English " the head chief,"[1] was born, according to both the accounts of him we possess, in East Lothian.   The legend in the older life (Chart. Glas., p. lxxx.) is, that King Loth (Leudonus), a semi-pagan from whom Lothian (Leudonia) is named, had an unmarried daughter, called Thaney.[2]   This young woman, the biographer says, was a devoted Christian, who meditated much upon the character of the Virgin Mary, and was filled with admiration of her ; in which way she became free from every unchaste thought.   This young lady had a suitor, a young man of much attrac- tion, descended from the most noble family of the Britons ; his name was Ewen, son of Erwegende, called by writers, Ewen, son of King Ulien.[3]   This Owen was one of the most famous of the British chiefs, and was son of Urien of Reged, whose name has been so often sung by the bards of Cumbria ; but according to the legend his advances were repelled by Thenew.   The royal father

---

[1] The Welsh Tyern, and the Gaelic Tighearn, a lord or chief, are clearly identical with the Greek, τυραννος, and the Latin, *tyrannus.*

[2] Thenew, modernized into St. Enoch.

[3] Ewen ap Urien is the true British name.   Urien is a famous man among the British bards.   His son Owen is said to have slain Ida, the first king of the Angles of Bernicia.   He was called Dutyern, the dark chief.   He repulsed the Angles, but was himself slain by an assassin, " Llovan of the accursed hand." (Robertson's Scot. under her Early Kings, i., 4.)

of the lady insisted upon her receiving favourably the
suit of her lover, and presented her with the alternative
of being sent to reside with the king's swineherd. The
maiden chose the latter alternative, and cheerfully removed to the swineherd's dwelling. The swineherd
treated her with profound respect, being himself secretly
a Christian, and taught her what of the doctrine of Christ
he had learned from his teachers, whether at home or
abroad. Many attempts were made by Owen to change
the damsel's mind, but her final reply was so decided
that the lover remarked, "It is easier to change wood
into stone and stone into wood, than to recal the mind of
this young woman from the folly into which she has
plunged." At length it appears, under cover of a legend,
the young man secured by guile and violence what was
resolutely denied with consent. So soon as the consequences of her apparent incontinency appeared, the king
her father judged her worthy of death, in accordance
with the laws of the nation. She was still pure and
chaste as ever, but nothing less than her life could atone
for her apparent transgression. When about to be stoned
to death, no man would venture to cast a stone at one
of the royal race. She was therefore brought to a hill
called Kepduff (*Ceap dubh,* ' the black heap '[1]); but being
cast from the summit, she escaped unhurt, while a beautiful fountain gushed forth at the spot where the head of
the wheeled carriage in which she was bound, struck the
earth. Three miles from Kepduff lay the sea at Aber-
lessie, probably Aberlady in East Lothian, interpreted
ostium fetoris, from the quantity of fish caught there.[2]
It was determined to commit her to the sea, and thus let
the winds and waves decide her fate.

---

[1] There is a Kilduff near Traprain-law.

[2] This hardly corresponds with the present condition of Aberlady, which
would scarcely accommodate one fishing boat.

Meantime the king sought vengeance of the swineherd, but in his attempts to put him to death, the swineherd, in self-defence, seized a javelin and slew his master. On the spot where the king died, a great stone was erected surmounted by a hollowed stone above, as a *regale signum* which, says the writer about 1150, still stands about a mile south of Dunpelder.[1]

The maiden was borne by the sea to the isle of May. Here the fish did her homage, and ever since her day, Aberlady, as the port where she was so cruelly dismissed, was deserted by all kinds of fish, while the isle of May, which gave her a night's shelter, became famous among the fishermen of England, Scotland, Belgium, and France. Next day she was carried by the sea to the neighbourhood of Culross (Collenros), and cast ashore upon the sands. Here Kentigern was born, and carried by shepherds to the presence of Servanus, who at that time taught the law of Christ at Culross. They told him how they had found the child. His reply was, *A dia cur fir sin*, which, says the writer, means, 'I wish that it were so ;' or as the meaning would be in modern Gaelic, 'O God, that this were true.' The youth progressed in the knowledge of divine things, and the writer thanks God at the close for having conferred so great a boon upon Britain.[2]

The other and later life by Joceline of Furness differs somewhat from this earlier one (Vit. Ant. Sanct. Pink., p. 198, &c.) According to it Kentigern was derived from the royal race in the northern part of Cambria. This Cambria or Cumbria, as it should be, included the Lothians. If we bear in mind that in the heart of this territory of the Britons lie the Pentland or Pictland hills, we will be

[1] Traprain-law in East Lothian.

[2] It will be observed that the language attributed to Servanus here is Scottish Gaelic, and that this event occurred nearly 100 years before the coming of the Dalriadic colony from Ireland, according to the most approved chronology.

aided in arriving at an accurate conclusion with respect
to the Picts. Here a daughter of the royal family, like
another Mary, was found with child. One writer com
pares her case to that of the daughters of Lot, whom he
calls Loth, and suggests the idea that the Loth of the
second life is identical with the Loth of the older life;
from which, he says, the name Lothian originated. Here
we learn nothing of Owen ap Urien, probably from the
desire of the biographer to make the birth of his hero as
far as possible resemble the birth of our Lord. The
maiden is condemned to death as guilty of incontinency,
and brought to the summit of Dunpelder, from whence
she is cast down, but escapes unhurt. She is then sent
to sea in a skiff and, wonderful to relate, is carried in
safety to Culross. Joceline makes no mention of the
adventure at the isle of May. At Culross Kentigern was
born and brought by shepherds or fishermen to Servanus.

So soon as he saw the child, a holy smile beamed
on the countenance of the saint, and he exclaimed,
" Mochohe! Mochohe!" These words, says the writer,
were " patria lingua," *in the language of his country,* and
are interpreted *Care mi, Care mi,* ' My dear one, my dear
one.' The words are obviously the Gaelic words, *mo
chaoimh! mo chaoimh!* ' my dear! my dear! The
older life makes it clear that the language used by
Servanus was a dialect of the Gaelic, but, as has been
shewn, mingled largely with the British, and which seems
to have been the character of the speech used by the
Caledonians or Picts. Both mother and child were baptised, and the former called Tanew, the latter Kentigern,
capitalis dominus, or ' head chief;' the latter word being
either British or Gaelic. The boy grew and was carefully
instructed by his patron in the mission school at Culross.
Nay, he became so much an object of affection and esteem
to the saint that latterly he gave him the name of Munghu

(Mun cu), interpreted, *Carus amicus,* or 'Dear friend,' and synonymous with the Gaelic *M'aon caomh,* or '*My dear one.*' Indeed it is impossible to say whether the words are British, that is, Welsh, or Gaelic, but they have been generally held to be British. The name, we need hardly add, is known in the Scottish calendar as Mungo, and Glasgow has long been famous as having been St. Mungo's seat.

The legend in this life by Joceline is expanded by a large intermixture of the miracles of the saint. Kentigern made one of a number of pupils who received instruction at Culross. This, there is reason to believe, is historically true, inasmuch as these early missionary institutes were in a large measure educational. Here the youth of a barbarous people received "the benefits of knowledge and the blessings of religion." In the absence of universities, and even schools, there was no other mode of supplying a sufficiently learned clergy, and with all the miracles that later writers attribute to those early missionaries, they do not attribute to them the power of being able to substitute miracles for a competent share of knowledge. The mission institutes of the early Church were all educational. In this school at Culross it happened on an occasion that a favourite bird of the superior was put to death. Grieved at the affliction likely to be suffered by his beloved master, Kentigern put forth his hitherto untried power, and restored the bird to life. So says Joceline, in detailing Kentigern's first miracle, in which we have a fine exhibition of the young missionary's benevolence and love of his master, but a humbling exhibition of historical narrative.

The cook of the establishment at a later period sickened and died. Servanus, now an old man, was much afflicted by his death, as were all the disciples. After the interment the disciples pressed upon their master to urge upon Kentigern to attempt raising the dead. After the most solemn adjuration the young man proceeded to offer up prayer, pleading with God that he should raise the dead man, as he had done Lazarus. "*Res nimium stupenda!*" says the writer, 'most stupendous event!' The dead man revived, and lived for seven years longer in the capacity of cook to the establishment, although a much changed man, as might well be supposed.

The holiness and miracles of Kentigern excited the jealousy of the other pupils, and at length his position became so uncomfortable that he found himself compelled to remove from Culross. He retired secretly, having God as his guide, travelling towards what Joceline calls the Frisian shore (Frisicum littus), which some students of our antiquities suppose to be the shore of the Solway Firth, others that of the Firth of Forth.[1] The name as given by Joceline is said to exist to this day in that of Dumfries, or the fort of the Frisians. Here the "Mallena," or high spring-tide prevented his crossing, but by Divine power, the water was divided, and a path opened up for the saint; the place, says Joceline, is called *Pons Servani*, or 'Serf's Bridge,' a name which, in the course of time, seems to have been lost. On reaching the other side, Kentigern looked back and saw the tide filling the channel; he also saw Servanus, who was in pursuit of him, standing on the opposite bank brandishing his staff, and exclaiming, "Why hast thou left me?" After a little explanation the saint became satisfied that his young disciple had a mission different from what he would have assigned him, and sent him away with his blessing. In this part of his narrative, Joceline mistakes the words *mallena* and *ledo*, 'spring and neap tides,' for

---

[1] Vit. Ant. Sanct., p. 212, and Paper by Mr. Skene on Frisian Settlements in Scotland in Trans. of Scot. Ant., vol. iv., part 1.

the names of two rivers, indicating that he must have been transcribing from some older biography.

A certain man named Fregus lived in a village called Kernach, probably Carnwath, in the valley of the Clyde. This man was grievously ill; he was a just man, strong in faith, of holy conversation, and intent on heaven. Like old Simeon, he sought and prayed that he might see Kentigern ere he died, and he was privileged to see him on the very day on which he left Servanus ; a remarkable fact, if we are to understand that the saint travelled that day all the way from Dumfries, but quite possible if he journeyed only from the banks of the Forth.   Having seen the saint, the old man died.   Next day, having attached two unbroken bulls to a new cart, Kentigern laid upon the cart the dead body of Fregus, and prayed that the bulls might be directed toward the place where it was the divine will· that it should be buried.   The bulls moved on submissively, and never halted until they reached Cathures, which is now called Glasghu, and there the interment took place near a cemetery which had been consecrated by Saint Ninian.   In this narrative we have the ancient legend of the selection of Glasgow as the site of a church, and afterwards of a bishoprick.   "The former name," says Joceline, "was Cathures," probably from the British *Cathair*, 'a town,' a word appearing in Caerlaverock, Caermunnock, and other places on the Clyde, and indicating that at that early period Glasgow was entitled to be called a *Cathair*, or 'Town.'   The transition from Cathures to Glasghu will appear in another part of the life.   This was the first sepulture there, and it is added, that the grave is to this day surrounded with a delightful grove of trees, in token of the sanctity of the person interred.

Thereafter Kentigern resided with two brothers, one of

whom was called Telleyr, the other Anguen. Anguen was most friendly to the saint, and was blessed accordingly; Telleyr was the very opposite, and in an attempt to carry a block of wood far above his strength he fell and was killed on the spot.

About this time the king and clergy of the Cumbrian kingdom,[1] with other Christians, although they were few in number, met, and having consulted about the improvement of the condition of the church, which was very low at the time, agreed with one consent to ask Kentigern to become their pastor and bishop. Who this king was Joceline does not inform us, though he furnishes the names of other kings ruling the Strathclyde Britons. We meet with Morken (Morgan) who was the opponent of Kentigern; and also with Rhydderch Hael, his fast friend, but the name of the king who called him is not given. We have learned from his life by Ailred, that Ninian baptized Tuduvallus or Totáil, a king of the Strathclyde Britons; that would have been between the years 390 and 400. The reign of the king who called Kentigern could not have commenced for nearly a century and a half later, indicating how impossible it was that Rhydderch Hael, who was one of his successors, could be the son of Tuduvallus, converted by Ninian. It is probable that during this period the names of Urien of Reged and his son Owen, come into the order of succession among the kings of Strathclyde; if so, we meet with one reason why the king would have favoured Kentigern, inasmuch as he must have been a near relative of his own. Ritson, no doubt, maintains (Ann. of Caledon., II, 58) that it is probable that Rhydderch was the son of Tuduvallus, and quotes in support of his view Adomnan, who, in his "Life of Columba" (Book i., c. 15), refers to *Rodercus filius Totail, qui Petra Cloithe regnavit,*

---

[1] Pinkerton uniformly uses Cambria for Cumbria. See Chart. Glasg. Int.

'Roderick son of Totail, who reigned at Dunbarton,' and Williams, who in his notes on the "*Æræ Cambrobrit.*" at the end of "Llwyd's Commentariolum," quotes an old Welsh genealogy, in which he is called *Rhydderch Hael ab Tudwal Tudglad,* 'Roderick Hael, son of Tudwal Tudglad.' Nennius (Hist. Nenn., c. 64) mentions the following four kings as having fought against the Saxons, " Urbgen (probably Urien), Ryderthen (Rhydderch) Guallane, and Morcant." Ritson's view is perfectly untenable, if the chronology usually assigned to these events be accurate. Ninian, who baptized Tuduvallus, was born about the year 360; the baptism of Tuduvallus, making all due allowance, would have taken place about the year 400, and the probability is that, at furthest, this king could have lived only to about the year 440. If Rhydderch (Roderick) was born about the year 420, he must have been 110 years old when Kentigern was born, and yet we are told that in the old age of Kentigern he was his friend. Joceline gives us to know, at the same time, that the saint lived to be either 160 or 185 years old. It is clear that if Rhydderch was the son of Tudwal, he must have been son to an entirely different Tudwal from him of Ninian's age. Pinkerton (Pink. Enq., i. 74) says that Joceline makes Rhydderch the son of Morken. This is incorrect, as Ritson observes, but it is more consistent with probability than Ritson's own opinion. Either the father of Rhydderch was not the Tuduvallus of the year 400, or Joceline and others have entirely misdated Rhydderch's reign. The Welsh genealogy quoted makes him to precede Morken, while Columba's prophecy respecting Rhydderch would indicate his period as posterior to 563, the era of Columba's mission. If Rhydderch was the son of Tuduvallus, there is nothing in Adomnan that throws more suspicion on his whole work than this pretended prophecy about a man who must have been dead a hundred years before Columba left Ireland. There seems some reason to take the Welsh genealogy as correct, and to hold Urien, Rhydderch, Guallane, and Morcant as successive kings of Strathclyde, although it is remarkable that there is no notice of Owen, who slew Ida the Angle chief. If this be correct, the likelihood is, that the name of the monarch who joined in the call to Kentigern has not come down to us, and that Owen was slain by Llovan before his father's death.

It is interesting to observe the character of Kentigern's call. During the primitive ages of the Church the thought does not seem to have been entertained that any pastor could be admitted to the oversight of a congregation, except by the call of the members ; and pastors continued to be so called till the age of Constantine.[1] Then, in the attempt to regulate the power of the Church generally, the rights of the people came for the first time to be assailed. (Mosh. Cent. iv., c. 2). The initial step in the changes which took place was an entire exclusion of the people from all part in the administration of ecclesiastical affairs. This was done chiefly by the bishops, who at the same time deprived presbyters of their ancient privileges, that they might have it in their power to exercise an unlimited sway in the government of the Church. We have the clearest testimony from the early fathers, especially Clement, as to the calling of a pastor being the sole right of the members of the Church, and it is somewhat remarkable, as has been observed, that those who profess to venerate the fathers, shew but little respect for their testimony on this question. It is manifest that in Britain the right to call a pastor was held to belong to the Church membership, in the middle

---

[1] It is unnecessary to cite authorities for a statement which has not been questioned, but the reader may consult the late Principal Cunningham's Hist. Theol., vol. i., p. 104.

of the sixth century, and when a call was given to Kentigern, the king, the clergy, and the Christian people, united with one accord in giving it.

Kentigern at once closed with the call which was tendered him. A bishop was sent for from Ireland and he was ordained. It appears that he had not his ordination from Servanus, who is said to have been ordained by Palladins, but from one of the pastors ordained by St. Patrick in the Irish Church. It is diffi-- cult to account for this proceeding. There were surely clergy at the time in the Scottish Church; but this was the era of the war between Aidan, King of the Dalriads, called by the Welsh chroniclers Aidan Fradawg or the Robber, and the Strathclyde kingdom (Ritson's Ann. of Cal., vol. ii., 164); and it may be that the intercourse between the two nations was arrested; while the communication with the east of Scotland would have been interrupted by the irruptions of the Saxons; in the year 600 (Annal. Tigh.) we read of a fierce battle between the Saxons and Aidan, whose territories lay beyond Strathclyde. The Angle kingdom of Bernicia was at this time thoroughly established over the ruins of the ancient Pictish power in this portion of Pictland. But however this may be, Kentigern received his ordination from an Irish bishop, a fact which shews that his orders were not received from Rome.[1] Ninian and Palladins might have valued the episcopal orders of the Roman See, but it would appear that they had no special value in the eyes of Kentigern, or the Church which called him. Nor did he shew any respect for the principles which regulate the canons of the Church of Rome, else he would not have received his orders from the hands of one bishop.

[1] Dr. Todd in the Introduction to his Life of St. Patrick, p. 79, points out that the canons of the Council of Nice, on the subject of ordination, only referred to the Church within the limits of the empire; but we will find that these Scottish orders were held invalid by the Augustinian Church of England notwithstanding.

Joceline refers (Vit. Kent., cap. xi.) to the peculiar mode
of consecration in use among the Britons, but accounts
for it by their remote situation, and states that it did not
detract from the efficacy of the rite ; yet such a thing
would not be permitted in his day. Thus do mediæval
ecclesiastics ever strive to link themselves to the early
British Church, at one time denouncing, and at another
excusing its peculiarities.

Kentigern fixed his residence in the town (villa) called
Deschu, which Joceline adds is interpreted the *dear family*
(cara familia), and is now called Glaschu. The latter
syllable here is obviously the Welsh *cu*, or the Gaelic
caomh 'dear.' The first syllable of either word is not so
easily recognised. The Welsh *Des* does not signify a
family, nor does the Gaelic *Deas*. In the form Glaschu,
the *Glas* is probably the Celtic *glas, a stream*, and the
whole name is most likely *the dear stream*, referring to
the stream now called the Molendinar Burn, which ran
close by the early seat of the mission. But " cara familia "
is not recognisable in the word Deschu ; it must have
been understood, however, as having this signification in
the days of Joceline. We thus find Cathures, Desehu,
Glaschu, as the successive appellations of Glasgow, the
two last being very manifestly of ecclesiastical origin,
while the former as already said, is but the British *caer*,
'a town.'

The diocese of Kentigern, according to Joceline, was
co-extensive with the Strathclyde kingdom ; it extended
(cap. xi.) along the wall built by Severus (this is a mistake for Antonine, and indicates the inaccuracy of Joceline's narrative) from sea to sea, reaching to the Forth
(flumen Fordense), and separating Scotland from England.
This statement is not consistent with what we know of
the existence and extent of the Angle kingdom of Bernicia
in the sixth century ; and the probability is that Kenti-

gern extended his labours to the Strathclyde Britons, whatever the extent of their territory at the time might be.

Joccline tells us that Kentigern was ordained at the age of twenty-five, and lived for 160 years more. To this long life the mode of his living was conducive. An account of this may not be uninteresting. He sustained rather than gratified his body by food; the food itself was of the simplest kind, bread, milk, cheese, butter, and pulse; his fasts were long and frequent; he abstained usually from flesh, blood, and wine, like a Nazarite; if he happened to be on a journey or sat at the royal table he then moderated the rigour of his abstinence, but afterwards, as if in expiation of a crime, he added to its rigour the more.

He was clothed first of all with a rough garment next the skin, then a second of goat's hair, above which he wore an overcoat (cuculla) like a fisherman's; over this was placed a white alb, with a stole about his neck. He carried a pastoral staff without any adorning of gold or gems; it was a plain piece of wood bent at the top.

He lay at night in a large stone trough hollowed like a sepulchre; the bottom was strewed with ashes, and a stone was placed under his head. Thus he strove to have his bed resembling the sepulchre of Christ. In the morning he went out clothed in a light garment (Sabba) and plunged into the neighbouring stream however cold the water might be; he sat there until he chanted the whole Psalter, and this being finished, he came out pure as a dove washed in milk, and sat, until dry, on the top of a hill called Gulath.[1] So says his biographer.

He had in a great degree the power of being silent, speaking seldom, and always with effect. His speech

[1] This must have been near the present site of Glasgow Cathedral.

was truly seasoned with salt. Joceline gives a long account of his mode of celebrating the divine mysteries as he calls it,—an account taken from the practice of the Church in his own time, and not from that of the age of Kentigern. He also tells of his retiring to a desert place, at a certain period, before the Lord's supper ; and of the general cheerfulness of his expression, the result of the life he lived.

His biographer gives a short account of Kentigern's missionary labours. He says that clothed with the shield of faith, the helmet of hope, and the other portions of the spiritual armour, he assailed the devices of the devil, cast down idols, built churches, dedicated them when built, divided parishes, ordained pastors, dissolved unlawful marriages,—much of it the work of a bishop of Joceline's time, but not of that of Kentigern.

We have an interesting notice from Joceline of the disciples of the saint, of whom he tells us there were many ; he says that they strove to resemble their patron, emulating his life, doctrine, mode of worship, fasts, and vigils. Farther, we learn that after the manner of the primitive Church, possessing nothing, they lived piously and soberly apart, in small dwellings (*casulis*) of their own, and there, like Kentigern himself, matured wisdom, whence, says the writer, they were called. single clergy (*clerici singulares*), and in common speech (*vulgo*) Culdees (*Calledei*). This view held in the twelfth century is instructive, as helping to shew whence the term Culdees was derived, and that it was a word belonging to the common language of the country, pointing to the Celtic *Cuiltich*, or 'men of the recess,' as its probable origin.

We have a fuller account from Joceline of the saint's miracles than of his labours. In the New Testament the power of miracle-working is confined to Christ and his apostles ; in the middle ages, it offered too ready a means of exercising influence over an ignorant and superstitious community, not to be claimed for those whom the Church denominated saints. This power is said by his biographer to have been largely possessed by Kentigern.

When, on one occasion, without oxen to draw his plough, a wolf and a deer came both miraculously under the yoke, and supplied the place of his usual team, and when about to sow the land thus ploughed, he found that he had given all his grain to the poor; but choosing sand, he sowed it, and reaped an abundant harvest, to the amazement of all. This story is told of St. Machar, as has been related already (Vit. Kent., cap. xx.).

A tyrant of the name of Morken (Morgan), (*ib.*, cap. xxi.), became at this time King of Strathclyde; this monarch was no friend of the holy man. Kentigern being in want of food for his household applied to the king for a supply of corn. His application was scornfully refused, but miraculously the river Clyde rose, swept round the barn of the king, and floated it with all its contents across, and up the Molendinar burn, where it was landed near the dwelling of the saint. At another time, the saint petitioned the king for a measure of wheat; the king not only refused the food, but ordered the saint with insult out of his presence, to which conduct he was instigated by his counsellor, a man of the name of Cathel. Kentigern endeavouring to remonstrate, the king rushed upon him and kicked him severely. The insult and the injury were both patiently borne; but soon after Cathel (Cathen here) mounting his horse was thrown off, and killed before the king's gate. The king himself, who had lifted his foot against the saint, died of disease in the foot, and his race became subject to gout from that day forth. Morken was buried at a place called Thorpe-morken, on which

Ritson remarks, that it is absurd to think that a Saxon name would be given to a Celtic place ; and yet the Celtic *Tre* or *Baile* might have become the Saxon *Thorpe* at a later period.

Kentigern being persecuted in Strathclyde took refuge in Wales, and resided for a considerable period with St. David in Menevia, or in what is now called the diocese of St. David's. We read of his remaining for a time at a place called in English Crossfelt, or the New Cross ; of his enjoying the friendship of King Cathwallan, who reigned in Wales about A.D. 600 ; of his being led by a wild boar to the place called Elgu, now St. Asaph's, and building a church there, notwithstanding the opposition of an Angle called Melcoind Galganius, who was struck blind ; of Asaph when a boy carrying burning coals without suffering from it, and being afterwards made successor to the saint.

Joceline favours his readers with an account of Kentigern's seventh journey to Rome, where he had the privilege of intercourse with Pope Gregory, who filled the Papal Chair from 590 to 604. If, as Ussher says, Kentigern was born in 514, he must have been 76 years of age when Gregory was chosen Pope. He remained at Rome, we are told, for a long period in much comfort, and with much enjoyment,[1] at the same time ruling his diocese in Wales well. There is no other evidence whatsoever of this visit to Rome. In fact, at the time such a visit was almost impossible. The state of Scotland had undergone great change since the days of Ninian ; for Rome was no longer accessible as the capital of an undivided empire extending to the Firths of Forth and Clyde ; the barbarous nations of the north had crossed the Alps and swarmed on the plains of Italy ; and the Saxons had entered England and had occupied a large

[1] Vit. Kent., cap. xxviii.

extent of its territory, bringing back heathenism along with them, and overturning all the symbols of the Chris tian faith. At such a time the visit of Kentigern was almost an impossibility, and yet the statement of the fact is additional proof of the desire of the ecclesiastical writers of a later period to link the early British Church with Rome; and their misstatements on the subject show that they felt the difficulty of doing so, so long as they adhered to the simple truth of history.

After a long period spent in Wales Kentigern was recalled to Strathclyde. Rhydderch Hael, or Roderick the bountiful, is said to have succeeded to the throne. We cannot say whether he was the son of Morken or not, but it is most probable, as said above, that he was not that Morken, and was an usurper who seized the crown either before or after the reign of Roderick. Roderick, perceiving the low state of the Church in his domi- nions, resolved, in conjunction with the other Christians there, to recal Kentigern. Messengers were despatched to Wales, and Kentigern, accompanied, as his biogra- pher says, by 620 disciples, returned to Glasgow. Asaph was constituted his successor in Wales, and from him the diocese of St. Asaph's takes its name. He was received by his countrymen with great joy, and many great works were immediately accomplished. At a place called Holdelin (Hoddam) many were converted by the preaching of the saint and his disciples, the level ground rising and forming a hill in commemoration of the event. King Roderick was so much influenced by veneration for the saint that he made the civil power in all matters subject to the ecclesiastical; in this indicat- ing the significance of Kentigern's name as Ceann Tig- hearna, *Caput Domini*, which, Joceline says, is Albanice, 'the Head of the Chief,'—where the word is made to be Gaelic, and not British. This legend is manifestly the view of an ecclesiastic of the twelfth century, an age when the conflict for supremacy between the civil and ecclesiastical power was keen and protracted. Joceline also tells us that Kentigern had the privilege from the Pope of being subject to no other bishop, a statement also very ingeniously, if not ingenuously introduced, to meet the long-standing claims of the See of York to supremacy over that of Glasgow.

In return for his beneficence, Rhydderch was favoured with a son, after being long childless. This child was baptized by Kentigern, by the name of Constantine, and excelled all his predecessors in wealth, glory, and honour. To this day he is called Saint Constantine.

The cathedral seat of Kentigern was first set up at Holdelin (Hoddam), where the mound rose miraculously during the preaching of the Saint, and his disciples. This place is understood to have been Hoddelme, the modern Hoddam in Dumfriesshire, which must have been at the time within the territories of the kingdom of Strathclyde. From Holdelin the cathedral was removed to Glasgow, a transportation in all likelihood not hard to accomplish; and one which would not a little have surprised the Saint himself, were it described to him as the transportation of a cathedral.

We have an interesting narrative from Joceline of Kentigern's missionary labours. Having cared for his own peculiar charge, he extended his labours elsewhere; first of all seeking to instruct his nearest neighbours. Thereafter he visited those more distant, and as Joceline relates (Vit. Kent., cap. xxxiv.) reached Galloway (Galwethia), the territory of the Picts (Pictorum patriam); Galloway being thus understood to have been a Pictish territory in the seventh century, by the writers of the twelfth. He visited also Albania, which lay beyond the line of the wall, and is the equivalent for modern Scotland. Nor did he confine his visits to his own country, but reached the Orkneys, Norway, and Salanda, the latter probably the modern Iceland. This account is rhetorical, and must be taken as of no historical value, though the journeys of these early missionaries were very remarkable.

The most famous legend of Kentigern is that which gave its heraldic arms to the See of Glasgow. The queen of Rhydderch, called in one place Langueth and in another Languoreth by Joceline, the mother of Constantine, (Vit. Kent., cap. xxxvi.) was guilty of improper intercourse with one of the military attendants of her husband. She foolishly gave this man a golden ring, probably the king's signet, which the king had, in his affection, entrusted to her. The king, hearing of it, and finding the man asleep at a hunt, plucked the ring from his finger, and threw it into the Clyde. On his return home, he demanded the signet of the queen, who, in her extremity sent for St. Kentigern. He bade her send a man to fish in the Clyde, which she did; and her messenger casting a hook into the river, caught (esocem) a fish, which is commonly called salmon. The fish being opened the ring was found in its stomach; being brought to the queen she handed it to the king, and thus secured impunity for her crime. In most of those legends the moral is good; it is not so in this case, and the wonder is that the event it records should have had so prominent a place given to it in the after history of the Church in Glasgow.

At a late period, apparently, Kentigern enjoyed ·a visit from Columba, who, during the ministry of the former in Glasgow, had established a mission institute in Hi or Iona. Accompanied by a large body of his disciples, Columba set out for Glasgow. When he reached Mellindonor, or as it is called in modern times Molendinar, he divided his followers into three bodies, and sent a messenger to announce his coming to Kentigern (Vit. Kent., cap. xxxix.) The latter at once proceeded with a body of attendants to receive him, and he was saluted with spiritual songs. Joceline describes the intercourse of these two worthies as having been highly gratifying and edifying ; ere they parted they exchanged their pastoral staves, and that of Columba given to Kentigern is said to have been preserved in the church of St. Wilfred at Ripon in the twelfth century (Vit. Kent., cap. xl.).

A number of noble crosses were said to have been erected by Kentigern ; and the description of that at Glasgow by Joceline is exceedingly graphic. The size of it was immense, and the mode of its erection by the combined strength of men and machines, affords an idea of how the great single-stone monuments throughout the country were set up, though it would appear that in this case the aid of an angel was requisite. Another cross was erected at Lotherwerd, which was famous for its cures.

Kentigern died at Glasgow, having attained, according to one of his biographers, the age of one hundred and eighty-five years. If, according to Ussher, he was born in 514, this would bring him to the year 699, and make him the cotempary of Adomnan. Were this true, it is hardly possible to conceive that Adomnan would take no notice of so remarkable an event as his death ; nor would he have failed in seeking information respecting Columba of one who had had such close personal intercourse with him ; and in relating the interview which took place between the two good men, he would hardly have failed to relate that Kentigern was still in life, or had but recently died.

But the whole of the chronology of the life of Kentigern demands examination. Let us allow with Ussher that Kentigern was born about 514 ; Palladins came to Scotland in 431 or 432 ; he then found Servanus living in the country, and professing the faith of Christ ; let us grant that Servanus was twenty years of age when Palladius set him apart to the Christian ministry ; in 514, when Kentigern was born, Servanus would have been 102 years old ; and yet we learn that, after that he instructed this young disciple and prepared him at Culross for the work of a missionary.   The whole narrative is incredible, and can be only accounted for by taking into account the effort of a later age to maintain the absurd delusion of apostolical succession.   There is no reason to doubt the mission of Servanus, nor that of Kentigern to the Strathclyde Britons, but a credible chronology is entirely wanting to make these men stand in the spiritual relation in which mediæval ecclesiastical writers strove to make them stand to one another.   Of Kentigern the truth seems to be, that he was born in East Lothian, was educated at Culross, most likely in the mission school established there by Servanus, was called to be pastor of the church among the Strathclyde Britons, whose king at the time was his relative, that he received ordination from the Irish Church, spent some time among a kindred people in Wales, and died in the time of Rhydderch Hael in Glasgow, where the Church became a memorial of his name and worth.

CHAPTER XI.

SCOTLAND had undergone remarkable changes during the
period between the departure of the Romans and the
middle of the sixth century. So soon as the Roman
legions were removed, Valentia became a prey to the
tribes of Picts and Scots, the natural result of which
was, that the Pictish territory was extended again as far
as the southern wall; indeed we learn of the struggle
between the Romanized Britons and the Picts, as
carried on in the very heart of England. The Britons
of the Roman province were originally the same people
with the Picts, and any changes they had undergone were the result of Roman influence. The unsettled nature of the Roman power in Valentia, and the
comparative shortness of its duration, would have rendered this influence less effective than in the southern
provinces; but even there Roman possession must have
produced sufficient change to have led to marked differences between the people within and the people without
the wall. The very name Picti or Picts, as observed
already, is indicative of this change, as it shews that the
tribes of Valentia had so far conformed to Roman customs as to have desisted from the national practice of
painting their bodies, whence it arises that it is only at
a late period of the Roman empire in Britain that the

name Picti appears at all. Time was necessary to produce that distinction between the habits of the two populations, which led to the application of this name to the portion of them which followed the ancient custom of the nation. The removal of the Roman troops brought the Picts again within the wall. Their former countrymen, without much resistance, appear to have succumbed, and to have readily acquiesced in the establishment of the ancient national government; and whether the former practice of painting was restored or not, the name crossed the wall, and the Picti of the Romans retained, throughout their territory, the name applied to a portion of them by their former neighbours. The Pictland or Pentland hills, a name which could only be given at this period, inasmuch as previously the name Pict did not exist, and soon thereafter the territory ceased to be Pictish—given, too, by a Teutonic race, is evidence of the fact that the Picts extended their sway over Valentia after the departure of the Romans. The Scots would have been largely intermingled with them, as the two seem to have carried on their warfare, not as a separate, but as a united people.

The Britons of the south were more Romanized than those of Valentia. They had tasted more deeply of the sweets of civilization, and to them the inroads of the northern barbarians would have been associated with all that was to be feared. In an hour of weakness these Britons, as is said, under Vortigern their king, summoned the ocean rovers of the opposite coast of Europe to their aid. Nor was the summons unheard or unheeded. A force of Saxons soon appeared on the English coast. These were not the first of the Teutonic races who had come to England, for the " Littus Saxonicum " had existed in the Roman period, but the early Saxons had made no great figure in the national history.

Hengist and Horsa are said to have led the force of the professed allies, and by their means the inroads of the northern marauders were soon checked. But the allies of the Britons discovered that in helping their distressed neighbours, they had found an opportunity of helping themselves; and, summoning reinforcements from the opposite continent, they proceeded to take possession of the country which they had come to defend. This first coming of the Saxons is variously dated from 374 to 449.[1]

There is a remarkable resemblance between the manner in which the Teutonic races came to the possession of England and Ireland. In the middle of the fifth century, Vortigern or Guortigern, king of the Britons, being afraid of the power of the northern tribes, of the same blood and lineage with himself, called in the Saxons to his aid. They came, they repelled the invaders, but soon became themselves by far the more dangerous foe of the two; in like manner, about the middle of the twelfth century, Dermot M'Murrough, king of Leinster, was at feud with his neighbours of like blood and lineage with himself. He summoned to his aid Henry II. of England. The aid was readily furnished; a body of English troops was sent to Ireland. But the allies again became invaders in their turn, and the same scene became enacted in Ireland that was enacted in England 700 years before.

Like eagles gathered together where the carcase lies, the nations of the north descended in flocks on the shores of Southern Britain. The Jutes or Goths from Jutland, occupied Kent; the Saxons occupied the western and midland counties of England; and the Angles made their descent on the region north of the Humber. These latter

---

[1] See Mon. Hist. Brit. Pref., 114; Bede, H. E., c. 15.

are the race to which Scotland owes the greater proportion of its Teutonic population, although it is to England
that they have given its name.

It is worthy of notice that while this Teutonic invasion,
as usually described, may have taken place in accordance
with the summons of Vortigern, there is reason to think
that it is not altogether to be attributed to that cause.
The whole of northern Europe was at the time in a
state of motion; in 409 Rome was sacked by the Goths,
and the Heruli, the Franks and the Vandals, were all
aroused. In 427 Genseric, with the latter of those nations,
penetrated into Africa, seizing the Roman territory for
himself; and in 447 Attila, "the scourge of God," with
the Huns, swept over Italy, carrying devastation whithersoever he went. The Spanish peninsula was seized by
those fierce and warlike nations; in fact the whole western
empire was at the time looked upon by them as one great
object of prey. And what was to exempt Britain, not
the least fertile possession of the west, from a similar fate,
when these hordes of marauders found that nothing could
resist their strength? There may indeed have been some
connection between the summons of Vortigern, and the
coming of the Teutons, but it is doubtful whether this
descent would not have been made upon the country,
whether the summons had been sent or not.

To the north of the Humber the Angles made rapid progress in extending their dominion. They pressed forward
both to the north and west, and gradually extended their
conquests as far as the Forth, in the one direction, and the
borders of Galloway in the other. The Pictish power
gradually gave way, and this, in all probability, presents
us with the period when the Catrail or Picts-work ditch,
crossing the country in a south-westerly direction, from a
point to the south of Edinburgh, onwards towards the
valley of the Liddell, was erected as a protection from

the inroads of these new found foes. The Britons had been taught the art of building such walls by the Romans, as a defence against their northern enemies, and it is probable that they exercised it in the case of the Catrail, for the purpose of now providing a defence against their invaders from the south.

The most famous of the Angle leaders (Anglo-Sax. Chron. A.D. 547) was Ida. Under his leadership his countrymen won many battles from the native tribes. But the resistance they met with was firm and persistent, and in one of those fierce fights, the Angle leader fell, slain, as the British annalists inform us, by Owen ap Urien, the reputed father of Kentigern. (See Rob. Scot. under her early kings, vol. i., p. 4). The fall of Ida was the prelude to numerous victories by the Britons. Gradually their territory was won back, and Bryneich, the Gaelic Braigh or Braes, and the Latin Bernicia, fell again under the dominion of the native tribes. But Owen, too, fell, slain by the hand of an assassin, and from the day of his death the tide of battle changed. Again Bernicia, extending to the western borders of Dumfriesshire, and northwards along the eastern boundary of Lanarkshire, became subject to the sway of the Angles.

It is difficult at this period to decide precisely upon the line of separation between the different nations and tribes that inhabited Scotland, or even the period of their settlement. Some writers think that a portion of the Frisians, who with the Jutes and Saxons, seized upon the south-eastern and midland counties of England, had settled in Scotland at a very early period. And it has been held that the name of the town of Dumfries, supposed to be the castle of the Frisians, is a memorial of Frisian possession. If so, it is a somewhat unusual combination of Gaelic and Teutonic words, the Dun being

Gaelic, and the Fries Teutonic. The whole word has a distinct meaning in Gaelic, being the Castle in the Copse, but the combination of two separate languages in the same topographical term, is not so unusual as to make it any very tenable argument against the theory of Frisian possession on the Solway. The same people are said to have pushed their conquests beyond the Firth of Forth, and to have occupied a portion of the southern coast of Fife. The older topography of Fife is so purely Celtic, that this territory must have been held for a very short period by these settlers, if held at all.[1] It is manifest, however, from unquestionable authorities, that about the middle of the sixth century the Angles had seized from the Picts, after a possession of about 150 years, the whole of the eastern portion of what was the Roman province of Valentia, and formed it into a province of their own, usually called Bernicia.

Along side of this was the kingdom of the Strathclyde Britons, at one time joining with the kingdom of Cumbria, the modern Cumberland, as well as with the Lothians,[2] and forming an extension of the ancient British territory from Wales northward; but now detached by the interposition of the Angle province, which included Roxburgh and Dumfries shires. Galloway was at the time a Pictish territory—Roman civilization had not succeeded in suppressing there the practice of painting the body; and this is just what, from the locality, might have been antici-

---

[1] See a paper by W. F. Skene, Esq., on Early Frisian Settlements, in Trans. of Scot. Ant. Soc., vol. iv., part i., p. 176. In this paper Mr. Skene makes some ingenious observations on the site of the city of Giudi, referred to by Bede, inclining towards the opinion that it was a Frisian city. It is perfectly obvious, however, that Bede, from whom alone we know anything of Giudi, speaks of it as one of the cities either of the Picts and Scots, or of the Britons, for he makes no allusion to the existence of any other people in the vicinity.
[2] Vit. Kent., p. 224.

pated. Distant and inaccessible, this southern region was exposed to similar influences with that beyond the wall to the north ; and the language as well as the dress of the people, would have been less conformed to the Roman model than those of the more accessible kingdom of Strathclyde, although previous to the Roman conquest the people were the same. To the north and east of the wall extending to the Pentland Firth lay the Picts or ancient Caledonians, with one royal seat placed in the neighbourhood of Perth, at Forteviot, Abernethy, or Scone, and another to the north in the neighbourhood of Inverness. To the west, apparently extending from the valley of the Leven to the valley of the Lochy, lay the Scots, a less numerous and weaker nation than the Picts, but destined in time to absorb the latter and to unite both under one monarchy. How or by whom the Scots were governed we know not ; that they must have had governors of some sort is indubitable, and that, judging from analogy among Celtic races, that government, under certain limitations, was monarchical, is most probable. Whether Boece's list of kings previous to Fergus the son of Erc, ever had any real existence, is hard to say, but if it be absurd to place any faith in Boece, it is no less absurd to imagine that the Scots would have been without kings previous to the arrival of the Dalriadic emigrants. We may not know who they were, any more than we know who the kings of the Britons were previous to the arrival of Julius Cæsar, but that by no means proves that such persons did not exist in the one case any more than in the other.

Bede's account of the coming of the Scots into Britain is as follows. Having (Hist. Eccl., B. i. c. 1) given some account of the immigration of the Picts, who, he says, first of all reached Ireland, and being directed by the Scots inhabiting that country, crossed over and settled in Scotland, he adds, "In process of time Britain, besides the Britons and the Picts, received a third nation, the Scots, who, migrating from Ireland under their leader, Reuda, either by fair means or by force of arms, secured to themselves those settlements among the Picts, which they still possess. From the name of their commander, they are to this day called Dalreudins; for, in their language, Dal signifies a part." He adds, "There is a very large gulf of the sea which formerly divided the nation of the Picts from the Britons; which gulf runs from the west very far into the land, where to this day stands the strong city of the Britons called Alcluith. The Scots arriving on the north side of this bay, settled themselves there." The bay here referred to must be either Loch Fyne or Loch Long, most probably the latter. It cannot mean the Firth of Clyde; for Alcluith, the modern Dunbarton, is on the north side of that estuary, and could not be described as lying within the Scottish territory.

This is the only account given by Bede of the immigration of the Scots from Ireland. Gildas makes no reference to it at all; and Nennius only gives us the story of Partholan bringing the Scots from Spain. While Bede furnishes us with no other notice than this of the arrival and settlement of the Scots in Britain, it is worthy of notice that in the account given there is no reference whatever to dates. There is no means of determining what the date of the movement was, save that the whole manifestly refers to the first settlement of the Scots in Britain; and it is clear, that the reference is to a much earlier event than the arrival of the three sons of Erc, and their settlement in Argyll in the sixth century. If Bede's account is of any value, it is as indicating a very early settlement of the Irish Scots in Argyll, and so far goes to corroborate the story of our earlier Scottish historians; in fact the names of Fergus, Lorn, and Angus do not appear in the pages of Bede at all; the only name given being that of Reuda, and as this same Reuda (Ruighe-fhada, or Long-arm) gave its name to the Dalriada of Antrim, at a very early period, Bede's reference must have regard to events long previous to the sixth century. The fact is, it is impossible otherwise to understand many of Bede's statements regarding the Scots; for while his account supports the view that the Scots were an Irish colony, it is utterly inconsistent with his narrative that that colony should have migrated from Ireland so late as the year 502. Indeed all our earlier authorities are opposed to this view. If Servanus spoke Gaelic in Fife as the language of his country, which Joceline says he did, in the fourth century, it is manifest that the Albanian Scots are a more ancient body of settlers in Scotland than the more favoured modern theories of their settlement allow. Some of these theories would not admit of that language being spoken in Scotland at all in the days of Servanus. Our older authorities, and those in consequence the most reliable, give us, on the other hand, ample reason to believe that it was spoken over a large portion of Scotland long before that period. Nor can anything opposed to the testimony of Bede be found in the Irish annals, for while the earlier of these note the emigration of the sons of Erc in 502, they do not indicate, by any means, that they were the first of their race. And even were it otherwise, we cannot forget that Tighernac, the earliest of the Irish annalists, belongs to a period more than 300 years later than that of Bede, and that we have no reliable account of authentic materials from which he composed his annals; while the Four Masters belong to the seventeenth century, and are of no more authority, unless supported by earlier testimony, than Fordun or Buchanan. At the same time,

Tighernac has generally been held, and perhaps justly so, to be the best authority we possess on events of early Irish and Scottish history, although we cannot lose sight of the distance of time at which he chronicled events, from that at which the events themselves are said to have occurred, in the earlier portion of his annals.

From Tighernac we learn, under the year 502, that "Fergus the Great, son of Erc, with the Dalriadic race, held a part of Britain, and died there." This is the first notice we meet with of the settlement of the Irish Scots in Britain in the sixth century, and upon it alone has been built the whole story of the Dalriadic invasion in 502. This is an entirely different story from Bede's, who refers to the settlement of Reuda, the founder of the "gens Dalriada," or Dalriadic nation. Tighernac makes no mention of Fergus, Lorn, and Angus; Fergus alone, he says, in 502 possessed a part of Britain. Nor does he inform us what kind of possession it was, or how it was obtained. Bede tells us of Renda, that he obtained possession either by force of arms or the favour of the inhabitants; Tighernac gives us no distinct information on the subject, but the character of the information he gives affords a strong presumption that the possession of Fergus was peaceably obtained, and held; the *tenuit*, or held,' giving no indication of a struggle, and an uncertain tenure. It is quite consistent with the belief that some members of the reigning family of Irish Dalriada crossed the Irish sea about the end of the fifth or beginning of the sixth century;[1] and that they arrived among a kindred or friendly race, where they received protec-

---

[1] It has not been adverted to sufficiently by writers on this subject, that it is the death of Fergus that is recorded by Tighernac, as occurring in 502; and if so, that the immigration from Ireland might have taken place many years before. There is no room for believing in the conquest of a people who were capable, along with the Picts, of coping with the power of the Roman empire fifty years before the period of Fergus Mac Erc.

tion, and an inheritance, and where, whether by marriage or otherwise, they rose finally to the throne of the nation.

The notice given by Bede, and the entry in Tighernae's Annals, have been largely expanded by later writers. Ussher quotes a life of St. Patrick, by an unknown author, which says (Ussher, Eccl. Prim., p. 587), that during the reign of Constantius, the son of Constantine, the Scots laid waste the Roman empire in Britain, under Neil of the nine hostages, their king in Ireland; and that, after a time, they drove out the inhabitants of the northern part of Britain and inhabited their territory. It was by these invaders, it is added, that St. Patrick was taken prisoner. For this story there is no authority whatsoever given ; and St. Patrick, in his "Confession," makes no mention of King Neil in connection with the account of his captivity.

Camden (Brit. p. 707) cites an ancient author, who says that "Fergus, the son of Erc, was the first of the race of Conair, who reigned in Alban, from Brunalban to the sea of Ireland and Inchegall (the Hebrides). And from that time the kings of the race of Fergus reigned in Brunalban or Brunhere, to the time of Alpin, the son of Eochy."[1] The Conair here referred to was Conair the Second, of the Clann-Deaghaidh of Munster, of the race of Heremon, who reigned about the year 212 (O'Flaherty II. 404). His son was Cairbre riada, or Cairbar of the long arm, of whom Bede speaks as Renda, from whom Dalriada, whether in Ireland or Scotland, derived its name. The Scottish kings of Alban were Heremonians of the race of this Conair. From Conair was descended Eochy Muinreamhar, or *thicknecked*, whose son was Erc, the father of Lorn, Fergus, and Angus, the reputed leaders of the Dalriadan Scots.

---

[1] This passage is in the tract *De situ Albaniæ*, Inn. Crit. Ess. 772.

Fordun, Boece, and Buchanan give us a different story from the Irish chroniclers. From them we learn that Fergus was an exile in Scandinavia, and that he was re-called thence in order to lead his countrymen against the Romans. He ascended the throne, according to these authorities, about the year 404, fought many battles in conjunction with the Picts against the Romans, and was slain along with Durstus or Drust, the Pictish king, in battle, after a reign of sixteen years. There is little in common between this account and that of the Irish annalists. Fergus is introduced merely as one of the succession of legitimate Scottish kings, and nothing is more clear than that these writers never thought for a moment that the Scots of Alban were an Irish colony of the sixth century. The very king under whose leader-ship it is maintained .that these colonists arrived, is placed by them more than a century before the period ascribed to that event by Irish writers ; and Fordun professes to have derived his authority from ancient documents.

Our earliest Scottish authority is Adomnan, who wrote his life of Columba about the year 680, or little more than a hundred years after the time of the sons of Erc. From him we learn of Donald and Fergus Mac Erc, but they were Irish monarchs (Vit. Col., Lib. i. c. 6). In the same chapter he informs us of the name of a Pictish king, Eochy Laib, but he was an Irish Pict. We learn, however, of Conall, son of Comgall, king in Britain, and of King Aidan, and of Arthur, Eochy Fionn, Domangart, and Eochy Buidhe, his sons. These, we may believe, are truly historic names. Tighernac places the reign of Conall about 560. Adomnan furnishes no dates ; as, for the most part, a relater of miracles, dates were a matter of little consequence to him. Yet it is impossible to believe that he would have invented names, especially the names of men so prominent as the kings of the nation, and men whose names would at the time have been fresh in the national traditions. The names of Aidan, Conall son of Comgall, Comgall himself, Domangart, and Eochy Buidhe, may be held to be authenticated by Adomnan as among those of the early Scottish kings.

Our next earliest Scottish authority is the Albanic Duan (Trans. of Iona Club, p. 71), said to have been sung by the royal seanachaidh or genealogist, at the coronation of Malcolm Ceannmor in 1057. Pinkerton's opinion of this literary relic is, "that it is the most ancient monument of Dalriadic history remaining, and deserves the greatest credit." Its historical statements have much to entitle them to respect. Malcolm the Third was the last king of Alban who reigned in accordance with the purely Celtic system, and, as down till his time, the royal bards, or seanachies, existed as an important part of the royal household, a hereditary account of the king's genealogy would have descended to Malcolm's days.

The poem begins with the words, *A eolcha Albain uile,* 'Ye learned of all Albin,' and proceeds to give an account of the royal race. Its earlier portion agrees very much with the account of Geoffrey of Monmouth. Britain is called "Albain," and is said to have taken its name from Albanus, the son of Isiocon. He was expelled by his treacherous brother, Britus, who drove him over the sea of Iochd,—the Iccian sea, or straits of Dover. Britus took Albin to the territories of the Fiaghnach Fothudain, a term in which the word Fian or Feinn may be very distintly discerned. This territory would appear to have embraced the northern part of Britain. After Britus came the race of Neimhidh, usually called by Irish writers the Nemedians. These were the descendants of Nemeth, who arrived in Ireland from Scythia,

and was the second foreign invader who seized its territory (O'Flaherty's Ogygia, vol. i. p. 8), according to some
writers, and the third according to others (Misc. of Celt.
Soc., p. 2).   The period of Nemeth is fixed by O'Flaherty
about A.M. 2038.   The Nemedians were expelled by the
Fir bolg, and settled partly in Scotland.   These Nemedians, the Duan says, acquired Earglan, probably the
eastern portion of Scotland, till after the building of the
Tower of Conaing, the locality of which is in the north
of Ireland.

The race of Neimhidh or the Nemedians, were succeeded by the Cruithne or Picts, according to the Seanachaidh, who came from Erin of the plains, and acquired
the western land.   North Antrim is known to have been
Pictish territory, and it is somewhat remarkable that it
is from that Pictish region that the Scottish colony with
its kings came.   This goes very far to prove the original
identity of the Scottish and Pictish races.   Of this Pictish race seventy kings possessed the Cruithnean plains or
the Pictish territory in Scotland, the name of the first
being Cathluan, and the name of the last Cusantin.
Cruithne, the first king of the Picts and the father of the
seven princes, Cait, Cé, Ciric, Fiu, Fidhach, Fodhla, and
Fortreim, who gave their names to the seven provinces of
Scotland, was not according to this authority a king of
the Scottish Picts.

Next came, says the Seanachaidh, the race of Eathach
or Eocha, the descendant of Conair, whose son Erc was
father of Lorn, Fergus, and Angus.   Of these Lorn was
eldest and reigned for ten years.   Fergus succeeded him,
and reigned for twenty-seven years ; to him succeeded
Domangart, his son, who reigned for five years ; Comgall
succeeded his father Domangart, and reigned for twenty-
four years ; Gauran succeeded him, and reigned two
years ; and after him Conall the son of Comgall, who

reigned eight years. If Tighernac be accurate in fixing the death of Fergus in 502, the Dalriadic invasion and the reign of Lorn Mor, according to this account, must be fixed thirty-seven years before, or in 465. If we add the periods of the succeeding reigns, we will find that Conall, son of Comgall, reigned till the year 541. But it is useless to attempt reconciling the various accounts given of those early events. Tighernac makes Fergus the first king of Dalriada; the Scottish Seanachaidh tells us it was his elder brother Lorn, and these two authorities were almost contemporaneous, being both of the eleventh century. They agree, however, with respect to Fergus, and both bring his family from the Scoto-Irish line of kings, and from this we may safely infer that Fergus was king of what is now Argyll in the beginning of the sixth century, having his residence in some portion of what is called Knapdale, either at Castle Sween or Dunmonaidh, an ancient fort whose ruins may be traced not far from the mouth of the Crinan Canal. In estimating what this king was, it must not be forgotten, as already stated, that, at his period and long after, every Celtic chief, and even the leader of an army among the Celts, was a king, and that we form most erroneous conceptions, in judging of these kings by monarchs of the modern type. Tighernac calls Domangart king of Alban, which he certainly was not.

From Adomnan we learn that about the middle of the sixth century Brude, son of Meilochon, was king of the Picts (Vit. Col. lib. c. 1). Bede informs us that, in the ninth year of this king, Columba visited him at his palace near Loch Ness (Hist. Eccl. L. iii., c. 4). If this visit was in 563 Brude commenced his reign about 554. In the Pictish chronicle first published by Innes in the appendix to his " Critical Essay " (Crit. Essay, p. 779), the name of this king appears as forty-ninth in succession of the Pictish monarchs. He is called "Brides filius Mailcom." He is also represented as successor to Necton Morbet filius Erp, or Neachdain mòr mac Eirp, who gave Abernethy to Dairlughdach as a gift to God and St. Bride, and who was monarch of the southern Picts. From this it appears that there were not two lines of Pictish kings, as generally believed, or if so, that they are so intermingled in this chronicle as that the separate lines are inextricable. Tighernac notes the death of Cendaladh, king of the Picts, in 580.

We have, then, pretty reliable authority for believing that, about the middle of the sixth century, there was in what is now called Scotland a Pictish people, of whose history we know almost nothing, in Galloway; an Angle kingdom extending over the Lothians, and embracing the modern shires of Roxburgh and Dumfries; a kingdom of Strathclyde Britons, whose king was Rhydderch Hael, or Roderick the bountiful; a kingdom of Picts, said by some to be divided into northern and southern Picts, although we have no evidence of the existence of two lines of monarchs; and a kingdom of Scots in Argyll, ruled by Conall the son of Comgall. There is reason also to believe that the Orkney islands had some time previously been occupied by a Saxon race, and that they formed a sixth division of the Scottish population.

CHAPTER XII.

THE MISSION OF COLUMBA.

AT the period of which we have been writing, Christianity had made extensive progress in Scotland. The Picts of Galloway, said to have been converted by Ninian, were at least nominally Christians; so were the Britons of Strathclyde, who had at this very time called Kentigern to minister among them. The southern Picts were also in a large measure Christianized, and one of the oldest missionary institutions in Scotland is said to have been founded at Abernethy, on the Earn. The Pictish chronicle attributes the founding of this institution to king Nectan, of whom mention has been made already, and who granted to a disciple of St. Bridget's a large extent of land in the neighbourhood of Abernethy, the boundaries being "from the stone in Apurfeirt (Aberfarg) to a stone near Cairfuil (Carpow), that is, Lethfoss, and thence upwards to Athan (Ayton)." (Inn. Crit. Ess. App., p. 778.) This account ascribes the founding of Abernethy to the year 454, or, according to the Pictish chronicle, 101 years before the time of Brude Mac Meilochon, and about 100 years after the death of Ninian. Nectan, it is said, was constrained by the enmity of his brother, Drust, to spend a part of his life in Ireland, where he became acquainted with the disciples of St. Patrick, and among others with the saintly Bridget, whose pupil, Darlughdach, appears to have followed him to Scotland, and become a female missionary among the southern

K

Picts. This tradition, to which reference will be made at an after period, would indicate that Abernethy was the earliest foundation of the kind north of the Tay, and preceded Iona by about a hundred years.

But while the south-west, and centre of Scotland, were thus christianized in the middle of the sixth century, it was otherwise with the south-east, and north. The early Christianity of the province of Bernicia had been extinguished by the heathen Angles, and that region, once under the influence of the true faith, had been reduced again to a state of Paganism. The Christianity of Britain suffered much at the hands of the Saxon invaders; theirs was the period of its martyrs, and not that in which the Christian faith was first planted in the land by early missionaries. A reference to the pages of Gildas is enough to shew how dire were the sufferings inflicted on the British Church by these northern invaders. Hence it happened that the south of Scotland stood as much in need of the labours of Christian missionaries in the sixth century, as it did in the first. In the north the Picts beyond the Grampians were also generally heathens; the Christian faith had not as yet been accepted by the nation beyond that great mountain barrier; not that the people had never been brought into contact with Christianity; that would have been impossible in the circumstances; nay, it is probable that they were to some extent leavened with Christian truth, for we cannot on any other reasonable hypothesis account for their rapid conversion by Columba. But the king was still heathen, and heathenism manifestly was largely predominant among the body of the population; while the leaven of Divine truth was at work, and required but the energy and faithfulness of Columba and his disciples to cause it to penetrate the whole mass. It was about the year 563 that a mission to this northern nation was undertaken from Ireland.

The missionary was Colum Mac Phelim, usually called Columba, a descendant of the kings of Ulster, and a near relative of Conall, the son of Comgall, the reigning Scottish monarch.

Columba was born at Gartan, in the barony of Kilmacrenan, county of Donegal, in the year 518, according to Tighernac ; although Colgan, Ussher, Reeves, and others, give different dates on to 522. His father Feidlimid or Phelim was son of Fergus, son of Conall, son of Neill of the nine hostages, head of the great house of O'Neill, and king of Ireland. His mother was Eithne or Aethnia, daughter of Mac Nave, a Leinster chief, connected also by blood with the royal family of Ireland. His father was grandson by the mother to Lorn mòr, son of Erc, one of the three leaders of the Dalriadic colony, and thus he stood nearly allied to the royal family of Dalriada (Vit. Col. Reeves, p. lxxi.).

Columba's first name was Crimthan, as some say, and he received the name of Colum from the Latin *columba*, a dove. Dr. Reeves says, he was baptized by the presbyter Cruithneachan, by the name of Colum (Vit. Col. Reeves' App. to Pref., p. lxxii.), to which the addition of *cille*, that is, *of the church*, was afterwards made. In his youth he was taught by Finnian of Clonard, usually called the Wise, and a celebrated instructor of the Christian youth of Ireland. He studied theology under Gemman in Leinster, and, as some writers say, though his own biographers do not, he was sent to Etchen, a bishop in Meath, to receive ordination. There is a curious legend preserved respecting his ordination (Note on Feilire Ængus, translated into Latin in Colgan's Act. Sanct., p. 306, *b.* n. 17. Reeves' Vit. Col. App. to Pref., p. lxxii.), which relates that the bishop by mistake conferred priest's orders only on Columba, when he intended to confer episcopal orders. This seems to have been a method suggested by a later age of getting quit of the difficulty respecting Columba's ordination, upon the theory of the early Church being, in the modern sense, an episcopal Church. The constant attempt of writers of that Church to make it so has led them into many difficulties from which a fair representation of the case would have kept them free. Columba received the orders that were conferred at the time, receiving from Etchen the orders which he possessed himself; the likelihood is that Gemman, though a Christian teacher, was a layman.

Our only reliable authorities for the facts of Columba's life and mission are his biography by his successors, Cumin Fionn and Adomnan, and the Ecclesiastical History of Bede; to these may be added the Irish Annals, which, however, as they have come down to us, are the work of a much later age. It has been already said that Tighernac, the earliest writer of them, compiled his annals in the eleventh century, and that we know not whence he drew his information, although it is generally believed that there were earlier annals in the Irish Church; Adomnan wrote his life about the year 695 (Reeves' Vit. Col. App. to Pref., p. xlix.), or about one hundred years after Columba's death; Bede wrote about forty years after. There was sufficient room in the period that elapsed between the death of the Saint and the age of those writers for the growth of a large mass of fable; and judging by the work of Adomnan, the soil was abundantly fertile, for a greater congeries of absurdity and pure fable does not exist within the range of literature, civil or sacred, than his life of Columba. It would be an insult to human intelligence to endeavour to represent it in any other light; while it is incidentally full of the most valuable information regarding the real events of Columba's life. In searching for those, however, it is necessary to bear in mind that Adomnan was a convert to Rome, and that he is not to be taken altogether as a representative of the ancient Scottish Church. He and Bede were at one in their adherence to Rome, and being a convert, we may believe that the Scot was not the less ready of the two to yield to any bias which he might receive from his newly adopted views. Much of Adomnan's work must be read in the light of this fact in his own history, if we would understand it aright, and really reach the truth.[1]

It is said that after his ordination Columba entered among the brethren at Glas naoidhen, now Glasnevin, near Dublin. His companions there were Comgall, Cainneach or Kenneth, and Ciaran, all of whom are well known in the ecclesiastical topography of Scotland. In 566 he founded what is called the monastery of Derry, although monasteries were not then what they afterwards became, and are misnamed by the use of the word. Durrow, founded about 553, became the most famous of all the Columban institutions in Ireland. Columba was only twenty-five years of age when he founded the former of these, so that from his earlier years he exhibited a truly missionary spirit.

Although a Christian missionary, Columba is accused of having been engaged in many family feuds in his native country. Keating tells us that Diarmad, son of Fergus Cerrbheoil, king of Ireland, held the feast of Tara, and that at the feast a chieftain was killed by Curnan, son of Aodh, son of Eochaidh Tiormcarna. Curnan fled to the protection of Columba; but notwithstanding the protection afforded, Diarmad seized him and put him to

---

[1] The recent edition of this Life by Dr. Reeves of Lusk, is an invaluable work to the student of early Church history. It is a perfect wonder of erudition, and affords an admirable example of laborious preparation to those engaged in similar work. If it have a strong leaning towards Ireland and the Irish, Scottish scholars may readily forgive it for the sake of the real value of the book.

death. Upon this Columba collected his friends, the Clann
Neill of the north, and attacked and routed Diarmad and
the Connaught men at the famous battle of Culdreivne.
There is a different story told of a book belonging to
Finnian, from which Columba had made a transcript. The
book was a copy of the Psalter. Finnian, as owner of the
book, claimed the transcript as his own. The matter was
referred to Diarmad, who gave judgment against Columba,
saying that, "to every cow belonged her own calf."
Hence the feud and the consequent battle. (Reeves' Vit.
Col., p. 248). There are other two battles said to have
been instigated by Columba—that of Cuil rathan or Cole-
raine, in connection with the feud which produced the
battle of Culdreivne, and that of Cuil feadha, in consequence of a murder perpetrated in violation of Columba's
sanctuary, Baodan Mac Ninneadh, king of Erin, having
been assassinated thus by Cuimin, son of Colman.

These feuds were held to be discreditable to a man of
Columba's religious profession, and accordingly his proceedings were taken up by a synod of the Irish Church,
where it was decreed that he must bring as many converted Gentiles to Christ as there were men killed in
those battles (Colgan's Acta Sanct., p. 645). This sentence is said to have been proposed by Molaise of Devenish, to whose arbitration the case was referred.[1] O'Don-
nell, quoted by Dr. Reeves (Vit. Col., p. 252), says that
Columba himself, in penitence for the share he had in
those battles, resolved to devote himself to the work of
a missionary among the heathen.

That Columba devoted himself to the work of a missionary is the more probable account of the origin of
his mission, and is the account most consistent with
the testimony of our more reliable authorities. The

[1] Maol Laise, or the servant of the flame or fire, whose name is commemorated in Lamlash, or Eilean Maoil Laise, an island off the coast of Arran.

legends respecting feuds among the different sections of the great O'Neill family, to which he belonged, may have some foundation in truth, but of their details we know nothing from credible testimony. Adomnan refers to the battle of Culdreivne, but gives no account whatsoever of the causes which led to it; and of the other two battles he makes no mention at all—that of Culdreivne he uses merely as a date.

Adomnan's account of the origin of Columba's mission is short and simple (Vit. Col. Pref.). He tells us that two years after the battle of Culdreivne, willing to go abroad for Christ, he sailed from Scotia (Ireland) into Britain. This is generally understood to have been about the year 563, or about 1300 years from this date. Bede's account is that he left for the purpose of " preaching the Word of God," and makes the date 565 (Hist. Eccl., Lib. iii., c. 4). The missionary was then forty-two years of age, and had been an active and successful minister of Christ in his native country. He was accompanied, it is said, by twelve disciples, whose names are still preserved. Dr. Reeves (Vit. Col., p. 245) quotes a note appended in an old handwriting to one of the existing codices of Adomnan's life of the saint in which they are given as follows:—The two sons of Brendan, Baithen, who, with Conin, was successor of St. Columba; Cobhtach, his brother; Ernaan, uncle to St. Columba; Diarmad, his servant; Rus and Fechno, the two sons of Rodain; Scandal, son of Bresail, son of Endens, son of Neil; Lughaidh Mocutheimne; Eochaidh; Tochannu Mocufir cetea; Cairnaan, son of Brandubh, son of Meilge; and Grillaan. These all seem to have been blood relations of the missionary. Brendan, the father of his two successors, was his father's brother.

These brethren left Derry in a *currach* or wherry made of wicker work, covered with hides, and tradition

informs us that they landed first on an island which is
usually understood to have been Colonsay.   In this
island there is a hill called to this day *Carn cùl ri Eirinn,*
or the ' hill where the back was turned on Ireland.'   It
would appear that upon ascending this hill and looking
southward, the shore of Ireland was still seen in the distance, and the voyagers concluded that they had not yet
reached a point where they might be said to have entirely
forsaken their native country.   They accordingly put to
sea again, and crossing the wide reach which separates
Colonsay from Iona, they landed in the latter, which has
since been made so famous by their labours.   It is said
in Scottish tradition that approaching this island, the
saint exclaimed, *Chi mi i,* ' I see it,' whence the island
derived its name of I, or Hy, by which alone it is called in
the Gaelic language.   Be this as it may, the name is a
curious one, and is not explained by the common asser-
tion that " I " means *an island* in that tongue.   Were
the term merely *an island,* it would, like the neighbouring island of Inchkenneth, always called by the natives
An Innis, ' the island,' have the article prefixed to
it ; besides, there is no authority whatsoever to shew
that the Gaelic " I," like the Scandinavian " oe," means
an island.   Dr. Reeves has shewn beyond controversy
that the island of " Tir iodha," or *Tyree* means ' the land
of corn.'   It is not unlikely that the name of I has some
connection with its fertility, *iodh,* ' corn,' with its relative
verb *ith,* ' to eat,' and *iodhlann,* ' a cornyard,' having all
sprung from the same root.   The modern name of Iona,
as already observed, has been shewn by Dr. Reeves (Vit.
Col.) to be but a corruption of the Latin *Iova,* the adjective form of the Gaelic " I;" the whole idea of *Iona,* ' a
dove, and *I thonna,* or ' island of the waves,' however
pleasing to the imagination, being founded in deficient
knowledge of the real history of the word.

Columba landed in a shallow bay at the south end of the island. To the west of this bay rises a hill called like its neighbour in Colonsay, " Carn cùl ri Eirinn," for on ascending its summit it was found that not a vestige of Ireland could be discerned from it. Had the saint lived till now he would have found that what his eye could not discern, might be discerned by modern telescopes,—the instruments of the officers conducting the government survey of the island having very recently enabled them from that very spot to discern the coast of Ireland. But these were not the days of telescopes, and Columba was satisfied with the testimony of his eyes. Ireland was now invisible ; the sacrifice of a much-loved native land was complete, and the spot was reached where the tabernacle of the missionary was to be pitched. Near the landing place, called in the native language *Port a Churaich,* or the *wherry port,* is a heap of earth and stones not unlike a boat in shape ; here it is said the saint and his followers buried their *curach ;* they feared lest if they retained it they might be tempted, as they encountered difficulties, to return again to Ireland ; and to secure themselves against temptation, they buried their only means of transport deep in the earth. When this was done they were prepared to commence their great work. According to the annals of Innisfallen under the year 555, it was on Whitsunday that Columba landed in I.

Bede relates that the island of I was given to Columba by Brude Mac Meilochon, whom he styles the powerful king of the Pictish nation (Hist. Eccl., Lib. iii. c. 4) ; Tighernac, on the other hand, in relating the death of Conall, son of Comgall, King of Dalriada, in the year 574, adds that it was he who gave the island of Ia to Columba. The question regarding the donor of the island has given rise to some controversy, and the controversy has, in its course, upon the whole, favoured

Bede. He is the older writer, and was likely to be well informed, besides having no national predilection connected with the question. In addition to this, the period of Columba's arrival was one of disaster to the Dalriadic kingdom; three years before (Ann. of Tigh. A.C. 560), a great victory had been won by Brude, over Gabhran, the son of Domangart, the King of the Dalriads, in which battle Gabhran himself seems to have perished. In 568 we read of a piratical expedition into the west by the Dalriadic king Conall, son of Comgall, in company with Colman beg Mac Diarmaid (Ann. Ult. 567). Neither of these entries represents the Scottish kingdom as flourishing, and this would lead to the inference that Conall had it not in his power to make a grant of Hy. Besides, Columba's mission was directed to the northern Picts, and it is not likely that he would have fixed his institute within the territory of another and a hostile kingdom. If the northern Picts were favourably disposed to Christianity, as does appear, it may account for the grant on the part of Brude, or it may be that the grant was not really made till after the conversion of the Pictish monarch. This last is Bede's account (Hist. Eccl., Lib. iii. c. 4).[1]

Having established himself and his companions in Iona, Columba set forth to visit the Pictish king. His residence was then in the neighbourhood of Inverness; as Dr. Reeves thinks, in the vitrified fort on the summit of Craig Phadraig, a rocky elevation which forms one of the summits of the romantic range of hills stretching along the north side of the river Ness, westward from the town; or, as tradition maintains, in the stronghold called *Caisteal Spioradan;* or, as the word is inter

---

[1] From Dr. Reeves giving no decision on this question, it may be inferred how the evidence tends, as that able critic makes no willing concession on any point that may contribute to the honour of Scotland, as opposed to Ireland.

preted, though apparently inaccurately, 'The Castle of Spirits,' lying in the fork between the west end of Loch Dochfour and the river Ness, where the latter enters the loch. The ruins of a stronghold remain there to this day, though much diminished by the necessary cuttings for the Caledonian Canal. Tradition seems in this case to be in the right, for there is no evidence, either written or oral, to connect Craig Phadraig with the memory of Brude, and where there is not, tradition is entitled to be heard respecting the other locality.

It is a very curious thing that Cumin "the fair," in his life of Columba, and he wrote at an earlier period than Adomnan, makes no mention of the conversion of the Pictish king. Cumin wrote about 657, or sixty years after the death of Columba, and his silence on the subject is very remarkable. Whether really the mission to the Pictish king assumed less dimensions in the days of the immediate successors of the saint, or whether Cumin judged nothing worthy of relation but miracles, is hard to say; but the former conjecture is by no means an improbable one, if, as has been suggested, the leaven of Christianity had been introduced among the northern Picts before the period of Columba. Let this, however, be as it may, Columba's mission was one of paramount importance to the people among whom it was undertaken, and hastened mightily the gathering in of the whole nation to the Christian fold.

The mission itself was one requiring no ordinary zeal and courage. The residence of King Brude lay at least 150 miles distant from Iona. The journey is even now, in the absence of steamboats, a troublesome one; what it was in the sixth century it must be difficult for us to conceive. In proceeding on his journey, Columba would have had, first of all, to cross the sound of Iona, a strait about a mile and a-half in breadth; thereafter a long journey of fifty miles through the southern part of Mull, to what is usually called the Green point, succeeded. Here a ferry of four miles broad brought the traveller to the island of Kerrera, and from that a ferry of a mile wide led to the mainland, four miles south of Oban. A land journey, with intervening ferries, succeeded, through Lorn, Appin, Duror, Lochaber, Glengarry, and by the north shore of Loch Ness, to the royal residence. This journey through such a country, and among a people largely Pagan, implied no little labour and suffering. Adomnan mentions in one place (Vit. Col., Lib. i. c. 34), that Columba's journey was *trans dorsum Brittaniæ*, 'across the ridge of Britain.' This could hardly mean the summit of the Grampian hills, and must be held to be the low summit level between the east and west coasts of Scotland, which must necessarily have been passed over by travellers across the country. This summit level is found between Loch Oich and Loch Lochy, and it is curious to observe that at that spot lies a place called 'Achadrom,' *Ager dorsi*, or 'the field of the ridge.' This was the only practicable way across 'Dorsum Britanniæ,' or Drumalban. Adomnan further relates (Vit. Col., Lib. iii. c. 14), that in one of those journeys, travelling near Loch Ness, the saint came to a place called Airchartdan, where an old man named Emchatus was found dying, who being converted and baptised, rose to heaven in the company of angels. His son, Virolecus, and his whole house, were also baptised, on their believing. This Airchartdan is the Gaelic 'Urchudain,' or the English 'Urquhart' of the present day; it is the valley usually called Glenurquhart, which lies beautifully embosomed in hills on the north shore of Loch Ness. The name has descended unchanged since the sixth century, and enables us to trace with accuracy

the usual course of the missionary's journey in one portion of it.

Adomnan gives us no information as to Columba's com
panions, nor does he so much as say whether he had any.
Other writers say that two of his disciples, Comgall and
Cainneach, accompanied him (Reev. Vit. Col., p. 152 n.).
Bede gives no names of any coadjutors with Columba in
his work, and as he and Adomnan are our earliest and
most reliable authorities, we are without any authentic
information as to who his companions were, while we
have no reason to doubt that some of his friends would
have accompanied him in his arduous undertaking.

On arriving at the residence of the Pictish monarch,
Columba met with immediate resistance from those
whom Adomnan calls Magi (Vit. Col., i. 37). It appears
that the saint and his companions joined with loud
voices in celebrating the praise of God in the immediate
vicinity of Brude's palace. Adomnan calls this exercise
vespertinales laudes, or vespers. The Magi, which some
translate Druids, approached, and endeavoured to prevent
them, lest the sounds should reach the ears of the people,
upon which the saint began to sing the forty-sixth psalm,
and his voice becoming miraculously loud as thunder, the
king and people were both struck with terror.

The king, however, was still undisposed to admit the
missionary. Filled with pride, he refused to open his
gates (Vit. Col. Lib. ii., c. 35) ; upon which Columba and
his friends drew near, and the former having made the
sign of the cross upon the gates, and striking them with
his hand, they at once, of their own accord, flew wide
open, and admitted the missionaries. The king, struck
with fear, along with his attendants, came forward to
meet them, and from that day the Christian missionary
was treated with all honour.

We are furnished by Adomnan with the name of one

of those Magi, and have an account of part of the saint's intercourse with him. This was Broichan, whom some translators call a Druid. The name is said by Dr. Reeves to be a British one (Vit. Col., Lib. ii., 33 n), and if so it goes to shew the relation of the Picts to the Britons, for Broichan is called *"nutricium,"* probably the tutor, or as it would be called in a Christian age, the chaplain of the king.[1] This Broichan had a slave, whom Adomnan calls *Serva Scottica,* 'a Scottish slave,' a captive taken either from the Irish or the Albanian Scots. This slave the saint required the heathen priest to liberate. The request was refused, upon which the saint threatened the priest with severe judgments. Soon after, the priest was seized with a dangerous illness, and the king sent messengers to ask help of the saint, who had gone down to the banks of the river Ness. A pebble was taken from the stream, which, provided the slave were liberated, would, he said, by being dipped in water and the water drunk, restore the rich man to health. The conditions were agreed to ; Broichan was healed, but we do not find that he was converted to the Christian faith, for immediately after he is represented as hostile to the missionary.

Columba was about to return to Iona, when Broichan threatened to prevent him by raising a contrary wind, and causing a great darkness over the water. Columba replied that the omnipotent God ruled all things. On the day fixed for the departure of the missionary a large crowd attended him to the shore of Loch Ness. The day was dark and the wind violent and unfavourable. Nevertheless the saint embarked in a frail skiff, and ordered the trembling crew to raise their sail. The order being obeyed, the vessel at once moved forward, and ran with extraordinary speed against the wind ; the weather soon

---

[1] Dr. Reeves says their is a Castle Brochain in Raasay, but in that case the word is Brochaill, and not Brochain.

became favourable, and Columba reached his journey's end that night in comfort. Thus were the Magi overcome, and victory obtained for the truth. The probability is, that the power of the Magi had been long on the wane; four hundred years of Christianity in the southern and midland parts of Scotland could not but have had its influence in the northern section of the country, and the likelihood is, as said before, that the way was paved by a large previous leavening of the public mind for the coming of the Iona missionary. Heathenism must have been on the decline ere it could have so readily given way, unless we are prepared to believe in the miracles related by Adomnan. What would we not now give for an authentic account of Columba's intercourse with Brude and his Magi! Could we but have it from his own hand, we would have something in simplicity like the "Confession of St. Patrick," which contrasts so markedly with the fabulous narratives of his more recent biographers.

One other legend of Adomnan's may be quoted as interesting from its topographical references, and its allusion to the popular beliefs of the period. Columba had to cross the river Ness on one occasion, where he saw a concourse of people engaged in burying the body of a man who had been killed by a monster that lived in the river.[1] The Saint, notwithstanding, ordered one of his followers to swim across and bring the ferry-boat from the other side. Lugneus Mocumin at once obeyed, plunging into the water. The monster, seeing him, darted after him with a terrible roar; the spectators were stupefied with

---

[1] From this it appears that sepulture was the usual way of disposing of the dead among the Northern Picts, and that the sepulture took place in any con_venient locality, which accounts for the number of solitary graves found scattered throughout the country.

fear ; but the Saint raising his hand, and making the sign
of the cross in the air, commanded the monster to desist.
At this command he retired more quickly than if he were
pulled by ropes, although he was within the length of a
spear-staff of Lugneus.   All Christians and pagans were
struck with wonder on witnessing this event.

Such are the events which Adomnan relates as taking
place in connection with the conversion of Brudeus and
the northern Picts.   The only other point of interest connected with the narrative has reference to Columba's
means of communication with the Picts.   In most of the
cases in which a detail is given by his biographers of his
intercourse with them, there is nothing to indicate that
he could not hold direct communication with them.   But
there are two cases in which Adomnan speaks of the use
of an interpreter.   (Vit. Col. Lib. i. 33, and Lib. ii. 32).
In one of these cases the event narrated took place in the
island of Skye.   An aged man received the word of God
from the Saint through an interpreter.   In the other it
took place "in provincia Pictorum," *in the province of
the Picts,* without any express statement as to the locality.
In this case a peasant with his whole family believed the
word of life through an interpreter, the Saint being preaching.   It is very obvious that the references here are to
the fact that the language of the missionary was unin-
telligible to the Picts, although it has been maintained
that the interpretation meant was the interpretation of
the Scriptures, and that such interpretation was needful,
as the word of God was then only in the Latin language.
But it is perfectly clear that there is no reference to reading.   In the second case quoted, it is distinctly stated by
Adomnan that Columba was preaching, and that it was
the preaching that required an interpreter.   If it was
merely the interpretation or translation of the Latin Bible
that was necessary, the Saint could furnish that himself,

and had no need of another to aid him. The statements of Adomnan go thoroughly to corroborate that of Bede, that the Pictish language was not identical with that of the Scot, however they might have sprung from the same root, a statement, as already observed, borne out by such words of the Pictish tongue, as have come down to us, and also by the existing topography of the Pictish portion of Scotland.[1]

---

[1] Dr. Reeves (Vit. Col. Lib. i. 33 n.) quotes three Pictish words as known, viz., 'Cartoit," which Cormac in his Glossary calls Beurla Cruithneach, or Pictish, and explains by "dealg," *a pin;* "Penfahel," or *the head of the wall,* now Kinneil; and "Scollofthes," (Scologs), certain ecclesiastics among the Picts. In addition to this, Ritson quotes the word "Geone," used as some writers think to indicate a body of armed men; while others think it means the island of Gunna. Such proper names as Alpin, Conall, Angus spelled Hungus, Neachduin spelled Nectan, and Kenneth, found in the Pictish Chronicle, are common among the Gael to this day; while others such as Broichan, Drostan, &c., may be found in British Chronicles; the proper names in use among the Picts thus corroborating the testimony of topography, as to the mixed British and Gaelic character of the Pictish language.

CHAPTER XIII.

THE monastic system found its way into Western Europe during the fourth century. It is generally thought to have been introduced by the famous Martin of Tours, with whom tradition has connected Ninian of Scotland and Patrick of Ireland by affinity of blood. The system itself originated in the East, and sprung not from a Christian but from a heathen source. It has not the shadow of a foundation in the Bible; the Jewish system, as revealed in the Old Testament, had no place for it, and acknowledged none of the principles on which it rests; the New Testament, as containing the teaching of Christ and his apostles, gives not the slightest warrant for it in any part; its source must be sought for among the writings of heathen philosophers; and there no doubt, and especially among those of the Platonic school, will be found the doctrine that human nature may be refined and purified by a certain process of self-denial, with respect to the ordinary cravings of human appetite and human ambition. It would appear to have sprung from a sense natural to the mind of man, that there is need of some means for expiating sin and purifying the heart; and in the absence of those means provided by God himself in the Gospel, men had recourse to such means as they themselves might devise, in ignorance of the real requirements of the case. The remarkable thing is that such a system should ever have become associated with

Christianity, and one can only suppose that it was in circumstances in which the true nature of the Christian faith came to be utterly obscured, that such a system could ever have been appended to it.

The first monks were men who retired to deserts, and in consequence received the name of eremites or hermits (ἔρημος). These were solitary, and hence were denominated monks, from μόνος the Greek *alone*. Their apparent piety and devotion acquired for them the highest regard ; their life had so much of the appearance of being a holy one, that while most men felt constrained to commend it, the more far seeing, such as Jerome and Augustine, were deterred from denouncing it. They felt, as men sometimes do, that a system which has the semblance of devotedness, or self-denial on the face of it, is very difficult to assail, however abundant may be the seeds of future evil which they see concealed in it. The world was captivated with the apparent piety of those early monks, although that piety contained the germs of the whole system of mediæval monkery. This is a warning to the Church of Christ to hold by the word of God, with the assurance that whatever is really for the good of mankind, will be found prominent there. Gradually monks came to form themselves into societies, but it was the fifteenth century ere the monastic system had reached its full growth.

In Britain and Ireland was found, in the fifth century, the only portion of the Christian Church which lay beyond the boundaries of the Roman empire. Hence occurred features peculiar to itself in the Church of those parts, and, more especially, an unwillingness as settled, and as resolute to acknowledge the supremacy of spiritual Rome, as their fathers had shown to acknowledge that of civil and political Rome. The very monachism of Celtic Britain had features of its own, and these continued to distinguish it, in some measure, till the close of its existence. These will be best brought out by presenting as full a view as possible of Columba's establishment at Iona.

The institution at Iona may be said in one sense to have been a monastery, although there was no vow taken by the inmates either of celibacy, poverty, or obedience. There was no rule constituting the brethren into a regular order, and any such attributed to Columba has been shewn to be the work of a later age, and to be of no historical value. The principle which lay at the foundation of this institution was not that which gave its origin to monasticism generally, viz., the personal improvement of the monks themselves. The early monks elsewhere retired for their own spiritual benefit ; that they might live more separate from the world ; that they might crucify the flesh more effectually ; that they might hold closer fellowship with God, and enter with less distraction on the study of His word. Here the main object was the benefit of others. Bede tells us that Columba went abroad for Christ ; it was to preach the Gospel he visited the country of the northern Picts, and the establishment' at Iona became not a monastery in the modern sense of the term, but a great mission institute. Were we to search for that which resembles it most in modern times, we would find it in those great educational and mission establishments which the Scottish Churches have planted in India, where a body of earnest, enlightened men, are engaged in teaching and preaching the Gospel, paying occasional visits to outlying towns and villages, and having occasional interviews with princes, for the purpose of communicating the knowledge of saving truth. Columba and his followers may be called monks, but the use of the term may lead to a very serious misapprehension as to the nature of the position which they occupied in the

Church, and the nature of the work which they had undertaken.

The head of the institution was the Abbot, called by Adomnan, abbas, pater, and sanctus pater or senior, and in the case of Columba, patronus (Vit. Col., Lib. i. c. 1), he being the original founder. This abbot had jurisdiction over all the inmates of his house, a jurisdiction which extended to all the subordinate institutions connected with it, whether in Scotland or Ireland, and all of which combined, formed the "parochia" of the abbot. The election of the abbot lay with the brethren of the monastery, although Columba was allowed to nominate his own successor (Vit. Col., Lib. iii. c. 23); a fact which shews that there was no fixed rule on the subject, but that general acknowledged principles were acted upon by the community, in their elections. This abbot was uniformly a presbyter. Bede's statement is, *Qui non episcopus, sed presbyter extitit, et mònachus,* 'Who was not a bishop, but a presbyter and monk.' The distinc tion between the bishop and the presbyter, which does not appear in the Bible, and which could not have existed when St. Patrick succeeded in planting 300 bishops in Ireland, or one to every Church, came to be fully established in the days of Bede. Its growth may be easily traced in the natural development of the influence of the larger cities, and larger congregations, with metropolitan Rome at their head. *Chorepiscopi,* or 'ministers of rural congregations,' sprung up, and became suffragans or subordinates to the ministers of the larger cities, who were the episcopi, or originally the ministers of the whole charge; and gradually a different jurisdiction, and a different kind of orders came to be introduced and acknowledged in the Church. There is nothing more easily traced in the writings of the early fathers than the development of the idea of episcopacy,

or superiority of rank, order, and jurisdiction on the part
of certain of the clergy. It was the twelfth century
before the system of diocesan episcopacy came to be
established in Scotland, but the distinction between the
bishop and the presbyter was acknowledged in England
in the time of Bede, and in some sense the 'episcopus'
or bishop came to be acknowledged in the Scottish
Church. ·It is impossible to read Adomnan's life of
Columba without being constrained to acknowledge this.
Bede (Hist. Eccl., Lib. iii. c. 4) tells us "that the island
(Iona) has for its ruler an abbot, who is a priest, to
whose direction all the province, and even the bishops,
contrary to the usual method (*more inusitato*), are subject, according to the example of their first teacher, who
was not a bishop, but a presbyter and monk." Almost
every clause in this sentence has been made subject of
controversy. The "presbyter," the "bishop," the "province," the "unusual manner," have all afforded matter
of prolonged dispute, the nature and result of which may
be learned by consulting Lloyd, Stillingfleet, and Innes
on one side, and Blondell and Jamieson on the other.
The passage is quoted for the purpose of shewing that it
was known by Bede that there were bishops in his time
in the Scottish Church.

In regard to those bishops, however, it is essential to
observe, first of all, that they were not diocesan bishops.
From all the authorities of any value on the question
this is clear, and that whatever functions they possessed
had no reference to any particular charge. The
abbot had his "parochia," extending not only to a definite portion of territory around his monastery, but to
all the affiliated monasteries connected with the head
institution, but there is no sign of any such charge as
appertaining to the bishop. Bede's notice does indicate that there were bishops when he wrote, but his

work gives no evidence of any specific territory as being assigned to them as a charge. Secondly, it is just as clear that the bishop had no jurisdiction. The passage already quoted from Bede makes this manifest. Lloyd and others attempt to twist the passage into all kinds of shape in order to deprive it of its force as against the principles of diocesan episcopacy. Lloyd shews that special privileges were in ancient times enjoyed (Lloyd on Ch. Gov., p. 164) by certain monasteries in Africa and elsewhere, entitling them to select their own bishop, and securing them exemption to a large extent from episcopal jurisdiction. This, however, rather strengthens the general argument from the practice in the Scottish Church, by shewing, that at an early period the practice was not confined to it alone, besides that the Scots sought no authority for their system from any source beyond themselves. Others take example from the English universities, and maintain, that as in the case of these a bishop, if a member of the university, is subject to the jurisdiction of its head, so these bishops of the early Scottish Church were similarly situated within the monastery, with respect to the abbot. This might serve the purpose if it could be shewn that the Scottish bishop had jurisdiction anywhere else, but the jurisdiction of the abbot extended throughout "the province," which Lloyd very weakly endeavoured to shew meant only the island of Iona. When men are driven to such shifts as these, they are ill off for arguments. It is perfectly clear that these Celtic bishops had no separate jurisdiction, and a bishop without either diocese or jurisdiction is an anomaly indeed. Bishops in modern times may class these men with themselves as enjoying the title of bishops, but they would feel it a grievous degradation, were they to be stripped both of their jurisdiction and their diocese, and reduced to the same position with them although they do reckon them as brethren. But thirdly, they did not possess orders such as Episcopalians are warranted to acknowledge. Innes (Civ. and Eccl. Hist., p. 177) feels constrained to give up the jurisdiction of those ancient bishops, but maintains that a bishop is a true bishop so long as he has the power of ordination ; that this and this alone is essential to the episcopal order. It is his prerogative alone to transmit valid orders in the Church. But the orders of these men were not generally held valid in the early Church. The first council of Nice, in its eighth canon, denounces irregular ordinations, which had very obviously been frequent in the Church prior to that date. Theodore, Archbishop of Canterbury, applies this canon to the British and Scottish bishops, saying (Concil., Tom. vi., Col. 1877, as quoted by Lloyd, p. 126), "They which have been ordained by the bishops of the Scots or Britons who are not united to the Catholic Church in their Easter and Tonsure, let them be confirmed again by a Catholic bishop by imposition of hands." In like manner, the consecration of Ceadda to the See of York was objected to by Theodore, as being the taking of another's office like a robber (Vit. Wilfr., by Heddius, c. 15). Ceadda was ordained after the manner of the ancient Scottish Church ; but his ordination was disallowed as not being in accordance with the canons of the Apostolic See, and Wilfrid, who was canonically ordained in France, was placed in his room.[1] Thus the bishops of the early Scottish Church

[1] When Columbanus, the great Irish missionary in the seventh century, began to found mission houses on the continent, he was charged by the local Church with irregularities in the matter of ordination and other observances. He quoted, in reply, the second canon of the Council of Constantinople, held in 383, which ordained that "the Churches that are without the Roman empire should be governed by their ancient customs, &c." But the ancient British Church was within the empire, and this canon was not held as sufficient to justify the Scots by the successors of Augustine of Canterbury.—(See Paper in "The Ecclesiastic" for April 1864, on Dr. Todd's St. Patrick.

might have had that name, but their orders were not acknowledged by the supporters of the Roman See. These orders were looked upon just as the Roman Church looks upon Presbyterian ordination now. This is a fact which cannot be gainsaid, so that even the right to ordain, for which Innes contends so strenuously, was disallowed at an early period by the Church to which he himself afterwards professed to belong. Lloyd makes little of this, satisfied that if they were bishops it makes entirely for his case, as himself an opponent of the claims of Rome. But if the orders of the Protestant Episcopal Church are prized as canonically transmitted from the apostles by regular succession, these orders, condemned and repudiated by the western Church, cannot be held as equally valid with those which the canons allowed. There is nothing in the constitution of the modern Episcopal Protestant Church to leave room for the admission of an episcopacy so conferred and transmitted as this, which seems to have belonged to the early Scottish Church.

But so far as Scotland is concerned, we have no evidence of the existence of bishops at all in the early Church, as a necessary part of its organization. There were bishops at a later period, as Bede testifies; but from Adomnan's testimony, which is the most valuable we possess, they do not seem to have been in an earlier age essential to the carrying on of the work of the Church at all. It is very true that on one occasion a bishop in disguise visited the institution at Iona. Adomnan's story is that Cronan, a stranger from the province of Munster, came in disguise to the saint; that being invited on a certain Sunday to join him in celebrating the Eucharist, so that two priests might be engaged, the saint suddenly looking him in the face as he stood at the altar, said, " Christ bless thee, brother, consecrate alone, according to the Episcopal rite, for I know thou art a bishop. Why didst thou disguise thyself till now, so that due honour was not given thee?" On hearing these words, the humble stranger wondered exceedingly, and worshipped Christ in his servant, and the bystanders gave glory to God (Vit. Col., Lib. i. c. 44). So Adomnan says. From which it appears manifestly that the bishop came from Ireland, that the presence of a bishop was a rare event in Iona, and that consequently there was no fixed bishop resident there, or any episcopal jurisdiction exercised. The whole ecclesiastical jurisdiction was in the hands of the presbyters of the existing institution, and their presbyter-abbot. That there were bishops in the Irish Church of which the mission in Iona was a branch is true, but the number of these ordained by St. Patrick indicates very distinctly, that they must have been a very different class of men from diocesan bishops of a more recent date, and possessed very different functions. The story of the visit of Bishop Cronan, as related by Adomnan, is a curious one. Its object is to bring into view one of Columba's numerous miracles; the strange part of the story being the miraculous discovery of the disguised bishop. Pennant says that Columba had the second sight, and this looks very like it. It must be borne in mind that Adomnan was a convert to the Romish school, and allowance must be made for this here as in many other cases in reading his work; for as being so, the Iona arrangements respecting jurisdiction could not have been agreeable to him, and we can readily conceive how glad he would have been of an opportunity to elevate the episcopal dignity. But there is much in his story to render it altogether incredible. Two presbyters were not necessary in the early Church to consecrate the elements, as this story would imply; and the saint's high veneration for the episcopal office is not consistent with the apparent worship which he seems to have willingly accepted from his visitor. The miracles of Columba we must regard as non-historical, and as having sprung from the veneration of a superstitious age; and this story, relating a 'miracle, can only be received in so far as it shows, that the Iona brethren were visited by an Irish bishop of the name of Cronan.

Thus notwithstanding all that has been written on the subject, a reference to the older authorities shows that there was no early episcopacy among the northern Picts. And the reason is sufficiently obvious. Christianity had been established in Ireland since the days of St. Patrick. Hence its more complete organization, so that throughout the country regular pastors were stationed. These were the bishops of the country, exercising their functions apart from the monastic institutions, which, since the days of Martin of Tours, had been spreading throughout Ireland and part of Britain. Among the northern Picts there were as yet no clergy exercising those pastoral functions. There was but this mission institute in Iona; a mission institute, however, distinguished by this, in which it differed from most of the continental monasteries, that all the inmates were ecclesiastics. Their head was the supreme ecclesiastic, whom the brethren venerated, and we can easily understand how men holding this power would feel jealous of any rival power seeking to exercise supremacy over them. The contest did finally terminate in the general supremacy of the episcopal order, but it certainly had not approached that stage at the period of which we write.

Some writers have endeavoured to find in the organization of the early Scottish Church a state of matters altogether analogous to that of modern Presbyterianism. Presbyterian writers have done their cause no service by pushing this analogy farther than it can bear. That the

Iona brethren were presbyters and only presbyters, no writer on either side has ever denied. That the abbot was a presbyter Bede distinctly states, being too honest to make a statement which he knew to be inconsistent with fact. That the presbyter-abbot exercised jurisdiction, no doubt with consent of the brethren, as will be seen hereafter, over the whole body of brethren wherever located, is universally acknowledged,—that jurisdiction extending at a later period over bishops. But it is utterly vain to look among those establishments for anything like what is called a presbyterian organization. Nothing like kirk-sessions, presbyteries, synods, or general assemblies as now constituted, appear in the pages of Adomnan. Nor could it be otherwise. The brethren at Iona were not the regular ministers of an organised church; they were missionaries whose object was to preach the Gospel, and plant the Church of Christ in an almost pagan country. To this they applied themselves as opportunity offered. They preached and administered the sacraments, spreading themselves over the land for that purpose. That they sent forth ministers, as distinct from the planting of monasteries, is clear from their dealing at a later period with the Saxon populations of the north of England; and that they ordained those ministers whom they sent forth is quite as clear, these ministers holding their commission from them, assuming the name and performing the functions of bishops. Thus far then they were presbyterians, that they were presbyters themselves, and that as presbyters they exercised jurisdiction in the Church, and, as will be seen hereafter, conferred orders involving the episcopate, although these orders were afterwards rejected by the Roman Church.

It has been already said that in the east, where the monastic system originated, the earlier monks were laymen. From this it followed that they had to look beyond themselves for the privileges to be derived from an ordained ministry. Among the Scots the early monks being in reality missionaries, were all in orders themselves, as presbyters associated together for the great purpose of converting the ignorant to the faith of Christ. Being thus ordained they possessed all necessary ecclesiastical functions within themselves. Whence originated the so-called anomaly in the early Scottish Church, of the supreme power being in the hands of the abbot or head of the Culdee College. It has been said that the monastic system of the Southern Picts was derived from Rome, and accordingly was in conformity with that of Rome, while the system among the Scots and Northern Picts was derived from Gaul, where there was always more or less antagonism between the Church and that of Rome.[1] It is doubtful, however, how far this is sufficient to account for the peculiarities of the Culdee monastic system, inasmuch as we can find nothing in the early monasteries of Gaul at all analogous to the peculiarities which distinguished the Culdees of Scotland and Ireland. The nature of the Scottish episcopate is brought out by an entry in the Annals of Ulster at A.D. 724, " Oan princeps Ego mortuus est," *Oan Bishop of Eigg died.* Dr. Reeves (Vit. Col., p. 307 n.) translates princeps by *superior.* The translator in the Transactions of the Iona Club makes it *bishop;* and with more accuracy, for we have nothing to shew that there was any monastic institution in Eigg. If so, what could the bishop of Eigg be but the ordinary pastor ?

---

[1] Skene's Highlanders, vol. i., p. 194.

CHAPTER XIV.

THE DOCTRINE AND DISCIPLINE OF IONA.

THE doctrine of the early Church forms one of the most interesting and important subjects of inquiry in connection with early Church History. But it is hard to get at anything like a correct view of it. The events which befel the Church are so wrapped up in the coverings furnished by the ignorance, superstition, and wilful perversion of a later age, that it is hardly possible to unfold them. The same fate has befallen the doctrines of the early Church. So soon as we leave the Scriptures we find ourselves in a mist of human folly and ignorance, and know not very well how to grope our way towards the light. That the doctrine of the early Church was largely different from what has been represented by Romish writers must be true unless we are to believe in an immediate and tremendous defection so soon as the apostolic age passed away. It is hardly consistent with the usual course of human events, that such a defection, which without doubt did take place, should be anything but gradual in its progress.

We have few remains of the early Celtic Church from which to judge of the doctrine which prevailed ; but so far as we have any, one thing is obvious : the Holy Scriptures were held to be the one standard of truth, and were made by the missionaries a subject of close and constant study. In his early life, Columba is represented as attending upon the instructions of Bishop Findbar (Vit.

Col., Lib. ii., c. 1), said to be St. Finnian either of Moville or Clonard, both having been his teachers successively. While thus engaged we read that he was "sapientiam Saeræ Scripturæ addiscens," *learning the wisdom of the Sacred Scriptures.* His preaching was "verbum Dei," *the Word of God* (Vit. Col., Lib. i., c. 33), and this he proclaimed through an interpreter. His own home-work and that of his disciples was transcribing the Scriptures. The very story of the Psalter copied from that of St. Finnian, and upon which the king adjudicated, as already related, proves that this was a favourite occupation; while it is told us by his biographer, that this was the last employment of his life, for he died while engaged in transcribing the 33d Psalm (Vit. Col. iii. 23). These early missionaries were thoroughly Biblical. Columba's life by Adomnan represents him, in almost every page, as familiar with the word of God, and ready to quote it on all occasions as of supreme authority. Bede informs us (Hist. Eccl. Lib. iii., c. 4), that they received those things only which are written in the writings of the Prophets, Evangelists, and Apostles.

These missionaries were warmly devotional, and had much faith in prayer. From this feature in their character the very name of Culdee, by which they came afterwards to be distinguished, seems to have been derived. This word has been traced to various sources, as, "Gille Dé," the Gaelic words for *servant of God;* "Cultores Dei," the Latin term for *worshippers of God.* Some writers have derived it from "Culla," the Irish name for a *cowl,* whence "Culdee," *the black monk,* the cowl being usually black (Nic. Hist. Acct., p. 139). Goodall (Int. ad Scotichr., p. 68) holds that it is derived from the Greek κελλεωται, or *men of the cells.* Toland (Acct. of an Ir. MS., p. 51), says it is from "Ceile Dé," *the spouse of God.* The word in its earliest Latin form is Kaledei.

Among the native Celts it .is uniformly Cuildich.   In
Iona is a hollow called " Cobhan nan Cuildeach," or the
Culdee's chest, to this day.   Cuildeach can have but one
meaning.   It is derived from " Cuil," a *recess*, or secluded
corner, and can only be descriptive of the habits of those
to whom it refers.   As interpreted by the language to
which this word belongs the Culdee was nothing else than
the man of the recess.   Jamieson is confirmed in his belief
that this is the accurate etymology by the close relation
between this word and " Cille," or " Kil," the term applied
by the Gaelic Celts to a church.   But the words have no
connection whatsoever, the latter being simply an adaptation of the Latin Cella.   They may be philologically
related, but they have no historical relation.[1]   Bishop
Lloyd says that it was an usual thing about the thirteenth
century to find out Latin derivations for words of which
men did not know the origin ; whence Culdees were
said to be Colidei, or " the worshippers of God."   But as
all Christians were Cultores Dei, the word could have no
special meaning as applied to this class of missionaries,
but in " Cuildich," or *men of seclusion*, we have a descriptive name, and the description borne out by what we
know of the history of the men.

It was characteristic of these missionaries that they
sought out for themselves islands on which to fix their
residence.   Iona itself affords a remarkable instance of
this, and it is but one of many.   One reason why such

---

[1] Most Gaelic ecclesiastical terms are derived immediately from the Latin, as
Eaglais, from *Ecclesia ; Sagart*, from *Sacerdos ; Pearsa*, or *Pearsoin*, from *Per-
sona ; Aoibhrionn*, ' the mass,' from *Offerens ; Caisg*, 'Easter,' from *Pascha ; Fao-
said*, ' to confess,' from *Confessio ; Reilig*, ' a burying place,' from *Reliquiœ ;
Ifrionn*, ' hell,' from *Avernus ; Nollaig*, ' Christmas,' from *Natalis ; Calain*, ' the
new year,' from *Calendœ ; Dìseart*, ' a hermitage,' from *Desertum ; De dòmhnaich*,
' the Lord's day,' from *Dies Domini*, &c.   Other words, although not from the
Latin, are ecclesiastical, as *De ceud aoine*, ' Wednesday, the day of the first fast ;'
De eadar da aoine, ' Thursday, the day between two fasts ;' and *De h-aoine*,
' Friday, the day of the fast.'

places were selected was probably the security they afforded to men, who, from the nature of their work, were exposed to the enmity of an ignorant and superstitious people. But seclusion seems to have been sought as well as security, that time and opportunity might be found for prayer. The religion of these men was less obtrusive than we often find it. It sought for concealment rather than display; and exhibited itself primarily, not in forcing itself, with little sense of modesty, upon the notice of men, but in urging its subjects to closer and more continuous intercourse with God. We find one good man (Cormac Ua Liathain), (Vit. Col. Ad. Lib. i., c. 6), seeking a place of retirement among the islands of the west, and returning three several times to Iona, not having found such a place as he sought. In this manner many of the islands of the Hebrides became their resort. The island of Tyree was one of the localities singled out; Inch Kenneth in the mouth of Loch nan Keal, or nan Ceall, (the Loch of the Churches) in Mull, was another; Oransay to the south of Colonsay became famous in Culdee history; and St. Kilda has several remains of those early places of worship. Forty miles to the north of the Butt of Lewis lies the island of Rona; thither Ronan, an early missionary, was wont to retire; the oratory[1] said to have been erected by him, of which a sketch is now

---

[1] In presenting a few sketches of the remains of ancient oratories still existing among the Hebrides, the author has to acknowledge his obligations to the author of the interesting and valuable work on the "Characteristics of Early Church Architecture in Scotland," and to Messrs. Edmonstone and Douglas, the publishers, for the readiness with which they permitted the use of these sketches for this volume. The sketches themselves are full of interest, as presenting us with the style of architecture adopted in Scotland so soon as stone became substituted for wood in church building. The same change appears to have taken place in civil architecture, the ancient crannoges passing into what are called the Pictish towers, and a comparison of the style of the two kinds of building will shew that the ecclesiastical oratories and the Pictish towers must

furnished, is still in existence. To the west of the island

TEAMPULL RONA
INTERIOR WEST END ELEVATION.

of Lewis are the Flannan islands, the retreat of the famous Flann, also an early missionary of the Scottish Church. The remains on one of these islands are represented below. The Orkney islands were sought out, and in some cases used for similar purposes, of which the several Papas are ample evidence ; while, in the course of

have been of the same period. There are the low doors, the walls inclining, and the stones similarly laid without mortar. Both these classes of building belong apparently to the seventh or eighth centuries.

their peregrinations, the brethren reached Iceland, where their footprints are still to be traced. When we bear in mind that these stormy northern seas were traversed in the tiniest craft, without chart or compass, by men actuated solely by religious zeal, we have ample evidence of the power which this great principle is calculated to exercise.

TEAMPULL SÙLA SGEIR, SOUTH SIDE

Many of these expeditions took place at a later period than that of Columba, and are adduced here as illus trative of the character and work of the Iona mission aries.

The retirement thus sought was evidently for prayer and communion with God. These men believed, as did Luther, that prayer was the best preparation for preaching, and hence much of their time was devoted to that exercise. The buildings, whose ruins still existing, are memorials of the period, are clearly oratories, and nothing else ; oratories, first used as places for prayer by these early Christians, and afterwards used more generally for the same purpose, in a later and more superstitious age.   One of these singular buildings exists

TEAMPULL BEANNACHADH
WEST END
Flannan Islands.

on the island of Inchcolm, in the Firth of Forth, not far
from Edinburgh   (See interesting notice of this relic, by
Professor J. Y. Simpson, in Trans. of Scot. Antiq., vol. ii.
p. 489.)   In this manner prayer and preaching were
mingled in the labours of these good men.   They had
learned the important truth that prayer was the great
means of ensuring a successful ministry, although they
carried to a dangerous extreme the idea, that to obtain
opportunity for prayer, it was necessary for a time to
seclude themselves entirely from the fellowship of others.
In this they helped to lay the foundation of much
future injury to the Church ; yet they never dissociated

their retirement from the activities of their missionary life, but sought the one to qualify them the more fully for the other. We cannot conceive a more interesting object, in that rude age, than one of these holy men retiring to some lonely island of the sea, and there, in solitude, with none of the comforts, and a small share of the necessaries of life, spending his time in holding communion with God, and pleading earnestly for His blessing on the great work in which he was engaged; and then strengthened and stirred up to more earnest zeal, by his intercourse with heaven, going forth among an ignorant and barbarous people, warning them to flee from the wrath to come, and calling upon them with earnest voice to believe and be baptized.

This practice of taking possession of secluded islands continued to characterise the Culdee system, and was carried by the missionaries sent forth from time to time whithersoever they went. When Aidan at a later period was sent to preach the Gospel to the northern Saxons, he fixed his residence in Lindisfarne, and thence went forth to preach the Gospel to the surrounding population; Lindisfarne, or the Holy Isle, becoming to the north of England what Iona was to the north of Scotland. In this there was a marked difference between the emissaries of Iona and those of Rome. When Augustine was sent from Rome he seized upon Canterbury, in the very heart of one of the richest counties of England, and there established himself. Paulinus, in like manner, settled in York, the capital of the north of England. Thus did these men represent the ambitious, grasping spirit of their system, covetous of place and power; while the humble missionaries of Iona and Lindisfarne represented the spirit of their own system, covetous of exalting Christ, but crucifying self. In nothing does the distinc-

tion between the Church of Rome and the ancient Scot
tish Church appear more clearly than in this.

The great subject of the teaching of those early missionaries was the simple truth of the Gospel of salvation.
It was *Verbum Dei*, 'the word of God.' Adomnan
says of Columba, that from his boyhood he was instructed
in the love of Christ (Vit. Col. Pref. Sec). When he
resolved upon his missionary expedition to Scotland this
was the great principle which governed him ; he sought
a foreign country " for the love of Christ." For thirty-
five years, his biographer tells us, he lived " a good
soldier of Christ " in his adopted island. He was in
every sense a missionary of Christ, and there can be no
room to question that, like the great Apostle of the Gentiles, " Christ, and Him crucified," was the great subject of
his teaching. To the work of the Holy Spirit his
biographer gives ample place. He tells us (Pref. Sec.)
that by the " grace of God " he preserved the integrity of
his body and the purity of his soul, and, in detailing the
experience of the saint, he attributes it to " the Holy
Spirit which filled his inmost soul." From all this we
can gather what the nature of the faith of these early
missionaries was, and the nature of the instruction which
they conveyed to others.

While this much may be gathered of the positive
belief of these men, there are some doctrines to which
the Church gave prominence in an after age, the want of
any reference to which, in the accounts of them that
have reached us, is abundantly significant. Thus there
is no reference to the worship of the Virgin in the whole
of Adomnan's work, whence it is obvious that the adora-
tion received by her at a later period was not offered to
her at this time, at least in the Scottish Church. This
is a remarkable and instructive fact regarding these
missionaries ; and the fact is further borne out by

what is well known in regard to the early dedication of churches in Scotland. They were uniformly dedicated to native saints, and there is not one instance in Scotland until a comparatively recent date of a dedication to the Virgin Mary.

Nor is there the slightest evidence of saint worship. Good men were held in high esteem, but such esteem as is warranted by the Scriptures, and as all Christian men count it a privilege to cherish. Columba entertained the warmest affection for other good men. Thus we read (Vit. Col., Lib. i. c. 41) that he sent two of the brethren to Cailtan, who lived in a cell near Loch Awe, asking him to come without delay to visit him. The saint on seeing him said among other things, "I sent for you because I loved you sincerely." In like manner, Baithean, among Columba's immediate disciples, was an object of very warm affection, and as his own death approached, the saint appointed that he should be his successor as head of the institution. But in all we read of these men in the pages of Adomnan, we read nothing of saint worship, or of their having recourse to the intercession of the saints with God, unless we accept as evidence of the contrary an address of a somewhat formal kind put into the mouth of Columba, by his biographer, on his death-bed ; an address which savours, however, too much of the work of the panegyrist to be so accepted. The Church was as yet not prepared for the introduction of such a change in the faith as this implied.

Nor do we find in the biography of Columba any reference to the doctrine of purgatory. Where the faith in Christ was so entire, and the love to Christ so ardent, there was no room for such a doctrine as this. The all-sufficiency of the atonement made by the Divine Saviour, and of the grace of the Divine Spirit, afford the one unanswerable argument against the doctrine of purification by any other means. The completeness in which these doctrines were held by the Iona missionaries necessarily excluded their belief in the doctrine of a purgatory. From the same cause we find no regard to other more recent doctrines and practices. Thus there is no reference in the account given of Columba's death to his having received extreme unction. Roman Catholic writers account for this by the suddenness of his death, but according to his biographer (Vit. Col., Lib. iii. c. 23), he knew the very day of it, and foretold it to his servant Diarmad, and if he held the doctrine of extreme unction, he would have surely asked that sacrament, as it is called, for himself.

It is at the same time manifest that there is in the biography of Columba, by Adomnan, an account given of certain observances and forms of worship, and of terms used, which differ from those used among Protestants. Thus the tonsure was in universal use, and in this we find one evidence of the change from apostolic times. We read nothing concerning the tonsure in the Divine record, but by the seventh century it came to be a matter of much importance in the Church. There were several kinds of tonsure in the early Church. The Greek tonsure was total, and was usually styled that of St. Paul, though for what reason it is impossible to say with any truth. The Roman tonsure, usually called that of St. Peter, extended only to the crown of the head, and was called coronal. The tonsure in use in the Scottish Church was from ear to ear, the hair being shaved from the forehead backwards to a line joining the ears across the top of the head. This tonsure was made a subject of bitter reproach by the adherents of the Romish Church, and was called the tonsure of Simon Magus. Its history, as originating in the East, is too well known to allow room for believing that there is any ground for the reproach, but no means were left unemployed for bringing the Church in Scotland and Ireland, with respect to this matter, into conformity with that of Rome[1] The controversy which arose at a later period on the subject of the tonsure, will appear in its own place. In the meantime, it is merely meant to note that the tonsure was practised by Columba and the other missionaries of Iona.

The words made use of in regard to the service of the church would seem to indicate that these missionaries held the doctrine of transubstantiation. There was an altar in the church (Vit. Col. Lib. I., c. 44, &c.), and the officiating minister is said *Sacra Eucharistiæ consecrare mysteria,* 'to consecrate the sacred mysteries of the Eucharist' (Vit. Col. Lib. III., c. 17), and *Christi corpus conficere,* 'to form the body of Christ' (Vit. Col. Lib. I., c. 44). Nor was this language by any means unknown in the church at the time.[2] And yet the language cannot be understood as implying that the doctrine of the conversion of the bread and wine into the body and blood of Christ as now held by the Church of Rome, was held by the ancient Scottish Church. Christ himself calls the bread his "body" and the wine his "blood" at the very time that he was himself in the body. To "form the body of Christ," then, does not necessarily imply that the bread and the wine in after times became changed into the flesh and blood of Christ any more than at the first supper. The use of the term "mystery" is quite in accordance with Scripture usage, so that it is necessary

---

[1] It is from the tonsure in use at the time that St. Patrick is said to have been called *Tailginn,* a name so common in the old Ossianic fragments. The word is understood as meaning 'a tonsured one,' either from *Tail,* 'to shave,' synonymous, as Dr. Todd thinks, with the French *Tailler,* or from *Tàl,* 'an adze,' the tonsure assuming somewhat of the form of that implement.

[2] Dr. Reeves has shewn by quotations from various sources that this form of expression was used even so far back as the days of Jerome (Vit. Col. p. 85, n).

to exercise caution in the interpretation we put upon
Adomnan's phraseology. It is certainly phraseology
which no Protestant would now use, but it is phraseology which must not be made to mean more than was
really intended. We know from unquestionable authority that the doctrine of transubstantiation as laid down
by the council of Trent did not receive general acceptance
until about the ninth century, and even then was strenuously resisted by many able and learned men (See Cunningham's Hist. Theol., vol. I., p. 205). Wine was used
in the Scottish Church along with the bread, so that the
communion was manifestly in both kinds (Vit. Col. Lib.
II., c. 2).

Easter was regularly observed in Iona. This season,
the name of which in English is, according to Bede,
derived from the heathen goddess Eostre, and which cor-
responded to the period of an ancient Saxon festival, is
called by Adomnan "Paschalis solemnitas" (Vit. Col.
Lib. ii., c. 39). The custom of observing it was like the
name "Pascha," originally derived from the Jewish passover. Yet dissensions as to the time of its observance
broke out at a very early period, between the Jewish
converts in the church and those who had been brought
over from heathenism. In Asia Minor the churches observed their Easter on the day of the Jewish Passover,
or the 14th day of the first month, which began with the
appearance of the moon. These were on this account
called Quartodecimans. In their way of observing the
festival the day commemorative of our Saviour's death
did not necessarily fall on a Friday, nor did the day
commemorative of his resurrection necessarily fall on a
Sunday. In Rome the fast was so extended as that the
weekly commemoration of the resurrection on the Lord's
day and the annual commemoration at Easter coincided.
The Easterns held that they had received their mode of

calculation from the apostles John and Philip, Polycarp, and others. After a keen controversy between Victor, Bishop of Rome, and Polycrates, Bishop of Ephesus, the question remained unsettled, various sections of the church following their own method of observing the season. In A.D. 325 Constantine endeavoured to get this with other questions settled in the council of Nice. After discussion, it was ordained that the death of Christ should be uniformly commemorated on Friday, and his resurrection on the first day of the week. But the followers of the Quartodeciman rule refused to concur, and they continued to observe their Easter on the 14th day of the month Nisan, without any reference to the day of the week. Great difficulty in fixing the period of Easter arose from the kind of calculations necessary in order to find the precise day in each year. This difficulty was less felt in the East from the prevalence of mathematical and astronomical learning. It was different in the west; but finally in the sixth century, and chiefly through the exertions of Dionysius Exiguus, a Roman abbot, the Alexandrian mode of calculation was introduced in Rome. The British churches did not accept this new method of calculation, which fixed the day of the Easter festival by the nineteen years' cycle of the moon, and the twenty-eight years' cycle of the sun, but continued to adhere to the ancient cycle of eighty-four years. They also held that the festival commenced from the 14th day of the month and extended to the 20th, while in Rome it was now held to commence on the 15th and to extend to the 21st day of the first vernal moon. They differed, however, from the Quartodecimans in this, that they uniformly commemorated the resurrection on the first day of the week. They thus differed both from the churches of Asia Minor and that of Rome (Hist. Eccl. Bede, Lib. v., c. 21). This difference often led to a

difference of a whole month in the day of observing
Easter. A violent controversy arose between the Roman and British churches on this subject, which came to a
close in A.D. 716 by the latter conforming to the Roman
method. The progress of this controversy will be traced as
we proceed. Meanwhile it may be well to observe, that
although the word Easter does occur once (Acts xii. 4) in
our translation of the Scripture, there is not a sentence
in the Divine record which warrants such an observance
at all. It would be as warrantable to maintain that the
Jewish ordinance of circumcision was still imperative in
the Church of Christ, because enjoined on the Jews, as
to maintain that the Jewish Passover was to be retained
in the form of the Christian Easter. If the one has
passed into the Christian sacrament of Baptism, surely
analogy would lead us to hold the other as represented
in the Christian sacrament of the Supper. That is the
true commemoration of Christ's passion. The festival of
Easter was however observed in the institute at Iona.

We can gather little from Adomnan of the peculiar
form of worship in use among the Iona missionaries—
whether they made use of any peculiar "cursus" or
liturgy, and whether the service, if there was such, was
chanted or read. We have no evidence to shew that any
liturgy or form of prayers was used in the Christian
Church before the fourth century; although some writers
maintain that a traditional form of observing the Lord's
Supper, handed down from the apostles, was in use. This
could only be traditional, as the Arcani Disciplina would
not suffer anything belonging to Christian worship to be
written, lest the heathen should discover it (see Riddle's
" Manual of Christian Antiquities "). Without adverting
to the Clementine liturgy, or that of Basil still used in
the Eastern Church, we find no evidence of the existence
of a liturgy in the west before the time of Gregory the

Great, in the end of the sixth century. There is no reliable evidence of any such having existed before his time, and it is to that date we must ascribe the Roman missal. If so, there can be no reason for supposing that anything of the kind existed in the Scottish Church at this time, although the Gallic liturgy came afterwards into use. In fact, the only books of which we read as existing at Iona, are the Bible in both canons, and *Scripturæ tam liberales quam ecclesiasticæ*, works of general literature as well as ecclesiastical. But there is no word of a missal or liturgy, and among all that is said of transcribing books, this could hardly have escaped Adomnan, if such a work existed. The fair inference is, that there was no such thing, although it may be very true that certain fixed modes of worship did exist. The missionary work in which these men were engaged required a large amount of freedom from the restraints imposed by liturgic forms and ceremonial worship ; the "cursus" or "synaxis" would in all probability consist in passages selected from the Word of God, intermingled with extempore prayer.

The sign of the cross was in use—another practice which had crept into the church without Scripture warrant, although it is very probable that those who used it first had the full belief that its use was not only justifiable but commendable in Christians. "The sign of the cross was generally employed as a *signum salutare*. Hence it was customary before milking to cross the pail ; before tools were used, to cross them. The sign of the cross was considered effectual to banish demons, to restrain a river monster, to prostrate a wild beast, to unlock a door, to endow a pebble with healing virtues. Hence the readiness to erect the substantial *vexillum crucis* on the sight of any remarkable occurrence, a tendency which got full credit for its development when Hy was celebrated for her 360 crosses (Vit. Col., Dr. Reeves' add. notes, p. 351). It must not be forgotten, however, that this account is taken from the writings of Adomnan, whose statements are coloured by the practice and beliefs of his own age, and who cannot be held as an accurate historian, when the question of a miracle is concerned. It is not safe to conclude from his account to what extent Columba used or relied on the sign of the cross.

One of the most remarkable features about the ancient Scottish Church was the extent to which it was pervaded by the principle of clanship; in so much that, at a later period, office in the church became a matter of hereditary succession. Columba and his followers belonged to one clan, and the succession in Iona continued for a long period to be limited to that clan. This was the Cineal Connell or race of Connell, the descendants of Conall Gulban, son of Niel of the nine hostages, the founder of the great northern Irish family of O'Niell; Columba himself was great grandson of Conall Gulban. It is from this Conall that Tirconnell in Ulster takes its name. It has been maintained (see Dr. Reeves' List of the Abbots of Iona and their connection with the chief families of Tirconnell. Vit. Col., p. 342) that all the Abbots down to the union of the Scottish and Pictish kingdoms were of one or other of the families of Tirconnell, with one exception; and in another case it is only said that the pedigree is not preserved. The evidence upon which this statement is made is not of a kind that bears to be looked into very minutely. Documents drawn up from 400 to 600 years after the events occurred to which they relate, are not very reliable as evidence of facts. Yet this principle of clanship did run through the old Scottish and Irish Church; so much so, that some of the monasteries in Ireland were named after the clan among which they were placed. In Scotland it has been shewn that to a large extent the early monasteries occupied the districts belonging to distinct tribes, which afterwards became the territorial divisions called Earldoms. (Skene's Highlanders, vol. I., 202, in which the following table has been drawn out to shew this) :—

Culdee Monasteries.	Tribes or Earldoms.
St. Andrew's	Fife.
Dunblane	Stratherne ; Menteith *(not an old Earldom.)*
Scone	Gowrie.
Brechin	Angus ; Mearns *(formerly part of Angus.)*
Monymusk	Mar.
Mortlach	Buchan.
Birney (Moray)	Moray.
Rosemarkie	Ross.
Dornoch	Caithness.
Iona	Garmoran.
Dunkeld	Atholl ; Argyll *(part of Atholl.)*

The likelihood is that this principle was first admitted in order to secure all possible influence in Christianizing the people, the very principle which led Columba to visit and seek the conversion of the Pictish king. Family influence was in the highest degree powerful, and to secure it on the side of Christianity was but a policy which the warmest zeal and the most consummate prudence dictated. This principle would also have been admitted for the sake of security. All these institutions had powerful family influence around them on every side ; no man could assail them without calling down the vengeance of the clan, and all men would in consequence forbear ; while they were capable of repay-

ing in full the benefit they received, and became finally
of so much importance from their wealth and influence,
that no family would willingly quit its hold of them.
They thus became hereditary possessions in the hands of
the great families of Scotland and Ireland, and even
came to be so situated as that the lands of the monastery
were in the hands of a layman, while the ecclesiastics of
the community occupied the house and conducted the
services.

The question has been frequently discussed whether
these early missionaries held themselves at liberty to
marry or not. Dr. Reeves, in his Notes (Vit. Col., p.
344), says, "Though St. Columba was desirous to pro-
mote conjugal happiness, and he was held in veneration
by the other sex, there can be no doubt that celibacy was
strictly enjoined on the community, and the condition
"Virgo corpore et virgo mente," held up for imitation.
Hence we find a monk discharging an office usually
assigned to women, and hence the total want of anything
like hereditary succession in the abbacy of Hy. A
learned and ingenious writer in a modern journal (Rev.
R. King, author of " Memoir of the Primacy of Armagh),
has proved to a demonstration, from the native annalists,
that a lineal succession of abbots existed in many of the
Irish monasteries during the ninth and following centuries, but he has failed to include the coarbs of Columba
in the class. . . . Marriage, no doubt, existed among
the secular clergy, but the practice seems to have been
disapproved of by the regulars." Whether Mr. King has
failed or not, Dr. Reeves has certainly not succeeded in
shewing that celibacy was practised by Columba and his
disciples. The chief proof which he adduces in the above
extract is that of a monk performing on one occasion a
service which is usually assigned to women. But surely
so important a question is not to be decided on such

evidence as that. It might be true that a monk on several occasions had to act in such a way as is described, but if a man's doing a woman's usual work is to be looked upon as evidence that the men who allow it are to be held as opposed to marriage, the doctrine of celibacy will extend over a breadth of surface for which the excellent editor of the life of Columba is not perhaps prepared. Adomnan does not inform us on the subject, and we need not wonder, inasmuch as the practice of clerical celibacy was not held at the time by any large number of men in the Church. And we know from irrefragable evidence that, in the Scottish Church, which looked to Iona as its source, the marriage of the clergy was practised to a late age. And the Culdees in that Church are to be held as the successors, not of the secular but of the regular clergy, in so far as they might be called regular, of the early period. There is a Gaelic adage which tradition professes to hand down from the times of Columba, to the effect that " Where there is a cow, there will a woman be, and where there is a woman there is a curse," *Far am bi bo bithidh bean, agus far am bi bean bithidh mallachd;* but this adage savours of a much later age than Columba's. The references in Adomnan's biography, however, to the existence of cows in Iona are sufficiently numerous. We read of the *Bocetum*, or pasture for cows ; we read of Columba's blessing the milk pail ; we read of milk as entering into the ordinary diet of the monastery ; and if the existence of cows necessarily implied that of women, the latter must have been numerous in Iona.

It cannot be denied that the idea of the superior purity of a state of celibacy found its way to some extent into the Church at an early period. Even Tertullian could speak of one who married once, as " falling from the high state of immaculate virginity. This was probably founded on a misapplication of St. Paul's statements in his First Epistle to the Corinthians, in which he clearly refers to the exigencies of the existing times, just as if these existed with reference to the ministers of the Church at all times. But however that may be, the idea gathered strength, until it was embodied in a Papal decree which was issued between the years 385 and 398, by Siricius, who was then Pope. Papal decrees did not, however, at the time bind the Church in Britain and Ireland ; and it is obvious that in this, as in other matters, the Papal injunction was disregarded. We have sufficient evidence to show that at a later period the Scottish Culdees resisted it, and continued to marry until they ceased to exist, while there is nothing of the slightest value in the way of proof to show that they did not follow the same practice in their earliest period. Indeed, the fair inference from the later practice is that they did.

CHAPTER XV

COLUMBA died in the year 597, after midnight, between
Saturday, then called Sabbath, the 9th June, and the
Lord's day following.   Adomnan says that, previous to
his death, he addressed his companions, saying, "This,
dear children, is my last advice to you—that you preserve with each other sincere charity and peace ; and if
you thus imitate the example of the holy fathers, God
the comforter of the good will assist you, and I being
with Him will intercede for you, and He will not only
give you sufficient to supply the wants of this present
life, but will bestow on you likewise the eternal rewards
that are prepared for those who observe the divine pre-
cepts."   The doctrine of intercession here propounded
savours of a different age from Columba's ; in fact, such
addresses are of no more historical value than the
speeches furnished us by Livy and Tacitus.

As the midnight bell tolled he arose, hastened to the
church, and entering first, knelt down in prayer before
the altar.   Diarmad, his attendant, who entered at this
moment, saw the whole edifice filled with light, which
fell upon the saint.   The faithful attendant entered the
church, the light having soon disappeared, and exclaimed,
"Where are you, father ?"   He found him in a recum-
bent position before the altar.   It was soon clear that he
was dying, and the brethren who had gathered in began
to weep.   The saint, with a motion of his hand, as he

could not now speak, indicated that he gave them his blessing, and soon after his spirit passed away. His body was carried back to his cell, and for three days his obsequies were duly celebrated. After that period, being wrapped in a shroud of fine linen, the body was placed in a coffin, and buried with every mark of respect.[1] It is related that he foretold that none but the monks of the island should be present at his obsequies, and it is said that such a storm of wind and rain arose, and continued for three days and three nights, that no one could venture to cross the ferry to join in their celebration (Vit. Col. Lib. iii., c. 23). This would seem to shew that there were no people at the time in Iona but Columba and his brethren.

His biographer adds, "After reading these three books, let the diligent reader observe how great in merit, how high in favour before God must have been our holy and venerable abbot; how often he was blessed by the bright visits of angels; how full of the prophetic spirit, how great his power of daily miracles; how frequently, during his mortal life, he was surrounded by a halo of heavenly light; and even since the departure of his happy soul from the tenement of his body unto this day, the place where his sacred bones repose is frequently visited by the holy angels, and illumined by the same heavenly light, as has been clearly manifested to a select few. And this too is no small honour conferred by God on his servant of happy memory; that though he lived in this small and remote island of the British sea, his name has not only become illustrious throughout our own Scotia and Britain, the greatest of all the islands of the globe,

---

[1] The grave is now shewn close to the door of the cathedral in Iona, but undoubtedly the grave of Columba must be sought in Relig Oran, the oldest place of sepulture in the island. If kings sought their sepulture here, it must have been in order to be laid in the same place with Columba, which would not have been if he were interred where his grave is now pointed out.

but has also reached Spain, remarkable for its triangular form, and Gaul; and penetrated into Italy beyond the Alps, and even to the city of Rome itself, the head of all cities" (Vit. Col. Lib. iii., c. 23).

Dr. Reeves says (Vit. Col. App. to Pref. p. lxxviii.), " Three Latin hymns of considerable beauty are attributed to him (Columba) and in the ancient Liber Hymnorum in which they are preserved, each is accompanied by a preface describing the occasion on which it was written. His alleged Irish compositions are also poems; some specimens of which will be found in the following pages. There are also in print his ' Farewell to Aran,' a poem of twenty-two stanzas, and another poem of seventeen stanzas, which he is supposed to have written on the occasion of his flight from king Diarmad. Besides these there is a collection of some fifteen poems, bearing his name in one of the O'Clery MSS., preserved in the Burgundian library at Brussels. But much the largest collection is contained in an oblong MS. of the Bodleian library at Oxford, Laud, 615, which embraces everything in the shape of poem or fragment that could be called Columba's which industry was able to scrape together at the middle of the sixteenth century. Many of the poems are ancient, but in the whole collection there is probably not one of Columcille's composition. Among them are his alleged prophecies, the genuineness of which even Colgan called in question. Copies of some of these compositions have been preserved in Ireland." There are three Latin poems still extant of which there is sufficient reason to believe that Columba was the author.

It must not be forgotten that while Iona was a missionary institute it was a school of learning too. For a long period it will be seen that it supplied Scotland and a great part of England with learned missionaries. The Latin language seems more especially to have been cultivated to a great extent, and was not only read but written with accuracy and freedom. Columba's own compositions, which are still extant, as the hymn beginning with " Noli, Pater, indulgere," or that beginning with "Altus prosator, vetustus," are sufficient evidence of this. The works of *Cuimean Fionn,* or 'Cumin the Fair,' and Adomnan are sufficient to shew that the learning of the institute was maintained for generations. Adomnan might speak of the barbarous sounds of his native Gaelic, and yet it would appear that these men, imbued with classical learning, cultivated at the same time their own ancient tongue, and made it the vehicle for communicating not the knowledge of religion alone, but also that of history and science. The Irish annals sufficiently attest this.

We may close our notice of Columba and his work by observing that to this day among the native Gael he is known as Columcille, pronounced Columkille, the plain meaning of which word is Colum of the Cell, or as the word "cill" is now applied, Colum of the church. The name originated unquestionably in the fame acquired by his devotional habits. Dr. Reeves has traced Columba's name in fifty-three places in Scotland, both among Scots and Picts, where it is commemorated either in wells or churches dedicated to him (Vit. Col. Reeves, pp. 289, &c.).

Upon the death of Columba he was succeeded in the abbot's seat by his disciple and relative, Baithean. Several incidents regarding him are related by Adomnan. He had accompanied Columba on his first expedition to Iona, and continued with him until his death. He was the son of Brendan, who was brother of Feidhlimidh, father of St. Columba, and brother to Cobhtach, another of the disciples of the saint (Vit. Col. Reeves, p. 245). Baithean was on one occasion transcribing the Psalter, and having finished the work, he asked of Columba

that one of the brethren should examine it.   The
saint remonstrated with him on the unnecessary trouble
he was giving, and said that there was nothing wanting
in the whole book but one letter *I.*   On examination it
was found that such was the case.   This is a specimen
of the laboriousness and accuracy of the scribe.

Like others of the brethren, Baithean sought an *Eremus*
or 'hermitage,' the Gaelic "Diseart," and found it in the
island of Tyree, the Terra Ethica of Adomnan (Vit. Col.
Lib. I., c. 30).   Here he became superior of a subordinate
institution at a place called "Campus Lunge," in Gaelic
Magh luinge, or 'the Plain of the ship.'   The modern
name is supposed to be Soroby, towards the south-east
part of the island, where there are to this day ecclesiastical remains, some of them very ancient, (Characteristics of
Ear. Ch. Arch., p. 157).   In this manner was the influence of the institution at Iona gradually spread over the
whole north of Scotland.   Baithean occupied the abbot's
seat at Iona for a period of three years only, having died
on the 9th June, 600.   It is a somewhat remarkable fact
that he died on the same day of the year with his great
predecessor.

Another of the cotemporaries of Columba, whose name
is well known in the Scottish Church, was Cainneach or
Kenneth.   His name is found in such topographical terms
as Kilchenzie in Kintyre, synonymous with Kilkenny in
Ireland, Inch-Kenneth at the mouth of Loch nan Ceall in
Mull, Kennoway in Fife, and various other places throughout both Scotland and Ireland.—(See Paper by Mr. Skene
in Trans. of Antiq. Soc. of Scot., vol. iv., p. 1).   He is
called by Adomnan, Cainnechus Mocu Dalon, being a
member of the Clan Ua Dalann, a branch of the Clan
Rudhraidh of Ulster.   He was born in 517, and died in
600.   In the Aberdeen Breviary we are told (Brev. Aberd.
Oct. 11) that he was of Irish descent, and that coming to

visit Columba he surprised him with his wisdom, which he told him he derived directly, while in retirement, from Christ himself. Two visits to Iona are related by Adomnan, one by Kenneth alone (Vit. Col., Lib. i., c. 4), and another (Vit. Col., Lib. iii., c. 17), where an account is given of the arrival of Comgall, Cainneach, Brendan, and Cormac, who witnessed a remarkable light resting on the top of Columba's head, as he was, at their request, celebrating the Eucharist. The miraculous part of the story may be dismissed, but the fact of the visit still remains, and there is nothing incredible in the statement of the Aberdeen Breviary that Kenneth did surprise his friend and brother Columba with his learning and wisdom.

The account of him in the Aberdeen Breviary further relates that he visited Rome, when, being attacked by robbers, his prayers for aid were answered by the arms of his assailants becoming perfectly rigid. Thereafter, through his intercession, they were restored, and the malefactors filled with admiration. There is nothing to discredit the story of Kenneth's visit to Iona, but there is everything to discredit that of his visit to Rome. Rome was not at the time to the Scottish Church what this legend would indicate, nor did it become so for centuries after ; but the story suited the tastes and beliefs of mediæval Hagiologists.

Another of the cotemporaries of Columba, whose name is associated with Scottish ecclesiastical topography, is Ciaran, or *the dark complexioned man*, pronounced Kiaran. In Ireland he is called Ciaran of Clonmacnois, from his having founded, about the year 548, the monastery of that name. His usual patronymic is Ciaran Mac an t-saoir, *the son of the artificer*, a name represented by the modern Macintyre. In Scotland his name is associated principally with Campbeltown in Kintyre, the Gaelic name of which is Kilkerran or Cill Chiarain, *Ciaran's Church*.

In the neighbourhood is shewn his cave, amidst the rocks which line the coast to the south,—a gloomy recess close upon the sea, which was used as the retirement or "diseart" of the good man. The name is commemorated also in Kilkerran in Ayrshire, and other places in Scotland. Ciaran was born in the year 515, and died in 549, being then only 34 years of age. His piety and learning must have been of a very marked character to have, in so short a life, made so deep an impression on the popular mind in both Scotland and Ireland. We have no record of the period of his life spent in Scotland, but it must have been considerable. Irish records afford little help in extricating the ancient history of the two countries ; this being of itself sufficient to shew that they are for the most part productions of a later age, and not entitled to much credit as historical documents. The cotemporary documents that do exist, as well as tradition and topography, shew that the ecclesiastical history of Scotland and Ireland was at an early period, like its literature, closely interwoven, and that the names of most of the early missionaries are, like those of their early warriors, inseparably associated with both. Nor is there much faith to be placed in the theory that *all* these men were Irish. Scotland had been for centuries under the influence of the Christian faith to some extent, and it is not probable that a country that gave birth to St. Patrick was undistinguished by the name of other saints from amongst its growing Scottish population.

Another of Columba's cotemporaries whose name is linked with Scotland was Colum an eala, pronounced Colmonell, or Colum of Ela, a stream in King's County, from which his church, Lann Ela or Lynally, took its name (Vit. Col., Reeves' Note, p. 124). He was born in 555, and died in 611. In Scotland his name is commemorated in Kilcalmonell, in Kintyre, and in the parish of Colmonell, in Ayrshire. Adomnan calls him

Filius Beognai, 'Son of Beognai' of the O'Niells, and also Mocusailni or Mac na Seille, being descended from a tribe called the Dal Sailne, from Feidhlimidh Sailne, their predecessor. He seems to have been in frequent communication with Columba, as we read of two visits of his to Iona. In one of those (Vit. Col., Lib. i. c. 5), he was almost drowned in Corryvrekan, but we learn from Columba that his danger was only intended to stir him up to more prayer. On another occasion (Vit. Col., Lib. ii. c. 15), he and Baithean were both leaving Iona at the same time, the one for Tyree and the other for Ireland. By the intercession of Columba, both obtained a favourable wind, although proceeding in almost opposite directions. This was in 597, the year Columba died, for upon his leaving, Columba stated that he would see his face no more ; and we are told that the latter died the same year. It is interesting and important to observe, that, in relating the first of these incidents, Adomnan calls Colum an eala or Columbanus a bishop, and in the second he calls him a presbyter, showing pretty clearly that the distinction between the offices was not then held as it is now. Dr. Reeves supposes that in one case there is an error, but on what authority is not said (Vit. Col., Reeves, p. 125 note). This saint is, like the former, closely identified with the early Church history of Scotland, but we learn nothing from any trustworthy record at what period, or how much of his life was spent there. As in other cases, we have from the Irish records sufficiently minute accounts of his genealogy, going back for twenty-five generations previous to the sixth century, but no satisfactory account of the real life of the missionary himself. His name is, however, indelibly engraved on the ecclesiastical topography of Scotland.

Donnan is another of the cotemporaries of Columba

whose name is interwoven with the early topography of Scotland. It is found in Kildonan, a parish in the county of Sutherland, occupying a narrow valley stretching westwards from the modern village of Helmsdale. It is also found in the island of Eigg,[1] where the parish church is called Kildonan to this day. There are other localities where the name is preserved, but these two are the most important. Donnan's pedigree is not known, and he may have been either of Scotch or Irish descent. In the commentary on the Feilire of Ængus the Culdee, on his commemoration, it is said, "Donnan of Eig, *i. e.*, Eig is the name of an island which is in Alba, and in it Donnan is (the church of Donnan) ; or in Cataobh (Sutherland) ; and there holy Donnan, with his family (or followers) died, to the number of fifty-two" (Quoted by Dr. Reeves, Vit. Col., p. 304). Columba early foretold the martyrdom of Donnan according to this authority. Donnan's place of retirement was chosen in Eigg, as Baithean's was in Tyree. Here it is said by the Feilire, "they took up their abode in a place where the sheep of the queen of the country were kept. This was told to the queen. Let them all be killed, said she. That would not be a religious act, said her people. But they were murderously assailed. At this time the cleric was at mass. Let us have respite till mass is ended, said Donnan. Thou shalt have it, said they. And when it was over they were slain, every one of them." Other accounts are given, some placing the martyrdom in Sutherland, without knowing very well where Sutherland was, others attributing the death to the king[2] of the countries, and relating that Donnan was engaged in singing psalms at the time of the attack. The legend of the fifty-two dis-

---

[1] In some Irish MSS. this word is glossed by "fons," a fountain. Eigg is now obsolete as a word for a fountain.

[2] Governors, chiefs, and commanders, were called kings by the early Celts.

ciples may be very safely dismissed, and the truth will probably be found in the conclusion, that Donnan was martyred either in Sutherland or in Eigg, but most probably in the island of Eigg, about the year 617. This is the only martyrdom connected with the planting of Christianity among the northern Picts.

The name of Molaise is that of another of the cotemporaries of Columba which is celebrated in the topography of Scotland. It is from this saint that the corrupted name of Lamlash, in Arran, takes its origin, the real name being *Eilean Molaise*, or 'Molaise's Island.' There were three famous men in the early Scottish Church of this name. One of these was Molaise of Devenish (Daimhinnis), the same who is said to have imposed exile on Columba as a penance for having been the instigator of so many bloody fights. Some have supposed that jealousy mingled its influence with that of justice in leading Molaise to so severe a sentence, while others deny that ever such a sentence was passed. Molaise of Devenish is, however, a well known saint in the hagiology of Ireland.

Another of the name was Molaise of Innismurry (Innis Muireadhaich) on the north coast of Sligo. He is also said to have been the judge in the case of Columba, although his namesake of Devenish is generally thought to have been the party who really gave judgment in the matter. These two saints are separately commemorated in the Irish Calendar, the former on the 12th September and the latter on the 12th August.

The third saint of the name of Molaise was Molaise of Leighlin, whose name is commemorated, as has been already said, in Lamlash, in the island of Arran. This saint can hardly be called a cotemporary of Columba, although of his period. He was the grandson of Aidan, whom Columba consecrated King of the Dalriadic Scots, by his daughter, Mathgemm. His father's name was Caireall, whence Ængus, the Culdee (quoted by Dr. Reeves in Vit. Col., p. 436) says, "Mathgemm ingen Aedan mec Gabhran rig Albain mathar molaisi, ut dicitur :—

Molaise lasair tened,	' Molaise, a flame of fire.'
Cona chlasaibh comaidh,	' With his comely choristers,'
Abb Raithchilli agus ri an tenaid	' Abbot of Rathkill and king of fire,'
Mac Mathgemm Monaidh,[1]	' Son of Mathgemm of Monadh.'

This would throw the age of Molaise of Lamlash a little later than that of Columba, but he was one of that famous band which at an early period laid the foundations of the Scottish Church, and who were of kindred sentiments with the great missionary of Iona, and whose connection with Scotland, although it is difficult now precisely to determine its nature, ensured for their memory the highest veneration of the people.

---

[1] Dunmonaidh, the seat of the Dalriadic kings.

CHAPTER XVI

WHEN Columba came first to Scotland, the Scottish kingdom there was a dependency on the crown of Ireland. This arose naturally from the fact that the royal family was an offshoot from one of the families which filled the Irish throne. The death of Gabhran, son of Domangart, king of Dalriada, took place according to Tighernac in 560. He was brother to Comgall, son of Domangart, at the time the reigning monarch. Comgall was succeeded by Conall, his son, who, according to Tighernac and the Ulster annals, although this is more than doubtful, gave the island of Ia to Columba. Conall had a son called Duncan, of whom Tighernac relates that he was killed at the battle of Delgen, (called Telocho in the Ulster annals,) in Kintyre, in the year 574. It is stated that there fell, besides, many of the servants or allies of the sons of Gabhran. This seems to have opened up the succession to the sons of Gabhran, probably from the want of any other male heir of the family of Conall. It is not stated with whom the battle was fought in which the son of the king of the Dalriadic Scots fell, but subsequent events would indicate that it was with the Picts, and the probability is that the Scots were at the time engaged in resisting an invasion of their territory in Kintyre by the Pictish forces.

The successor of Conall was his cousin Aedhan, or as it is usually spelled in English, Aidan. He was apparently not the eldest son of his father, but Columba received an intimation from heaven to set him apart for the crown. The story told by Adomnan is (Vit. Col., Lib. iii., c. 5), that while at one time residing in the island of Hinba,[1] Columba saw in an ecstasy an angel of God, who held in his hand a " Liber vitreus," or *chrystal book* of the ordination of kings.[2] The angel instructed the saint to proceed immediately with the inauguration of Aidan as king. The latter declined, upon the ground, as many writers suppose, that Aidan was not the elder son, but as Adomnan says, " because he loved his brother Iogenan more ;" upon which the angel smote him so severely that the mark of the lash continued in his flesh all his days. The angel, at the same time, told him that he was sent of God, and that if he refused, he would smite him again. The appearance of the angel with the chrystal book was repeated for three successive nights, upon which Columba being assured that the thing was of God, crossed to Iona, and finding Aidan there, he ordained (ordinavit) him king as he was instructed, laying his hand upon his head ; and at the same time prophesying of his grandsons and great grandsons.[3]

Aidan soon after agitated for the independence of his kingdom of all connection with the Irish monarchy. From this originated the great convention at Drumceat in

---

[1] Dr. Reeves says the identification of the name is the great desideratum in Hebridean topography. He adds that it was clearly north of and not far from Hy. The locality which most nearly meets all the requirements of the case is the island of Inchkenneth, at the mouth of Loch nan Ceall, or the Loch of the Churches, nearly north-east of Iona. The Gaelic name is uniformly Innis, and if I or Hy could produce Iova in Latin, there is no doubt that Hinba might very naturally be deduced from Innis.

[2] The idea of the inauguration of Aidan is probably borrowed from that of David by Samuel, while that of the chrystal book, in all likelihood, is taken from Revelation, and is to be understood as indicating the existence of a heavenly, and not an earthly volume.

[3] This is a curious instance of the same form being employed in inaugurating a king as in ordaining an ecclesiastic.

Ulster, where the question of Albanie independence was fully discussed, and decided in favour of Aidan. This convention was held between the years 574 as stated by the Ulster annals, and 590 as stated by Colgan and O'Flaherty. The reigning sovereign of Ireland at the time was Aedh or Hugh, the son of Ainmire, and it is of this Hugh's son, Donald, that Adomnan relates that he was blessed of the saint while attending the convention, and that the prophecies of the saint then regarding him were amply fulfilled (Vit. Col., Lib. i., c. 10). The notices of historical events at so early a period must necessarily be scanty and incomplete, but such notices as reach us of this great meeting, shew that the claims of the bards, who, besides being extremely exacting, had set themselves up as the opponents of the rising Christianity of the country, were then settled, and the limits of their rights strictly fixed ; and that the new Scottish monarchy which had hitherto been a dependency on the Irish crown was thereafter to be altogether independent. It is from this period, then, we are to date the independence of the ancient Scottish monarchy. Columba's influence is clearly discernible in both these proceedings. That he was no friend of the ancient bardic order is clear from some incidents mentioned by Adomnan, although he resisted any unjust persecution of it ; nor is there reason to doubt of his anxiety to strengthen the hands of his kinsman Aidan as favourable to himself, and to the interests of the Christian Church in his adopted country. From the result of this course it is obvious that the cause which led to Columba's leaving Ireland was not one which permanently affected his influence with his Irish countrymen.

Aidan was worthy of his independence, being an able, vigorous, and prosperous ruler. Welsh writers attach the epithet " vraddog," the Gaelic " bradach," or *thievish* to his name ; but this epithet is one applied by enemies, and may be taken more as an indication of the feelings inspired in his foes by his character and actions, than as truly descriptive of the man. His conflicts with the Britons were many and fierce. About the year 520, Maelgwn, King of North Wales, said to be the nephew of King Arthur, wrested the Isle of Man from its ancient Scottish inhabitants.[1] He was succeeded by his son Rhun. In his reign, about the year 581, Aidan, probably for the purpose of recovering the island for the Gaelic race, made a descent upon it, and drove out the Britons, leaving his nephew Brandan as governor. Upon Brandan's death, at the battle fought with the Saxons at Fethanleg, Aidan appointed his own son Eochy (Eugenius) in his room, who was so much satisfied with his Manx subjects, that, upon succeeding to the Scottish crown, it is said he sent his three sons, Farquhar, Fiacre, and Donald, to be educated by Conan, an ecclesiastic in the island. He defeated the Saxons at Fethanleg in 584.

Besides this descent on the Isle of Man, several battles are recorded as having been fought by Aidan. Lhuyd (Comm., p. 143-4) mentions that of Arderyth (Airdrie) with Rhydderch Hael, the Strathclyde king. Another was the battle of Leithrigh fought in the year 584. The Irish annals neither relate with whom this battle was fought, nor who the victor was. The probability is that Aidan's opponents were the Saxons, whom he defeated. The place Leithrigh or Leithreid, as it is spelt in the Annals, it is difficult now to identify. The meaning of the word appears to be *the king's half,* and there are several names bearing some resemblance to it in the ancient British territory.

In 598 was fought another of the battles of Aidan, to

[1] That portions of Man were possessed by the British is clear from the topography. In the south-east portion of the Island, British names are numerous, although they are not found in any other portion of it.

which reference has been made. The year is marked as
that on which Eogan or Ewen, the son of Gabhran, the
elder brother of Aidan died. This battle is said to have
been fought at Chirchind. Here Aidan was vanquished
with the loss of four of his sons, Bran, Domangart, Eochyfinn, and Arthur. (Tigh. Ann.)[1] This battle is called by
Adomnan "Bellum Miatorum," a people whom Ussher
supposes to be identical with the Mæatæ of the Romans,
and to be the Southern Picts, whose territory extended
to the Grampian hills. The death of Aidan's sons served
for the accomplishment of one of Columba's prophecies as
related by Adomnan (Vit. Col., Lib. i., c. 9). Aidan
had asked of the saint which of his three sons, Arthur,
Eochyfinn, or Domangart, was to succeed him. The reply
was that neither should, but that a younger son should
be his successor, upon which he pointed out Eochy buy,
or Eochy the yellow. Soon after, says the biographer,
Arthur and Eochyfinn were slain in battle with the Miati,
and (differing in his account from the Annals) Domangart was slain in battle with the Saxons. Eochy buy
(Eochaidh buidh) succeeded his father.

Aidan's battle as related in the Annals, was that which
Tighernac under the year 600 designates, " Battle of the
Saxons with Aidan, where fell Eanfrait, brother of Etal-
fraich by Maeluma, son of Baedan ; in which he was
victorious," and the Annals of Ulster under 599 · "The
battle of the Saxons in which Aidan was vanquished."
Bede (Lib. i., c. 34) gives a fuller narrative of this event.
He tells us that Ethelfrid was King of the Northumbrians,
a "most worthy king, and ambitious of glory." He
extended the dominions of the Saxons far among the
Britons. Aidan jealous of this success, and fearing the

---

[1] Dr. Reeves supposes Chirchind to be Kirkintulloch, the ancient Cairpenta-
loch (Orig. Par.) This is, however, but the Gaelic form of the British word ;
and with merely Kirkin alone the word would be incomplete.

consequences to himself, came against him with a great army. But the Saxons were victorious; Aidan was beaten, and the greater part of his men were slain. Theobald, brother of Ethelfrid, called Eanfrait by the Celtic annalist, was killed with the greater portion of his men. This battle was fought at Dagsastan, thought to be Dalston near Carlisle, or Dawston near Jedburgh. Aidan, who had spent so many of his years in warring, both with the Pict and the Saxon, lived, according to Tighernac, for six years after this battle, and died probably at Dunmony in Knapdale, in the year 606, in the thirty-eighth year of his reign and the seventy-fourth of his age. He was by far the ablest king of the race of Gabhran who filled the Scottish throne.

During Aidan's reign the annalists note the death of three abbots of Iona, Columba in 597, Baithean, his immediate successor, in 598, and Laisrean, who succeeded him, in 605. They note also the death of Gartnaidh, King of the Picts in 599. He was the successor, but not the son of Brude Mac Meilochon. His usual appellation is Gartnaidh Mac Domelch, from which it would appear that the Tanaisd system by which the succession did not fall to the son, but to the chosen Tanaisd or *second*, as the word means, usually the next oldest brother, was characteristic of the Pictish more than of the Scottish Celt; for Aidan was made king only by the interference of Columba, and his elder son would have succeeded him had he not fallen in battle. In no case do the Pictish lists of kings present the son as immediately succeeding the father (see App. to Innes' Crit. Ess.).

During Aidan's reign an event of much importance to the interests of the Church in Britain took place. Pope Gregory sent Augustine to England to preach to the Saxons. It is a remarkable coincidence that, according to the Anglo-Saxon chronicle, this event took place in

the very year (596-7) on which Columba died, the same
year thus witnessing the death of the great apostle of the
Northern Celts and the advent of the great apostle of the
southern Saxons, the representatives of two systems
which were long to maintain a fierce and exterminating
war with each other.

Some years after the death of Aidan, about the year
617, great movements took place among the northern
Saxons. Ethelfrid, the scourge of the Britons, and the
monarch by whom Aidan was defeated at Dagsastan,
was slain by Redwald king of the East Angles (Bede
Eccl. Hist., Lib. II., c. 12). Redwald had gone to war
in the interest of Edwin King of Northumbria, a rival of
Ethelfrid for the throne. This Edwin became a Christian, having been converted by Paulinus, usually called
the first Bishop of York, a missionary sent from Rome
along with Mellitus, Justus, and Rufinus, to assist
Augustine in preaching to the Saxons of Britain (Bede's
Eccl. Hist., Lib. I., c. 29). Upon the death of Ethelfrid
Edwin succeeded to the throne of Northumbria. Edwin's
succession led to the dispersion of the family of Ethelfrid. The Ethelings or princes, Eanfrid, Oswald, Oswy,
Oslac, Oswudu, Oslaf, and Offa, fled to the Scots
and Picts for refuge (Anglosax. Chron.), and were
brought into contact with the missionaries of Iona. By
them they were instructed in the Christian faith, and
received the Gospel at their hands. Bede's language
is (Lib. III. Eccl. Hist., c. 3) that Oswald, afterwards king, "being desirous that all his nation should
receive the Christian faith—sent to the elders of the
Scots, among whom himself and his followers, when in
banishment, had received the sacrament of baptism,
desiring that they would send him a bishop, &c." The
family of Ethelfrid in fact had received the Christian
faith among the Scots. The period of their residence

was about seventeen years, which was the period of Edwin's reign. In that time they had even learned the language of the Scots, for we read of Oswy (Bede's Eccl. Hist. Lib. III., c. 25), that he was not only instructed and baptized by the Scots, but was "perfectly skilled in their language."

In the year 633 Edwin was killed in battle with the Britons at a place called Heathfield, supposed to be near Doncaster (Bede's Eccl. Hist., Lib. II., c. 20). Cadwalla, King of the Britons, supported by Penda, a Saxon King of the Mercians, rebelled against him, and in the battle that ensued he was slain, and his army dispersed. In the same battle his son Osfrid fell, and Eanfrid, another son, being taken prisoner, was some time after put to death by Penda. This event led to the return of Ethelfrid's family from Scotland. Deira or Southern Northumbria, fell to the lot of Osric, the first cousin of Edwin; Bernicia, or the northern division of the province, became the portion of Eanfrid, the eldest son of Ethelfrid. Both these kings renounced the Christian faith, and returned to their heathenism. Paulinus fled from York and established himself at Rochester, where he died. The reigns of both, however, were brief; like Edwin they fell by the hand of the British Cadwalla. The Britons made no question of whether the Saxons were Christians or heathens. To them they were the usurpers of their rights, and the unrighteous possessors of their territory. The language of Bede is (Eccl. Hist. Lib. II,, c. 20) that even to his day "it was the custom of the Britons to pay no respect to the faith and religion of the English, nor to correspond with them any more than with Pagans."

The death of Eanfrid opened the succession to the truly Christian Oswald, who ascended the throne of Bernicia, or Northumbria, between the Tyne and the Firth of Forth, about the year 635. But before entering

upon the events of his period—events so full of interest
in their connection with the early Scottish Church, we
may take a glance at the state of Scotland about this
time, with respect to its intercourse with the rest of
Europe. Adomnan relates (Vit. Col. Lib. I., c. 28) a
prophecy of Columba regarding a city in Italy which
was to be destroyed by fire, in addition to which he foretold that French sailors coming from France would bring
tidings of the event. Shortly after we read that Columba and Lugbeus Mocumin, the friend to whom he
uttered the prophecy, going to Kintyre, which forms
now the southern part of Argyllshire, met there a French
bark, the sailors on which told them of the destruction
of the Italian city. The event is a historical one. The
city destroyed was that now called Citta Nuova in Istria,
which was overwhelmed by an earthquake in the sixth
century (see Reeves' Note, Vit. Col. Lib. I., c. 28). From
this incident we gather that French ships traded with
Kintyre in the sixth century. The trade was probably
to a large extent in wine, as we find several notices of
the importation of wine to Ireland at the same period.
It is manifest, from such an incident occurring in the
neighbourhood of the Scottish court,—for the court was
at the time located in Kintyre, or in the near neighbourhood,—that the country was sufficiently civilized to require the importation of French commodities, probably
for the use of the court, but not for its use exclusively.

About the same period (A.C. 588) Columbanus, accompanied by Gallus, afterwards the famous St. Gall, and
other disciples, came to Columba at Iona. Father Innes
(Civil and Eccl. Hist., p. 209) supposes that these
brethren, who had been brought up in the monastery of
Bangor, under the supervision of Comgall, one of the
disciples of Columba, accompanied the latter from the
great convention at Drumceat. However that may be,

Columbanus, along with the favourite number of twelve disciples, passed over from Iona to France, where he was kindly received by Childibert II., King of Austrasia. Here he founded several religious houses upon the model of that of Bangor. Anegray, Luxeu, and others, were among the houses he planted.[1] At length his faithfulness in rebuking the vices of the court and nation, and his adherence to the usages of the Scoto-Irish Church, exposed him to persecution, the persecution being earnestly fostered by Queen Brunechilde, wife of King Theodoric. He was obliged finally to flee, and leaving St. Gall behind him, he took refuge in Italy, where he founded the famous monastery of Bobbio. This, as well as that at Reichenau, were fruits of the zeal of the early Scoto-Irish Church. Nor is there wanting in both these establishments to this day literary evidence, in the shape of MSS. of a very early date, of their connexion with that Church. It is remarkable that while Rome was sending her emissaries to Christianize the Saxons of England, the Celtic races of Scotland and Ireland were sending their missionaries to convey the gospel of salvation to France, Germany, and even Italy. Columbanus died at Bobbio about the year 615.

Another incident brings out the connection between Scotland and the rest of Europe at an early period. Adomnan, the biographer of Columba, who flourished about 680, wrote a book still existing, on the holy places of the East. It may appear almost incredible that, shut up as he was in a distant island of the Scottish Hebrides, he should have known much on the subject. Bede, who relates the fact, tells us that Arculfus, a French bishop, had accomplished a visit to the Holy Land, including

---

[1] For full notices of the continental establishments planted by the Culdee missionaries, see those in " Zeitschrift für die historische Theologie," 1862-3. by Dr. Ebrard of Erlangen.

also Damascus, Constantinople, Alexandria, and many islands of the sea. On his way home he was driven by a storm towards the western coast of Britain, and after enduring much suffering, he landed safely at Iona in the beginning of winter. Here he was hospitably received and entertained by the brethren. During his long winter stay on the island he detailed, for the instruction and entertainment of his hosts, all he had seen in his travels. Adomnan, who then presided over the institution, committed the information received to writing. Hence his book "De locis sanctis," of which Bede says, that he produced "a very useful book, especially for those who, being themselves far away from the places where the patriarchs and apostles lived, can only learn of them by reading." From the facts now narrated, some idea may be formed of the intercourse existing in the sixth and seventh centuries between Scotland and the rest of Europe. It will be seen that, so far from being in a state of utter barbarism, Scotland was not only receiving from continental Europe the fruits of its literature and commerce, but was, in conjunction with Ireland, able to reciprocate the former, by sending some distinguished men to extend over many portions of the continent the blessings of religion and civilization. There was a continental mission scheme in Scotland so early as 588.

CHAPTER XVII.

THE year 597 was famous not only for the death of Columba and the coming of Augustine into Britain, but for the death of Gartnaidh, King of the Picts, to whom reference has already been made as Gartnaidh, son of Domelch. Father Innes (Civ. and Eccl. Hist., p. 211) states that this Gartnaidh was famous as the restorer of the ancient church and monastery of Abernethy, which had been founded by Nectan I. about a hundred years before. In restoring these, he placed in them ministers of the Columbite order, afterwards called usually Culdees. It is beyond doubt that Abernethy was long a famous seat of the Culdees, and that it only gave place latterly to the more prominent and more famous institutions at Dunkeld and St. Andrews. But it is doubtful, as will be seen hereafter, whether Abernethy can claim such an antiquity as this would ascribe to it. The national history of the Picts is at this period somewhat obscure. Brude, the predecessor of Gartnaidh, dwelt in the neighbourhood of Inverness; it is not easy to discover how, if Innes be correct with regard to Gartnaidh, he should have jurisdiction in Abernethy, so long the seat of government in the southern province. True, there is but one list of kings given in the Chronicles of the Pictish sovereigns, for we find there no indication of separate monarchies; so that if there was only one, the seat of sovereignty would probably have moved south in the reign of this

Gartnaidh, transplanted from the banks of the Ness to those of the Tay. The inference from this is, that the Picts, though divided into two provinces, had but one series of monarchs, these monarchs fixing their seats in different localities, as suited their convenience, or served to secure their safety.

Gartnaidh was succeeded by Nectan, son or grandson of Irb, who reigned for twenty years, and died in 617. It is to him that the Register of St. Andrews attributes the restoration of Abernethy, although Innes maintains that the writer mistakes this Nectan for Nectan the First, the original founder of the institution. Kenneth, son of Luthrin, reigned till 628, and Garnard, the son of Wid or Fothe, and his brother Brude, reigned for nine years. Others succeeded, till we meet with Brude, the son of Bili, who died in 687 (App. to Inn. Ess., vol. ii., p. 780) ; or, according to another authority, in 696. This Brude was the victor in the battle of Dunnichen, where Egfrid, a Saxon king, was slain.

Aidan was succeeded on the throne of the Dalriadic kingdom of Scots by Eochy Buy, who reigned for sixteen years, his death occurring in the year 628. His successor was *Coinneach cearr*, or 'Kenneth the left-handed.' He is called son to Conall, in the chronicle of the Scottish kings appended to Innes' Essay. Fordun and other writers after him place him after Farquhar, whom they make successor to Eochy Buy. The synchronisms of Flann of Bute, written as they were in the eleventh century, and still existing in the MS. called "The Book of Leacain" (Lib. Roy. Ir. Ac.), a work in every way reliable, so far as modern readers can judge, follows the order of the Irish annals. This list of contemporary kings places Aedh Mac Ainmire, King of Ireland, as cotemporary with Aidan Mac Gabhran, but tells us that Aidan outlived Aedh by a period of two years.

If Aidan died in 605, Aedh died, according to this authority, in 603. The lists of contemporary Celtic monarchs are given by Flann thus :—" Aedh M'Annrech, Da ri don fir Albain, fisin, eadhon Conall M'Comgaill, agus Aedhan M'Gabhrain : II Bliadhna do Aedhan tareis Aedh M'Annrech ; Da ri don fir Ullthaibh, fisin, eadhon, Daigh M'Cerbhall, agus Aedh dubh M'Suibhne agus ise ro marbh Diarmaid M'Cerbhail. Da ri don fir Laignibh, &c. :" which is, that during a period including the reign of Aedh M'Annrech or Hugh the son of Henry,[1] there were two Scottish kings, Conall, son of Comgall, and Aidan, son of Gabhran ; two kings of Ulster, David son of Cervall, and Black Hugh' son of Sweyn, and it was he that killed Diarmad son of Cervall. Two kings of the men of Leinster, &c., giving cotemporary lists of the kings of Ossory, Leinster, and Connaught. In the succeeding period to the above Flann states, that sixty-three years elapsed between the death of Aedh M'Annrech and the death of Donald M'Aedha, King of Ireland, about 663. In this period he tells us there were six kings of Ireland, four kings of Scotland, four kings of Ulster, three kings of Leinster, three kings of Ossory, four kings of Munster, and three kings of Connaught. The four Scottish kings set down as contemporary with the Irish monarchs of the period are, " Eocho buidhe, agus Conadh ceir a mhae, is leis adrochar M'Demain, agus Ferchar, agus Domhnall brec M'Ethach buidhe ; which is, Eochy Buy, and Kenneth the swarthy, his son, it was by him that the son of Deman was slain, and Ferchar and Donald "breac" or the spotted, son of Eochy Buy. With this succession the Albanic Duan agrees, placing the name of Kenneth after Eochy, and attributing to him a reign of three months only. All writers on this period make the reign of Kenneth brief, but the Irish annalists extend

[1] M'Eanraic or Henderson is still a common name in the Highlands.

it to some years. Under 627 Tighernac notes the battle of Ardcoran in Dalriada, in which Lachtnen, the son of the abbot Toirbene, was victorious, and Fiachna, the son of Deman, the same referred to by Flann, was slain by Conad Cerr, King of Dalriada. In 629 he notes the battle of Fedaeoin, in which Maelcath, son of Seandail, King of the Cruithne, was victorious. "The Dalriads fell. Conad Cerr, King of Dalriada, was slain, and Dicuil, the son of Each, king of the cinel Cruithne, was slain. Eochbuidhe, the son of Aedan, was victorious, &c." According to this notice Kenneth was slain before his father and predecessor, after his being at least two years king. The Ulster annals note the death of Eochy Buy as taking place at this battle. Both these battles were fought with the Irish Cruithne or Picts, and the only way of reconciling the account of them with the statement in the Albanie Duan and elsewhere is, with Chalmers, to consider Kenneth as Tanaisdear in the battle of Ardcoran, and to hold the entry regarding his father in the notice of the battle of Fedeaoin as incorrect. The account of the Albanie Duan is probably correct, which gives Kenneth a reign of three months after his father.

Kenneth was succeeded by Ferchar, or as now spelt, Farquhar, who, according to the Albanie Duan, was his son, or as in Innes' Chronicon (Crit. Essay, vol. ii., p. 789), the son of Eu. The Duan attributes to him a reign of sixteen years, which would bring his death to about the year 638.

It was in this reign that Oswald, son of Ethelfrid, who had been converted among the Scots to the Christian faith, succeeded his brother Eanfrid on the throne of Bernicia. His first act was to punish the Britons, whom he vanquished under their King Cadwalla, having erected a cross ere he engaged in battle, and prayed earnestly to God for victory. About the year 635, desirous for the conversion of his subjects, Oswald sent to the elders of the Scots for an instructor. The Scots replied most favourably to the request, and it is said sent Cormac, one of their number. Being too stern, however, for a rude, uninstructed people, Cormac was constrained to return, upon which Aidan, who remonstrated with him for his severity, was sent in his room, as a person likely to be more accommodating, and therefore more attractive. Bede mentions nothing of this episode, but states that Aidan was immediately sent, and adds, that he was a man of singular meekness, piety, and moderation, zealous in the cause of God, though not altogether according to knowledge; for he was wont to keep Easter Sunday according to the custom of his country from the fourteenth to the twentieth moon.

The king appointed Aidan the island of Lindisfarne, or Holy Isle on the east coast of Northumberland, as his residence. This may have been done at the request of the missionary himself, for these men always sought such retreats, and in selecting Lindisfarne, Aidan followed the example of Columba in choosing Iona, and of Baithean in choosing Tyree. How different from the Roman emissaries Augustine and Paulinus! The one chose Canterbury, the other York; fit emblem of the ambition of the one religious system, and the humility and self-denial of the other. Aidan himself was a monk of Hii (Bede's Eccles. Hist., Lib. iii., c. 4) or Iona, a monastery, adds the historian, for a long time the chief among the Northern Scots and the Picts. He was followed by many Scots, who, coming to Britain, with great devotion preached the word to those provinces of the English over which King Oswald reigned.[1]

---

[1] Bede's use of the word Britain here does not imply that these men came from Ireland, any more than Aidan, though it does not by any means imply the contrary. But Britain was often opposed to Scotia on either side of the Channel.

Segenius presided in Iona at the period of Aidan's mission. He was the fifth abbot there after Columba, and is said upon Irish authority to have been of the same lineage with the illustrious founder, in accordance with the system pursued in the early Scottish Church of confining the succession in each monastery to a certain family. Segenius appears to have been a man of like spirit with his great predecessor. The Irish annals inform us that in the year 634, "Seigine," which may be presumed to be Seathan, the Irish *John*, "abbot of Ie, founded the Church of Rechrain or Rathlin," (Tigh. Ann.), another of those island strongholds of the Christian faith. We may understand how grateful to a man filled with the spirit of a true missionary would be the application of Oswald for a teacher of the still heathen Saxons of Northumbria, and with what readiness he and his brethren would respond to the request.

The account given of Aidan by Bede (Hist. Eccl., Lib. iii., c. 5) is full, and presents a deeply interesting picture of those early missionaries. He received his dignity of a bishop in Iona, but from whom Bede does not precisely say. He tells us it was in the time of Segenius, but he does not say it was from Segenius, who was a monk. He tell us, however, that upon hearing Aidan's reproof to Cormac, all the brethren concluded that Aidan ought to be made a bishop, and accordingly being ordained, they sent him to their friend King Oswald, to preach. If so, it must have been by those "elders of the Scots" from whom the bishop was asked, and who were the parties to send him, that he was ordained. Bede's bishops, like the miracles both of Bede and Adomnan, must be received with a measure of caution. But putting this question aside, Aidan is represented as "leaving the clergy a most salutary example of abstinence or continence ; it was the highest commendation of his doctrine, with all men, that he taught no otherwise than as he and his followers had lived." He travelled usually on foot, and wherever he met any man, whether rich and poor, he asked him earnestly, if an unbeliever, to embrace the Gospel; if a believer, he sought to strengthen his faith. Bede adds, "his mode of life was so different from the slothfulness of our times, that all those who bore him company, whether they were tonsured monks or laymen, were employed in meditation, that is, either in reading the Scriptures, or learning Psalms.". From which it appears that these early missionaries were men learned in the Scriptures. His humility and almsgiving are duly recorded; in addition to which we learn that he was endued with singular discretion, which is the mother of other virtues.

Oswald and his subjects profited much by the preaching of the Scottish missionary; the king acting as interpreter for his people, while at the same time the nation was attended with much outward prosperity. We learn (Bede's Hist. Eccl., Lib. iii., c. 6) that "Oswald brought under his dominion all the nations and provinces of Britain, which are divided into four languages, viz., the Britons, the Picts, the Scots, and the English," a statement which we know is not literally true, although to be understood as indicative of the firmness and success with which he governed the mixed nations which composed his kingdom. We know for certain that his dominions never crossed the Firth of Forth. Bede, in fact, in the very chapter succeeding that in which this statement is made, calls Oswald the "victorious King of the Northumbrians." Oswald reigned for nine years, including the one year during which his predecessor filled the throne. He was killed in battle with Penda, the Pagan King of the Mercians, at a place called Maserfield, either in Shropshire or Lancashire, in the thirty-eighth year of his age.

The miracles wrought by his relics, as related by Bede, are just as absurd and incredible as any related by Adomnan. There is reason to believe the writer himself to be sincere in his faith in them, but if credulity on one point is sufficient to vitiate the authority of a writer through out, the authority of both these writers is utterly worth less. To deny them all authority, however, would be just as unreasonable as to believe, upon their authority, state ments which are fabulous upon the very face of them.

Oswald was succeeded by his brother Oswy, who had also received the Christian faith among the Scots, although the murder of his cousin Oswin, who reigned in Deira, was an act of detestable cruelty. Oswin was much beloved by Aidan, who only survived him twelve days, this great apostle of the Northumbrians dying on the 31st August 651, nine years after the death of Oswald. Bede relates numerous miracles wrought by him, of equal credibility with those related of his friend and patron Oswald.

Finan was sent from Iona to succeed Aidan, and continne the mission among the Saxons of Northumbria. Previous to his time, Fursey an Irish missionary had begun (A.D. 633) to preach to the East Angles. He had come in the time of King Sigibert, who had himself been instructed and baptized in France, and who gladly welcomed the services of the Scottish preacher (Bede's Eccl. Hist., Lib. iii., c. 19). In 653 Peada, son of the notorious Penda, King of the Middle Angles or Mercians, received the Christian faith. Being a young man of high promise, he sought the daughter of King Oswy of Northumbria in marriage. One condition of obtaining his request was that he should embrace the faith of Christ. On hearing the Gospel preached he declared that he would embrace it, although the damsel were refused to him. The influence of Alfred, King Oswy's son, and Penda's brother-in-law, was exercised in favour of the new faith, and Peada and his followers were all baptized by Finan. He received four missionaries to instruct his subjects, Cedd, Atta, Betti, and Diuma ; the latter of these was a Scot. The same year the East Saxons were anew received into the Christian Church, having fallen away from the profession made under the preaching of Mellitus. Their King Sigibert, a friend of King Oswy, was baptized with his followers by Finan. Finan recalling Cedd from his duties among the Mercians, sent him to preach among those Saxons whose territory extended to the Thames, in what is now Essex. (Bede's Eccl. Hist., Lib. iii., c. 22). Thus do we find that the Gospel was carried by the missionaries of Iona among the Northumbrians, the Middle Angles, the Eastern Angles, and the East Saxons, or throughout the whole eastern part of England, from the Firth of Forth to the Thames.

In the early part of the seventh century two famous ecclesiastical institutions were established in what is now the south of Scotland ; one at Melrose, on the Tweed, the other at Coludi or Coldingham. The first mention made of the former by Bede is in connection with Eata, one of the twelve Saxon boys whom Aidan trained in the Christian faith, and of whom the historian relates, that he was, about A.D. 660, abbot of Melrose. The other he mentions in connection with Queen Ethelrida, the wife of Egfrid, King of Northumbria. Ebba,[1] sister of King Oswald, presided over the nuns at Coldingham, and was there joined by Ethelrida, who had long sought for a life of retirement. The establishment at Melrose was purely Scottish in its constitution, being an offshoot from Iona, but there being no reference in Adomnan or writers of his period to female monastic establishments among the Scots, it is curious that the queen is represented by the

---

[1] From whom St. Abb's Head.

historian as receiving the veil from Wilfrid, a Saxon bishop (Bede, Hist. Eccl., Lib. iv., c. 19). Melrose became famous towards the close of the century as associated with the name of Cuthbert, one of the most notable of the early Scottish missionaries.

We thus find that at a period so early as the middle of the seventh century, or about one hundred years after the coming of Columba to Scotland, several large and influential monasteries or rather mission schools were in existence. Iona, Abernethy, according to some authorities, and Melrose, were all in a flourishing condition; Iona among the Northern Picts, Abernethy among the Southern Picts, and Melrose among the northern inhabitants of Northumbria; while Lindisfarne rose into importance among the Northumbrians of the south, and Glasgow flourished under the successors of Kentigern. It would appear, too, that there was a religious establishment at Abercorn, dispensing the benefits of religion and education to the Saxons on the south side of the Firth of Forth, including, as some suppose, a Teutonic population to the north of it; while there is reason to believe that Servanus had his successors at Culross, and that the fruit of Ternan's labour had not perished in Aberdeen and Forfar. The institution at Whithorn would appear at this time to have been shorn of much of its pristine glory under Ninian, and yet there is no reason to suppose that the Gospel and Gospel influences had disappeared from Galloway.

Ferchar, the first of the race of Lorn, who held the sceptre of Dalriada, died in 637. It was during his reign that Aidan was sent to Northumbria. If Eochy Buy the Scottish king, dealt kindly by the banished children of Ethelfrid, who had been his father's bitter enemy, it is no less true that his successor Ferchar shewed no opposition to the desire of Oswald to obtain from Iona a Christian missionary. The expedition of Aidan could hardly have taken place without the consent of the king, more especially as the few notices we have of Ferchar represent him as a man of enterprise and firmness.

Ferchar was succeeded by Donald " breac," or *speckled,* of the race of Gabhran, who reigned for a period of sixteen years. It was he who led the combined forces of the Scots, Picts, Britons, and Saxons in the famous battle of Magh Rath, in Ulster. In this battle he was shamefully defeated, as he deserved, having taken up the cause of Congal-claon Mac Scanlan, the assassin of Suibhne meann, king of Ireland, who had been for some time a fugitive in Kintyre (Ir. Ann.). Donald was no more successful in a battle fought the succeeding year, at a place called Glenmairison, by Tighernac, supposed by some to be Glenmorison, near Loch Ness. Being associated, however, in the Annals with the siege of Etain, later inquirers having come to look upon this Etain as represented by Carriden, in West Lothian, suppose Glenmairison to be situated in that part of Scotland likewise. The place would indicate that the battle was fought with the Saxons, and yet it is difficult to make this consist with the relations maintained by Oswald with the Scots. If fought with the Saxons it must have been provoked by some sudden and uncalled for irruption of the Scottish king. It is just as likely that the battle was fought with the Picts of the north, between whom and the Scots there was at the time frequent war, although it is most probable of all that the battle of Glenmairison occurred in the war between Donald and the Britons of Strathclyde, whose territory extended far enough to the east to admit of its embracing Carriden and the neighbourhood. The last battle fought by Donald breac was that of Strathcarron, probably in the neighbourhood of Falkirk, where he was slain, according to Tighernac and others, by Hoan, or

Owen, King of the Britons, who was the successor of Rhydderch Hael. Donald was unfortunate in his family. His son, Catusaigh, died in 650 (Tigh. Ann.); Doman gart, another son, was slain in 673; and Drost, apparently another son, perished in 678.[1]

"After Donald breac of renown," the Albanic Duan tells us, "Conall and Dungall reigned for ten years." Conall was of the race of Fergus, being grandson of Conall son of Comgall; Dungall was of the race of Lorn, which race first acquired the sceptre in the person of Ferchar. These were rival monarchs, but success attended Conall, whom the bard of the Albanic Duan calls, *Conall nan creach,* or 'Conall of the spoils.' Conall, usually called *Crandomhna,* 'Heir of the Crown,' died, after a reign of ten years, in 652. He was succeeded by his son, Donald *donn,* or 'the brown haired,' who died in 665, after a reign of thirteen years. To him succeeded his brother *Maolduin,* or the brown bald man, a name not unknown among the Scottish Celts.[2] In this case we have an instance of the brother succeeding according to the Tanist law. Whether the murder of Donald breac's son, Domangart, in 672, or of Conall, son of Maolduin, in 675, had anything to do with a struggle for the maintenance of Maolduin's power, we know not; but the Gaelic bard was quite entitled to speak of Maolduin's succeeding his brother, even in preference to a son, as being *gu dligheach,* or 'lawfully,' according to

[1] There is much confusion in the chronology of Donald's reign in the Irish annals. His death is entered both by Tighernac and the Inisfallen annalists in 642. Tighernac, again, as well as the Ulster annalists, enters the death of Donald breac at the battle of Calistros, in 678. This second Donald we would naturally take to be another person, but in 686 we again find, both in Tighernac and the Annals of Ulster, a notice of the death of Donald breac, son of Eocby Buy, by Hoan, King of the Britons. It is impossible to make all these entries correspond. The Albanic Duan brings the date of his death to 642, which cor-responds with the earliest of the Irish entries.

[1] See Geneal. Lists in Trans. of Iona Club.

the Tanist law. These events, however, are sufficiently indicative of a barbarous age, and a people little under the influence of a Christianity, which they had nominally adopted, and whose missionaries at the period, emanating from Ireland and Iona, were covering much of the known world with their labours. The claims of Christianity were then, as now, little owned by kings and governments, although there were as there are noble exceptions.

Ferchar Ifada, or 'Farquhar the tall,' succeeded to Maolduin. He belonged to the rival race of Lorn, and was descended from the first Ferchar of that house, being probably his grandson. This king reigned for twenty-one years, and died about 702. The annalists relate few of the events of his history, but he is famous among the lists of Highland seanachies, as from him are deduced some of the most ancient and most distinguished of the Highland clans. This is not the place to give those genealogies which terminate in *Fearchar Ifada righ Albain*, 'Farquhar the tall, King of Scotland;' but of the number may be named, the Macgregors, the Mackintoshes, the Maormors of Moray, the Macnaughtons, the Macquarries, and the Macphees (Trans. of Iona Club, pp. 53, 55, 57).

Seigine, who died in 652, was succeeded in the Abbacy of Iona by Suibhne, the son of Cuirtre, who filled the chair till 657. He is the only Abbot of Iona whose genealogy the Irish annalists profess themselves unable to trace. To him succeeded Cuimean Fionn, or Cumin the Fair, the earliest biographer of Columba. He is, like Adomnan, a relater of miracles more than of real events. His work is, however, interesting on many accounts, although most of its statements are adopted by his more voluminous successor, and included in his biography. Cuimean was sainted, and has his name associated with the several Kilcummins (Cille Chuimein) in Scotland,

besides being probably preserved in the now common
name of Cumming, the first of which name had, in all
likelihood, as was common among the Celts, derived it
from that of the saint. Cuimean is called by Tighernac,
Cumaine Ailbe, a manifest corruption of the Latin "albus."
In 679 died Failbe, Abbot of Iona (Ann. Tigh.) To him
succeeded Adomnan the wise, the biographer of Columba,
who filled the chair till 704, when Tighernac says of him,
Quievit in Christo, ' he rested in Christ.'

Adomnan or Adhamhnan, the diminutive of *Adhamh,*
' Adam,' was the son of Ronan, son of Tinne, the direct
descendant of Conall Gulban, King of Ulster. His
mother, Ronnat, was one of the Cinel Enna, from whom
the Irish Tirenna takes its name. Little is known
of his early years, there being no certainty even as
to his birthplace, but an old duan (Reeves' Vit. Col.,
App. to Pref., p. 43), says that he became " Anam-
chara," or soul-friend, that is spiritual guide, to Fiann-
achda fleadhach, or Fiannacht of the feasts, King of
Ireland. In 679 he was chosen head of the institution
in Iona, whither he seems to have proceeded forthwith.
Several interesting events in his life are related. Egfrid,
the Saxon king, had, in 684, made a cruel and unpro-
voked descent upon the north of Ireland, and had carried
away a large amount of spoil and prisoners. Adomnan
was requested to become intercessor with the Saxons for
the restoration of the prisoners. He was the more likely
to succeed in this, from having met and formed a lasting
friendship in Ireland with Aldfrid, one of the Northumbrian princes. He proceeded at once on his mission of
mercy, and succeeded in restoring a large body of captives to their country and friends. But besides these
captives, Adomnan carried away from Northumbria new
views on the points of difference between the Celtic and
Roman Churches. He was led by the reasonings and

remonstrances of the Saxon brethren to go over to the Roman view on the subject of Easter and of the tonsure. (Bede Hist. Eccl., Lib. v. c. 15). Bede gives as his reason for doing so, " that he was a good and wise man, and remarkably learned in the Holy Scripture." On returning to Iona he endeavoured to bring his brethren there to an agreement with him on these points, but with no success. Crossing to Ireland he made the same effort with his countrymen there, and to a large extent suc ceeded. Bede says, he " brought almost all of them that were not under the dominion of Hii to the Catholic unity." The Scottish Church, however, maintained its own prac- tice till after his death. Adomnan was known in Ireland as a legislator, having secured a law for exempting women from war, and a certain tribute called " Cain Adhamh- nain" being long raised by authority of regulations passed at a convention where he was present. After a long stay in Ireland, attracted probably by the greater readiness of the brethren there to follow him in his change of sentiment, he returned among his refractory friends at Iona in 703, and died there in the year 704. Bede speaks of him as an author, referring particularly to his work " De Locis Sanctis;" but he is chiefly known by his " Vita Columbæ," or Life of Columba, a work bearing all the marks of authenticity, although, as already said, a humbling exhibition of human credulity. One is not surprised at the author of such a book finding little difficulty in forsaking the principles and practice of the ancient Scottish Church.

Ten churches have been reckoned in Ireland as com memorative of the name and fame of Adomnan ; while eight have been enumerated in Scotland. The Scottish churches which have been dedicated to him are Furvie, in the parish of Slains, Aberdeenshire ; Forglen, in the same county ; Aboyne, also in Aberdeenshire ; Tanna-

dice, in Forfar; Inchkeith, in the Firth of Forth; Sanda
to the S.E. of the Mull of Kintyre; Kileunan, near
Campbellton in Kintyre; and Dalmeny, in the county of
Linlithgow. The name appears as Teunan, Eunan, and
even Skeulan (Reeves' Vit. Col. App. to Pref., pp. 65, 66,
67). It will be observed that most of these churches
are situated in what is now the Scottish Lowlands. Six
of the eight are in the ancient territory of the Picts,
which shews how thoroughly Iona was the metropolis of
the Pictish Church. Dr. Reeves remarks that the surname of M'Lennan in Scotland is derived from the name
of Adomnan, the clan being in an ancient Gaelic genealogy deduced from a certain M'Gille-Adhamhnain. A
modern Gaelic Celt would be more disposed, from the
pronunciation of the word, to derive it from St. Finnian.

A fast friend of Adomnan's was found in his cotemporary, the Pictish king, Brude the son of Derile. Brude,
though on no satisfactory authority, is said to have been
present at the convention of Tara, where Adomnan proposed his improvements in the social and political econ-
omy of Ireland. This king succeeded to the Pictish
throne about the year 678, and was a worthy successor
of his famous namesake, the disciple of Columba. Egfrid
was at the time King of Northumbria, a man fond of
war, and greedy of spoil. It was he that sent his general Behrt on the expedition to Ireland in 684, which
occasioned Adomnan's visit to Northumbria. The success of his arms in that case seems to have whetted his
appetite for war, for in 685 he led a great expedition
against the Picts; he crossed the Frith of Forth, and
in the neighbourhood of Dunnichen in Angus, met the
forces of King Brude. The Saxons had obtained many
advantages over the Picts in war, but if so, the result of
the battle of Dunnichen was ample retribution for them
all. Egfrid and his army were totally routed. The king

was himself slain, and few of his men returned to tell the tale. Egfrid's body was interred at Iona, the one Saxon king who is said to have been buried there (Bede Hist. Eccl. Lib. iv. c. 26). Another battle in 699, in which the Saxon troops were led by Berht or Bertfrid, was no less fatal in its result, and from that time the Picts not only extended their territories southward, but lived as did their neighbours, the Britons of Strathclyde, undisturbed by the inroads of the Saxons (Bede Hist. Eccl. Lib. v., c. 24). In this battle Berht was killed (Anglo-Sax. Chron. 699); and in 706 King Brude died (Ir. Ann).

The defeat and death of Egfrid led to the downfal of the ecclesiastical influence of the Saxons in what is now Scotland. In 678 Theodore, Archbishop of York, added two bishops to the number under his supervision, Tunbert at Hagulstad or Hexham, till then united to Lindisfarne, and Trumwine, in the province of the Picts, which at that time was subject to the English (Bede Hist. Eccl. Lib. iv., c. 12). In 685, after the battle of Dunnichen, the strength of the English crown began to waver; for the " Picts recovered their own lands, which had been held by the English and Scots that were in Britain, and some of the Britons their liberty, which they have now enjoyed for about forty-six years." At the same time Bede says, "Trumwine, who had seven years before been made bishop of the province of the Picts subject to the English, retired with his brethren from Abercurnig or Abercorn, which was seated in the country of the English, but close by the arm of the sea which separates the lands of the English and the Scots." There is confusion in this statement between the province of the Picts and the country of the English, and between the Picts and Scots. But the obvious meaning is, that the Pictish territory of the Lothians was then subject to the Northumbrian Saxons, who sent a bishop there, and that the Scots had pushed their conquests eastward along some portion of the Firth of Forth, over the territory of the Picts. There is no evidence in Bede's statement of the Saxon territory having embraced one foot of the northern coast of the Firth of Forth. Trumwine retired to the monastery of Streansalch or Whitby, bringing to a sudden end the Saxon institution at Abercorn. The Picts, like the Britons, seem to have had little regard even for the religion of their Saxon neighbours, who had come as lawless marauders to seize and hold their territory (Bede Eccl. Hist. Lib. iv. c. 26).

About the middle of this century we meet with the name of Cuthbert, one of the most devoted and faithful of the missionaries of Scotland. Little is known of his early life but that he was born on Tweedside, and that when young he entered the mission institute at Melrose. Here he was instructed by Eata, a holy man, who had himself received the instructions of Aidan. Upon the death of Boisil, who succeeded Eata when removed to Lindisfarne, Cuthbert was chosen to fill his place at Melrose. Cuthbert was no contemplative monk, but an active missionary. "He strove to convert the people around him far and near," and in a time of plague, when the country people were having recourse to their old superstitions, he denounced them faithfully. He travelled both on horseback and on foot through the neighbouring towns, and "preached the way of truth." It was the custom then among the English "when a clerk or priest came to a town to flock together to hear him; while they both heard and practised what he commended. Such was Cuthbert's eloquence and such the weight of his character, that all men openly confessed to him their sins" (Bede Hist. Eccl. Lib. iv., c. 27). It was the custom of this good man to resort to the villages among the high and mountainous parts of the country, where the people were poor and ignorant, staying sometimes for a month preaching the Gospel of God's grace. It would appear that, like other missionaries of the Scottish school, he sought after a time for a " diseart " or place of retirement, which it is sufficiently obvious he did not find in what is called the " monastery " of Melrose, and withdrew to the island of Farne, about nine miles south of Lindisfarne in Northumberland. Here King Egfrid found him, and in 685, the very year of the king's death, removed him to Lindisfarne, where he was appointed abbot. It is related that when in Farne, Cuthbert erected an earthen fence round his dwelling so high that he could see nothing when he looked out but heaven ; a curious specimen of what Christians of the period held to be a crucifying of the flesh, and not without its lesson too to Christians of a more enlightened age, among whom the tendency is to the secularizing of religion, bringing heaven down to earth, and not earth up to heaven. Cuthbert was removed with difficulty to Lindisfarne, having resisted the translation until all men urged him to agree to it. Cuthbert's first election was to Hexham, but having expressed a preference for Lindisfarne, Eata removed to Hexham, and Cuthbert was placed in Lindisfarne. After being an ornament to his office by his virtuous actions for two years, he returned to his little oratory at Farne to die. Here he closed his life on the 20th March 687, and was buried at Lindisfarne, though his own preference was for the humbler island. It is useless to record his miracles as related by Bede. They are worthy of a credulous age, nor can we make any distinction in regard to this feature of the period between the Celtic abbot of Iona and the Saxon monk of Jarrow. Both seem to have esteemed their heroes according to the miracles they were capable of performing, or others

of coining for them. The name of Cuthbert is commemorated in the west church of Edinburgh, usually
called St. Cuthbert's ; in Kirkcudbright or Kirkcuthbert
in Galloway ; in a church in Glencairn, in Dumfriesshire ;
in Ballantrae in Carrick ; and in a chapel in Sorn, in
Ayrshire (Chalmers' Caledonia, vol. I., p. 325, note).
These churches are confined to what was clearly the territory of the Northumbrian princes.

Another famous missionary of the seventh century,
Maolrubha or Malrue, appeared in the north-west of
Scotland. In 671 we read in the Irish annals, *Maelrubha Benchorensis in Brittaniam navigavit,* 'Malrue of
Bangor sailed to Britain.' The name, however, by which
he was usually known was Malrue of Applecross. This
famous missionary was born in January 642. His father
was Ealganach, a direct descendant of Niell of the nine
hostages, King of Ireland. His mother was Suaibhseach
or Subhtan, sister of Comgall of Bangor, of the race of
Irish Picts. He was trained at Bangor, probably under
the eye of his uncle. At the age of twenty-nine he left
Ireland, and, like Columba, adopted Scotland as the field
for his missionary enterprise (Ann. of Tigh.) Two years
after, or in 673, he founded the church of Applecross
among the northern Picts. Here and in the neighbourhood he continued to labour for fifty-one years, dying in
the year 722 at the age of eighty. The Aberdeen
breviary differs in its account of the saint from the Irish
annalists ; it makes no reference to his birth, but attributes his death to a body of Danish pirates who slew
him at a place in the neighbourhood of the present
Urquhart or Ferrintosh.[1] His body is said to have been
interred in Applecross. Tradition still points to a place

---

[1] The common topographical word Urquhart would seem to be of British derivation. "Urchudain," as in the vernacular, would appear to be composed of
Urch, 'a knoll,' and *Din,* 'a fort,' *the fort on the knoll.*

near Conan Bridge where Maolrubha is said to have been slain, and this tradition may rest on some basis of truth, but it could not have been by the Danes, who had not begun their descents on the Scottish coast for a century after the death of the saint. Maolrubha established himself on the little island of Croulin, off the coast of Applecross, which became to him and his followers what Iona was to Columba. From this he extended his influence over the neighbouring region, probably as far as the eastern coast of Ross-shire. Few of the parishes around are without some memorial of Maolrubha. Natural objects became associated with his name, among others the fairest of Scotland's lakes, Loch Maree, which, with its island famous for its chapel, its cemetery, and its well, bears to this day the honoured name of the early missionary. The name itself, *Maol rubha,* 'servus patientiæ,' or the servant of patience, has assumed various forms in the course of centuries. It has become Marou, Mulrruy, Mourie, Maorie, Maree, Mary, Arrow, Marie, &c., in the Lowlands taking the form of Sammareve. Besides the church at Applecross, called in Gaelic *a chomaraich,* or 'the sanctuary,' so named from the girth or sanctuary existing there as a refuge for debtors or criminals, there were numerous churches commemorative of Maolrubha throughout the north of Scotland. These will be found usually as Kilmaree, in the parishes of Gairloch, Lochcarron, Strath in Skye, Portree, Bracadale, Arasaig in Ardnamurchan, Harris, Muckairn, Craignish, Kilarrow in Islay, Strathlachan in Lochfineside, Forres, Fordyce, Keith, Kinnell in Forfar, &c. The number of these indicates the esteem in which his name was held in the early church. Later times have converted the missionary into a Druid or necromancer. Men will invent rather than be held ignorant. Not to know is more to be dreaded than to design falsehood, and truly no human invention could be more inconsistent with historical fact than that which could convert a faithful self-denied missionary like Maolrubha, a worthy follower in the footsteps of Columba, into a necromancer or a heathen priest. The mediæval church in its practice led to this, in attaching to these men's names a superstitious veneration which they themselves would have been the first to spurn.[1]

The names of Ernan or Marnock,[2] and Ronan, the former appearing in several Killearnans, Kilmarnock, and Inchmarnock, and the latter in the islands called Rona, besides such churches as Kilmaronock and Kilmaronan, belong to the seventh century. They, too, formed a part of that great band of missionaries who at this time devoted themselves to the Christianization of Scotland. The lustre of their fame has been darkened by that of the confessors and martyrs of a later age; yet do they merit being held in lasting remembrance.

---

[1] See Dr. Reeves' notice of Maolrubha in Trans. of Ant. Soc. of Scot., vol. III., part 2d.

[2] Ernan became Marnock, as Maith Ernan òg, pronunced Maernanog, or the young Saint Ernan.

CHAPTER XVIII

SOME reference has been made already, in discussing the character of the institution at Iona, to the differences that existed between the Scottish and Pictish churches and the rest of the western churches, on the subject of Easter and the tonsure. A fuller statement is however necessary, in order to explain the question at issue.   •

Several changes were introduced in the early church in the manner of calculating the day on which Easter Sunday fell, or the day in the year which properly represented that on which our Lord rose from the dead. The knowledge of these things had either not reached Britain (Bede, Hist. Eccl. Lib. iii. c. 25), or having reached, the church there did not feel called upon to acquiesce in them. It is hardly possible to conceive, notwithstanding Bede's statement to the contrary, considering the intercourse then existing between Britain and the rest of Europe, that such changes were unknown among British Christians. The cycle of nineteen years, by which the more accurate Roman calculations were made, was introduced by Pope Hilarius in 463, and it is not possible to con ceive that this continued unknown in Britain and Ireland for a period of two hundred years.

The Roman and Scottish systems came into collision not only in Britain, but on the continent. Columbanus, in the end of the sixth century, carried the Scottish system into France, and by his earnest advocacy of it made his own position so uncomfortable that he had to flee. In Britain the question arose soon after the arrival of Augustine and the other Romish missionaries. Augustine was succeeded in the see of Canterbury by Laurentius (Bede, Hist. Eccl. Lib. ii. c. 4), who, while devoting his attention chiefly to his English charge, endeavoured to extend his influence also over the Scots and Picts. More especially did he condemn their holding Easter on the Sunday, which fell between the 14th and 20th day of the April moon, instead of that between the 15th and 21st. The conjoint letter of Laurentius, Mellitus, and Justus to the Scottish churches complains that so strong was the feeling on the subject, that Dagan, a Scottish ecclesiastic, said to be from Bangor in Ireland, refused to eat meat with those Saxon brethren. It is very probable that national feelings, strongly excited, in ancient as in modern times, by jealousy of Saxon power and fear of Saxon oppression, had somewhat to do with Scottish views on the subject.

In 634 the question excited interest at Rome. The appeal of Laurentius had not been altogether in vain, for in the south of Ireland many of the Scots adopted the Roman period of celebration, and some time after the whole churches there acquiesced. But at a synod held at Magh-Lena about 630, the northern brethren withstood the change and resolved to follow Iona rather than Rome. To these Pope Honorius in 634 addressed a strong appeal, pleading the smallness of their numbers in comparison with the rest of the Church, a method of establishing truth more frequently used than legitimate or convincing. His successor Severinus was pope but for a few months; but his successor again, Pope John, took up the subject earnestly, and sent a long admonitory epistle to Cromanus, Dimanus, and Baithanus, bishops; Cromanus, Hernianus, Laistranus, Scellanus, and Segenus, priests ; to Saranus and the rest of the Scottish doctors or abbots,[1] health, &c.   In this letter the pope condemns their rejection of the Catholic Easter, and whether justly or not, charges them with maintaining the Pelagian heresy.   The latter charge is probably like that made against the Scots of practising the tonsure of Simon Magus, and was intended to give these poor Scots a bad name in the eye of the Catholic world.   We do not find that these remonstrances had the slightest effect.   It could not be that this was owing to ignorance, for these several letters must have informed the Scots fully f the error with which they were charged ; yet notwithstanding, they continued to hold by the practice of Columba, to whose authority they deferred in preference to that of the Roman pontiff.

In 655 the question was brought to an issue in the Northumbrian Church (Bede, Hist. Eccl. Lib. iii. c. 25). Visitors from Kent and from France came and found grievous fault with the Scottish mode of observing the season.   Among others was a Scot, Ronan, brought up in France and Italy, who disputed with Finan, then abbot of Lindisfarne, on the subject.   Finan refused to yield on account, as Bede says, of his hot and violent temper ; but a party adhered to Rome, and the strange anomaly occurred of the king and his followers observing one day, and the queen who belonged to Kent observing another ; or as Bede puts it, when the queen and others were fasting on Palm Sunday, the king and those of his mind were feasting on Easter.

Finan was succeeded by Colman, also a Scot, and wedded to Scottish customs.   After his appointment the controversy waxed hotter, and at last King Oswy and his son Alfrid resolved upon calling a synod.   King Oswy was taught by the Scots, and held their view

---

[1] The abbots were just teachers according to this epistle.

strenuously ; Alfrid was taught by the Saxon Wilfrid, and held the Roman view as he was instructed. The synod was convened at Whitby, and was attended by Oswy and Alfrid. Agilbert, bishop of the West Saxons, being on a visit to Alfrid and his friend Wilfrid, was present with Agatho, a priest, Wilfrid, James, a deacon, and Romanus, on the one side. Colman and his clerks, supported by the Abbess Hilda, in whose monastery they were met, were present on the other ; while Cedd, Bishop of London, or of the East Saxons, who spoke the Gaelic language, and who favoured Colman, acted as interpreter.

King Oswy commended unity in the Church, and said it was desirable to know the truth, requesting Colman to describe his system. Colman answered, that he derived his system from his forefathers, men beloved of God, and added that they followed the practice of John the Evangelist. At the request of the king, Wilfrid stated the opposite view, giving an account of what was practised at Rome, where Peter and Paul taught and suffered, and of the practice in the rest of the Western Church, as well as in Asia, Africa, Egypt, Greece, and in fact all the world, except the Picts and the Britons.[1] Colman again referred to St. John, when Wilfrid replied, that John observed the Jewish mode of calculation, beginning to keep Easter on the 14th day of the month, whether the succeeding day was the Lord's day or not, while Peter taught at Rome that it could only be duly kept by beginning on the first Lord's day after the 14th, which was the day the Lord arose from the dead ; thus shewing that the Picts and Britons followed neither St. John nor St. Peter, for they began to keep Easter on the Lord's day, but calculated so as to include the 14th in their Easter if that day was a Sunday. Colman continued to refer to the practice of such holy men as Columba, whose

[1] Bede, Hist. Eccl. Lib. iii. c. 25. The Scots are not named by Wilfrid.

example they were bound to follow. Wilfrid acknowledged the holiness of these men, but with reference to Columba said that he transgressed in ignorance, and that in consequence his transgression was forgiven him, but that now when light had come, they could not continue to transgress without contracting great guilt in the sight of God. Wilfrid appealed most earnestly to the decrees of the apostolic see, and asked Colman whether he was prepared to resist them, and thus prefer the authority of Columba to that of St. Peter.

The king upon this asked Wilfrid whether Christ had really given the keys of authority to Peter? Wilfrid answered in the affirmative, and was joined by Colman, who could not claim a similar right for Columba. Upon which the king, expressing very decided reverence for Peter as the door-keeper, who might prevent his access to heaven, gave his decision in favour of Wilfrid and Rome.

Colman was put down but not convinced, and being joined by a body of men of similar sentiments, returned to Scotland, where the ancient Scottish Easter and the ancient tonsure were still observed. He afterwards retired to Ireland and settled with his followers in a small island on the north-west coast, called *Inis-bofin*, or the ' Island of the white cow.'

We have a remarkable account of the simplicity and self-denial of these Scottish missionaries during the thirty years of their existence in Northumbria. Few houses but the church were found at Lindisfarne on their removal. They had no money, but cattle. The king, when visiting them, partook of their simple fare ; for their whole care was to serve God, not the world—to feed the soul and not the belly (Bede, Hist. Eccl. Lib. iii. c. 26). Colman's successor, Tuda, adopted the new tonsure, and the new method of computing Easter, accepting, although a Scot, the Roman computation. His incumbency was, however, short, for he died within a few years of his appointment. He was the last of the Scottish abbots of Lindisfarne, which became afterwards a bishoprick of the Romish Church. It is worthy of notice that the Scottish practice of filling the chief offices in a monastery with men of the same family does not seem to have been carried out in the case of Lindisfarne. Cuthbert had no relation to the Iona missionaries, nor have we any evidence to shew that there was any blood relation between the others. This throws some shade of suspicion upon the statement as to the practice, although it is generally accepted by Irish writers and applied to Iona, in order to shew that all its abbots were of Irish extraction,— a very curious fact, if true, in the case of a Scottish monastery.

Reference has already been made to Adomnan's visit to Northumbria during the reign of Egfrid, for the purpose of obtaining the deliverance of certain Irish prisoners. Among other things the Easter question, then probably the great question of the day among ecclesiastics, came up. The reasoning of the Saxon clergy convinced Adomnan, and he resolved to adopt both the Romish tonsure[1] and the Romish computation for Easter. His efforts for the conversion of his brethren in Iona were, however, ineffectual. Notwithstanding his position and influence as abbot, he was sternly resisted, and the Church continued to hold its own course. There must have been a large amount of sturdy independence among the members of this Church, judging from this case, in which the clergy were able to withstand the influence of the Romish

---

[1] The tonsure originated in the practice among early Christians of cutting the hair short, in order to the crucifying of the flesh, by rejecting all conformity to worldly vanity and fashion. The development of the practice affords ample evidence of the simple and even commendable beginnings from which corruptions in the Church may spring.

see and that of their own abbot in a matter held to be of
the highest importance. More than this, their abbot left
them and retired to Ireland, and yet they persisted. No
jurisdiction was felt to be entitled to submission as opposed to the mind of the brethren. If this be not presbytery, it is wonderfully like it. It may not indicate
the details of modern presbytery as existing among these
early Christians, but it certainly indicates a constitution
implying in it the fundamental principles of presbytery,
in the independence of individual ministers, and the
supreme authority of the collected mind of the brethren.
It is perfectly impossible to escape from this conclusion
in studying the history of the Easter controversy. These
men were not to be overborne by authority, even that of
the Apostolic see.

Meantime Naitan or Naughton, King of the Picts, had
been led to adopt the Romish system in the observance
of Easter. His frequent meditation on ecclesiastical
writings had led to this result (Bede, Hist. Eccl., Lib. v,
c. 21), a statement testifying to the scholarship of the
Pictish king, and hardly consistent with a state of barbarism. Hitherto, since the time of Brude, the Picts had
received their instructors from the Scots, but this remarkable revolution in the mind of the king led him to look
for instruction to their old enemies, the Saxons. It was
but five and twenty years after the destruction of Egfrid
and his army at Dunnichen that Naitan sent messengers
to Ceolfrid, abbot of Jarrow, asking information on the sub-
jcet of Easter and the tonsure, and requesting masons to
be sent to Scotland to aid him in building a church after
the Roman fashion.[1]

Ceolfrid's letter as given by Bede (Hist. Eccl., Lib. v.,
c. 21) is long, and filled with the usual arguments for

---

[1] The Scots built their churches of wood, and thatched them with reeds.

observing Easter after the Romish mode. He explains fully the Jewish method of computation, and the points both of difference and resemblance between it and that adopted at Rome. He also explains the method of the cycles as calculated by Theodosius of Alexandria, Cyril and Dionysius Exiguus, inasmuch as it was necessary that the Paschal full moon should be observed after the vernal equinox. He agrees that men may differ as to the tonsure, quoting Job, who shaved his head in the day of trouble, and Joseph, who was shorn when he was delivered from slavery, as shewing a difference of sentiment among good men : but urges strongly the example of Peter, who he says was shorn in honour of the passion of our Lord. He presses men to bear the form of the crown of thorns upon their heads that Christ may bear the thorns and briars of their sins. He makes the common charge against the tonsure of the fore part of the head by the Scots, that it is the tonsure of Simon Magus, and detestable. Ceolfrid quotes his conversation with Adomnan at the time of his visit to Northumbria, and adds that Adomnan would have amended the Scottish tonsure if he could.

The remarkable thing about this long and laboured letter of Ceolfrid of Jarrow to King Naitan is that the only authorities to which he refers in the question are the Scriptures and the example of St. Peter. He bases his whole calculations as to Easter upon the law of Moses, and quotes on New Testament authority that of St. Peter. His whole epistle is an appeal to the reason and conscience of Naitan. He strives to convince but never ventures to command. There is no reference to the supremacy of the Romish See, and he acknowledges the liberty of private judgment on the part of the Pictish king and people as much as if his letter had come from the pen of Luther.

Naitan was convinced, or rather had his previous convictions confirmed. The cycle of eighty-four years was suppressed, and that of nineteen years adopted, and all the ministers and monks among the Picts received the coronal tonsure. But the Scottish ecclesiastics established among the Picts resisted the authority of the king. Ceolfrid's letter was written in 710, and in 717 we read of "the expulsion of the family of Iona beyond the ridge of Britain (dorsum Brittanniæ) by King Nectan" (Tigh. Ann.) For seven years these stubborn Scots were borne with, not, in all likelihood, without means being used for their conversion ; but in vain, and they are finally driven as incorrigibles out of the Pictish kingdom. The tenacity of the Scot is no new feature of his character. He could suffer in the eighth century as he could in the seventeenth for conscience sake, and did so at the hand of a persecuting Pictish king.

But the minds of the Scottish brethren were gradually yielding to the pressure from every side brought to bear on them, and finally they were induced to yield to the appeals of Egbert, a Saxon monk. The history of this Egbert is full of interest. We learn that about the middle of the seventh century many of the nobles and common people · of the English nation, forsaking their native island, retired to Ireland, either for the sake of Divine studies, or of a more continent life ; some of them devoting themselves to a monastic life, and others applying themselves to study, travelling from master to master. The Scots willingly received them all, supplying them with food, with books, and with instruction, gratis. (Bede Hist. Eccl, Lib. iii., c. 27).

Among others who so visited Ireland was Egbert, one of the youth of the English nobility. With a friend who had accompanied him he studied in the Irish monastery of Rathmeilsige, now Melfont, where his companion died of the plague which ravaged both Britain and Ireland at the time. Egbert, though seized, recovered, having vowed to devote his life to God's service if it was spared. A portion of his vow was that he would never return to Britain again, that he would, besides canonical singing, repeat the Psalter once every day, and that he would every week fast one whole day and night. His character, his industry in teaching, and his authority in reproving sin gave him much weight among his adopted country-men, and under him the northern Irish first received the Romish Easter and tonsure. From Ireland he crossed to Iona, where by his character, and wisdom in dealing with them, he induced the Iona brethren also to conform to the Romish practice. Bede remarks upon the interesting nature of the fact that they who had, without envy, com-municated to the English people the knowledge of the true Deity, should afterwards by means of the English nation, be brought where they were defective, to the true rule of life. This change took place in the year 716, when Dun-chadh was abbot of Iona, or about eighty years after Aidan had been sent to preach to Northumbria. (Bede, Hist. Eccl., Lib. v., c. 22).

The only party in the kingdom who now held by the old forms as to Easter and the tonsure were the Britons, of whom Bede says, that they never conferred any spiri-tual benefits upon the English, and were now left, inve-terate in their errors, "exposing their heads without a crown, and keeping the solemnity of Christ without the society of the Church." The boon which the English bestowed on the Scots in return for the Gospel, and which the Britons rejected, is one whose value none but a dis-ciple of Rome will hold in high estimation. Truly the Saxons have in this case, as in some others, repaid their obligations to the Celt in coin sufficiently valueless. It is a remarkable thing, with what readiness the liberty-loving Saxon succumbed to the pretensions of Rome on all religious questions; nor is it uninstructive to observe how certain features of character adhere persistently to a nation; for to this day the Englishman, with all his love of civil liberty, is usually as indifferent to ecclesiastical liberty as any man out of the pale of the Church of Rome.

The main interest in the whole controversy regarding Easter and the tonsure, in modern times, lies in the light which it throws on the relation in which the early Scottish Church stood to that of Rome. To a large body of Protestants it matters not on what day Easter is observed, a Quartodeciman being, in their estimation, just as orthodox as any other observer of the day; to a larger number it matters not what the form of the tonsure was or is; but it is a question of very deep interest indeed, whether the early British churches acknowledged the authority of the Roman See. Nor can it but be sufficiently obvious to any candid student of this portion of the history of the Church, that in the whole controversy we have been relating, the Scottish brethren never once acknowledged that the authority of the Romish See was entitled to their deference and obedience. They acknowledged the authority of Holy Scripture, and of apostolic example, but they never acknowledged any other. Nor was it in deference to Papal authority, that they finally succumbed. What they refused to the letters of Popes, they yielded to the reasoning and persuasion of a Saxon monk. The question at issue was one which to many Protestants is of the very utmost insignificance, but it involved principles of the highest importance to the well-being of the Church, and which are still of the deepest historical interest. The ancient Scottish Church was not Papal in its constitution. It loved unity and by its desire for unity was led to conform to a practice which it had long resisted, but the unity it sought was not the unity of Rome. The Scot and the Pict had no reason to love civil Rome ; they withstood, for many a year, with no little determination, the claims of ecclesiastical Rome. Even when finally yielding in the matter of Easter and the tonsure, it was to reason and not to Rome that they professed to defer. Bede makes the real position of the Scottish Church with reference to that of Rome sufficiently clear in one sentence in which he says of Oswy, that, "*though* brought up among the Scots, he understood quite well that the Roman was the Catholic and Apostolic Church." Oswy knew this, but the Scots had never taught him so. (Bede, Hist. Eccl., Lib. iii., c. 29).

CHAPTER XIX.

THE EVENTS OF THE EIGHTH CENTURY.

In the MS. containing the synchronical kings of Ireland and Scotland, said to have been written by Flann Mainistreach, or Flann of Monasterboice, and already referred to, we find it said, "V bliadhna agus cend o bhas Domhnaill M'Aedha gu bas Aedha Allain M'Eargaile. Ceithir ri deg fir Eirin fisin Conall agus Cellach du mac Maelcoba, &c. IX ri don fir Albain fisin Congall crondomna, agus Duncadh M'Dubain, agus Domnall donn Mailduin Mac Conall agus Fercar foda agus Eocho rianamhail agus Anbcellach M'Fercair agus Selbach M'Fercair agus Eochaigh Angbaigh a medhon a laithusa cath muigh seiredh adrochar Aedh allain." That is, "There were one hundred and five years from the death of Donald, son of Aedha to the death of Aedh Allain, son of Eargail. Fourteen kings of Ireland, viz., Conall, and Cellach the swarthy, son of Maelcoba, &c. Nine kings of the men of Albain (Scotland), viz., Congall Crondomna (heir of the crown), and Duncan, son of Dubain, and Donald donn, and Mailduin, son of Conall, and Ferchar the tall, and Eochy Rianamhail (with the high nose), and Ainbhcellach, son of Ferchar, and Sealbhach, son of Fercair, and Eochy Angbaigh (Ardfhlaith? *great chief*), in the middle of his days Aedh allain was slain." Ferchar fad dying in 702, we have as succeeding him in this century on the Dalriadic throne, Eochy, latinised Achaius, son of King Domangart, distinguished by his aquiline nose. The Gaelic bard characterises him as "Eochaidh nan each,"

Eochy of the Steeds, a name which conveys a pretty accurate idea of the man as a warrior and a huntsman. All authorities are agreed as to this succession. His reign lasted only two years, but long enough to secure for him from the bard the epithet of "calma," or *bold,* a feature in his character which probably aided in shortening his days. He made war on the Strathclyde Britons, and unsuccessfully, for we read under 704, "Strages Dailriada in Glen lemnæ," the slaughter of the Dalriads in Glen Leven (Tigh. Ann. and Ann. of Ulster). This weakening of his power seems to have encouraged his successor, Ainbhcellach, son of Ferchar fad, to endeavour to seize the reins of government. This he did and ascended the throne in 705. The bard of the Albanie duan calls him Aincheall maith or Aincheall *the good,* a quality not adapted to the period in which he lived, for his brother Sealbhach, a man of the very opposite character, displaced him at the end of a year, and seized the government. Eochy was of the house of Fergus ; Aincheall and Sealbhach of the house of Lorn. The Scottish throne seems for a long period to have oscillated between these two houses, the strongest always holding it for the time. This rivalry appears to have disturbed the succession of the Scottish kings more than the Tanist law. The Gaelic bard, who probably held that Duncha beg of Kintyre, whom he calls Duncha dion or *the resolute,* was the lawful king, makes no mention of the name of Sealbhach, but the Irish annalists and Flann are incontrovertible evidence as to his reign. Sealbhach is described so early as 701 as destroying the castle of Dunolly (Ann. Ulst.) The event is associated by the annalist with the slaughter of the tribe of Cathboth ; from whence it is probable that, though in his native province, Dunolly had been seized or was held by a hostile tribe, who had provoked his opposition. A feud existed during Sealbhach's reign between himself and Duncan beg, a scion of the rival house of Fergus, who retained sovereign authority in his own part of the Dalriadic kingdom. In 719 the two tribes met in naval warfare at a place called Airdeanesbi (probably Ardaness in Melfort), when the race of Lorn under Sealbhach were worsted by the race of Gabhran under Duncan. In 719 Duncan died. Other events are related as occurring in the reign of Sealbhach. In 711 the Britons of Strathclyde were overcome in a battle fought at Loirg ecclet, probably Largs, famous in after times for the defeat of King Haco, by Alexander the Third (Tigh. Ann.) In 713 Sealbhach built the castle of Dunolly, which he had previously destroyed. In 717 another battle took place in the chronic warfare between the Scots and the Britons. They met at Minvircc, a word whose first syllable is obviously the British "Maen," a stone; "ad lapidem," says the annalist, called "Minvircc." Here the Britons suffered another defeat. A border warfare seems to have been carried on during the whole of this period along the lower reaches of the Clyde. Private feuds were also rife. Ainbhcellach, whom Sealbhach his brother had dispossessed, remained long in Ireland, but in 719 made an attempt to recover his kingdom. The two brothers met in a place called Finghinn (Tigh. Ann.) thought to be Glen Fine at the head of Loch Fine. Ainbhceallach was worsted and slain, leaving to Sealbhach undisputed possession of his crown. Sealbhach in 723 entered the Church (Tigh. Ann.), although he appears in a great battle in 727 at Irroisfoichne with the family of Donald. He was succeeded by another Eochy, under whom the two provinces of the Dalriads were again united.

It is remarkable that during the period we have been describing the great ecclesiastical questions between Rome and the Scots and Picts were being discussed and settled. These seem to have progressed undisturbed by the perpetual warfare that raged around. It is likely that religion had sufficient authority at the time even over the most warlike or the most barbarous of the inhabitants of Scotland, to secure the safety of its ministers in all quarters. Still there was much awanting of having the public mind leavened by Christian and civilizing influences. How true it is that civilization is of slow growth, and that even after men think they have attained it, human nature still shews itself in its own colours. What are the animosities, and feuds, and wars of modern times better than those of the Picts, and Scots, and Britons of the eighth century?

Eochy the Second was son of Eochy Rianaval. The annalists record few of the events of his reign, which closed in 733, after a period of four years. Two events, however, are noted. The one is a battle between the Cruithne and the Dalriads "cum murbulg," with the *murbulg,* in which the Cruithne were overthrown. It would appear that war had broken out between Eochy and the northern Picts, in which the former was entirely successful. The three neighbouring races of Scots, Picts, and Britons appear to have been in a state of continual warfare among themselves, and to this period must, in all probability, be traced the erection of many of those "raths" or round-hill forts which are studded so numerously over the Highlands. The other event is an expedition of Flaithbeartach into Ireland with the Dalriadic fleet. In this expedition Conchobar, son of Lochen, and Branin, son of Bran, and others were drowned in the Bann. Eochy himself was slain. Ireland shared in the existing feuds (Tigh Ann.).

To Eochy succeeded, according to Flann's synchronisms, Dungal. Innes excludes him from his list, but his reign is admitted by some of the oldest authorities. The Albanic Duan, which places him after Ainbhceallach calls him Dungal "dion," or the bold; the synchronisms of Flann call him Dungal M'Sealbhaich. The date given in the Irish annals places the death of Dungal in the same year with that of his predecessor, Eochy, and associates it with an invasion of the Pictish territory. The entry of the Irish annalist is "Dungal the son of Sealbhach dishonored Toraic when he drew Brude out of it, and at the same time he invaded the island of Culenrigi;" an entry which one writer interprets as a seizing by force Forai, daughter of Brude, brother of Ungus or Angus, the Pictish king. (Chalmers' Cal. v. 1, p. 293). Dr. Reeves considers Toraic to be Tory island, in the north of Ireland, and Culenrigi to be Inch, off the coast of Inishowen. There is very considerable difficulty in reading the Irish annalists, in distinguishing between the Scottish and Irish Cruithne or Picts. Hence the very different interpretations of Scotch and Irish writers (Reeves' Vit. Col. p. 384, n.)

Dungal's reign appears to have closed with this event, and he was succeeded by Alpin. At least so the Albanic Duan and Flann's synchronisms both say. The words of the Albanic Duan are, "Four years to Alpin." Both Chalmers and Innes exclude this king altogether, holding that the Sennachies have by mistake inserted the name of a Pictish king.

To Alpin, or, according to Tighernac, to Eochy, succeeded Muireadhach or Murdoch, called by the Bard of the Duan "maith," or good. His reign extended but to three years. He is called by Flann, Muireadhach Uadaithe, or O'David. Tighernac calls him the son of Ainbhceallach. The chief authorities agree as to his existence, and they agree also in fixing the commencement of his reign in 733. In his time the Picts, probably enraged by the cruel and shameful assault of Dungal M'Sealbhaich, retaliated with terrible severity. The Pictish throne was filled at the time by one of the ablest men that ever occupied it, Angus the son of Fergus. In 734 Dungal, probably the son of Sealbhach, appears defending the castle of Dunleven, some *rath* (fort) probably in the valley of the Leven (Tigh. Ann.). The castle was taken, and Dungal, wounded, fled from the power of Angus, and took refuge in Ireland. Angus extended his foray, and laid waste the territory of the Dalriads, penetrating as far as Dunad, in Argyll, which he took, with great booty. Here he found Dungal, who seems to have returned from Ireland, and Feradach, sons of Sealbhach, and threw them, in chains, into prison. Soon after, Brude, the son of Angus, whose seizure by Dungal seems to be the real event narrated in 733, when Culenrigi was attacked, died. He had been probably kept in prison and ill-used by Dungal, which occasioned his death. Angus' foray terminated at Knock Cairpre, at Calatros, on the shores of the Linne,[1] where a great battle was fought. Here Talorgan, the son of Fergus, brother to Angus, defeated Muireadhach, who fled, after many of his nobles had been slain (Tigh. Ann.) Murdoch died in 736, probably at the battle of Knock Cairpre, and was succeeded, according to Innes and Chalmers, by Eoghan or Ewen, his son, and according to the Albanic Duan and Flann of Bute, by Aodh fionn, or fair, called by Flann, Aedh aireatach, or *the noble*. Ewen's reign extended, like that of his father, over three years, during which the annalists note nothing belonging to the civil history of the Dalriadic kingdom. The probability is that the nation, wasted by the inroads of the powerful Angus, was glad to be at peace.

Aodh fionn, or Hugh the fair, succeeded, according to

---

[1] Linn Chaladair is an old name for Loch Lomond. Dr. Reeves supposes this to be Culross, in Perthshire.

all the authorities, in 739. He was son to Eochy III., and grandson to the famous Eochy rianamhal. The term "'n a ardflaith," in the 'Duan,' of which Chalmers makes so much (Caled. i. 295), as applied to this king by the Gaelic bard, implies nothing personal to the monarch, but merely tells us that he was sovereign. The translation of the line is, "Thirty years was Aodh sovereign." This king was of the race of Fergus, who now again succeeded the rival house of Lorn on the throne. Fergus and Lorn were the York and Lancaster of the early Scottish kingdom.

Under Aodh, notices of battles which had ceased under the reign of Ewen, appear again. The first recorded is that of Drumcathmail, or Eathmail, between the Cruithne and the Dalriads (Tigh. Ann.), under Inreachtach. Peace between the Scots and Picts had not been of long dura-- tion, and the Scots under Aodh made vigorous efforts to avenge their defeats at the hand of the great Angus. The locality of this battle has not been fixed, but Drumcathmail is a Gaelic word, the "Drum," signifying a *ridge* or *rising ground*, and was probably within the Scottish territory. The battle was unfavourable to the Scots, who were totally routed by King Angus.

In 750 the Britons and Picts engaged in war, for in that year a battle is recorded at a place called "Cato hic" by the Irish, and Mocetauc or Maesydauc, by the Welsh. The real name, as used by the Scottish Celt, seems to have been Magh Ceataig, or the plain of Ceataig. Here Angus' forces were defeated, and his brother, Talorgan, slain. Angus died in 761, and soon after we find his successor, Ciniod or Kenneth, at war with the Dalriads. A battle was fought between Aodh and Kenneth in 768. Aodh's reign was one prolonged war with the Picts; at first with Angus, a serious opponent to deal with, and latterly with a weaker man, Angus' successor,

R

Kenneth. Later writers have attributed a code of laws to Aodh fionn, by which the Dalriadic kingdom was long governed. Aodh died in 769,[1] and was succeeded by his son, Fergus. The Gaelic bàrd here introduces Donald, but Flann agrees with other chroniclers in entering the name of Fergus. Three years was the period of his reign, during which no important event is recorded.

His successor, according to Innes and Chalmers, was Sealbhach; according to the Albanic Duan it was Donald; and Flann of Bute records Eochy, called Annuine, a corruption of the Gaelic *an nimhe*, or 'poisonous;' bitter or cruel when applied to character, as his successor. These are remarkable incongruities in the case of a reign like that of Sealbhach, to which a period of twenty-four years is attached. But Lorn and Argyle had so many subordinate chiefs or reguli, many of them almost equal in power to the sovereign, and all of them called "righ," or king, in the vernacular of the country, that there is no cause of surprise in some confusion of the kind appearing among chroniclers, who might have their own predilections among these several claimants to the title and rights of monarchy. Sealbhach's reign seems to have been a period of peace, and closed in 796. Eochy Annuine, in whose existence all authorities except the Albanic Duan agree, began his reign in 796. This king, usually called Achaius, has been famous in Scottish history. He was the cotemporary of Charlemagne, and the tradition has long existed that he and that great founder of the French monarchy entered into a treaty of alliance. This tradition has been derided by modern writers, but upon as little authority at least as that upon which it is said to be founded. Nothing on the subject can be averred with any confidence;[2] but this we have shewn that so early

---

[1] Tighernac dates his death in 778. This cannot be made to agree with a reign of thirty years begun in 739.

[2] Mr. Hill Burton is disposed to date the French alliance from the period of Sir William Wallace.—See " The Scot in France," vol. i.

as the days of Columba there was intercourse between Kintyre and France, and we know that a belief in the existence of such an alliance led to the cherishing of a very cordial feeling of kindness towards each other, by both Scotland and France for many generations. If the alliance was, as some historians maintain, with an Irish prince (Chalm. Cal., p. 299, n.), Scotland will lose nothing by being deprived of the honour of a treaty which went to make her the hired ally of the French king.

Scottish historians agree that in the domestic relations of Eochy, the Scottish and Pictish royal families became first united. The wife of the Scottish king was Urgusia, daughter of Urguis or Fergus, and sister of Constantine, the King of the Picts. In virtue of this marriage a claim was afterwards successfully founded on the part of Kenneth M'Alpin to the Pictish crown. Eochy died in 826, twelve years after the death of Charlemagne.

During the period now under review, feeble as the light is which history sheds on the Scottish monarchs and their actions, it is somewhat feebler still in the case of the Picts. The latter were farther removed from the country of the Irish annalists, and their actions were less known to them in consequence. Besides, as it happens that the same word Cruithne is applied to the Picts of Scotland and those of Ireland, it is difficult to decide to which country their notices refer. In this century the annalists appear first to apply the name Pictones to the Picts, their country afterwards assuming the name of Pictavia. This name has been thought to apply to the southern Picts only, while the name Cruithne was reserved for those of the north. The first use of the word Pictones appears in Tighernac under the date 750, where it is translated into the Gaelic Piccardach. The Latin word seems to have been formed by the annalist to rhyme with the word Britones in the same sentence, and the Gaelic word was afterwards formed from the Latin. The language of the early Scottish ecclesiastical writers is full of similar conceits, and no historical inference of any value can be founded on them. That there were northern and southern Picts is undoubted, inasmuch as there were Picts south of the Grampians and Picts north of them, but these were not separate nations, nor were they governed by a separate succession of kings. As already shewn the seat of the monarchy might vary, and some of the subordinate reguli might assume to themselves regal power, but there was but one list of kings over the whole people. Angus M'Fergus appears in the annals as *Rex Pictorum*, 'King of the Picts,' and once as *Righ Albain*, 'King of Scotland' (Tigh. Ann.) ; while his subjects are indiscriminately called Cruithne, Picts, and Fortren. But to shew that there were among the Picts of Scotland as in Ireland, and among the Dalriads powerful provincial reguli, we read in 739 that "Talorgan son of Drost, King of Athole, was drowned by Angus." The Picts, north and south, were obviously one people, with one monarch and several subordinate rulers of districts.

Brude the son of Derile, who died in 710, was the last of the Pictish kings whose reign came under review as belonging to the previous century. He was succeeded by Nectan, Naughton, or Naitan, whose name is associated with the adoption of the Romish Easter and tonsure among his people. He was brother of Brude, and succeeded in accordance with the Pictish law. His reign extended for fifteen years till the year 725.

Nectan's reign was marked by a renewal of the war with the Saxons of Northumbria. In 710 an assault was made on what the Irish annalist calls the tribe of Comgall, when the two sons of Nechtan M'Doirgarto were slain, and when Angus the son of Maelan was slain upon the island. This region of Comgall, whose name is probably derived from *Com,* in the British language 'a hollow,' and *gall*, 'a stranger,' lay most probably along the shore of the Lothians. In this quarter there is a barony named in charters, called Congalton.[1] It includes a portion of the district around North Berwick. The reference to the island where Angus M'Maelan was slain, adds to the evidence in favour of this locality.[2] The Picts had obviously crossed the Firth and carried the war into their ancient territory of Lothian. In 711 a battle was fought in the plain of Manand, probably Slamannan, in Linlithgowshire, when the Picts were overpowered, and Findguine the son of Deleroith slain. The war continued on the same side of the Firth, notwithstanding this defeat; for in 712 Tiarpairt Baetten, or Boitter is said to have been burnt. This has been shewn very distinctly to have been Tarbert in the neighbourhood of North Berwick, which was an old stronghold in that quarter.[3] Nectan or Naitan was not without civil disturbances in his kingdom. In 713 Kenneth the son of Derile, and his son Mathgeman were slain. These were brother and nephew to the king, and were probably aspiring to the throne which he filled. Nor were others of his family altogether submissive, for Talorgan the son of Drostan, afterwards called King of Athole, and drowned by King Angus, is said to have been bound by his brother Nectan (Tigh. Ann.) Nectan was a man of religious earnestness, and interested himself in the religious wellbeing of his people, although he opposed the Scottish Church, and adopted from the Saxons the Romish view of Easter and the tonsure, besides, like them, placing his

---

[1] It is quite possible that Congalton derives its name from Congal, who was slain there.

[2] See Paper by Mr. W. F. Skene in Trans. of Scot. Ant., Vol. IV. p. 1.

[3] See Mr. Skene's Paper. Mr. Skene understands the Baetten or Boitter to be identical with Elbotle, a name recently in use as applied to a neighbouring estate.

kingdom under the patronage of St. Peter. It is strange to find him learning from the Saxons at the very time that he is carrying on war against them. But the religion of the period does not seem to have influenced much, any more than now, the policy of nations, although its influence largely pervaded the community with respect to the arrangements of social life. Nectan drove the Scottish missionaries away, nor did they return to the Pictish territory until the union of the kingdoms in 843. Nectan is said to have re-established the monastery of Abernethy. He entered the church in 724, and was succeeded by Drust. This king, not very sure of his throne and jealous of Nectan, notwithstanding his assuming the garb of a monk, put him in chains in 726, but had himself a struggle with another pretender in the person of Alpin or Eilpin, who succeeded him, and is the king whom some writers hold (Chalm. Cal. I., p. 294) to have been introduced by mistake into the lists of Scottish kings. Alpin was opposed by Angus the son of Fergus, and both at the battle of Monid croib or Moncrieff, near Perth, and that of Scone, was routed, and Nectan restored to his liberty and his throne (Tigh. Ann.). In 729 the Picts suffered great loss in the wreck of 150 of their ships. The place where the wreck took place is called Ross-cuissine, the situation of which is probably in the Firth of Forth. Fife Ness was called Muck Ross, and there is a Ross which appears to have been the ancient name of the present Pettycur, where the ferry between Fife and the Lothians long was kept, and where it is quite possible that with an easterly gale such a fleet as that of the Picts might have been lost. In 729 Angus Mac Fergus attacked Nectan as he had done Alpin, and was victorious. A battle was fought at Monith-carno, near the lake of Loogdae.[1] Angus obtained a vic-

---

[1] Perhaps the mount near Lochee, in Forfarshire.

tory, and Nectan's officers, Bisceot the son of Moneit, and his son, Fingan the son of Droitan, and Ferot the son of Finguine with many others, were slain.[1] Having overcome Nectan, Angus turned his forces against Drust, who was still in the field, and a battle was fought at a place called Dumdearg Blathmig,[2] which Chalmers identifies as lying in Perthshire on the Isla, where Drust was slain.

In 731 Nectan the son of Derile died, and Angus the son of Fergus, called Ungus by the chroniclers, succeeded to the Pictish throne. As already related in connection with the reign of the Dalriadic king Aodh fionn, Angus carried war and desolation into the territory of the Dalriads, and in 741 the following graphic entry is found in Tighernac's annals : " Percussio Dalriati la Œngus Mac Ferguso," *the smiting of Dalriada by Angus son of Fergus.*

War was also carried on against the Strathclyde Britons, for in 750 was fought the battle of Cato hic or Magh Ceataig already referred to. In this battle the Picts were worsted, and Talorgan, brother of Angus, slain. Nor were internal feuds unknown. In 752 a battle was fought in the land of Circi, thought to be the modern Forfarshire, so called from Circi, son of Cruithne, the first king of the Picts, between the Pictones themselves, in which Brude, son of Malcolm, was slain.

Nor was Angus at peace with his southern neighbours, the Saxons of Northumbria. He carried his forces across the Firth of Forth, and like some of his predecessors gained decided advantages for his kingdom. It was on this occasion that the legend arose which gave to Scotland her patron saint. The legend varies, but the scope of it is, that previous to a great battle in Lothian, St.

---

[1] One of these names is just the modern M'Kinnon.
[2] Blathmig is a man's name (see Ann. of Ulst., 825).

Andrew appeared to the king, either in a dream or during
the battle, with the figure of a St. Andrew's cross in the
air, told him that he was his defender, and that upon his
return home he must devote a tenth part of his kingdom
in honour of St. Andrew.   Angus gained a great battle,
and the Saxon general, called Athelstane, fell at a place
called, in memory of that event, Athelstaneford.   It has
been shewn very clearly that at this period St. Andrew
became the patron saint of Scotland.[1]   Bede, who died
in 731, relates that the patron of Scotland was St. Peter.
From the days of Angus it was St. Andrew.   To this
Pictish king then Scotland owes the selection of her patron
saint, and in this at least we can trace the footprints of
Pictish influence.   Angus died in 761, and the Chronicle,
appended to Bede's history, sums up his character in a
single sentence—" Angus, king of the Picts, who a blood-
thirsty tyrant, led a life of cruelty and crime from the
beginning to the end of his reign, died."   This passage
shews in what estimation the Pictish monarch was held
by his Saxon neighbours, who had suffered so much from
his power and military skill.   He was unquestionably the
greatest king who ever filled the Pictish throne, although
many of these men were men of enterprise and ability,
and men who, although it has not been much recognised
by later writers, left largely the impress of their talents
and character on the future history of Scotland.   There
is more of what is Pictish in the influences which have
moulded the social system of Scotland than has been
generally acknowledged by writers on our early history.
Changes of dynasties do not necessarily change the manners and habits of subjects.

Angus was succeeded by his brother Brude, the son of
Fergus, who reigned for two years.   Kenneth succeeded

[1] See paper by Mr. Skene in Trans. of Soc. of Scot. Antiq., vol. iv., part i.,
pp. 304-5.

Brude, and reigned from 763 to 775. Under date of 768 the Irish annalists enter, "War in Fortreim between Aedh and Kenneth." Aedh, the Dalriadic king, recovering from the chastisement inflicted by the warlike Angus, carried war into the Pictish territory.

To Kenneth succeeded Alpin, the son of Uroid, who reigned for three and a-half years, and to him succeeded Drust, the son of Talorgan, who reigned for four or five years, his reign closing about the year 780.[1] The next king was Talorgan, the son of Angus, who filled the throne for two and a-half years. In 782 the annals of Ulster relate that "Dutolarg, or Tolarg the black, King of the Picts on this side the Mount,[2] and Murdoch, son of Huargail, Stewart (equonimus) of Iona, perished." The date given in this place corresponds exactly with that which may be gathered from the Chronicle already quoted, as that of the death of Talorgan. To Talorgan succeeded Canaul, son of Tarla, or probably Conall, son of Charles, who reigned for five years,[3] and to him succeeded Constantine, who is said to have been the seventy-first king of the Picts. Constantine began his reign in 789, and reigned for thirty years, or till the year 819. His accession is thus noted in the Ulster annals—"789, Battle between the Picts, where Conall, the son of Taidg,[4] was conquered and escaped, and Constantine was victor." Conall was driven from his throne, which was seized by his successful rival, Constantine. Conall retired to Kintyre, where he remained till 807, when he was slain by another Conall, the son of Aedhan.

The great event of Constantine's reign was the commencement of the inroads of the Vikings, or pirates of the

---

[1] Chron. Pict. in App. to Innes' Crit. Ess., p. 780.

[2] The northern regulus seems at this time to have assumed independence. The Maormors of Moray often strove for independence of the king.

[3] Chron. in Inn. Essay.

[4] This is evidently Canaul, son of Tarla, of Innes' Chronicle.

north.   For four hundred years a portion of the Teutonic
race held a great part of Britain, their territory being
almost commensurate with that formerly held by the
Romans.   A new section of the race drawn from a more
northern source and severer climate now assailed the
whole island.   Saxon and Celt became equally the prey
of the hardy northman.   The Vikings, or men of the bays,
descended upon such portions of the western shores
of Europe as lay exposed to their depredations.   It is
not supposable that it was the poverty and barbarism of
the land that attracted them.   Scotland must have had
sufficient wealth to present to these marauders a motive
for crossing the stormy seas that divided their own land
from her shores.   Nothing is more indicative of Scotland's
having attained to a considerable share of material wealth
than the descents of these northern spoilers.   In 794 the
following significant entry appears in the Annals of Ulster ;
"The ravaging of all the islands of Britain by the Gentiles,"
and of the same date in the Annals of Inisfallen ; "The
ravaging of Icolmkill."   In 795 Rathlin was laid waste,
and the Church founded there by Seigine, abbot of Iona,
spoiled.   In 798 the whole islands of Scotland and Ireland were wasted.   This new enemy must have borne
heavily upon the Pictish territory, lying as it did more
immediately exposed to their depredations ; and it is not
at all unlikely that the weakening of the Pictish power
by these incursions of the northmen prepared the way
finally for the union of the Pictish crown with that of
the Scots.

During the eighth century we have few intimations of
the condition of the Strathclyde Britons, save that they
seem to have had frequent wars with their northern
neighbours, especially the Dalriadic Scots.   In 722 Bili,
son of Alpin, King of Alclutha, died (Tigh. Ann.)   A
battle was fought at Loirgeclet in 711, in which the

Britons were vanquished. Another battle between the same parties was fought at Minvircc, in which the Dalriads were again triumphant. In 750 a battle was fought with the Picts, when Talorgan the son of Fergus, and the Picts were overcome. This was the battle of Magh Ceataig. These battles have been referred to already. In 780 Ailclutha or Dunbarton was burned about the end of winter, but by whom is not recorded (Ann. Ulst. 779).

Galloway, in so far as it did not belong to Northumbria, seems during this period to have belonged to the kingdom of Strathclyde, for in 823 we read that "Gallo way *of the Britons* was laid waste, with all its houses and its church, by Feidhlimidh" (Ann. of Ulst.)

Having thus given a sketch of the civil history of Scotland during the eighth century, let us advert to its ecclesiastical condition during the same period. Turning to Iona we find Conamhail succeeding to Adomnan in 704. He is called Conamhail Mac Failbhe by Tighernac. His period was much disturbed by the controversy with Rome, and Duncan his successor, and the first conformist to the Roman practice as to Easter, seems to have assumed power in the Iona institution in 707, three years before the death of Conamhail, who died in 710. Dun can, who succeeded Conamhail, died in 717. It is diffi cult to understand some of the notices of ecclesiastical affairs given by the annalists during his time. In 713 we learn (Ann. Tigh.) that Dorbene obtained the chair of Iae, and retained the primacy for five months, when he died. In 716 we learn (Ann. Tigh.) that Faelcu, son of Dorbene, obtained the chair of Columba in the seventy-fourth year of his age. Dr. Reeves supposes this to mean that there was schism in the community during a part of Duncan's presidency. The annalists do not say so, but they do indicate that there was during that period a

change in the presidency. That a violent internal controversy reigned in Iona at the time cannot be doubted.
Duncan agreed with his predecessor Adomnan in his
views of the great question then at issue. The brethren
were divided. It had defied Adomnan to bring them to
conformity, but the matter was evidently making progress, and the opinions of Adomnan and others were
leavening the community. The different factions would
naturally seek the elevation of their own friends. Thus
Dorbene would represent the friends of the ancient prae-
tice, and he was raised to the chair in 713. In 716
Faelcu, who is called son of Dorbene, had the same
honour conferred on him. Being son to Dorbene, he
would naturally hold by the opinions of his father, and
would be raised to the dignity of abbot by the same
parties. During all this time Duncan was abbot, and
the interesting point in the whole is, that the office of
abbot was not necessarily permanent, and that being
originally elective, the brethren felt themselves entitled
to elect another at any time, when circumstances demanded of them to do so. Thus during the presidency
of Duncan, the brethren, or a portion of them, elevated
Dorbene, and afterwards Faelcu to the chair. Notwithstanding this, however, the visit of Egbert was successful
in subduing the opposition of the brethren, and upon the
death of Duncan in 717, Faelcu, who was apparently
his rival, succeeded quietly to his office.

Faelcu was seventy-four years of age, when he was
raised to the abbot's chair first (Tigh. Ann.), during the
life of Duncan. He succeeded finally at the age of
seventy-five, a period of life when most men are glad to
withdraw from the burden of public duty. The first
notice, under his rule, by the annalists refers to the expulsion of the Scottish clergy from the territory of the
Picts. It would seem that these men among the Picts

had not acquiesced in the change adopted by the mother Church. Nectan the Pictish king had followed the example and teaching of the Saxons. The Scots in his territory were between two fires. Both Picts and Scots as nations had departed from their ancient testimony; but upon being pressed, these brethren yielded to the claims of kindred, and chose to face the opposition of their own Scottish brethren, rather than that of a race with which they had little connection by blood. It is probable that in time these men followed the example of their countrymen and adopted the Roman cycle. It would appear that the coronal tonsure was not adopted in Iona contemporaneously with the Roman Easter, but in 718, two years after, when Tighernac notes "*Tonsura coronæ super familiam Iae*," 'the coronal tonsure on the family of Iona.'

In the year 722, two years before the death of Faelcu, Maolrubha of Applecross died. By that time the Gospel had pervaded the northern part of Scotland, penetrating by the west, and reaching the eastern coast.

An event similar to that which occurred in the closing years of Duncan's presidency, occurred in that of Faelcu. Feidhlimidh held the presidency for two years previous to his death (Tigh. Ann.) Dr. Reeves supposes him to have been coadjutor bishop. It is far more likely that the existing schism had not entirely disappeared, and that Feidhlimidh was to Faelcu what Faelcu and his father Dorbene were to Duncan. One thing is clear, that Feidhlimidh did not finally succeed to the chair.

In 724 Faelcu died and was succeeded by Cillean fad, or Killen the tall. He occupied Columba's chair for a year only, during which the most important event narrated is, that Nectan the Pictish king entered the Church. Oan (Owen) minister of Eigg died in 725.

In 725 Cillean fada was succeeded by Cillean drochaiteach, or Killen of the bridges. He is said to have been an anchorite (see Reeves' Vit. Col., pp. 382). His period was a stormy one, the Scots and Picts being both in a continual state of war; at times intestine, and at others with one another, or with the Britons of Strathclyde, or the Saxons of Northumbria. Several events interesting in the history of the Church are recorded by the Irish annalists. In 734 Caintigern, the daughter of Ceallach Cualann, died. She is the St. Kentigern commemorated in Inchcaillich, one of the islands in Loch Lomond. She is said to have been sister of St. Comgan of Turriff, and mother of St. Fillan of Strathfillan (Aberd. Breviary). Another event is the death of Ronan, called in the annals "Abbot of Kingaradh," the name given to the south end of the island of Bute, where the remains of an ancient chapel are to be seen to this day. This event occurred in 737. Ronan's was a famous name in the early hagiology of Scotland, and is commemorated to this day in several Ronas,—islands scattered over the Hebridean group. Besides the island of Rona off the Butt of Lewis, with its interesting remains already referred to, other relics of Ronan are pointed out. On this island are shewn certain scratches on the rocks, said by the vulgar to have been caused by the claws of the evil spirit when Ronan was engaged in expelling him. These are the traditions of a later period, and are to be accepted only as indicating the esteem in which the memory of the saint was held (Characteristics of Early Church Arch. of Scot.) A few other events are narrated as occurring during this period. The relics of Adomnan were in 727 brought to Ireland; in 730 they were returned to Scotland. The early annalists do not give the reason for this movement, but the calendar of Donegal states that the object was to aid in the reconciliation of the races of Conall and Eoghan. In 737 Failbhe, the son of Guaire, or as it would be in modern times Failbhe

Macquarrie, who succeeded Maolrubha in Applecross, was drowned with twenty-two of his crew. This is said to have taken place " in profundo pelagi." He was perhaps on the outlook for a desert island to which to retire. In 749 a serious loss of life seems to have taken place at Iona, marked by the significant notice, *Dimersio familiæ Iae*, ʻThe drowning of the family of Iona' (Tigh. Ann.) The intercourse with Ireland was at this time so frequent that the brethren must often have been in great danger crossing the stormy sea that intervened, in their fragile vessels. In 752 Cillean died.

His successor was Slebhine, son of Congal. He is said to have been a descendant of Lorn, son of Fergus, and was thus probably of Scottish birth. (Reeves' Col. Vit., p. 385). Few events of his life are recorded. In 307 Cumine the grandson of Becce or O'Becce "religiosus Ego," or an ecclesiastic of some kind in Eigg died. This small island is frequently noticed in the earlier annals of the Scottish Church. We have " Princeps Ego" and " Religiosus Ego" spoken of, both titles being probably applied to the same office. It is clear that there was a regular succession of ecclesiastics in the island.

At this period it is obvious that Ireland contributed largely to the support of the Columban Church. A tribute was imposed by authority of what was usually called " Lex Columcille," or " Columba's law." This impost was rigidly exacted. In 753 it was introduced by Donald, son of Dermait Mac Cerbhail, King of Ireland, and in 754 Sleibhine visited Ireland apparently for the purpose of enforcing its exaction. In 757 Sleibhine, still in Ireland, seems to have secured its universal acceptance, for the annalists enter, " Lex Columcille per Sleibhine." In 767 Sleibhine died.

His successor, who seems to have been chosen to the office in 766, was Suibhne, pronounced Sween, a name still known in the Highlands.   He filled the office for five years, dying in 772.

Suibhne's successor was Breasal, called the son of Seigh ine.   For twenty-nine years he filled Columba's chair,—years the latter of which were among the most momentous in the history of Iona.   We learn little during the early period of his incumbency from the Irish annalists, but such entries as the following shew that a regular succession of ministers was kept up throughout the country,—Ann. 775, "Conall de Magh Luinge obiit," *Conall of Magh Luinge died;* Ann. 776, "Mors Maelmanach abbatis Cinngaradh," *The death of Maelmanach abbot of Kingarth.*   The kind of state maintained in Iona appears from such an entry as, Ann. 782, "Muredach Mac Huairgaile equonimus Iae quievit," *Murdoch, son of Huairgaile, steward of Iona, died.*   In 795, however, appear those ominous notices, "Vastatio Iae Colum-cille," *The devastation of Iona;* and, "Combustio Rechrainne a Gentibus, et scrinia ejus confracta et spoliata sunt." *The burning of Rathlin by the Gentiles, and its shrines violated and spoiled.*   The northern hordes seem to have made a sweep through the Western Isles, and shewn no reverence either for sacred places or things.   The chief of the institution at Iona seems not to have long survived these mournful events, for in 801 "Bresal, the son of Seighine, abbot of Iona, fell asleep in the thirty-first year of his incumbency." (Tigh. Ann).

In the early part of the eighth century, the See of Galloway was restored by the Saxons, and Pecthelm, whom Bede calls "that most reverend prelate" (Hist. Eccl., Lib. v., c. 18), and "first bishop of the See" (v. 23), was appointed bishop.   Galloway was at the time part of the Northumbrian kingdom, and Aldfrid the reigning monarch was a warm friend of the Church.   Galloway was one of four dioceses erected in connection with and subordinate to that of York. It was apparently the first of the kind erected in Scotland, where as yet the idea of attaching a territory to the function of a Christian pastor does not seem to have entered the minds of the rulers, in either church or state ; nor did it for four hundred years more. It is even questionable how far it had yet taken shape in the mind of the Saxon Church, notwithstanding its strong sympathy with Rome. Whithorn, which was merely the locality of his mission, gave his distinctive title to the first Saxon Bishop of Galloway. Pecthelm's fame had extended far as a man of learning and piety, for Boniface, called the "apostle of Germany," addressed to him his consultation on the subject of marriage, a high tribute to his acquaintance with the laws and discipline of the Church. Pecthelm died in 735, and was succeeded by Frithewald.

Frithewald's incumbency continued till 764. This period seems to have been a peaceful one, although Saxon Galloway presented strong temptations to the Scots of Ireland and Argyll, nor do these seem to have been altogether resisted. To Frithewald succeeded Pectwine, who filled the See of Galloway till 777 (Inn. Civ. and Eccl. Hist., p. 329), and he was succeeded by Ethelbert, who died in 791.[1] The successor of Ethelbert was Beadulf, of whom William of Malmesbury says, that he is the last recorded bishop at the time, as Galloway was thrown into confusion by the incursions of the Scots and Picts. Innes (Civ. and Eccl. Hist., p. 331) quoting a MS., which he found in the Cottonian Library says, that another Eadredus or Heathored, as in the Chronicle of Florence of Worcester, is on record ; but this period seems to have been that when a hostile population from the coasts of Ireland and Argyll assailed Galloway, and that province came

---

[1] App. to Chron. of Flor. of Worces.

again into possession of a Celtic race, after having been for two hundred years under the dominion of the Saxons.

In Strathclyde we have few notices of the state of the Church during this century. Among no race did hatred to the Saxon so prevail as among the Cumbrian, whether of Scotland or Wales. To them therefore no change could be acceptable that was advocated by the foe they feared and hated most. Hence when Pict and Scot had accepted the Roman Easter with the coronal tonsure, the Briton still held out, and followed the fashion of his fathers. But even he at length yielded, and in 768 or fifty-one years after the change was adopted in Iona, the Britons accepted the Roman Easter (Ann. Cambriæ). In the Welsh Annals (Brut y Tywysogion) the change is referred to the year 770, and the person instrumental in bringing it about is said to have been "Elbot, a man of God." In the Annales Cambriæ the same man is called Elbodugo. Innes (Civ. and Eccl. Hist., p. 317) quotes from the Register of General Councils, a notice of a council held at Rome in 721, the resolutions of which were signed by Sedulius subscribing himself a "Bishop of Britain, of the race of the Scots;" and Fergusius or Fergus, a Pictish bishop of Scotland ; and farther adds, that although Langhorn thought that the seat of Sedulius was Dunbarton, his opinion was that he was one of the successors of Kentigern at Glasgow. It may be so, but the conjecture is not supported by any evidence. If it be correct, however, we have here a glimmer of light thrown on the ecclesiastical condition of the people of Strathclyde. One of their bishops was in Rome three years after his nation had accommodated its religious observances to the practice of the Roman Church, perhaps as a token of reconciliation with the Roman See.

Among the Picts several important events occurred affecting the condition of the Church during the eighth century. The early history of Scotland has hitherto been so entirely held to be the history of the Scots that it is of importance to keep these in view, for where this is done, it will appear that the great Pictish nation has left its footmarks as deeply impressed upon the history of our early Church as did the Scots. Nor could it be otherwise, when we reflect that three such institutions as Abernethy, St. Andrews, and Dunkeld existed among them, while Iona alone was distinguished among the Scots ; and farther, that Abernethy is said to have existed for more than a century before Iona, although for a time it fell into decay.

In the early part of the century the most important event in the Pictish Church was the adoption of the Roman Easter and tonsure as already narrated. As in the case of the Scots it was a Saxon priest (Ceolfrid) who finally led Nectan or Naitan, the Pictish king, to acquiesce in the change. Ceolfrid and Egbert might well boast of the influence which made them the instruments of bringing about so great a revolution, and Rome might well have their names in high esteem. The change took place in 710. The expulsion of the Scottish clergy followed, although it is sufficiently probable that this expulsion only extended to such of the Scots as were obstructive. The Picts might well have treated the Scots with tenderness and consideration. They had received from them the Gospel. From the Saxons they had received hitherto nothing but the fruits of devastating wars ; yet now they became their willing debtors for what was in some measure to subject them to the pretensions of the rising hierarchy of Rome. The admission of the one influence, and the expulsion of the other, was not ominous of good for the Pictish nation ; and yet it is perfectly true that there was hitherto no avowal of submission to Rome in the change. The name of the Pope does not appear in the discussion, shewing how gradually and with how little observation the Papal claim became developed.

We have already narrated the erection of the ecclesiastical institution at Abernethy by Nectan or Naitan, the son of Erp, in the fifth century. It is well to observe, however, that the Register of St. Andrews attributes the erection to another Nectan, the successor of Gartnaidh, in the beginning of the seventh century. Boece follows Fordun in attributing the foundation to Gartnaidh, and mentions a nun called Marota, celebrated in the Scottish Calendar on the 22d December as connected with the institution. The ancient notice in the Pictish Calendar (Inn. App., p. 780), while attributing the foundation to " Necton morbet filius Erp," adds that the cause of it was that Nectan was expelled by his brother Drust, and fleeing to Ireland had recourse to St. Bridget, who interceded for him, and secured for him his inheritance ; in commemoration of which he erected this monastery in honour of the Saint. Now there is evidently confusion here, for in 726 Tighernac relates that Nectan, son of Derile, was put in chains by Drust the king, and immediately afterwards, in the same year, we read that Drust was expelled from the kingdom of the Picts. It is difficult to believe that this is not the event recorded in the notice of Nectan I. It may be said indeed that Bridget was the cotemporary of St. Patrick. But it is quite possible that Nectan's appeal was to the shrine of the saint, and not personally to herself. But it is not easy to suppose that there were two Nectans and two Drusts in precisely similar circumstances. From this the inference is a very natural one, either that Abernethy was originally founded by Nectan, the son of Derile, in the eighth century, or at least that it was renovated and reorganized by him. The character of Nectan as a religious man, and one who finally adopted a religious life, would strengthen the evidence for his being the real founder, and it is perhaps to him we owe the erection of the round tower there, a work which bears all the marks of being as old as his period.

To this century is to be traced the foundation of St. Andrews, under that name, the founder being the great Angus, the son of Fergus. The tradition of his having seen St. Andrew's cross in the air during the battle with the Saxons at Athelstaneford, has already been referred to. It is pretty clear, however, that St. Andrews was at a very early period the seat of a Christian Church. Angus, the Culdee, in his "Festology," relates that St. Kenneth had a church "at Kilrymont in Alba." The Aberdeen Breviary says it was at Kennoquhy, which is near St. Andrews, and obviously derived its name from St. Kenneth. The ancient name of the district in which St. Andrews stands is Muckross, a name derived from "Muc" a *sow,* and "Ros" a *forest.* The word has been accurately rendered in the chroniclers by "Nemus porcorum," and in English by "The boar's chase." It extended from Fife Ness to a line running directly north from Largo. The locality of St. Andrews itself was called Kilrymont, a corruption of what Tighernac more accurately writes "Cindrighmonaidh," or Ceann righ Monaidh, *the end of the king's hill.*[1] From its relation to the sow the spot was probably a sacred one in pagan times, and for this reason may have been early occupied by Christian missionaries. At all events there is reason to believe that there was an establishment of Christian teachers here before the beginning of the seventh century. From this spot some of the recusant Scots may have been expelled by King Nectan, and thus a way opened up for a new foundation.

---

[1] By no ingenuity can Regulus be converted into Righmonaidh. The modern Kilreymont or Cill rimhinn is obviously a corruption of Cindrighmonaidh.

The command which Angus received in the vision at Athelstaneford was to dedicate a tenth part of his inheritance to St. Andrew. We have already stated how the Picts had adopted the views of the Anglo-Saxon Church on the subject of Easter and the tonsure so early as 710. The result of this was, that the Saxon clergy felt no misgiving, when circumstances urged it, in taking refuge with them. Hence the flight of Acca, Bishop of Hexham, to the territory of the Picts in 732. Hexham, since the days of Wilfrid, had venerated St. Andrew. The flight of the bishop, for what cause we know not, seems to have been attended with the removal of the relics, and in 736 a foundation, dedicated to St. Andrew, seems to have been instituted at St. Andrews by the Pictish king, Angus.[1] This was the origin of what came finally to be the metropolitan church in Scotland. In this way Abernethy was founded or renovated by Nectan, and St. Andrews by Angus, both Pictish kings, in the eighth century.

It may be well here to quote from Bede his account of the state of the Northumbrian Church in this period, as throwing some light on the tendency of the Church generally in Britain at the time. The account is found in the historian's letter addressed in 734 to Egbert, Archbishop of York. Among other things he says that the monasteries were often filled by men of irregular lives, that these foundations were too numerous, not leaving sufficient estates for laymen of condition; and farther that men who were no monks bought land on pretence of founding a monastery, and got a charter of privileges signed by the king and bishops, and others; that thus they acquired large estates, and adopting the name and office of abbots, and filling their pretended monasteries

---

[1] See an admirable piece of Historical Analysis connected with this subject, by Mr. W. F. Skene in Trans. of Scot. Ant., vol. iv., part i., pp. 300.

with unworthy monks, they indulged in all kinds of excesses ; bringing their wives into the monasteries and even setting up monasteries of women, over which they set their wives as abbesses. He adds that there were scarce any of the lieutenants or governors of towns in Northumbria who had not seized the religious jurisdiction of a monastery and put their wives into the same criminal posts ; that the custom had spread to the king's inferior officers, and that consequently the same parties were, most inconsistently, often at once abbots and officers of state, men being trusted with the government of religious houses without practising the obedience and discipline belonging to them.[1]

This account of Bede's indicates how readily a system in itself erroneous may develop itself in the production of the most abominable fruits. And we have here an insight into some of the steps which led in after times to deterioration in the monasteries of Scotland.

---

[1] It is to be borne in mind that this account refers, not to the time when the Culdee Church existed in Northumbria, but after the establishment of the Church of Rome among the Saxons by Augustine.

CHAPTER XX.

THE ninth century, which we have now reached, was an important one both in the civil and the ecclesiastical history of Scotland. The throne of the Dalriadic kingdom was filled in the earlier part of it by Eochaidh Angbhaidh, usually called Achaius, who died in 826. After his death there appears great confusion among the chroniclers in their lists of his successors. The synchronisms of Flann of Bute, give Domhnall, Custantin, Donall reime, Aengus, Aed, Eoganan, Ailpin M'Echach, Eoganan, Cinaeth M'Alpin; the Albanic Duan agrees pretty nearly with this, giving Donald, Conall, another Conall, Cusantin, Angus, Aodh, Eoganan, Kenneth. It is pretty clear that in both these chronicles there is a mixing up of the Scottish and Pictish kings. The Constantine and the Angus are plainly borrowed from the Pictish lists, and this fact shows how much the history of the two races was mingled in the later annals of the *seanachies*, especially during the latter portion of their separate existence. The Colbertine MS., as quoted by Innes, gives Dungal, Alpin, and Kenneth as the successors of Eochaidh, and Chalmers agrees with Innes in holding this to be the accurate succession. Eochy, according to all the lists, was succeeded by Donald, called also Dungal.[1] He was son of the second Sealbhach, and was descended of the house of Lorn. Few of the

---

[1] The ancient form of the name Donald is clearly Donnghal, like Dubhghal, Conghal, &c.

events of his reign, which extended from 826 to 833, have been recorded, and his name does not appear among the Irish annalists. But it is clear from incidental notices in their pages that the period was a stormy one. In 829 we read, " Diarmaid, Abbot of Iona, came to Scotland (Alba) with the relics of Columcille" (Tighernac). In 831 " Diarmaid came to Ireland with the relics of Columcille " (Tighernac). Why this scattering of the relics of the great Scottish saint, which has given rise amongst the Scotch and Irish to a dispute regarding their possession ? The reason will be found in the continued inroads of the Northmen. Although these inroads have generally been attributed to the dislike of the Norwegians to the government of Harold Harfager (Fair-haired), they commenced, as already related, at a period considerably earlier than his time, for in the last decade of the eighth century Iona was spoiled by these marauders. It is true the rule of Harold might at a later period have stimulated the migrations of the Norse, and he himself might have followed the migrating hosts either for purposes of revenge or conquest, but the inroads had begun previously, and became continuous ; and to these alone can be traced the scattering of the relics of Columba during the reign of Donald.

Donald was succeeded in 833 by Alpin. He belonged to the rival race of Gabhran, and was son of Eochaidh Angbhaidh and of Urgusia, the sister of the Pictish king, Constantine. In him, then, were united the blood of the Scottish and Pictish royal races, while he had the advantage, as regarded the Picts, of having his descent by the female side. The Albanic Duan extends his reign to four years ; other authorities make it only three. The Chronicle of Dunblane and the Register of St. Andrews both point to Galloway as the place of his death. He had carried an army across the Clyde, and laid waste a large portion of the modern county of Ayr. At a battle at a place called now Laicht, in the parish of Dalmellington, he was slain, and his body interred. Chalmers has shown pretty distinctly (Caled, vol. i. p. 302, *n*) that the place called Pitalpie, in Forfarshire, and long held to commemorate the death of this king, is really commemorative of the death of the Pictish king of the same name, who was killed a century before. Alpin is famous among the Scots not only as father of Kenneth, who united the two rival sovereignties of Scots and Picts in his own person, but among Scottish genealogists as the progenitor of some of their most famous clans. The clan Alpin, embracing as they do such races as the M'Gregors, the Grants, the M'Nabs, and the M'Kinnons, are said to have taken their generic name from this monarch. Alpin's death took place in 836.

Kenneth, son of Alpin, known in history as Kenneth Mac Alpin, succeeded his father. The Albanic Duan calls him *Cionath cruaidh*, 'Kenneth the hardy.' In Flann's synchronisms he is noted as *Cinaeth M'Alpin, in ced righ ro gab righe sgoinde do gaidhelaibh*, 'Kenneth M'Alpin the first king who obtained the kingdom of Scone for the Gael.' In the earlier part of Kenneth's reign his neighbours of Pictland would seem to have been much harassed by the Northmen. In 839 we read, "War by the Gentiles against the men of Fortrenn, in which fell Eoganan son of Angus, and Bran the son of Angus, and Aedh son of Boanta; and others almost innumerable." (Tighernac.) This weakening of the Pictish royal family, and the power of the nation, must have paved the way for the union of the Scottish and Pictish crowns. During the early part of his reign Kenneth vindicated his claim to the title of *cruaidh*, or 'hard,' by subduing under his complete control the territories of Argyle and Lorn, and carrying his armies into Galloway, where his father had been slain. But in 843 took place the great event of his reign, when he became monarch of the united kingdoms of the Scots and Picts. In his person he became the representative of the three monarchies of Ulster, Dalriada, and Pictland, a privilege which he transmitted to his successors, down to the present Queen of Great Britain. Kenneth became the first King of Scotland, although modern Scotland embraces the ancient kingdom of Strathclyde, which did not own his sovereignty.

The beginning of the ninth century found Constantine occupying the throne of the Picts. He dying in 821, was succeeded by another Angus or Ungus, the son of Fergus. Of his reign we have no notice but that it closed in 833; although by many writers this king has been mistaken for his great predecessor of the previous century. Angus was succeeded by Drest, the son of Constantine, who seems to have been associated in the government with Talorgan, the son of Uthoil. This reign was contemporaneous with that of Alpin over the Scots, and closed in 836. Owen, Uven, or Eoganan, the son of Angus, succeeded, and was slain, along with his brother Bran, by the Northmen, in 839. Wrad succeeded, and reigned till 842, and Boed followed, filling the throne till 843, and thus closing the long and famous line of Pictish kings, the true descendants of the ancient Caledonians, the brave resisters of the Roman power, and men who influenced the after history of Scotland more than the historians of the race who supplanted them ever gave them credit for. It should never be forgotten, in studying this portion of the history of Scotland, that the *Sennachies*, or retailers of the ancient history of the country, were the dependants of a royal family who had descended directly from an Irish origin, and who, whatever was in reality the origin of their subjects, were under strong temptations to derive them from the same source with their masters. It is not to be doubted that Scottish history received much of its Irish complexion after the union of the crowns in 843.

Kenneth, after the union, removed the seat of government to Forteviot, the ancient capital of the Pictish king dom. This, like the removal in more modern times of the seat of the British government from Edinburgh to London, was an indication of the superior power and consequence of the Pictish nation. From Dunstaffnage, or any other of the western strongholds of the Dalriadic kingdom to Forteviot, or to Scone, as Flann has it, was a gain in every respect. Tradition will have it that Kenneth extirpated the Picts; but the early annalists make no reference even to war between the two nations. It is pretty clear that the invaders from the north had struck terror into both nations, and the decline of the royal family of the Picts, with Kenneth's legal claims to the succession, through his grandmother, would have led them both to see the advantage of combining their strength for resistance. The extirpation of the Pictish race is utterly inconsistent with notices in the Irish annalists, referring to the Picts down throughout the ninth century and farther. In fact, in 876 we find the Ulster Annals referring to Constantine, Kenneth's son, as King of the Picts, so that for a time the name of the united kingdom would seem to have oscillated between that of the Picts and that of the Scots.

Kenneth's reign was a troubled one. He had indeed no inducement to attempt the extirpation of the Picts, as other races threatened to do it to his hand. The Lothians, called Saxonia in the chronicles, was long a disputed territory between the Picts and the Northumbrians. Kenneth endeavoured to make his claim good, and carried war across the Firth of Forth. He burnt the castle of Dunbar, and spoiled Melrose Abbey. At the same time he was himself invaded from two opposite quarters. The Britons of Strathclyde entered his kingdom from the west, burning the town of Dunblane, a town which had taken its name from the earlier St. Blane. The Scandinavians, under the famous Ragnar Lodbrog, entered from the north, extending their devastations to within a few miles of his capital. Kenneth, it is said, removed the famous stone which now sustains the coronation chair at Westminster Abbey, from the ancient seat of the Scottish monarchy in Argyle, to Scone. Notwithstanding recent doubts thrown upon its history, the probability is that this ancient stone was brought from Tara, and that it had been used as a coronation chair by the Irish monarchs. Kenneth's services to.the Church will appear when we treat of its history during his reign. He died at Forteviot in the year 859, leaving one son, Constantine, who afterwards succeeded to the throne, and a daughter, Maolmuire, or the servant of Mary, who married Aodh Fionnlaith, the King of Ireland (Ann. of Ulster). He was buried in Iona.

According to the Tanist law of succession, Donald, the brother of Kenneth, ascended the throne upon the death of the latter. He is called in the Register of St. Andrews, quoted by Innes, Dovenald Mac Alpin. The Albanic Duan applies to him the epithet of *dreachruadh*, or 'ruddy-faced.' The Colbertine MS. attributes to him the restoration of the laws of Aodh fionn, the son of Eochy (Inn., App. ii. 783). This would seem to indicate the introduction of these ancient laws among the Picts. They were probably such laws as those found still existing among the ancient Brehon laws of Ireland. Donald died at a place called in one catalogue Belachoir, in his palace; in another called Veramond, this Veramond being but a corruption of the word Inveralmond, a place at the mouth of the Almond river, in the vicinity of Perth, where the ancient kings had a "rath," or stronghold.

In the year 863, Constantine the son of Kenneth succeeded Donald. The Colbertine MS. (Innes Ess. ii. p. 784) states that three years after Constantine's succession, Olave or Aulay with his people, wasted Pictavia and its inhabitants from the calends of January until St. Patrick's day, a period of nearly three months. The writer adds that the Northmen remained for a year in Pictavia. In the neighbourhood of Dollar in 872 Olave was slain by Constantine in one of the many battles fought at the period. The Northmen would seem to have encircled Scotland by the north and west, seizing the Orkneys and the Hebrides, and making these a stepping-stone to the acquisition of Ireland. From Ireland they issued forth on plundering expeditions, sometimes descending on the coasts of Cumberland· and Westmoreland, and at others on those of Galloway and Kintyre (Munch's Chron. of Man.) At the same time the east coast of Scotland was not overlooked, for every frith and bay formed an inlet for these barbarous and powerful marauders. To the northern hordes must be largely attributed the breaking down of the power both of the Picts and of the Strathclyde Britons. The statements of the Ulster Annals make this sufficiently evident. In 866 "Olave and Auisle went into Fortreim with the Gall (strangers) of Erin and Alban, and laid waste all the Cruitintuait (northern Picts) and carried off hostages." And in 870, "Siege of Alclutha (Dunbarton) by the Northmen, that is by Olave and Ivar, the two kings of the Northmen; they besieged that citadel, and after four months destroyed it, and plundered." In 871 they "return to Dublin from Alban with 200 ships and a great booty of men, Angles, Britons, and Picts." This was the age of Thorstein, who subjected the northern half of Scotland to himself (Annals of Ulster). Constantine is said by the best authorities to have reigned for eighteen years, his reign closing in 881, when, according to the Register of St. Andrews, he was killed fighting with the Northmen at a place called Merdo-fatha, or Werdo, probably the present Perth. His body was conveyed for sepulture to Iona (Inn. Ess. vol. ii., p. 801). The uneasy throne of Constantine was occupied by his brother Aodh or Hugh. The Gaelic bard gives him a reign of two years, which he characterises by *Bu daor a dhath*, 'sad their complexion.' Aodh was slain in a civil broil. Girg or Grig Mac Dungal was Maormor of Mar, the province extending from the Dee to the Spey. Grig became competitor with Aodh for the crown. A battle was fought between the rival candidates in Strathalan (Reg. Prior. of St. And.) where Aodh was slain. The Colbertine MS. places his death at Nrurin (Inverury), the account most likely to be accurate, as the Maormor of Mar was the rebel; but if so Strathalin is probably a mis-reading for Strathdon. Aodh was interred at Iona.

Grig, Girg, or Grigor, as he is variously called, seized the sceptre of Aodh. By the writers of the St. Andrew's Register he is said to have reigned alone for twelve years, to have subdued Ireland and England, and to have been the first king to give liberty to the Pictish Church, which had hitherto been in a state of bondage in accordance with the constitution of the Pictish kingdom. Mr. Robertson understands this to mean the transference of the privileges of Dunkeld to St. Andrew's (Hist. vol. i., p. 50). He is said by this authority to have died at Dundurn or Durrisdeer in Aberdeenshire,[1] and to have

---

[1] There is a Dunearn, a place of note, on the banks of the Findhorn, above Forres which may be Dundurn.

been buried in Iona. The Colbertine MS. (Inn. Ess. 11, 784) states that, apparently to give some legality to his claim, he associated with him on the throne Ku, King of the Britons, a grandson of Kenneth Macalpine, along with whom he was finally expelled from his kingdom. Grig could hardly be destitute of all claim to the throne, as we find that from him is deduced by the seanachies one of the oldest and most powerful of the Scottish clans, the clan Gregor, who are traced through him up to King Alpin, and in virtue of this descent they claim connection with the royal line of Scotland. *Is rioghail mo dhream,* 'royal is my race,' is the ancient motto of this famous clan. If there be exaggeration in the praise bestowed on Grig by the St. Andrew's monks, there may be undue depreciation by the writer of the other account. Innes sets no value on the latter account, and seems in this to be more accurate than Chalmers, who does, but who is always glad to get a charge against Buchanan, who gives a laudatory account of the reign of Grig. Grig died in 897.

To Grig succeeded Donald, the son of Constantine and grandson of Kenneth Macalpine. The Gaelic bard calls him *Cain*, or 'beloved.' History, so far as it exists, shews him to have been brave and patriotic. He lived and reigned during the very heat of the invasions of the Vikingr, and taught these northern spoilers to fear a Scottish foe. Their first assault was from the east, with the apparent determination of reaching the very heart of the Scottish kingdom. They were met by Donald at Collan,[1] a place said by Chalmers to be in the near neighbourhood of Scone, and were defeated with great slaughter. In 904, under Ivar O'Ivar, they invaded Scotland again, as Chalmers thinks, from the west, and were again defeated. Ivar was, according to the Ulster Annals, slain by the men of Fortrenn with great slaughter of his

[1] Innisib Ca''an. Colb. MS.

followers. Chalmers thinks Donald was killed in this battle. The Irish Annals say he died in 900 ; the St. Andrew's Register says he died at Forres, which Chalmers thinks is a mistake for Fortrenn. Donald Mac Constantine or M'Causlan, as now pronounced, was apparently slain in battle by the northmen about the beginning of the tenth century, after a reign of from six to ten years. Conflicting authorities render it impossible to be more accurate in our details.

Let us now return to the Picts, who, in the beginning of this century, were still a separate kingdom. Constantine, the son of Fergus, had ascended the throne in 791, and reigned, according to the Pictish chronicle (Inn. Crit. Ess. ii., 780), for thirty years. He was the friend of the Church, although harassed by the hordes of northern Vikingr. In the Annals of Innisfallen is the following entry for the year 820, " Constantine, son of Fergus, King of Alban died ;" in the Annals of Ulster he is called " King of Fortrenn," where we see the Scottish nomenclature in the process of absorbing the Pictish, a process which extended to the peoples and the languages without the annihilation of the Pictish race maintained by tradition.

Constantine was succeeded by the second Angus Mac Fergus, to whom has been attributed by mistake many of the actions of his great namesake of the previous century. His reign was disturbed like that of his predecessor by the irruptions of the northmen, and after a period of twelve years, according to the Pictish chronicle, it was closed by his death about 835. Under 834 the Ulster Annals note, " Angus Mac Fergus King of Fortrenn died."

Events were telling sorely upon the great Pictish kingdom at this period. Constantine was succeeded by his son Drest, with whom was associated Talorgan, the son of Uthoil. Their conjunct reign lasted but for three years.

Eoganan or Ewen, sometimes spelled Uen, the son of Angus succeeded, but a fierce battle with the Northmen ended in his death, with that of Bran his brother, Aodh son of Boanta, and many others in 839.

Four years were filled up by the precarious reigns of Urech, son of Bargoit, and Bred, when every circumstance conspired to favour the union in 843 of the two great kingdoms of Picts and Scots, probably representing the ancient division of Caledonii and Meatæ, or Deucaledonii and Vecturiones, under the sway of Kenneth Mac Alpine. If the Picts were destroyed, it was by the sword of the Northmen they perished, and not by that of the Scots. Their union with the latter seems to have been the means of their preservation. Scot and Pict had long been at feud, the presence of a common enemy compelled them to unite. Thus closes the history of the great kingdom of the Picts!

There are few notices among the annalists of the Strathclyde Britons during the ninth century. Such as are present them as still maintaining their territory in the midst of frequent conflicts with the Scots, the Picts, the Ulster Cruithne or Picts, and the Northumbrians. In 816 Conan Mac Ruadhrach, *son of Roderick*, king of the Britons, died (Ir. Ann.). In 856 Ruaidhri Mac Merminn was king, for we read that in that year " Horm, leader of the Dubhghall or Northmen," was slain by him (Ir. Ann.). The Welsh annalists make this Roderick successor to his father, whom they style " Mervina Vrych" or Mervinn, the spotted. At this time Strathclyde, like the other neighbouring kingdoms, was suffering from the Vikingr. In 870 Alcluyd or Dunbarton, was beseiged by these marauders under Olave and Ivor. For four months did the seige last, when this ancient strength of the Britons was seized, spoiled, and utterly destroyed (Ann. of Uls.). For a time the monarchs of the united Scots and Picts seem to have had some form of alliance with the Northmen, for in 872 the latter slew Artga, king of Strathclyde, at the suggestion of Constantine Mac Kenneth. The same alliance seems to have given the Scottish monarch an opportunity of practising deceit upon his allies, for in 875 Oistin, son of Olave, was treacherously slain by the Scots. In 877[1] Roderick Mac Merminn fled to Ireland from the hostility of his northern enemies, and returning next year he was slain by the Saxons, who seem in his hour of weakness to have assailed him from the other side. The Cambrian annals associate his brother Guriat with him in his death. The Welsh chronicle calls him his son. The Strathclyde kingdom was gradually weakening under the assaults of the Northmen, thus preparing for its final decay, and like the Pictish, its absorption into the Scottish kingdom, and preparing also for admitting colonies of Irish Cruithne along its coasts in Ayrshire and Galloway, driven, as these probably were, out of their own country by the same invaders who were the means of providing for them a refuge.

Northumbria during this century continued to extend to the Firth of Forth and the boundaries of Strathclyde, extending along the Solway Firth to the borders of Galloway. Little effort was now made to extend its boundaries, the common foe from the *Viks* of the north extending their favours promiscuously to Celt and Saxon. The English coasts were at this time as much infested by the Danes as the coasts of Ireland and Scotland were by the men from the opposite shores of Norway.

During the period under review several important events occurred in the history of the Scottish Church.

[1] A year at least must be added to this date, in order to correct the chronology of the Irish annals.

In the reign of the Pictish king Constantine, a monastic institution was founded at Dunkeld. This was the third of the kind founded in the Pictish kingdom; Abernethy by Nectan in the beginning of the previous century, St. Andrews towards the middle of the same century by Angus M'Fergus; and now Dunkeld in the beginning of the ninth century by Constantine M'Fergus. "Hic edificavit Dunkelden," *He built Dunkeld*, is the statement of the Register of St. Andrews regarding this king. There is no reason to suppose that, as erected by Constantine, Dunkeld had any peculiar connection with Iona, although afterwards a very close connection was formed by the Scottish king. It is probable that like Abernethy or St. Andrews it was a token of the piety of its founder and nothing more. That it became afterwards a refuge for a portion of the relics of Columba is true, but that belongs to a later period in its history. Dunkeld was founded previous to 820, when Constantine died.

Bresal, son of Seighine, Abbot of Iona, died in 801. For thirty-one years, according to the Ulster annals, he filled the chair, and acquired the designation of "Bresal o dertaigh," or *Bresal of the oratory*. In his time pilgrimage to Iona became frequent, the stream of pilgrims becoming increased by the addition to the brethren of two Irish kings (Reeves' Vit. Col., p. 386). And yet it was also a period of sore trial, for the sacred and much loved island had become an object for the cupidity of the Northmen. Such a notice as "Vastatio Iae Colum-cille," *the spoiling of Iona*, tells its own tale. Feradhach Mac Seigine, apparently a brother of Bresal, died in 799, as abbot of Rathlin.

Bresal was succeeded by Conachtach. The annalists call him "scriba selectissimus et abbas Iae," *choicest scribe and abbot of I*. His tenure of office extended only to one year. He died in 802. In this year two events are recorded by the Irish annalists. The one is the burning of Iona by the Northmen, the other is the death of Mac Oigi of Applecross, abbot of Bangor, in Ireland. This Mac Oigi was one of the successors of Maclrubha, and this notice of him sheds some light upon a dark portion in Scottish history. As already noticed Failbhe Mac Guaire succeeded Maelrubha, and was drowned in 737. The death of Mac Oigi is recorded at 802, so that we have probably, with one exception, the succession of ministers at Applecross from the planting of Christianity there for a century and a-half. Maelrubha, belonged originally to the monastery at Bangor, and we see that the connection was kept up, for Mac Oigi was abbot of that monastery as well as incumbent of Applecross. Dr Reeves (Trans. of Soc. of Scot. Ant., vol. iii. pt. 2) thinks that this individual may be discovered in a Ruadhraidh Mor Mac Caoigean, who is known in Applecross tradition, and on whose grave stands a slab still having an incised cross sculptured on it. It is well known that the lands in connection with the early Celtic monarchies were hereditary in the kin of the founder, but not in the case of any individual of the kin, the appointments to office being elective. The lands, however, were usually farmed to a certain individual or family of the kin, who were called *herenachs.* These in the long run became secularized, and their lands became their own like other heritages. It seems that at an early period the O'Beolans, a branch of the same family with Mac Oigi, became herenachs of Applecross, and thus are the direct progenitors of the great family of Ross ; for O'Beolan was the family name until " Farquhar, born in Ross, was created Earl of Ross by King Alexander."[1] The seanachy adds that St. Rice or Rufus (Maelrubha) was of the same tribe with this O'Beolan, saying "they

---

[1] Hist. of M'Donalds in Trans. of Iona Club, p. 304.

were of the Menapii," which does not agree with the story of their Irish descent. There was in the fourteenth century a Sagart ruadh, or *Red priest* in Applecross, whose name was Gille padruig O'Beolan, whose daughter was married to Alexander, Lord of the Isles of Lochalsh, and was mother of Celestine. In this notice of Mac Oigi then we have some light shed on the origin of one of our great northern families. The name Ross, like many others, was assumed from the territory of the family in the age of feudal tenures and charters.

Ceallach succeeded Connachtach in Iona. During his incumbency in 806, the "family at Iona," as it is called, was slain by the Northmen. This seems to have led to an enlarging of the Columban establishment at Kells, or, in Irish, Cennanus, in the county of Meath, in Ireland. The notice of the annalist is, *Constructio novæ civitatis Columcille in Ceninnus*, 'The erecting of the new institution of Columcille in Kells.' This work was accomplished by Ceallach, who made Diarmad, the pupil of Daighre, president. In 815 Ceallach died.

Diarmad of Kells succeeded to the Abbot's chair in Iona, both institutions being apparently held as one. During his presidency the Northmen again laid waste the island. Among those who perished was Blaithmac, son of Flann, afterwards St. Blaithmac. He is said to have concealed the precious shrine containing Columba's relics, and refusing to reveal the place of its concealment, was cruelly put to death. But Iona was no longer a place of security for what was held to be so precious a charge. So in 829 Diarmad, with a portion of the relics, sought for a place of refuge in Scotland. In 831 he carried another portion to Ireland (Annals of Ulst).

The year of Diarmad's death, or of the succession of Innrechtach, is unrecorded. The latter is said to have brought a further portion of Columba's relics to Ireland, while Scotland again received her share, for in 849 "Kenneth, son of Alpin, in the seventh year of his reign, carried the relics of St. Columba to the church which he had built" (Chron. Pict., Inn. App.) Kenneth, it may readily be supposed, would earnestly seek the introduction of the Scottish clergy into his new dominions. Since the days of Nectan, who expelled them, they had probably been in bad odour among the Picts, and their place would seem to have been filled by the Saxon clergy, who, as in the case of Acca, were on the most friendly terms with the Pictish monarchs and people. St. Andrews had been established for a hundred years when the union of the Pictish and Scottish kingdoms took place, and had continued to retain the constitution given by its founder. The Aberdeen Breviary refers at this time to the coming in of Adrian, a Hungarian, with followers to the number of 6606, confessors, clergy, and others. These men finally settled on the Isle of May, where they suffered martyrdom from the Danes in the year 875. It has been conjectured that this was in reality the coming in of the Scottish clergy, with Adrian, sometimes called Odran, a name appearing in the surname of M'Gidran and M'Gladry, a priest of the diocese of Kildare, at their head. (Paper in Trans. of Scott. Ant., by W. F. Skene, Esq., vol. iv., part i., p. 318.) This Adrian is placed by some writers at the commencement of the list of the Bishops of St. Andrews, nor is it improbable that he was the first bishop, of the kind of bishops then existing, who presided over the institution there, after the succession of the Scottish kings to the Pictish throne. Thus did Kenneth restore the Scottish clergy to a place in the Pictish territory, and removed what was held among the Scots to be the reproach of their neighbours, that "they despised the service and precept of God, and were unwilling to hold others in equal esteem with themselves" (Colb. Chron., Inn. Crit. Ess. ii. 783), a charge clearly founded on their expulsion of the Scottish clergy. Innes remarks with truth, that it is utterly unjust to charge such men as Angus and Constantine, the Pictish kings, with impiety, when nothing distinguished the reign of both more than their favour for the Church.

The precarious condition of Iona, from the inroads of the Northmen, and the consequent decline of the institution there, together with the scattering of the relics which had attracted pilgrims thither, led to the rapid rise of other similar establishments. Whether it was to St. Andrews or not Kenneth removed the relics of Columba, it is true that Dunkeld, and not St. Andrews, became the head of the Columban establishments in Scotland, a fact sufficiently verified by the connection long known to exist between Iona and Dunkeld. For a long succession of years, even after the erection of dioceses in the west of Scotland, Iona was held to belong to the diocese of Dunkeld. From this the probability arises, that while Scottish priests were introduced by Kenneth to St. Andrews, the relics of the great Scottish saint were deposited at Dunkeld. And even there they were hardly safe, for in the reign of Kenneth himself the Northmen penetrated as far as Dunkeld (Colb. Chron.). Iona, it is very clear, was at this period rapidly declining in importance. Several causes would have conduced to this. The seat of the monarchy was removed to a much greater distance from it when that became fixed at Forteviot, or Scone. Even as a place of sepulture its inconvenience must have been strongly felt; then the union with the Pictish kingdom must have loosened the ties which bound the Dalriadic kingdom to the ancient Irish monarchies, and the relation with Ireland generally became less close; but more especially the inroads of the

Vikings, in whose path Iona lay as they threaded their way through the western isles, exposing it to constant spoliation, made the maintenance of it in its former grandeur almost a matter of impossibility. The place which the Norsemen had now attained is indicated by the entry at 853 in the Ulster Annals, "Godfrey, son of Fergus, Lord of Innsegall (the islands of the strangers or Hebrides), died."

In 854 Ceallach succeeded Innrechtach in the chair of Columba. He is called son of Ailill, and was Abbot of Kildare as well as of Iona, although the former was not a Columban institution. As the residence of St. Bridget, however, it was closely related to Scotland, which held this saint in high honour, her memory being associated with the institution at Abernethy. From Kildare came Adrian, the first Bishop of St. Andrews, and when Iona began to decline, the Abbot of Kildare became Abbot of the sacred island. Hence the relation between Iona, St. Andrews, Dunkeld, Abernethy, and Kildare. Ceallach lived during the reigns of Kenneth and Donald Mac alpine, and died "in regione Pictorum" (Ann. of Ulst.) in 865 or 866.

Feradhach succeeded. He was son of Cormac, and fell upon troublous times. Among the earliest entries of the annalists during his time is this "Tuathal, son of Artgusso, chief bishop of Fortrenn and abbot of Dunkeld, died." The whole of Scotland was full of war during his time. Vikingr attacked Scots, Picts, Britons, and Saxons indiscriminately, while the Scots attacked the Britons, and were attacked in their turn, the Saxons joining in the assaults of the Scots on their Strathclyde neighbours. The hounds of war have but once to be let loose, and they will find prey for themselves. Again is it recorded by the Ulster annalists in 878 that "the shrine of Columba with his relics, was carried to Ireland for protection from the foreigners."

For eleven years Flann, son of Maelduin filled the chair of Columba from 880, when Feradhach died. Little is recorded of him but that he died in peace. If so, it was peace amidst universal war.

To him succeeded Maelbrighde, or Malbride, the son of Tornan. He too held offices in the Irish Church, for he was abbot of Armagh and Raphoe. Nothing could exhibit more clearly than this the decline of Iona. He is said to have been " Head of the piety of all Ireland, and of the greater part of Europe" (Reeves, Vit. Col., p. 392.) Stone churches were at this time in existence. That at Kells was violated by the Danes in 920 (Ann. Ulst.) Nor is it unlikely that stone buildings of some kind existed at Iona. The oratories and other buildings found still in existence in the Hebrides and elsewhere, built without cement of any kind, and apparently from their style of architecture of the same age with the Pictish towers scattered over the north Highlands, would render this sufficiently probable. It is impossible to visit such remains as exist in North Rona, the Flannan islands, or Ealach naomh, without being convinced of the existence of stone buildings, of a very primitive kind, it is true, in the ninth century.

Malbride died in 927 or 928, after an incumbency of thirty-three years, during which the probability is that Iona was a name and little else. It was a name full of interest to the Irish and Scottish Churches, but the savage cruelty and cupidity of the still heathen northman had stripped it of all its real glory. Time, however, was preparing to work a change. The northman himself was to partake of the blessing which at first he contemned, and his ignorance and barbarism were to give way before the light of Christian truth. Like the Saxon of England in a previous age, so far from conferring benefits, he came to participate in the religion and civilization of the native inhabitants.

Such was the ninth century, a period among the most important in the history of Scotland, whether we consider the union of the two great kingdoms of the Scots and Picts, the inroads and conquests of the northmen, or the rapid and marked development of the Church, and growth of ecclesiastical institutions on the Scottish mainland. No period has been more important, save that of the Reformation, or that of the union of the Scotch and English crowns and kingdoms.

CHAPTER XXI.

THE EVENTS OF THE TENTH CENTURY.

ABOUT the beginning of this century Constantine II., the son of Aodh or Hugh, ascended the throne. Of him the St. Andrew's Register says that "having resigned the kingdom according to God's will, he became abbot of the Culdees in St. Andrews." Here we meet one of the earliest instances of the occurrence of the term Keledeus or Culdee in our chronicles. The earlier part of Constantine's reign of more than forty years was characterized by what was more significant of the steel helmet than of the mitre. He was a brave and sagacious man. Two events of historical importance distinguish his reign. The one of these was the famous battle of Brunanburgh; the other the placing of a member of the royal family of Scotland on the throne of Strathclyde. The Irish chron icles, in Ann. 904, note, "Imhar Ua h-Imhar slain by the men of Fortrenn and a great slaughter around him." This Imhar or Ivor was grandson of Ivor the northman, who had held large possessions in Ireland, and whose family had lost them. We have already noticed the death of Godfrey Mac Fergus, the King of Innsegall or the Hebrides. To him succeeded a person of the name of Caittil or Ketil, a Northman. His sons settled in Ireland, and the Hebrides became thereupon the prey of Vikings from the Scottish and Irish coasts, among others of the sons of Ivor, upon their expulsion from Ireland.

It was in one of their inroads they were defeated by Constantine in 904. After the death of Ivor, Reginald became their leader, and under his able leadership he and his brother Sitric possessed themselves anew of their Irish territory. Having established their power they sailed with a great expedition from Waterford to claim for their countryman Halfdan the throne of Northumbria (Robertson's Early Scot. Kings, vol. i. p. 57). The north-west of England was then in the hands of the Danes, who readily joined the expedition. With their assistance Reginald seized upon York. Edrid king of the Northumbrian Angles sought the assistance of Constantine, who readily consented to assist his neighbours, probably with the view of weakening a common enemy. A battle was fought at Corbridge on Tyne, in which the Angles and Scots were defeated, and Edred slain. Reginald retained his Northumbrian possessions, but the victory was so dearly won that no attempt was made to retaliate on the Scots, and the latter claimed the affair as a victory.

Reginald soon after died, and in 921 his brother Sitric succeeded him. Athelstan, King of England, desirous to secure the support of the Northumbrian Danes, gave him his sister in marriage, but Sitric, dying soon after, Athelstan claimed the territory of Northumbria as by right his own. Sitric left a son, Olave. His brother Godfrey governed the possessions of the race in Ireland. The latter sought the assistance of Constantine on behalf of his nephew, but Constantine preferred the alliance of Athelstan to that of the northern adventurers. Time, however, brought about changes in the relation of Constantine to the Danes. Olave, the son of Sitric, married his daughter, and from that time his relations with England were disturbed. Athelstan appeared with an army on the banks of the Forth, reached Forteviot, laying waste the province, while a fleet swept round the coast as far as the Pentland Firth.

In 937 Constantine, with two Olaves one the son of Sitric, the other the son of Godfrey, made preparations for seizing from the former of these the lands of Northumbria. Supported by allies from Strathclyde and Wales, they invaded the province. Athelstan hastily collected his forces, made up of mixed masses of Saxons and loyal Danes. At first success attended the invaders, the English forces being defeated in various skirmishes. Negotiations were attempted and broken off, and at length the rival armies met on the field of Brunanburgh. Here after a furious fight Constantine and his allies were defeated, and a glorious victory fell to Athelstan. Constantine retired with the loss of a son. This victory led for a time, but only for a time, to the establishment of the English power in Northumbria.

The other great event of Constantine's reign had reference to the kingdom of Strathclyde. The royal families of that kingdom and of Scotland had become related by marriage in the time of Kenneth Macalpine, whose daughter had married the existing King of the Britons. This lady had a son called Eocha, who afterwards succeeded to the throne of Scotland. In 878 a great migration of the Strathclyde Britons to Wales took place, leading, as it is thought, to the establishing of a part of the present British population in North Wales. But let that be as it may, it led to the weakening of the Strathclyde kingdom to such an extent, that Constantine secured the election of his own brother Donald as king, and as with the Picts, the way was paved for the final union of the kingdom of Strathclyde with that of Scotland, which took place a hundred years after.

In 943 Constantine abdicated his throne, and retired to St. Andrews, where he became abbot of the monastery,

an office, as has well been observed (Robertson's Early
Scot. Kings, vol. i., p. 67, note), not necessarily ecclesiastical, and where he continued for nine years, assuming the
sword for a short period, as is said, in 949 in a renewed
attempt of his son-in-law, Olave, upon Northumbria, and
dying about the year 952 (Reg. St. And.). Thus died
one of the greatest of the early Scottish kings, the cotemporary of Alfred of England, and one having not a little
in common with him, although history has done less justice to his memory. He thoroughly vindicated the skill
and courage of the Scot as against the Northmen, having
completely crushed the power of the latter in his dominions,
but wearied with the bloodshed of a turbulent reign he
sought for his declining years the peace and seclusion of
a monastery. He died at St. Andrews, and was buried
there and not at Iona.   (Inn. Chron. p. 802).

Constantine II. was succeeded in 943 by Malcolm the
I., son of Donald the II.   It was in the early part of his
reign that Constantine came forth from his monastic
seclusion, and assumed the sword on behalf of Olave, son
of Sitric, his son-in-law.   Malcolm had previously to this
received Cumberland from Edmund of England, on condition of his firm alliance.   This arrangement continuing
has been thought to have trammelled Malcolm in the efforts
in favour of Olave. (Rob. Early Scot. Kings i., 72).   At
a future period he joined his forces with those of the English and Britons against the Northmen, but unsuccessfully.
Olave had finally to retire to Dublin, where he established
his power, until broken by the battle of Tara in 980.
After this, like Constantine, weary of war and bloodshed
he sought for seclusion and peace, and retired to Iona.
In 954 Malcolm was slain at Uluru or Auldearn in Moray,
by the Moravienses, and was buried in Iona, according to
the Register of St. Andrews.   The MS. quoted by Innes
(Crit. Ess., p. 787) says he was slain by the men of Moerne

in Fodresach, that is Claideom. If Moerne stands for the modern Mearns, the two authorities differ widely. The long continued struggle between the northern Picts and the Scottish kings, together with the names of the places recorded in Uluru or Auldearn, and Fodresach or Forres, would indicate that Moray was meant by both the chroniclers. It has been remarked (Robertson's Scot. und. her early Kings, i. 75) that the slaughter of Ceallach, Maormor of Moray may have led to the death of Malcolm. At least the MS. quoted by Innes (Crit. Ess., p. 786) says that Malcolm proceeded to Moray with an army, and slew Ceallach in the seventh year of his reign.

Malcolm was succeeded by Indulf in 954. He reigned for eight years. This king is called in Gaelic Illolb, and Flann's synchronisms add "Constantin," making him son of Constantine. In his time we read that the town of Eden was vacated and left to the Scots. (Inn. Crit. Ess., p. 787). This may be either Carriden or Edinburgh. But whichever it is, the notice is indicative of the extension of a Scottish population into the Lothians. The same authority narrates that the fleet of the Sumerlids (Sumerlidiorum) was destroyed in Buchan. These were the Northmen, who, being summer visitors, received this name suggestive not of bloodshed, but of the warmth and verdure of summer. The name seems to have settled into an ordinary proper name, Somerled, well known in the history of the Clan Donald. Indulf was slain by the Northmen at Inverculan (Cullen), (Inn. Crit. Ess., p. 802) and was buried in Iona.

To Indulf or Illolb succeeded Dubh or Duff, son of Malcolm, called in one MS. "Niger," the Latin equivalent for the Gaelic Dubh or Black. Like several of his predecessors we find him fighting in the north. Duff was son of Malcolm I., but Indulf had left a son who represented a younger branch of the royal family. A feud would appear to have arisen between these two families, having its origin in a struggle for the crown. A battle was fought at a place called Dorsum crup (Crit. Ess., p. 787) in Latin, but in the vernacular Drum crup,[1] in which Duff was victorious. In this battle there fell Duncan, abbot of Dunkeld, and Dubhdubh Maormor of Athole. These seem to have been the supporters of Colin, who were drawn apparently from the district of Athole. At an after period Duff was dispossessed of his crown which Colin seized, and finally we read (Crit. Ess., p. 802) that he was slain at Forres, and his body hidden under the bridge of Kinloss, where it lay concealed, the chronicler reporting that during the period of its concealment the sun never made his appearance. Duff was interred in Iona, which in despite of the northern irruptions, still continued to be the depository of the dust of the Scottish kings. With whom his last battle was fought is not said, but the Moravienses had never hitherto been reduced to complete submission to the Scoto-Pictish throne, while it is not improbable that, as in the case of his predecessor Indulf, the enemies of Duff were the restless and adventurous northmen, who had now become a great power in the North of Scotland and the Isles.

His rival Colin, called Culen-rig or Colin the king, succeeded Duff, ascending the throne about the year 967. All we read of him in one MS. is, that he and his brother Eochy were slain by the Britons (Inn. Crit. Ess., p. 788), while another relates that he was slain by Andarch, son of Donald, in Lothian, on account of some insult given by the king to his daughter (Inn. Crit. Ess., p. 802).

Kenneth the II., brother to Duff, succeeded to the throne in 971. He carried an army into Strathclyde and ravaged the country as far as the heart of Cumberland,

---

[1] The place is called by some authorities Monaghard, which is understood to be Monievaird in Perthshire. If so the Drum crup or Drum craoibh, is in all probability the modern Crieff.

but mány of his troops were slain, and on his return he is said to have fortified the fords of the Forth. Immediately thereafter he carried an army into the territory of the Saxons, which he laid waste, carrying away captive a daughter of the king, probably of Northumbria. His last war seems to have been with his own subjects in the old Maormorship of Angus. Finella, daughter of Cunechat, *Kenneth*, or as some say, *Connor*, Maormor of that province, married, and had an only son. This son was slain by Kenneth at Dunsinane, whether in punishment of some crime, or for the purpose of weakening the power of his family, we can hardly tell. But the mother evidently had long studied revenge, and on a visit of Kenneth to her residence at Fettercairn he was slain. It has been thought that till this time the Maormorship of Angus was in some measure independent of the Scottish crown, never having thoroughly yielded to its supremacy, that the death of the young chief took place in course of an effort on the part of Kenneth for its reduction, and that Kenneth himself was on a visit to the quarter at the time of his death, for exacting the usual royal privileges of *cain* and *cuairt*, or a certain tax and certain provision for the king and his followers when on a journey, due by the chiefs or landholders of the kingdom (Rob. Scot. und. her ear. Kings, vol. i. 88, *n*). Under this king's reign several of our earlier historians have recorded the battle of Luncarty, when the famous Hay rallied the scattered Scots, and secured for them a victory over the Scandinavians, and when Scotland obtained her badge of the Thistle, which, pricking the sole of a Northman, constrained him to utter the cry which discovered the presence of the invaders to the unwatchful Scots.

Constantine III. succeeded Kenneth II. He was son of Colin, and descendant of Constantine II. The Chronicle (Inn. Crit. Ess., p. 802) so often quoted, says of him, that he was slain by Kenneth, son of Malcolm I at Rathveramon, or the castle at the mouth of the Almond, near Perth. His reign lasted for two years.

The successor of Constantine was his rival, Kenneth, usually called Kenneth III., who succeeded in 997. The MS. in Innes (Crit. Ess., p. 802), gives the name of Girg, probably a mistake for Grim, an epithet applied to this king, son of Kenneth here ; but Flann, the Albanic Duan, and all our chief authorities make Kenneth himself king—the Albanic Duan calls him " The son of Duff," giving four years to his reign. He seems to have reigned, however, till the year 1005, when he was slain at Monievaird, by Malcolm, son of Kenneth II.

During the whole of the century under review, the north and north-west of Scotland were exposed to the continual irruptions of the Northmen. Besides the " Goill," or foreigners from Ireland, irruptions were frequent from the Orkneys, Caithness and the coast of Sutherland, which with the opposite coasts of Moray and Buchan, were to a large extent under the sway of the Northern earls. Such names as Eric Blodœxe, Thorfin the skull cleaver, Einar, Liotr, and Thorstein, have left themselves indelibly engraved on the history of the century. Sometimes the foreigners entered into alliance with the native chiefs, as in the case of Thorfin, who married the daughter of Duncan Maormor of Caithness, or of Groa, sister of Thorstein, who married the same Duncan ; but usually their relation to the natives was that of cruel aggressors, who, however, found for the most part that the Scottish kings and their people were their superiors in war. It is interesting to notice, that in 976 Tighernac enters Cellach M'Findgaine (M'Kinnon) Cellach Mac Bairedh and Doncadh Mac Morgain (now M'Kay) as " tres comites Alban." These were Maormors.

The British population of Strathclyde had, during the century, emigrated largely to Wales, fleeing from the terror of the ferocious Vikings. They had now received a king, like the Picts, from the all-absorbing Scots, but their power was a declining one, their declension preparing them for a final union with their northern neighbours.

The south-east of Scotland was still Anglo-Saxon, but the Scots were pushing their way southwards, and encroaching rapidly on the Teutonic power, both in Northumbria and Cumbria.

The history of the Church during this century is shrouded in much darkness. A time of perpetual warfare is not one favourable to literature, and while we have still existing several literary relics of a previous age, of much value, we have few of this century. The chiefs of Iona were now resident in Ireland. The place was still famous, and the Scottish kings were still interred there, but it was desolated by the northern invaders, and its pristine glory was being overborne by the rising glory of St. Andrews and Dunkeld. It was natural to expect that the Scoto-Pictish kings would interest themselves in these recent institutions of their own founding.

Maolbrighde, with whom the former century closed as Abbot of Iona, continued to hold the office till 927, when he died. Being Abbot of Armagh, his connection with Iona must have been very much nominal. Hence, during his period, the Irish annalists relate few events belonging to the history of the Church in Scotland. During Maolbrighde's incumbency within this century, Constantine the Second was king. Like his predecessor of the same name, he was the friend of the Church, and was zealous for her power and purity. The Northmen had laid waste Dunkeld, but this did not hinder steps for the consolidating of the Church. In the year 906, Constantine,

along with Kellach, a bishop, and the Scots, bound themselves to observe the laws and discipline of the faith, and
the rights of churches and of the gospel on the hill of
the faith, near the royal city of Scone (Colb. MS., Inn.
Crit. Ess., p. 786). This has been called a council, and
by the same authority the bishop is said to have been
Fothad, Bishop of St. Andrews (Rob. Scot. und. her
Earl. Kings, i. 53). But the only authority of any
value, as quoted above, states distinctly that the bishop
was Kellach; and so far from making him Bishop of St.
Andrews, it makes him merely a bishop. Nor can we
call the convention a council unless we are prepared to
admit the laity to a place in ecclesiastical councils; for
in this case the Scots were present with their bishop
at the deliberations. Many authorities are quoted
with respect to this Kellach, fixing his See (Keith's
Bishops, pp. 5, 6, 7), but all of a date too recent to be
of any value. There was no such thing as a bishop of
St. Andrews in the tenth century. There was very
probably a bishop in St. Andrews, but no one who
values evidence can say that there was a regular
diocesan See of St. Andrews in the days of Constantine II. (See note, Reeves' Vit. Col., p. 393.) The
abbots were, according to the old Celtic system, the
heads of the ecclesiastical institutions, called now monasteries,—institutions, however, in which the monks were
not what monks afterwards became. Constantine himself, as already related, like some other monarchs,
weary of the burden of government, spent his last
years in St. Andrews, having, as the Colbertine MS.
relates, "assumed the staff in his decrepit old age, and
served the Lord."

This period is marked by the decease of Cormac
M'Cuileanan, the King-bishop of Cashel, said to be
the author of the Psalter of Cashel, and of the famous

glossary of the ancient Irish tongue, called · Cormac's Glossary.

In Iona Maolbrighde was succeeded by Dubhthach, called the son of Dubhan. He was Abbot of Raphoe, and as the Irish writers express it, was Coarb, or successor of Columba, both in Scotland and Ireland. He held the office for eleven years, and was succeeded in 938 by Robhartach. There is some confusion here in the succession of the abbots, but the office itself was purely nominal, Iona being no safe place of residence for unarmed ecclesiastics. Robhartach held the office till 954. He was succeeded by Dubhduin, who continued in office till 959. Dubhscuile succeeded him, and died in 964. During his time the following entry appears in the Annals of the Four masters for 963 : "Fothadh Mac Brain, scribe, and Bishop of the isles of Alban, died." Some writers call him Bishop of St. Andrews. In the Supplement of Fordun he is called "first Bishop of the Scots," and is said to have been expelled by Indulf, and to have lived eight years after his expulsion. If this story be true, the story of Adrian cannot be true, but the story of Adrian is better vouched for than that of Fothadh, who was not in the ordinary sense "primus episcopus" among the Scots. There was no "primus episcopus" in point of rank at the time, and there had been very many bishops among the Scots, such as bishops were, before the days of Fothadh. The latter was evidently a bishop among the Scots in the tenth century, but taking our different authorities together, he would appear to have had both St. Andrews and the islands of the west within the field of his labours. Keith has not a particle of authority for making him Bishop of St. Andrews. The "primus" in Fordun's Supplement may refer to Fothadh as being the bishop of most note among the Scots.

In 964 Mughron became head of the institution at Iona.

In his time Duncan, abbot of Dunkeld, was slain at the battle of Drum Crup (Crieff), an incident which lets us in to the character and position of churchmen at the period. A kind of episcopacy begins also to show itself even at Iona, where hitherto the abbot was supreme. "In 966 Finghin, anchorite, Bishop of Iae died" (Ann. of Ulst.) This was to be looked for from the union of the Scottish and Pictish crowns. The Picts had been long in friendly alliance with the Saxon Church, which had adopted the Roman model. The union provided for the extension of a similar influence among the Scots. Such unions have seldom left religion untouched, the peculiar beliefs and forms of the lesser kingdom being ever exposed to the modifying influence of the greater. Scotland has more than once in its history presented an instance of such influences, producing remarkable changes, and usually for the worse. In the tenth century Saxon England was exercising an influence over the Church planted by Columba, which was to culminate in the twelfth. In the Scottish annals under the reign of Colin, who was cotemporary of Mughron, we read that Leot and Sluaghadach went to Rome. Rome was beginning to draw the Scottish clergy towards her. Maelbrighde the bishop died, and Cellach ruled (Inn. Crit. Ess., p. 788.) Innes at once puts these down as bishops of St. Andrews without one shred of authority. No authority of the period acknowledges any bishop of St. Andrews. Another office appears at this time in the Columban Church, for in 978 Fiachra Ua h-Artagain "aircinneach" of Iona died. This is sometimes called "Erenach." The word is probably derived from *Air cheann*, meaning 'at the head of,' and denotes superiority. It is said to have indicated in the Church the person who held the local supremacy without being the successor in office of Columba (Reeves Vit, Col., p. 864).

Maelciarain succeeded Mughron in 980. The only important event related during his presidency is that which occasioned his death. It appears that he resided at Iona, and that in 986 the Danes made an unsuccessful inroad with three ships. Landing in Dalriada, 140 of them were taken and hanged and the rest slain ; but a new expedition was undertaken, in which Iona was laid waste, and on Christmas night the abbot and fifteen monks were slain. Even at this period the mass of the northmen were heathen.

Duncan succeeded Maelciarain in 986. In his period the Danes suffered sorely for their cruelty in Iona. They were assailed in turn by whom the annals say not, but probably by the Scottish king. Three hundred and sixty of these sacrilegious marauders perished. Two years after Godfrey, son of Harald, King of the Island Danes, was slain in one of these frequent conflicts.

Dubhdaleithe succeeded Duncan. He was abbot of Armagh, and was elected by the joint voices of the Scots and Irish as head of the Columban order in both Scotland and Ireland. During his period Kenneth M'Malcolm, or the Second, held the Scotch government in his vigorous grasp. We have already referred to his reduction of the province of Angus to submission, the final cause of his death ; and he gave the Church evidence of his extended power, for it was he who gifted Brechin to the Lord (Inn. Crit. Ess., p. 788). It is not by any means improbable that the round tower of Brechin, about which antiquaries have written so much, is of the period of this great king. If so, it belongs to a period 200 years later than the kindred tower at Abernethy, erected probably by the equally famous Nectan in the eighth century. Dubhdaleithe died in 998.

Muiredhach succeeded him. He was Bishop of Armagh, and successor both of Columba and Patrick, the two offices being now often united in the same person. But a change was manifestly passing over the state of the Columban Church, for during his presidency Maolbrighde Ua Rimhedha was abbot of Iona. It is very probable that as the Scottish Church was separating more and more from that of Ireland, the Scots would incline towards a clergy of their own nation. Nor would the Northmen, who were now founding their island kingdom, and becoming Christianized, be satisfied with entire dependence upon Ireland for a supply of clergy. Hence the nominal headship of the Columban order in Ireland, while Iona was coming again to enjoy the presidency of its own abbots. With Muiredhach in office the tenth century closes. He died in the year 1007.

The principal events in the history of the Scottish Church in this century will be found associated with the gradual separation of Scotland from Ireland, and the growth of the Scandinavian power in the west. This power came in, in fact, as a wedge between the two ancient Celtic kingdoms, and did more to detach them than any other cause. As the fruit of this the Columban Church became disunited. A portion of it became purely Irish and another Scottish. We have followed the Irish lists given by Dr. Reeves in our account of the Iona abbots, but these furnish us simply with the Irish heads of the order, and we have no warrant to believe that their authority was acknowledged in the Scottish Church. It is questionable whether during a long period in this century there was any abbot of Iona, but latterly we see an abbot alongside of the Irish president, as might be looked for in the case of a Scottish ecclesiastical institution. The Scottish Church was at the same time yielding to influences assailing it from the south and east, and thus preparing for the great changes awaiting it in the days of Malcolm III. and his son David.

CHAPTER XXII.

THE civil history of the tenth century closed with Kenneth III. upon the throne. He being slain in battle at Monievaird in Strathearn, was succeeded by his conqueror, Malcolm, son of the great Kenneth II. In the Register of St. Andrews Malcolm is called *Rex Victoriosissimus*, 'a most victorious king.' In the Colb. MS. it is said, " He fought a great battle at Carham. On that day he distributed rich offerings among the churches and the clergy." Malcolm began his reign by an attack on Northumbria, where Scottish influence was rapidly extending. His first raid was unsuccessful, as his attack was repelled by Uchtred, son of Waltheof the Ealdorman. The armies met at Durham, and the battle was fatal to many of the Scots, whose heads were exposed on stakes round the walls of the city.

At the same time Finlay Mac Rory father of Macbeth, Maormor of Moray, whose family had been the keenest opponents of the Scottish crown, was beaten in battle by Sigurd, the northern Jarl. The defeat was a relief to Malcolm, who gave his daughter to Sigurd in marriage. Of this marriage was born the great Thorfin, son of Sigurd. In 1014 Sigurd was killed in the famous battle of Clontarf, in which the Northmen were vanquished by Brian Boroimhe, King of Ireland, and Thorfin was confirmed by his grandfather Malcolm in the earldom of Sutherland and Caithness.[1]

In the meantime events were preparing in Northum bria for another invasion by Malcolm. Uchtred, his suc cessful opponent had been put to death, and Eadulf Cudel, his brother, a man of no vigour, succeeded him. Malcolm collected his forces and marched into Northum-bria. A comet had for many days alarmed the Northum-brians, but they met the army of Malcolm at Carham on the Tweed. After a disastrous defeat the Northumbrian commander sought for peace, and obtained it on condi-tion of ceding to the Scots all the territory north of the Tweed. Thus for the first time did Scotland extend to the banks of that famous river.

In 1031 Malcolm met a new adversary in the person of Canute the English king. The Anglo-Saxon chronicle states that " This year King Canute went to Rome. And so soon as he came home then went he into Scotland ; and the King of the Scots, Malcolm, submitted to him and became his man, but that he held only a little while, and two other kings, Macbeth and Jehmar." It is not easy reading this notice accurately, or deciding whether Malcolm became the vassal of Canute for the Lothians or his ally, but the transaction seems to have been one of little historical consequence.

In the year 1033 the Irish annalists notice that Mac mhic Boete mic Cineadha was slain by Malcolm Mac Cineadha. This has been thought to imply an attempt by Malcolm to secure the throne for his own immediate de-scendants, contrary to the old Scottish law of collateral suc-cession. If so the attempt would appear to have been suc-

---

[1] The battle in which Sigurd perished was fatal to several of the Scottish magnates. The Ulster Annals narrate that Donald Mac Eoghain, Mhic Coinnich, Maormor of Mar, and Murdoch, Maormor of Lennox, were killed fighting on the opposite side from Sigurd, called Sichfrith Mac Lodair iarla de Innsi h-orc.

cessful, for Malcolm was succeeded by his grandson (Rob. Scot. under her Early Kings, i. 97.) Malcolm is said to have been slain at Glammis in Angus in the year 1034.

ˑTwo important events belong to the reign of Malcolm; the first was the extending of the Scottish frontier to the Tweed, and the second was the amalgamating of the kingdom of Strathclyde with that of Scotland. The last king of Strathclyde of whom we read was Eoghan or Ewen, a direct descendant of the Scottish kings of that territory. On his death Duncan, afterwards king of Scotland, succeeded, and thus by natural succession did another crown fall into the hands of the Scottish kings. The invasions of the Northmen might have been a sore visitation for Scotland, but they manifestly contributed to the final consolidation of the Scottish kingdom. To them was owing the weakening both of the Pictish and Strathclyde kingdoms, leading to their final junction with that of the Scots. Malcolm II. is justly entitled to a place of no common eminence among Scottish kings.

To Malcolm succeeded Duncan, called in the Register of St. Andrews Donchath Mac Trini abbatis de Dunkeld, *Duncan, son of Trini (or Crinan) Abbot of Dunkeld.* According to Celtic law, the crown should have reverted at this juncture to the line of Kenneth III., son of Duff. Malcolm was the son of Kenneth the Second. The line of Kenneth III., the senior branch of the house of Alpin, was deprived of a male representative by the slaughter of the son of Boete or Bute, son of Kenneth, as narrated above. Malcolm had no son himself, and his elder daughter Bethoc was married to Crinan, abbot of Dunkeld. But Bute[1] left female representatives, too, one of whom Gruoch married Gilcomgain, son of Malbride Mac Rory, who is called by

---

[1] From some of these Butes the island of Bute is probably named.

the Irish annalists "Rex Alban," King of Scotland. In 1029 this Gillecomgain with fifty followers was burnt in his own house. He was at the time Maormor of Moray and transmitted the right to this hereditary dignity to an infant son Lulach, whom the Scottish annalists call "fatuus." Gruoch married a second time Macbeth Mac Finlay, himself a near relative of the house of Moray, being first cousin of Gillecomgain, and carried to him the rights of her father's house, as well as the guardian-ship of the young Lulach. Never were claims to an inheritance more righteous than those of Macbeth, whose memory has suffered much injustice at the hands of historians, as well as at those of the great English drama-tist. His wife was in fact the lawful representative of the ancient Scottish kings. But the house of Athole, to which Crinan belonged, being the representative of that ancient Maormorship, proved too strong for that of Moray, and the son of Bethoc, daughter of Malcolm the Second, succeeded his grandfather on the throne. This is the Duncan of Shakespeare's great tragedy.

Duncan had previous to his succession ruled Strath-clyde, so that he was not altogether ignorant of govern-ment, and he succeeded to a throne whose rights and dignity had been amply upheld by his predecessor. He had difficulties connected with the opposition of the family of Moray, but as a set off to those his cousin Thorfin, son of Sigurd and another daughter of Malcolm, ruled in Sutherland and Caithness and latterly in Orkney, and between him and the son of Finlay, the old anta-gonist of his father, there could be no peace. In this manner the northern Maormor was in some measure kept in check. Thorfin held his earldom from the Scottish king, but it soon became evident that such thraldom was distasteful to him; and refusing the service which his tenure implied, Duncan at an early period of his reign appointed Moddan in his place, and sent an army with him to enforce his claims. But the expedition was unsuccessful, and ended in the slaughter of Moddan himself in the neighbourhood of Thurso. At the time of Moddan's expedition the king made a raid into England, but it was unsuccessful. He suffered a defeat close to Durham, a place frequently unfortunate for the Scottish arms.

Meantime, upon the slaughter of Moddan, Thorfin carried his victorious troops across the Moray Firth, where Duncan lay on his return from an unsuccessful expedition to support Moddan with his fleet. A battle was fought in the neighbourhood of Burghead, in which the Scottish army was routed. The northern Jarl upon this, extended his devastations southwards, and wasted the country as far as the Firth of Forth. In the meantime Duncan had perished at Bothgowanan, said to be near Elgin, most probably by the machinations of Macbeth.[1] The Register of St. Andrews says he was slain by Macbeth Mac Finleg in Bothgowanan, and buried at Iona. Internal dissensions were more ruinous to the interests of Duncan than the enmity of the Northman. He perished by the hand of a countryman, a subject, and a relative, at the very time that he was contending against the common enemy of his country and his race. His death occurred in 1040.

Macbeth succeeded to the throne, which the murder of Duncan had rendered vacant, not without legal rights to it of the first order, although these were enforced in a manner so execrable. Much that is written of him is fiction, besides what was written by Shakespeare. The historians of rival races are not apt to be very particular in their narratives, which are prone to regard the stigma-

---

[1] There is a Boath between Nairn and Forres, close to the village of Auldearn, which may be the place of Duncan's assassination. The "Gowanan" is lost, a kind of change not uncommon in topography.

tising of an adversary more than the maintenance of truth. Macbeth did not enjoy his honours in peace. In 1045 the following entry occurs in the Irish annals :— "A battle among the Scots in which Cronan (Crinan), abbot of Dunkeld, was slain." There is little room to doubt that this was an attempt of Crinan in favour of his grand-children, and that the entry quoted chronicles his defeat by Macbeth.

In 1052 Macbeth got into difficulties with his neighbours of Saxon England. A hospitable reception afforded to fugitives from the court of Edward the Confessor provoked the ire of Earl Godwin and the hostility of the English power, and an expedition of the English against him headed by Siward, Earl of Northumbria, ended in the defeat of Macbeth, with the loss of 3000 men. (Ir. Ann. 1054). It is questioned and with reason (Robertson's Scot. under her early Kings, i. 123) whether it was Siward who reinstated the family of Duncan on the Scottish throne, the statement being made by English historians always wishful to establish the right of England to interfere in Scottish affairs. But however that may be, Siward's victory must have materially weakened the power of Macbeth, and paved the way for his defeat and death at Lumphanan, in the valley of the Dee. The entry in the Irish annals under 1058, is to the effect that Macbeth was slain by Malcolm, son of Duncan. A similar entry under the same year narrates the death of Lulach, Macbeth's stepson, by the same hand. There is no mention by these writers of Macduff, but it is quite possible that the Maormor of Fife had an active share in restoring the line of Athole to the throne of Scotland. Macbeth is said to have been a good king, and to have reigned during a period of much external prosperity. His reign terminated an era in Scottish history, for with his rival and successor, Malcolm Ceannmor, began a series of changes which converted Scotland from a Celtic into a Saxon kingdom, and laid a foundation for the introduction of the feudal system. In fact, feudal ideas had been making way for years in Scotland, and indicated their existence by the change in the mode of succession to the crown introduced by Malcolm II., although the arrangement then made was disturbed for a time by Macbeth.[1]

In 1058 Malcolm Ceann mòr, or *large head,* succeeded to the throne. It has been said that on the death of his father Duncan, the young prince was conveyed to England, and that he remained there until the success of the Northumbrian Siward against Macbeth opened his way to the throne. It has been farther said that it was to his early English training that Malcolm's future sympathy with Saxon ideas and customs was due. But this portion of Malcolm's life is extremely obscure, nor is there sufficient evidence to establish that he was in England at all at the time.

In the early part of Malcolm's reign the great Thorfin, son of Sigurd, died, leaving a young widow named Ingiobiorge. She became the first wife of the Scottish king. This is the earliest event we know in his reign. A period now approached, perhaps the most important in the early history of Britain—the period of the invasion of England by William the Norman. This period was one fraught with important consequences to Scotland. Internal troubles in Northumbria had previously sent some of the Northumbrian magnates across the Tweed, where they

---

[1] The name Macbeth—Macbeathadh or Mac Bheathaig—*son of Bethoc,* is a curious one. It is in the form of a surname, and is the only instance the writer knows of such a form in the case of a Christian name among the old Celts. It would describe Macbeth's rival Duncan, who was in reality the son of Bethoc, more accurately than Macbeth himself. Macbeth's mother, however, may have been Bethoc too, although the Gael rarely named a man from his mother. Fingal was called Mac Muirne from his mother. Macbeth may have been a clan name, though it is not likely.

met with a hospitable reception from the Scots ; but the government of William, stern and uncompromising towards the ancient races, whether Saxons or Danes, led to the flight of large numbers of the first families in England across the border. In 1068 Edgar the 'atheling' or *young prince*, with his mother and two sisters, sought refuge in Scotland. From Scotland Edgar attempted to repair his fortune. On one occasion Malcolm seems to have co-operated with him, for marching from Cumberland, then attached to the Scottish crown, he ravaged Northumberland and York, and carried away so many captives, that besides those who perished, every family in the south of Scotland could have an abundant supply of Saxon slaves. The Scottish king had in the meantime welcomed Edgar and his household to his court, where they met with the most hospitable treatment. Malcolm soon after married Margaret, the sister of Edgar, who was induced with some difficulty to agree to the union, although at first opposed to it from a desire to enter a monastery, her mind being deeply impressed by the misfortunes of her family.

The raid of Malcolm into the north of England was followed by a terrible famine, and a farther body of the inhabitants were impelled to flee to Scotland, some of them to sell themselves as slaves. Thus, in the reign of Malcolm, three things operated to fill Scotland with a Saxon population—the conquest of England by William the Norman, the escape thither of the English royal family with their followers, and the immigration of the people of Northumbria, some led as captives, and others impelled by famine. There is reason to believe that the number of English in the south of Scotland about the middle of the eleventh century, was greater than that of the original inhabitants.

William of England was no indifferent spectator of the acts of Malcolm, and with a view of punishing the active sympathy shown by him for his rivals, he marched an army into Scotland, penetrating as far as Abernethy, on the Tay. Here, instead of a battle, an agreement was entered into, Malcolm receiving twelve manors from William, and an annual payment of twelve marks of gold, and giving in return his eldest son, Duncan, as a hostage to the English king (Sim. of Durham). At this time Cospatrick, the founder of the great Scottish family of Dunbar, received the castle of that name, with the adjoining territory, from Malcolm.[1]

After this peace with the English Malcolm was constrained to carry his arms to the north. The men of Moray, although their head was dispossessed of the throne, were still restless and dissatisfied. In the Irish Annals, at 1085, we read that Malsnecta Mac Lulaigh, King of Moray, died. It is to this Malsnecta the Anglo-Saxon Chronicle must refer under 1077, when it says, that " Malcolm won the mother of Malslaye, and all his best men and all his treasure and his oxen, and himself hardly escaped." Malcolm would seem to have finally crushed the power of the Moray men.

It is not improbable that this was the period when Malcolm founded the bishopric of Mortlach, the first of the kind in Scotland, and commenced a long course of policy, which ended in the establishment of a complete hierarchy in the kingdom, including the supplanting of the old Scottish Church.

In 1091 William the Conqueror died, and was succeeded by William Rufus. A few years after William's death, Edgar, the brother of Queen Margaret of Scotland, who had received a grant of lands in Northumberland, was expelled from these by Rufus, and again retired to Scotland. Malcolm took up strenuously the cause of

---

[1] If Cospatrick was a Norman, the name is apparently Celtic.

his injured brother-in-law, and marched an army into England. He became soon alarmed, however, for the safety of his troops, and speedily retreated. An attempt of the English king to revenge this raid ended in the reconciliation of William and Edgar, with the promise of the restoration of the latter to his possessions, a promise which never was kept.

Malcolm having demanded the fulfilment of William's promises, it was arranged, in 1093, that the two kings should meet at Gloucester. Malcolm arrived, but found himself treated by the haughty Norman as if he had been a subject. Homage was demanded of him, which he refused, and indignant at the offered insult, he left the English court. Having drawn an army together, Malcolm marched across the border, and met De Mowbray, Earl of Northumbria, near Alnwick. Here Malcolm perished, along with his son Edward, as some say by the treachery of Morel of Bamborough (Sim. of Durham). His body was at first buried at Tynemouth, but afterwards, in the reign of his son Alexander, it was removed, to be laid beside that of his queen in Dunferm line. He was the first of the Scottish reigning monarchs whose dust was not laid in Iona, a change significant of greater and more important changes.

A sketch of Malcolm's reign would be imperfect without marked reference to the character and influence of Margaret, his queen. Margaret was a woman of no common character, judging by the notices of her life furnished by Turgot, her confessor, and other authorities. She was somewhat unwillingly hindered from entering a monastery by her marriage with Malcolm, and the latter repaid the obligation by unbounded devotion to her, and readiness to fall in with all her schemes. She was brought up in the Anglo-Saxon Church, as that Church was moulded by Augustine and other emissaries of

Rome, and was in consequence naturally opposed to many of the peculiarities of the Scottish Church, which was still without diocesan bishops, and had many things in its forms of worship peculiar to itself. She was farther ignorant of the Gaelic language, the language at the time of the Scottish Court, and required the services of Malcolm, who, from his frequent intercourse with England, knew the English tongue, in communicating with her new subjects. She aided much in hastening on the development of the Roman Church in Scotland, as will be seen in sketching the history of the Church at the time, a history which brings out, therefore, the curious fact, that it is to the Saxons that Scotland is indebted for the introduction of the whole system of ecclesiastical Rome. Ceolfrid first brought the Pictish Church to adopt the Roman Easter, Egbert brought about the same change in Iona; Margaret still farther promoted the same interest, and the whole system was set up by her son David acting in accordance with his mother's training. The Roman hierarchy of Scotland she owed entirely to the Saxons, a payment, as some say, of the debt due to the Scots for the first preaching of the Gospel to that people, but payment in a coin which Protestants would say had better be withheld. It was a poor equivalent for the gift which the Scots had been the means of conveying to the north and east of Saxon England. Margaret died the very day she received tidings of Malcolm's death.

But as the century almost closed with the reign of Malcolm, let us return to take a view of the condition of the Scottish Church during its course. Iona had now sunk into comparative unimportance. The Coarb, or successor of Columba, was usually an ecclesiastic of the Irish Church, having little connection with the ancient seat of that of Columba. Nor is there any reason to imagine that his authority or jurisdiction extended to any portion of the Church in Scotland. There appears at the same time to have been abbots in Iona itself, who most probably enjoyed the revenues of the institution there still, and who, in all likelihood, wielded any power left to the successors of Columba. The Irish successors of the great missionary would have occupied the place of power amidst the Churches of the order in Ireland, and might hence be called Abbots of Iona, but there is no evidence to shew that they had any power in Scotland, even in Iona itself. This might be anticipated from the relation in which Iona stood to Ireland since its occupation by the Northmen.

In 1002 Muiredhach, or Murdoch, son of Crichan, was appointed Coarb of Columba. He was rector of Armagh. But Iona had its distinct abbot, for in 1005 " Maelbrighde Ua Rimhedha, Abbot of Iona, slept in Christ." (Ulst. Ann.) On Muiredhach retiring from his office, or, as the Irish annalist narrates it, " relinquishing the heritage of Columba for the sake of God," which means, becoming a recluse, Ferdomnach succeeded, and to show how entirely his was an Irish ecclesiastical office, the annalist says, he succeeded, *consilio virorum Hiberniæ,* ' by consent of the Irish.' He lived but a year after his appointment, and was succeeded in 1008 by Maelmuire, who died in 1009. Dr. Reeves gives Maeleoin as successor to Maelmuire, but in 1025 the Ulster annalists narrate that Flanobhra, Coarb of Columba in Iona, died. This, then, was the real Iona succession, Flanobhra having in all probability succeeded Maelbrighde, who died in 1005. To Maeleoin succeeded Maelmuire. Iona was still famous as a place of pilgrimage, "for in 1026 Mael ruanaidh Ua Maeldoraidh, Lord of the Cinel Conall, made a pilgrimage to Iona."[1] (Ann. of Ulst.) It would appear that at this period the security which had been sought for the relics of Iona nearer the heart of the country and the seat of government had proved insufficient. Dunkeld was altogether destroyed by fire (Ir. Ann.) A.D. 1027. Constantine had imagined that Iona was no longer a place of safe keeping, and had sought for one in Dunkeld, but his precautions were no protection against certain foes. Whether the burning of Dunkeld-was an accident or the work of an enemy, is not clearly indicated by the chronicler, but in all probability it was the former, for Malcolm II. was not a man to suffer readily so near an approach of a foe to the capital of his dominions. Besides, Thorfin, the leader of the Northmen at the time, was his grandson, and the Maormor of Moray was reduced in strength by his conflicts with his Scandinavian neighbours. Fire was a source of as great a danger to the relics of Columba as the assaults of the Northmen. Malcolm had a peculiar interest in Dunkeld, his daughter Bethoc having married Crinan, the abbot. This Crinan was head of the Athole family, thus including in his own person both the civil and ecclesiastical authority of the Athole district. It is clear that he was no bishop, but merely an abbot, a married abbot, or head of the ecclesiastical college at Dunkeld.[2] Although no bishop, however, the abbot in the old Celtic Church must have occupied a high social position, else he never could have married the daughter of the king. It is clear that at this period the line of demarcation between the civil and the ecclesiastical was not drawn so clearly as under the regime of the Roman Church. Crinan engaged in war, raising troops, as we

---

[1] In 1034 the annalists note the death of Sweyn of Argyle. He is called Sweyn, son of Kenneth, King of the Gall Gaedhil. This was probably a native regulus, and may have been a predecessor of the succeeding Lords of the Isles. It is not improbable that he gave its name to Castle Sweyn, in Knapdale.

[2] Robertson's Scotland under her early Kings, i. 111.

find, on behalf of his grandchildren, and was slain on the battle field. This, with the fact that the clergy married, and certain peculiarities in their forms of worship, has exposed the ancient Scottish Church, or the Culdee Church,[1] to charges of corruption from writers of a later age, commencing with those in the interest of the Church of Rome. It has been averred, until others have ceased to contradict it, that the changes commenced by Margaret were loudly called for by the state of the ancient Church. The conduct of Crinan as a Churchman engaging in war is not to be defended, although Roman Catholic writers, with the history of their own Church before them, have no room to blame it, but generally speaking, most of the features which can be shown to have characterised the early Scottish Church, even at the latest period, were such as no true Protestant can censure—nay, in so far as they implied the absence of diocesan episcopacy, and a sacred indefeasible priesthood, they were such as to commend themselves to the Presbyterian. It cannot be shewn that there was one episcopal diocese in Scotland previous to the period of Malcolm Ceannmor and his queen, and it can be shewn that the Christian ministry was not a priesthood, was more identified with the general population, and hence more thoroughly patriotic than afterwards, when it became a mere pendicle of the Roman See. Crinan was slain in 1045, having survived his son, King Duncan, for five years.

In 1040 Robhartach succeeded Maelmuire in the seat of Columba, in Ireland. This was in the year that King Duncan was slain by Macbeth. It is manifest that at this time Scotland, too, had her famous ecclesiastics ; for in 1055 "Maelduin Mac Gillaodhran, Bishop of

---

[1] Dr Ebrard claims for the early Church in Scotland this name, maintaining that it was a Church entirely distinct from that of Rome. In many respects the claim is a perfectly good one.

Alban, and the glory of the Gaelic clergy, died."[1] Fordun makes this Maelduin, son of *Gillandris*, or 'the
servant of St. Andrew,' and makes him eighth Bishop of
St. Andrews. The Irish chronicle gives no warrant for
such a statement, and it is the only trustworthy authority we have on the subject. Maelduin was a Gaelic
bishop, no doubt, but the chronicler identifies him merely
by his connection with Scotland, and not with any
diocese in it.

In 1057 Giollacriosd[2] succeeded to the presidency of
the Columban order in Ireland. He is called "Coarb of
Columcille both for Ireland and Scotland" by the Irish
annalists. It was during the first year of his presidency
that Macbeth was slain, and the way opened for the succession of Malcolm Ceannmor to the throne. Macbeth
had been the friend of the Church. It was during his
reign that Maelduin flourished, and one tradition narrates
(Marianus Scotus) his liberal gifts to the poor of Rome,
without indicating whether the king was present there or
not in person. The statement is hardly credible, or if it
be true, it sheds a somewhat surprising light on the existing condition of the Scottish people, and their relation to
the rest of Europe. Macbeth and his queen are recorded
in the Register of the Priory of Saint Andrews as the
liberal benefactors of the Culdee institute at Loch Leven.
Such grants were now frequent, and these institutions
must have become possessed of considerable wealth.
The Book of Deer, a relic of the eleventh century
(Trans. of the Spalding Club), records several grants
of land by Maormors and others written in the Gaelic
language to the religious house at Deer in Aberdeen-

---

[1] Tighernac Annals. The name is *Maol Domhnaich Mac Gille Adriain*, or
'the servant of God (Dominus), son of the servant of Adrian.' The bulk of
Scottish names had now become ecclesiastical.

[2] Gilchrist, *Gille Chriosd*, servant of Christ.

shire. Kings and rulers of provinces united in enriching the Church.

At the opening of Malcolm's reign in 1058, the Scottish Church would appear to have been very much as it had been modelled by its early teachers. Ecclesiastical institutions, called monasteries, existed throughout the whole land. We can trace them in Iona, Abernethy, Applecross, Dunkeld, St. Andrews, Brechin, Loch Leven, Deer, while others must have no doubt existed. Besides these, many ecclesiastics, following the practice of the early missionaries, became " diseartachs" or *hermits* living alone, some in caves as at Dysart in Fife, and some in small stone edifices as that still to be seen at Inchcolm in the Firth of Forth. The lands of these institutions were sometimes held by an "aircinneach" or lay tenant, as at Applecross, in whose family they became hereditary. These institutions are called monasteries, but they have hardly any claim to such a name. There were no vows of perpetual celibacy and poverty taken by the inmates, for they could hold property, and there was nothing to prevent their being married. Ecclesiastical property and office came finally to be hereditary, the worst feature about the ancient Culdee Church, although the same feature characterises the livings in some modern churches. The existence of these marriages and their good repute are evidenced by such common Scottish names as Mac Nab[1] and Mackellar;[2] and one thing is clear about this ancient church, that it had the thorough and hearty support and confidence of the nation ; kings and their subordinates held it in high esteem, else whence those large contributions in lands for its support ? The marriage of Malcolm with an Anglo-Saxon Queen however altered seriously the prospects of this church. One reason

---

[1] Mac an Aba, *the son of the Abbot.*   [2] Mac Cealloir, *the son of the Superior.*

of this may be that the ancient church was too much the church of the people, and too little that of the monarch, in an age when feudal ideas of sovereignty were beginning to prevail; and another reason, and probably the chief one was, the devotion of Margaret to the Church of Rome, in which as an Anglo-Saxon she had been brought up. Turgot's account of Margaret's early efforts to reform the Scottish Church is as follows :—" When she had perceived many things in that nation (the Scots) contrary to the rule of the true faith and the holy customs of the universal Church, she appointed frequent councils, that in as far as she could, she might recal them, through Christ's aid, to the right way. In one of these councils particularly, she stood alone, with a few of her friends, against the supporters of the perverse practices, contending for three days with the sword of the Spirit which is the word of God. Like another Helena she convinced men from the Scriptures. In this conflict her principal assistant was the king, who readily did or said whatever she commanded ; and who, knowing the English language as well as his own, was a most vigilant interpreter throughout the whole controversy."

" Wherefore the Queen, as those seeking to preserve the unity of the Catholic faith, ought not to differ from that Church by adopting new and strange rites, first of all proposed" that the fast of Lent should count from Ash Wednesday, or extend to forty days. The Scots quoted Scripture rule in their own defence, but she replied that their practice was far from Scriptural, and finally convinced them of their error. The next point of difference referred to communicating on Easter Sunday. This the Scots had not done, lest, being such sinners, and communicating on so holy a day, they should eat and drink judgment to themselves. The queen instructed them to read the following clause, *not discerning the Lord's body,* which she interpreted by not distinguishing it from common food, and urged that except they eat and drink Christ's body and blood they must perish. She pointed out the real duty to be observed, and the real danger to be avoided, and induced them to adopt her view, which was the Roman view, that the fast of Lent with confession and penitence, prepared the transgressor of God's law for the Easter communion. The Scottish view of the period still exists to some extent in the Scottish churches.

Queen Margaret also set herself to accommodate the Scottish worship to that of Rome. Turgot tells us that the Scottish Church in many places celebrated mass in a way opposed to the whole practice of the Catholic Church, and by a barbarous rite unknown to him. Could this *barbarous* rite imply the use of the vernacular tongue? The word barbarous would seem to indicate something of this sort. We know that the *cursus* or form of celebration varied in the Roman Church at the time, but the term barbarous is hardly applicable to mere variations in the Latin service. At all events Margaret insisted upon the old form being discontinued, and an immediate adoption of the Romish ritual, in which her subjects acquiesced.

Besides these changes Margaret exerted herself to secure the due observance of the Lord's day. If Turgot's account be true, the ancient Scots were not duly impressed with a sense of the reverence due to the Sabbath. They therefore admitted of an amount of manual labour altogether inconsistent with the design of its institution. Margaret felt what men who are practically called upon to deal with it will always feel, whether they will or no, that there is no resting ground for a Sabbath at all between a sacred day and a day of labour. If not sacred to God it can never be preserved as sacred to man. The only authority for its observance at all is the Divine word, and the warrant there is only for a day to be kept holy to God. If that is given up the day must be given up. Hence Margaret argues for the sacredness of the Lord's day, as commemorative of the resurrection of Christ, and urges on the Scottish Church the duty of its more faithful observance. In this the Scots readily acquiesced, and it would be well if all her reforms were equally salutary.   •

Margaret further found that marriages with step-mothers were allowed, and marriage with a deceased brother's wife. In regard to both of these she exercised both her power of argument and her royal authority, and had both from that time suppressed. Such marriages, she said, "were to be avoided like death." Other prac tices, it is said, of a similar character were condemned in the same council, and ordered to be discontinued in the kingdom. Turgot adds, "That whatsoever she proposed was so supported from Scripture and the authority of the fathers, that no man could gainsay her; and putting away all opposition, and acquiescing in the soundness of her reasons, they all readily undertook the carrying out of her proposals."

These were the changes introduced by Queen Margaret into the Scottish Church. They did not go the length, as happened in the reign of her son David, of interfering with the organization of the Church, introducing a diocesan episcopacy, and prohibiting the marriage of the clergy, with other such radical reformation, but they were all, with the exception of her Sabbath legislation, in the direction of Rome, as the future history of the country amply shews. She had introduced the point of the wedge which her son David afterwards drove home to the head.

Margaret's personal character added much to her influ-ence in carrying these changes through. She was a person of remarkable piety. Much of her time was spent in prayer, a cave being still pointed out near Dunfermline, (*Dun Farlan,* 'Partholan's tower,') to which she retired for private devotion. Her fasts were frequent and rigid, so much so that her bodily health became affected, and her latter years were spent in much pain. She was lavish in her alms to the poor, of whom she supported a certain number statedly; and to provide for the comfort of pilgrims to St. Andrews, which was then becoming famous as a place of resort for such, she built houses of accommodation (habitacula) on both sides of the Firth of Forth, where they might rest and refresh themselves either after their journey or their voyage. Her death, which occurred immediately upon hearing of the slaughter of her husband and son by the English, was without a murmur of complaint. She was sainted[1] long after her death by the Romish Church, and few of the saints of that Church deserved it better at her hands (Vit. Marg., by Turgot, Pink. edition.)

The reign of Malcolm was signalized by the planting of an ecclesiastical institute in Moray. The planting of the Church at Mortlach is usually attributed to Malcolm II., and is said to have been commemorative of his victories over the Danes. But we know of no such victories in the reign of Malcolm II. The Maormor of Moray and his northern neighbours had serious conflicts, which were however all in the interest of Malcolm as tending to weaken his principal rival in the kingdom. But the Northmen he had secured by placing his grandson Thorfin in the earldom of Sutherland and Caithness. There were no victories over the northern Danes which this king had to commemorate. But Malcolm III. had victories to commemorate in the north, not however over the Danes, but over his own countrymen of the province of Moray.

[1] Called "Translatio" by mediæval writers.

In fact it was he who really for the first time fairly annexed that province to the Scottish crown. This was done by the entire overthrow of Maelsnectan, the son of Lulach, the last Gaelic Maormor of the province. What so likely as that, when thus put into possession of the territory, he should devote a part of it to pious uses? Nor is it improbable that the memorial stone at Forres, with its cross on one side significant of the Christianity of its author, and the symbols of war and victory, apparently among two kindred peoples, sculptured on the other, is commemorative of the same event, and represents to this day both the piety and the military skill of Malcolm Ceannmor. The Church of Mortlach and the Forres pillar may both in all probability be attributed to Malcolm III. Bishop Keith attributes the foundation of the Church at Mortlach to this king, but assigns a date to it (1010) long previous to his succession to the throne. It is somewhat difficult to decide whether the mistake is as to the date or to the man. Bishop Nicholson attributes the dedication of this Church to Malcolm IV., and if the charter of dedication as given in Bishop Keith's appendix be compared with others of Malcolm's charters, the resemblance is so strong as almost to induce conviction that they are of the same period. At least there is strong reason to think that the foundation may have been of the age of Malcolm IV., while there is none to think that it was of that of Malcolm II. The grant, judging from the charter, was not a new one, but made to an existing ecclesiastic in the locality, " Beyn (Baithean, whence MacBhaithein, *Macbean*), bishop of Murthelach," that he may set up an episcopal see there. All this savours of a later period than that of Malcolm III., and indicates the maturing of the design for setting up a diocesan episcopacy in Scotland rather than the commencement of it. At the same time, while this charter may be of the time of Malcolm

IV. granting certain privileges, with certain objects, to a church set up by his great-grandfather, the very fact of the grant being to an existing bishop, shews that the Church had existed in that place previously, although there was no "sedes episcopalis" (Keith's Bishop, App. G.) *Bishop's see*, there. The likelihood is, that Malcolm III. planted there a bishop of the old Culdee Church, and provided for him the needful ecclesiastical buildings and means of sustenance.

Reference has been made to the opinion that the ancient church had become so corrupt in the time of Malcolm as to call for reformation. Turgot records two instances of this corruption in detailing Queen Margaret's reforms, the desecration of the Lord's day by performing ordinary labour on it, and marrying within the degrees prohibited by Scripture. To these it has been added that the successors of the abbots became latterly the representatives of the lay founders, and that the monasteries became family heritages, the possession and patronage being vested in the great family of the district. If this statement be true, it may prove the corruption of the Culdee Church in its latter stages, but it proves just as distinctly that that Church was not organized after the Roman or Episcopal model. The state of things represented here was such as could not be reached by a church so organized. Besides, the anxiety of writers of the Roman school to represent the ancient church as so corrupt, shews that its organization could not be in accordance with their views. But it is questionable whether the corruption was such as these men represent it. To the marriage of the ministers of that church, protestants can take no exception, and hold that so far from being an evidence of corruption it is the very opposite. That much of the property of the Church should be held by laymen, was very natural, seeing the anxiety of laymen on all occasions, where possible, to obtain the property of the Church, of which the period of the Scottish Reformation in the sixteenth century affords ample evidence; yet it was not an unsuitable arrangement that the property of the different ecclesiastical bodies over the country should be managed by laymen who received one-third of the profits for their remuneration, thus relieving the Church from one of the most secularizing of the influences to which it was exposed. That the civil and ecclesiastical power became in some cases combined is clear from the case of Crinan of Dunkeld, and yet it is difficult to understand how in Scotland the churches should have become the mere appanages of the great families which founded them, as in Ireland, seeing that in Scotland all the principal churches were provided by the kings, and that there is not sufficient evidence to shew that they were appanages of the throne.[1] But, as already stated, the Church in the days of Malcolm had the entire confidence of the king and the people, and it required no little skill and patience on the part of Queen Margaret to get her changes effected. The country was covered with places of worship, the remains of which still exist, extending to the furthest distant of the Hebrides. These, as their remains testify, were of the Culdee period, and shew how all-pervading the influence of that Church was, and recently, specimens of the hymnology of that Church of the twelfth century have been brought to light (Dean of Lismore's Book. Poems by Muireadhach Albanach), shewing how thoroughly the country was influenced by religious truth. We do not mean to aver that the influence of the Roman system had not been felt down from the eighth century, but till this

---

[1] Mr. Robertson (Scotland under her early Kings, i. 332) thinks they were, and yet Dunkeld was a royal foundation, and is represented by him as an appanage of the family of Athole, when, as in the case of Crinan, in no way related to the reigning family.

period that influence had met with a large measure of resistance. In Queen Margaret's own case the resistance seems to have been resolute and tenacious. It is not denied that corruptions existed in the Culdee Church in the commencement of the eleventh century, and that the hand of a judicious reformer was necessary, but it is denied that that corruption existed to the extent which writers of a later period have maintained. The Culdee Church had pervaded Scotland with the knowledge of the Gospel, had filled the country with places of worship, and had raised Scotland to a place of no little note among the nations. One of her kings under that system was called "the lord and father of the west," and one of her ministers was called "the glory of the Gaelic clergy." The organization of that Church was no doubt peculiar, consisting mainly, as has been said, of great central institutes or colleges (monasteries, as they have been called, although it is hard to conceive what title men with wives and families and holding property in their own right, had to be called monks), with oratories or places of worship scattered numerously over the country. Here and there were the *diseartaich*, or 'anchorites,' who retired to caves and small oratories for meditation and prayer. These retreats, however, were not for life, but for certain periods, although some men seem to have retired altogether in the close of their days. There were no doubt bishops also, but as different from bishops of the modern type as the so-called monks were from the monks of Rome. There is some reason to believe, although the evidence is scanty, that the ordinary clergy, as distinguished from the members of the colleges, were the bishops of the early Church. We are safe in inferring this, if we judge of the later Church in Scotland by that of Ireland in the days of St. Patrick, when there were 300 bishops in that Church. And, if this be not so, we have no trace in existing documents of any secular clergy at all in Scotland, a state of things which one could hardly conceive of in a Christian country.

Donald O'Rafferty continued to occupy the chair of Columba in Ireland from 1062 to 1098, a period of thirty-six years. In the year 1065 the Irish annalists narrate the death of "Dubhthach Albanach," whom they style the "principal confessor of Ireland and Alban," placing his death at Armagh. This was in all probability the famous St. Duthus of the Scottish Church, whose name is commemorated at Tain and Dornoch. Scottish writers give his era in the thirteenth century, but Dr. Reeves gives good ground for believing that the Dubhthach of the eleventh century is the real person commemorated. Although styled "Bishop of Ross" by some writers, authentic documents give no warrant for such a title. There could not be a bishop of Ross before a bishopric of Ross existed.

Alongside of the Irish Coarbs we have occasional notices of the real occupants of Columba's Scottish chair. In 1070 Mac mic Baethen, abbot of Iona, was slain by the son of the abbot Ua Maeldoraidh. The cause of this outrage is not narrated, but the Ua Maeldoraidh tribe were Irish, and the difference might have arisen from national jealousy. The death of an archbishop of Alban is narrated at 1093. Fothadh, apparently the second of the name, is said by the Irish annalists to have died then. It is quite unnecessary to stay to shew that the title can not be taken to mean an archbishop in the modern sense of the word. If so it died with Fothadh himself, and was not resuscitated for generations after. That the bishop resident at St. Andrews should now be acquiring consequence at the expense of his brethren is very likely. It was perfectly in accordance with the design of Queen Margaret, and is in farther accordance with the process by which Episcopacy first grew up in the Christian Church. But it would be a mere waste of time to attempt to prove that there was no Archbishop of St. Andrews in the eleventh century.

In 1097 Magnus Barelegs, King of Norway, paid a visit to Iona (Ir. Ann.). He came with his fleet, and brought peace and security to the inhabitants of the island. He shewed the highest respect for the Church of Columba, and gave commands with respect to the reverence to be shewn to it, which were faithfully obeyed. In this respect, however, Iona stood alone (Johnstone's Antiq. Celto-Scand.).

The close of the eleventh century found Edgar, son of Malcolm Ceannmor, who succeeded his uncle Donald Bàn on the Scottish throne, Ferdomnach Coarb of Columba in the Irish Church, and Dunchadh Mac Mhic Maenaigh filling the presidency at Iona. Both the state and the church were undergoing a process of rapid transition, the one to feudalism, the other to Romanism, in both instances providing for that tremendous revulsion which a few centuries more brought about.

CHAPTER XXIII.

In the close of the last chapter it was stated that Malcolm
Ceannmor was succeeded on the throne by his brother
Donald Bàn the fair). This succession was not in accordance with the system, which Malcolm II. endeavoured to
introduce, and which led to the convulsions under Macbeth, nor was it in accordance with the system which
both Malcolm III. and his queen strove so eagerly to
establish. The great grandson and his Saxon wife would
fain have carried out the projects of the great grandfather. But it was in perfect accordance with the ancient
system of the Gaelic races. The Saxon Margaret, saint
as she afterwards became, was far from popular among
her Gaelic subjects. This became very evident in connection with her funeral. Her son Ethelred was glad to
take advantage of a fog which covered the country, in
order to carry the body of his mother quietly to its last
resting-place at Dunfermline. The dust of the Saxon queen
was not secure against dishonour from those to whose
customs and laws she had shewn so persistent a hostility.
It is no wonder, then, that the same spirit should indicate itself in connection with the succession to the throne.
The Gaelic people at once rallied around Domhnull Bàn
(Donald the fair), Malcolm's brother, and proclaimed him
king. Donald assumed the government, and took im-

mediate steps for the expulsion of the Saxons. But the sons of Malcolm were not to be easily dispossessed. His son Duncan, by Ingibiorge, widow of Thorfin, had been long in England, given originally as a hostage, and remaining latterly as a guest. Offering to hold Scotland in fealty to William if put in possession of his father's crown, William put him at the head of a body of troops, with which he marched northwards, expelled Donald, and seized upon the kingdom. The Scots, however, rallied, assailed Duncan's followers, most of whom they slew, but having no enmity to the family of Malcolm, they left Duncan in possession of the crown. Donald bàn in the meantime had taken refuge in the Mœrne, whose Maormor, Malpeder Mac Loen,[1] was friendly to his claims. He was joined by Edmund, son of Malcolm and Margaret, who was to share the kingdom with him, should he succeed in expelling Duncan. The effort was successful, ending in the death of Duncan, of whom the Irish annalist records that he was slain by his own brothers, *per dolum,* 'by treachery.' The Register of St. Andrews places his death at Monachedin, near Bervie, in the modern county of Kincardine, where a rough stone still marks the spot. The reigns of both uncle and nephew had each extended to a period of six months. Donald's second reign began in 1094, and till 1097 he reigned in peace; but in that year Edgar Atheling, Margaret's brother was sent to Scotland with an army on behalf of his nephew and namesake Edgar, son of Malcolm. Don-

---

[1] Maolpheadair Mac Gille Sheathain, or the devotee of Peter, son of the servant of John, a purely ecclesiastical name. This is the earliest instance we have of what became afterwards the surname M'Lean. The province of this official was probably what is now called the Mearns, the Gaelic Marairnn, perhaps Mòr earrainn, *the great province.* Mr. Skene, in his work on the Highlanders, points out the existence of a second province on the west coast of the same name, which is still retained in Morvern. This second province was usually called Garmoran *Garbh-Mharairnn,* or the Rugged Mœrne, a name sufficiently descriptive.

ald was defeated, and having his eyes put out, was kept a prisoner for the rest of his days at Roscolfin or Rescobie, in Angus. Edmund, his nephew and coadjutor, entered a monastery of Cluniac monks in Somersetshire. Some writers speak of the bitterness of his final repentance for his proceedings in Scotland. It is very well for those whose sympathies are all with the changes introduced by Margaret to magnify the causes of repentance among those who resisted her proceedings, but others who think that a nation is fairly entitled to make a stand for laws and customs distinctive of itself, especially if they be laws favouring the maintenance of civil and religious liberty, may be excused for holding that both Donald and Edmund were fairly entitled to act as they did, and deserved the gratitude of the nation and its support against men who came to seek the kingdom as the sworn liegemen of the English crown, and the devotees of the Roman see. Edgar succeeded his uncle. He was the first king of the Scots who bore a Saxon name. His reign was unmarked by any event of note, being in this not unlike himself, for he was a man of gentle disposition and a lover of peace. One portion of Scotland, however, although not at the time attached to the Scottish crown, suffered much during his reign. The Hebrides had long been an appanage of the kingdom of Man. One of the most vigorous of the kings who ruled this island territory, as well as a part of Ireland, was Godfrey Crovan, or Godfrey of the white hand. Godfrey died in 1095, leaving his dominions to be divided between his three sons. Magnus son of Olave, King of Norway, usually called "Barelegs," whose visit to Iona has already been narrated, resolved to add again to the Norwegian crown the island kingdom which had been lost for a time, and sailed with a powerful fleet for the west in 1098. First seizing the Orkneys, he sailed for the Hebrides, carrying fire and sword among the wretched inhabitants. Iona was excepted, for the Scandinavians were now nominally Christians, but nothing else indicated that Magnus had forsaken the tenets of his barbarous ancestors. He extended his incursion as far as Anglesey, thus establishing the Norwegian power over the whole islands of the west. It is said that, claiming by ancient right all the western islands, he was conveyed in his boat, with his hand on the helm, across the narrow neck of land between east and west Loch Tarbert, in order to prove that Kintyre was an island, and belonged to him. Edgar does not seem to have interfered, notwithstanding this outrage on a portion of the ancient Dalriadic territory, and Magnus was allowed to proceed undisturbed, until he met his death in Ireland in 1103, during an expedition against the Ulster men. Edgar died in 1107, bequeathing to his brother David the appanage of Cumbria, an event fraught with important consequences to the country in its future history. The place of his death is recorded in the St. Andrew's Register as Dunedin, the modern Edinburgh, and his body was interred in Dunfermline, the new state of things in Church and State involving changes in every department of the government; among the rest in the burial place of the kings.

Edgar was succeeded by his brother, Alexander I., who ascended the throne in 1107. The last act of Edgar, bestowing Cumbria upon David, excited early the jealousy of the new king, and he would have resisted the dismemberment of his dominions if he could. David, however, had powerful friends. His sister, Matilda, was married to Henry I. of England, son of the Conqueror. With her David had spent much of his time. She was a woman who had imbibed deeply the religious sentiments of her mother, and had perhaps as much to do as the latter with the moulding of the mind of David. From the English king, a man wise in counsel and powerful in the field, David had the promise of assistance, and the fear of such a power, as much as any sense of what was due to the bequest of Edgar, led Alexander to give a reluctant consent to David's retaining Cumbria, and continuing to be an English baron, rather than a Scottish subject.

Early in the reign of Alexander the Gaelic race made a new effort to throw off the Saxon power, and deliver their country from Saxon influence. The centre of the movement was in the north, where the men of Moray and the Mearns joined together and made a sudden descent on the king, then living at Invergowrie. Alexander was not unprepared for his assailants, and meeting them boldly with such troops as he had, he forced them to flee to their native hills. He even pursued them to the Moray Firth, where, at a place called Stockford, he crossed suddenly what was probably the river Beauly, and dispersed his opponents with terrible slaughter. Many of the more important events in the reign of Alexander were connected with the state of the Church, and will come to be related when we treat of the ecclesiastical events of the century. Alexander was married to Sibylla, a natural daughter of Henry of England. She died suddenly near Loch Tay, about 1122, where the remains of a convent still exist on a small island in the lake, where the body of the Scottish queen lies buried. Alexander died in 1124, after a reign of only seventeen years.

Alexander left no children, and was succeeded on the Scottish throne by his younger brother David, who was the fourth of the sons of Malcolm,[1] and the third of the

---

[1] Dr. Reeves, in his table of the Dalriadic kings, rejects the statement which makes David the son of Malcolm III., and deduces him through a certain Finghin, Duncan, and Malcolm, from Malcolm II., avoiding altogether Crinan of Dunkeld in the line of his ancestors. This is probably done on the authority of the old Gaelic MS. of 1450, but it would be unfortunate were it a specimen of the general accuracy of the table.

sons of Margaret who succeeded to the throne of his father. David had spent his earlier years about the English court, where he imbibed a love for English manners and those principles of government introduced by the Normans. Upon the death of Edgar he succeeded to the government of Scottish Cumbria, which he held as liegeman to the English king. He was thus exposed from his youth upwards to every influence calculated to mould his character in accordance with the Anglo-Norman type; while, although the descendant of a long race of Celtic ancestors, there was little save his descent, and more immediately a respect for his father's memory, to attach him to the Celtic race and Celtic manners. But the memory of their mother appears to have been cherished by the sons of Malcolm with far more warmth than that of their father, and this, combined with the attraction of the feudal system to a monarch like David, served to give to his mind its bias in favour of everything characteristic of the foreign race which was now rapidly filling the country, to the prejudice of the native Scoto-Picts. The suggestive fact has been referred to,[1] that the dignitaries at the court of Alexander were exclusively " Gaelic Maormors—Earls of Moray, Fife, Atholl, and Strathearn," with the ancient Scoto-Saxon nobility of the Lothians; whilst around David " gathered Moreville and Somerville, Lindsay and Umphraville, Bruce and Fitz-alan—Norman names destined to surround the throne of his descendants."

David, as an English baron, was early brought to intermingle in the great struggle for the English crown between Stephen and the Empress Maud, daughter of Henry I., and David's sister Matilda, a struggle which terminated in Stephen's retaining possession of the throne. While so engaged, however, David was not

[1] Rob. Scot. und. her ear. Kings, i. 184.

without his troubles at home. The Gael, ever jealous of what is characteristic of themselves, were far from satisfied with the changes taking place in their country. In the north, more especially, the feelings of the ancient inhabitants were deeply aroused, and were ready at any moment to break forth. The representative of the ancient Maormors of Moray in the days of Alexander was Aodh or Hugh, usually called Heth. He was now dead, but left two sons, Angus and Malcolm, who inherited, with his possessions, all the feelings of their father. Their mother was daughter of Lulach, son of Gruoch, daughter of Boedhe or Bute, son of Kenneth III., and consequently they held, and not unjustly, that their family had a preferable claim to the throne. These two brothers now raised troops to assert their claims, and prepared for a struggle. This was about the year 1130. David sent Edward, son of Siward, a Saxon, who, in accordance with Norman ideas, was made Constable of Scotland, with troops to meet them. The armies met at Strickathro, in Angus, when the northern men were utterly routed. Angus was killed, and Malcolm escaped to prolong the war for a few years amidst his native hills. David, alarmed lest this rebellion might assume more dangerous proportions, collected his forces from all quarters, including the Anglo-Norman barons of Northumberland and York, and a large body of troops were assembled at Carlisle. But the Moray men became alarmed in their turn, and falling upon Malcolm, they seized him and sent him prisoner to the king, who incarcerated him in Roxburgh Castle. The whole territory of Moray was thereupon forfeited to the crown, and redistributed either to Anglo-Norman settlers or such of the ancient people as were loyal to the crown. This was manifestly the period of the dispersion of the ancient Moravienses. Tradition has, with its usual inaccuracy and love of exaggeration, attributed the event to a period as far back as the reign of Malcolm II. But such historical statements as we now possess, and as are worthy of confidence, entitle us to attribute it to the reign of David. Never till then was the power of the Moray chiefs thoroughly broken, and only then were the inhabitants proscribed, and many of them expelled. The Murrays, afterwards so powerful, found their way to the south, carrying with them the name of their ancient country, and some of the tribes of Sutherland, as well as of Inverness-shire, who, there is reason to believe, belonged to the Scoto-Pictish inhabitants of Moray, removed their dwellings to those portions of the country which they have occupied ever since. The race of Mac Heth may appear among the Mac Heths or Mac Aoidhs, *the Mackays* of Sutherland, nor is this rendered less probable by the Morganaich or *sons of Morgan*, the ancient name of the Mackays, appearing in the Book of Deer as owning possessions and power in Buchan in the tenth century.

In 1136 David led an army into England in defence of the claims of his niece the Empress Maud. Stephen who had taken possession of the throne met him in Northumberland, but after a while peace was concluded without any battle. It was at this period that the title of Huntingdon, so famous afterwards in the great contest for the Scottish crown between the Bruces and the Balliols, was conferred, together with the fiefs of Carlisle and Doncaster, upon David's son Henry, the latter accompanying Stephen to England. A short time only elapsed, however, until the English barons, jealous of the young Scottish prince being raised to the place of honour at a court held by Stephen, left the court in a body; upon which David recalled his son to mark his displeasure.

In 1138 David marched an army into England. Two objects seem to have been sought by this movement; the one was to recover the throne of England for the Empress Maud, his niece ; the other to obtain for his son, Henry of Huntingdon, the earldom of Northumberland. David's wife was Matilda, the widow of Simon de St. Liz, and heiress of Waltheof, Earl of Northumberland. In right of her David claimed the earldom, which was at the time held by the crown, for her son Henry. A portion of the Scottish army, under the command of William, son of Duncan, the elder brother of David, advanced into Northumberland, and assailed Werk Castle, belonging to Walter Espec, the commander of the English army. But the assault failed, and David coming up soon after with the main army proceeded to lay waste Northumberland. On the approach of the English army the Scots retreated across the border followed by Stephen, who, after wasting some portions of the country, withdrew his troops again to the south of the Tweed.

Towards the close of spring David again marched southward. After seizing Norham Castle and laying siege to Werk he met the English at a place called Clitheroe, where the people of York and Lancashire had assembled to defend their country. The latter took alarm and fled ere the battle had well begun. In the meantime Stephen despatched a numerous army to repel the invasion under the command of Walter Espec. The two armies met in the neighbourhood of Northallerton, and there was fought the great battle of the Standard. The loss of the battle by the Scots is attributed to the Picts of Galloway, who, unwisely brave, insisted on leading the van and assailing the mailed troops of England, destitute of armour as they were. David yielded to this wish with the utmost reluctance, giving way latterly to the fear of mutiny. A sacred standard, from which the battle took its name, was erected in the midst of the English army ; it was composed of a ship's mast with the consecrated host on the summit, and the three banners of St. Peter, St. John, and St. Wilfred around it. About this standard the English fought. The cry of the Scots in advancing to the battle was Albanaich! Albanaich! and unarmed as they were the impetuosity of their attack shook the ranks of their opponents. But there is no equality between men in armour and men without it, and the Scots were driven back like chaff before the wind The armed knights of Scotland and their troops led by Prince Henry, were more successful, so much so that for a time the English army seemed on the brink of a total defeat. But while victory hung in the balances, the cry was raised among the Scots that their king was dead, and in despite of all David's efforts to rally them and restore their courage, the whole army broke and fled under a tremendous charge from the English troops. The Scots did not however become totally disordered, but retreated in a body until they reached Carlisle. It was three days after the king's arrival in Carlisle ere Prince Henry, extricating himself from innumerable difficulties, joined him ; the joy of David was great on finding that his son was alive. After resting his troops, the Scottish king recommenced the siege of Werk Castle, which after a brave resistance yielded to him.

Meanwhile Pope Victor IV. had sent to David a legate in the person of Alberic, Bishop of Ostra, the object of whose mission was to intimate to him the cessation of the division in the church, caused by the election of rival popes. David had adhered to the party of the pope who had resigned his pretensions ; and it was to secure his adhesion to the one pope that the mission was undertaken. The legate, however, while fulfilling the object of his mission was grieved to observe the wretched condition to which the war had brought the north of England, and offered himself as mediator between the two parties. He

had an advantage in so doing, for he had rescued William
Comyn the Scottish Chancellor, from the English who
had taken him prisoner at the battle of the Standard.
David, probably having his mind embittered by his
recent defeat, was long immoveable and resolved to continue the war, until at length the legate went on his knees
and besought him to accept his mediation with Stephen.
A truce was then agreed upon to last till St. Martin's
Day. Alberic, who immediately left Carlisle 'after the
arrangement of other matters at the English court,
pressed upon Stephen the duty of making peace with
Scotland. In this he finally succeeded, having the
warm sympathy and able support of the Queen Matilda,
herself the niece of the Scottish king. She took the
affair into her own hands, met Prince Henry in the
spring after at Durham, when the preliminaries of a
permanent peace were finally fixed, in which was included the investing of Henry with the great fief of
Northumberland, a grant which extended the Scottish
territory practically to the very heart of England.

David continued to mix himself with the English
troubles in the latter years of Stephen's reign, still retaining his interest in the cause of his niece, the empress.
At Winchester this interference almost cost him his life.

It is to this period that the rise of the great family of
Comyn in Scotland is to be traced : whether of Norman
descent, or taking their name like many of the Celtic
clans of Scotland from the saint of their name who is
commemorated in some of the Scottish churches, it may
not be easy to determine. It is not impossible that, like
the Livingstones and other Scottish families, there may
be two sections of the tribe—one deriving its origin
from a Norman family, and the other from Mac a
Chuimeanaich, or the son of Cuimin, some ancestor
of Celtic lineage and fame. William Comyn, the chan-

cellor of David, who was an ecclesiastic, seized upon the Bishopric of Durham, and retained it forcibly for three years, supported by the power of this Scottish prince ; and Richard Comyn, who is said to have been the founder of that name in Scotland, and whose wife, Hextilda, was directly descended from Donald Bàn, received a grant of the honour of Allerton. It is almost unnecessary to record that their power became afterwards well nigh paramount in Scotland, which may have arisen in some degree from the fact that the family of Richard were through their mother directly descended from the royal family of the country

It was in the latter years of David's reign that a pretender of the name of Wimund arose to disturb the peace of David's kingdom. Originally a monk of Furness in Lancashire, he was one of the first monks sent by the abbot of that monastery to plant a priory at Rushen in Man, in virtue of a grant for that purpose by king Olave. By degrees, although covering a nature utterly corrupt, his jovial, friendly, manners secured his elevation to the see of the Isles. His ambition became stimulated by success, and he began to give himself out as one of the sons of Heth, earl of Moray. He collected a body of islanders around his standard, with whom he spoiled large districts of the western coasts. David quieted him by making him a grant of the abbey of Furness ; but his proceedings were so outrageous that the people around seized him, and expelled him from his see ; and, having put out his eyes, and otherwise maimed him, he was allowed to linger out his life in another monastery. Thus ended the life of one about whom historians have written much that has no foundation in fact. His life shows the kind of events which may occur among an ignorant people, and how unsettled the best governments were in the twelfth century.

In 1152, David suffered the most grievous calamity that darkened the course of his life. His hopes for his kingdom had been all centered in his only son, Henry, usually called of Huntingdon, a young man of excellent disposition and of the highest promise. This young man, so much beloved by his father, and no less so by the nation, died in the summer of this year. His death gave a blow to his father, now an aged man, from which it is doubtful if he at all recovered, for within a year after, about the end of May, 1153, David himself was no more. Although David had no son but Henry, the latter left a large family. His wife was Ada de Warenne, a scion of one of the greatest of the Anglo-Norman families of England. By her he had three sons, Malcolm, surnamed the Maiden, afterwards king; William, called by the opposite name of the Lion, also king; and David, who long enjoyed the honour of Huntingdon; and three daughters, Ada, wife of the Count of Holland; Margaret, who was married twice, first, to the Duke of Bretagne, and secondly, to the Earl of Hereford; and Matilda, who died unmarried. Never did the Royal family of Scotland possess a higher European reputation than in the days of David I., nor was Scotland at any period of its history so powerful, in comparison with the neighbouring kingdom of England.

In the "Eulogium Davidis" by Ailred of Rievaux, the biographer of Ninian, and David's cotemporary, this king is spoken of in terms of the most unmeasured laudation. We must take this as entitled to all the weight due to a cotemporary writer. But we cannot help regretting that, while having the testimony of a firm supporter of the Roman Church and its claims, and of the system of government introduced into England by the Anglo-Normans, we have not alongside of it the testimony of some of the Ancient Culdee Churchmen, and of the friends of the ancient Scots, who were contending for the laws and liberties of their country. The points in the king's character to which his eulogist refers, are his unwillingness to accept the throne, his justice and kindness in conducting his government, his liberality to the Church, founding bishoprics and monasteries, a feature of his government which made his more worldly successor James VI. say, that he was a " a sair sanct for the eroun," his encouragement of horticulture and agri- culture, by which he strove to civilize a rude people ; his love of peace, his chastity ; his favour for the crusaders, his penitence and his patience, his adoring of the ebony cross of his mother, and his compassion towards them that would betray him; although it is fully acknowledged that he sinned in not repressing the cruelty of his soldiery.

For some time previous to the death of David, Scot- land had been undergoing great and remarkable changes. The old Gaelic kingdom had well nigh ceased to exist, and in its place there appeared a mixed population of Gael, Britons, Saxons and Normans. The north was the stronghold of the Gaelic race, although even there a Scandinavian population had intruded on their ancient domains in Caithness, where their descendants exist to this day. A mixed population of Celt and Saxon occu- pied the Lothians ; the ancient Britons still lingered in Strathclyde, and are addressed as a distinct race in the "Inquisitio Davidis," and Galloway was occupied by a Gaelic race, who had emigrated from Ireland in the ninth century, attracted by the weakness of the Britons, and impelled by the incursions of the Northmen, a race usually called the wild Picts of Galloway, although it is doubt- ful whether they were wilder than their neighbours who named them so ; at least, any knowledge we have of them represents them as zealous members of the old

z

Scottish Church. Few parts of Scotland are richer in ecclesiastical remains of the Culdee period than are Ayrshire and Galloway. But David's dominions included the northern half of England, held as fiefs of the English crown, and perhaps the temptation to extend his power to the south may have been one of the most urgent motives with him to denude himself of Scottish peculiarities, and to conform himself to the Anglo-Norman model. Scotland was never either before or since so extensive a kingdom as in the reign of David. Besides, the internal organization of the country was undergoing change ; the ancient maormor was becoming the modern earl, and the basis was being laid of the future sheriffdom. The maormor although a royal officer was, owing to the office being hereditary, a dangerous rival to the crown, and the sagacious king set himself with all due deliberation, but with inflexible resolution, to establish a system of government that would give greater influence to national law.

This was in all probability the period which gave origin to the system of Scottish clanship, a system which afterwards led to the deterioration of the Gaelic people. Hitherto there seems no reason to believe that any such thing existed. Names were patronymics. It was so in the case of the monarchs. Kenneth Mac Alpin was so named, not because there was a clan of that name, but because Alpin was the name of his father. So with Donald Mac Constantine and Kenneth Mac Duff among the Scots, and Angus Mac Fergus among the Picts. But two things served to give clan names permanence about this time : one of these was the decline of the Maormors, which admitted of the rise of smaller sections of the people with their leading men at their head. The ancient Celtic system was in fact breaking up ; and ere another had supplanted it there was ample opportunity for the growth of licence and of anarchy ; men being driven, in the absence of any supreme power possessed of paramount authority, to make the best provision they could for the defence of their persons, and the protection of their property. The other cause of the growth of clans and chiefship is to be found in the introduction of feudal charters. These necessarily required of the men that held them distinctive heritable names. Hence those of certain families assumed from their territories, as those of Murray, Sutherland, Grant, Innes, Ross ; and of others derived from the patronymic of the chief probably existing at the time, as M'Donald, M'Kenzie, Mac Dhomhnuill duibh or Cameron, Mackay and others. That this is the origin of these clan names is clear from the fact that their existence may be clearly traced back to the very period now under review, but no farther ; and that, save in public documents, they have been little known among the native Gael, save as applicable to the chief, till within the last century. No native Gael ever spoke of any man in the clan by the clan name, save the chief. The members of the tribe were uniformly known by their common patronymics. The state of the Gaelic population of Scotland during the 15th, 16th, and 17th centuries, was the result of those great changes in the 12th, which altered their government, and diminished their consequence in the kingdom, converting the ancient native population and mainstay of its strength into strangers, if not foes.

But as we propose closing our historical sketch with the end of David's reign, let us turn from the civil history of the first half of the 12th century to the history of the church during the same period. We have already adverted to the marked changes occurring in the reign of Malcolm and Margaret in the condition of the ancient Culdee church, and the progress made by the Roman See in establishing its power over its downfall. It must be borne in mind, however, that although the Culdee clergy felt that the change was a revolution, and gave it all the resistance in their power, it was not in the form of a revolution it was introduced by the monarch and his queen. To shew that she reverenced highly the saints of the ancient church, Margaret erected a chapel in Iona, the remains of which exist to this day, and in other ways indicated the highest reverence for the memory of Columba ; nor did this policy die with her, for her son, Alexander, on occasion of his being driven by a violent storm on Inchcolm, in the Frith of Forth, erected an abbey there, which he dedicated to Columba, to whom he attributed his deliverance. Indeed, if we believe Fordun, it was in answer to prayers offered up to St. Columba that Malcolm and Margaret obtained the gift of children. In this way national prejudices were as little violated as possible. Columba passed into the category of Romish saints, although there does not seem to be any evidence of his translation ; and the " diseartach," or hermit of Inchcolm, passed into a body of regular monks, while his little oratory, which still stands, became supplanted by handsome and costly monastic buildings.

The eleventh century closed with Ferdomnach, as Irish Coarb of Columba. In 1099 the Ulster annals note the death of Dunchadh, or Duncan Mac Mhic Maenaigh as abbot of Iona. This institution, although now in Norwegian territory, continued to retain its Celtic abbots. Nor is there anything to shew that these abbots had any connection with, or owed any subjection to, the Irish Coarb. The fact is now clear that Scotland and Ireland had each its successor of the great saint, as might be anticipated in the case of separate kingdoms with separate governments. It was not to be expected that the Scottish crown and people would willingly acquiesce in having their most important ecclesiastical institution filled from the Irish clergy. There is a curious notice on this subject by the Ulster annalists under the year 1164, when they relate that the "abbacy of Iona was offered to Flaithbertach O'Brolochan .by the magnates of the isles," stating at the same time that the Coarb of Patrick and the King of Ireland prevented his accepting it. Flaithbertach was at the timê Irish Coarb, and this entry plainly shews that that did not imply his holding of the Scottish office. It is interesting to observe that the annalists, in recording the election, give a list of the officials at Iona engaged in it as, *an sagart mòr Augustin,* 'the great priest Augustine;' *agus am 'fear-leighinn i. Dubside,* 'and the reader Dusith;' *agus an Diseartach i. Mac Gilladuibh,* 'and the hermit Mac Gilleduibh;' *agus cenn na Céile-n De i. Mac Forcellaigh,* 'and the head of the Culdees Mac Forcellaigh.' These parties, then, were all somehow interested in the establishment at Iona in the middle of the twelfth century. The O'Brolochans, of which tribe this Flaithbertach was one, were long famous in the Irish Church. The first of them, Maelbrighde ·O'Brolochan, who was called *Primh saer Erenn,* or 'the first artificer in Ireland,' is entered in the Ulster annals as dying in 1029 (Vit. Col. Reeves, p. 405, n.). The family seem to have been hereditary architects, for the name of Domhnull O'Brolochan is carved upon one of the pillars of the cathedral of Iona, as the architect who constructed it. This Donald died in 1202, his death affording the means of fixing approximately the date of the building.

Ferdomnach died in 1114, and was succeeded in the Irish chair by Maelbrighde. Dr. Reeves, in noting his succession, adverts to the fact that the title "Coarb of Columcille" is intermitted in the annals of this period, and adds that the most probable cause of this was the commencement of diocesan episcopacy in Ireland (Vit.

Col. p. 403). He farther adds that the title, although resumed afterwards, was "more an honorary than a real dignity." This goes to prove how the whole Scottish Church was, at the same period, undergoing a process of transition ; Roman influence, backed by the power of the Anglo-Saxons and Anglo-Normans, being rapidly over-bearing the distinctive principles and the power of the Church of Patrick and Columba.

At this period a remarkable man arose in the Church in the north. It has already been related how Magnus Barelegs led an expedition from Norway, which extended its ravages as far as Anglesea. In that expedition King Magnus was accompanied by another Magnus, whose fame has been perpetuated in many of the ecclesiastical build-ings of the north. The population of the Orkneys had been converted to Christianity under Olaus Trygvason in the tenth century. The Earl of Orkney at the time was Sigurd, who fell in the battle of Clontarf. The son of this Sigurd was Thorfin, who left two sons, Paul and Erlend, who divided the earldom between them. Erlend married Thora, daughter of Somerled, and by her had two sons, Magnus and Erling. Magnus was thus de-scended of the best blood in the Orkneys, while he could claim descent in the female line from the royal family of Scotland. Magnus from his youth was distinguished for his modesty and virtue among a group of turbulent relatives. In 1097 King Magnus made his expedition to the west. Having seized Paul and Erlend, the Orkney earls, he sent them as prisoners to Norway, placing his own son Sigurd, then a boy, over their territory. The sons of Paul and Erlend, Magnus, Erlend, and Haco, he ordered to join him in his expedition. At a great battle fought off the coast of Anglesea, Magnus, although present, refused to fight, saying that the men with whom they were about to engage never had done him any injury.

While the battle lasted, he sat down reading the psalter. This conduct enraged the king against him, and Magnus found it necessary for his safety and comfort to devise some mode of escape. When the Norwegian fleet, after their victory over the Britons, had returned to Scotland, Magnus on one occasion arranged his bed so as that it should have the appearance of being occupied, and escaped. His escape was soon discovered, and the king, resolving to have him taken, ordered his bloodhounds to be let loose. But Magnus, who had ascended a tree, was miraculously delivered, and finally found his way to the court of Malcolm.[1] It is related that he here remained for some time, having taken up his abode with a bishop. King Magnus in the meantime returned to the Hebrides, where he wintered, and having on the succeeding summer carried a large army to Ireland, he was slain in battle by the Ulstermen. Magnus having learned of the death of his father, which took place in Norway, proceeded forthwith to Caithness, where he was acknowledged earl. Here he at once assumed the place of an earnest Christian man, as his biographer says like another Saul becoming a Paul; exercising himself much in repentance for sin and such other exercises as belong to a truly religious life. Like another Moses he slew the man self, and buried him in the sand; and taking the images of Laban, he interred them under the roots of the trees. Magnus then became *Magnus*, 'great,' indeed, as his biographer remarks. His first cousin Haco in the meantime held the other half of the earldom. He was a man of the very opposite character from Magnus, violent in his passions

---

[1] Vita Magni, Pinkerton's ed., p. 399. According to the Irish Annals Malcolm Ceannmor was slain in 1093, and the expedition of Magnus Barelegs took place in 1097, so that the reference here could not be to Malcolm III. if the dates are correct. According to these the King of Scotland at the time of Magnus' escape was Edgar. Yet the dates may not be perfectly accurate, and Magnus may have sought the court of Malcolm for refuge.

and covetous of power and wealth. He had acquired more than his own territory by rapine, and held it in despite of Magnus the lawful possessor. Magnus earnestly sought for a peaceful settlement of differences, in which he finally succeeded, although in the case of Haco it was a settlement entirely destitute of sincerity. The two cousins are compared by the biographer of Magnus to Cain and Abel, and truly the issue was such as to justify the comparison. Being much troubled by the insidious enmity of Haco, Magnus sailed to England, where he put himself in communication with Henry I., the reigning monarch, by whom he was received with the utmost friendship. Here he remained for twelve months, commending himself to the admiration of all men by his modesty, his wisdom, and his piety. Laden with gifts, he returned to his own country, but found that Haco had taken advantage of his absence, and ravaged the whole of Orkney and Caithness, subduing the country to himself. On the return of Magnus, however, peace was made, and a new agreement entered into for the division of Shetland, Orkney, and Caithness equally between the two cousins. This agreement, however, was of short duration, for not long after Magnus was seized by Haco and his followers while engaged in worship in the church of Egilsay. Haco required of his cousin that he should at once proceed on a pilgrimage to Rome or to Jerusalem, in order to expiate both his sins and his own. This and many similar propositions Magnus firmly resisted, main-taining his right to his liberty and possessions. At length Haco ordered one of his followers to slay him on the spot. Struck with the aspect of the holy man, the man hesitated at first, but Magnus himself removing his scruples, he hewed him down with his axe. This murder, or as it has been called martyrdom, took place in the year 1110 (Vit. Magni. Pink. Ed., pp. 387,

435), according to Pinkerton, although the biographer of Magnus makes it 1104. And this would correspond better with what he says of Malcolm Ceannmor. It is to this Magnus that the cathedral of St. Magnus in Kirkwall is dedicated. His life stands out in marked contrast to those of the great body of the Scandinavian earls of the north, and indicates the growing power of religion among them.

There is no evidence of the existence of an episcopal diocese in Orkney and Shetland at this time. Indeed the earliest bishops of Orkney of whom we read were presbyters of York, who were ordained to the See by the archbishop of that diocese, in order to increase his own authority by extending the number of his suffragans. But we have no evidence of their ever residing there, or exercising spiritual jurisdiction. Such were Thorolf, Adalbert, and Rodolph, said to be bishops (Keith's Bishops, p. 219). Rodolph (Keith's Bishops, p. 220), is witness to a charter of David I., but as Keith remarks, not *qua Episc. Orcaden.* We have no satisfactory evidence of a fixed diocese in Orkney before the thirteenth century, or nearly three hundred years after the conversion of the Scandinavians to Christianity, and seven hundred years after the Christian faith was first planted in the Orkney islands.

The revolution, which had commenced under the auspices of Queen Margaret, may be seen proceeding with accelerated rapidity in the days of David I. For the most part, the change proceeded quietly, so far as we can see; but in such places as possessed Culdee establishments, it was more or less vigorously resisted.

Beginning at the Pentland Frith, there was no Bishop of Caithness or Sutherland previous to the close of David's reign, when we find, under the date 1150, Andrew, designated Bishop of Caithness (Keith's Bishops,

p. 205). Bishop Keith states, that it is certain that the diocese was erected long before the reign of Malcolm IV., but does not state upon what authority he says so. There does not appear to have been any resistance to the introduction of the bishop's authority in this quarter, the reason being, in all probability, that there was no leading Culdee institute within the bounds, perhaps owing to the long distracted state of the country. Not but that there was a Culdee church. Kildonan, in Sutherland, commemorates one of the most famous of the cotemporaries of Columba, indeed is said by some Irish authorities to have been the scene of his martyrdom ; and Culmailie, in Golspie, is commemorative of a saint of Scotland whose name was equally savoury on the banks of the Beauly and on the shores of Lochiel. In the same county we have Kilcolmkill, Kilmachalmaig, and other ' Kils,' all indicating the existence of Culdee worship to the north of the Dornoch Firth. The diocese of Andrew, Bishop of Caithness, seems from the beginning to have embraced the two counties of Caithness and Sutherland ; and although the earliest records of the country indicate the residence of the bishop as having been in Caithness, Dornoch would seem at the earliest period to have been the See of the diocese. The diocese appears to have been founded by David, although not without a measure of approbation and support from the Scandinavian earls of Caithness and Orkney.

The first bishop of the See of Ross we find styled " Episcopus Rossmarkiensis."[1] Opposite Fort George, on

---

[1] Winton's story of the founding of this See by St. Boniface seems quite apocryphal. Boniface, who is said to have come from Italy in order to conform the Scottish to the Roman Church in the eighth century, is never referred to by Bede, who gives a full account of the conversion of the Picts. The tradition originated, most probably, in the selection of Boniface as patron saint of the diocese. The story of St. Andrew is enough to throw suspicion on all such traditions.

the north side of the Moray Firth, lies the burgh of Fortrose. A little to the east is the modern village of Rossmarkie, which appears to have given his first title to the incumbent of the See of Ross, in all likelihood the existing minister of this, one of the most accessible and fertile of the parishes in the diocese. The first bishop is said to have been Macbeth, a Celtic minister. He witnesses a charter of David so early as before 1128 (Keith's Bishops, p. 184). Indeed David's charters are abundantly witnessed by bishops, and shew as if his purpose were, by having them about him, to give them all the consequence that could be conferred by royal favour. Feudal lords and Romish bishops became now the chief denizens of the Scottish court. Nor is it unlikely that if David's favour gave consequence, he sought a similar return for his court, by having it surrounded with dependent magnates of the country, whether in church or state. The purity of the church would, in such circumstances, become less a question of consequence than its power and grandeur. Now, then, the Culdees of Applecross disappear; we hear no more of the successors of Malrubha, but in their room we begin to hear of the consecration of bishops, for in 1161 Gregory was consecrated Bishop of Rossmarkie by Arnold, Bishop of St. Andrews, the Pope's legate (Keith's Bishops, Ross). Rome had now got a secure footing in the territory of the ancient Scots. The ancient Killearnan and Kilmichael were but a short distance from the new bishop's seat of Rossmarkie, places of more consequence than itself in former times, but the rising glory of an episcopal hierarchy was about to eclipse all the pristine glory of Scotland and its Church.

Passing southward we reach the province of Moray, separated from Ross by the Moray Firth and some of its tributaries. Here was the ancient seat of the Maormors of Moray, long related by the closest ties to the Scottish throne, and often rivals for its possession. This province received the Christian faith from Columba himself, for King Brude's stronghold, near Inverness, was within its bounds. From the reign of Brude Mac Meilchon then, or the middle of the sixth century, the inhabitants of Moray had possessed the faith of Christ. Of the manner of its maintenance we find no record. We read of no institutions like Abernethy, Dunkeld, or St. Andrews, but Iona was itself within the territory of the Pictish king, and was probably looked up to in the north as the source of all Christian privilege. That there were other institutions in the region is evident from the recent discovery of the Book of Deer, with its Gaelic charters and other records of the Culdee establishment of Deer in Buchan, so far back as the tenth and eleventh centuries.

Nor are we without some traditions at least of the planting of the Gospel in this quarter, in addition to what we have learned of Columba and Maelrubha. On the 30th October, according to the Aberdeen Breviary, was commemorated in the early Church, Talarican, confessor and priest. The Breviary tells us of this early missionary that he was of Irish extraction, but the name as Talorgan is so frequent among the Pictish annals that there is every probability of his having been a native Pict. Having devoted himself to the service of God, he also sought to commend it to other men, and preached the Gospel faithfully in the northern parts of Scotland, converting the inhabitants from paganism to the faith of Christ. Aberdeen, Moray, and Ross, were the provinces to which his labours were chiefly confined. In the north-west corner of the province of Moray, on the south side of the Beauly river, lies Kiltarlity, a church in which the name of this early missionary is commemorated.

The same saint is commemorated in the church of Portree in Skye.

Close by Kiltarlity, but in the diocese of Ross, lies Kilmorack, a church commemorative of another Celtic saint. The account given of this saint, whose day is the 8th November, in the Aberdeen Breviary is, that he was a bishop of Dunblane. Bishop Nicolson (Scot. Hist. Lib. App., No. 5) quotes a bull of Pope Adrian IV., addressed among other prelates to M. Bishop of Dunblane. Could this be the Morag or Moroc of the Breviary? Perhaps not, for the day of the "Kils" had passed in Scotland before the pontificate of this Pope Adrian. Besides, the authenticity of the bull is doubted, and Moroc, like Talarican, must be held to have been one of the old Scottish missionaries, perhaps from an institution of Culdees at Dunblane, who aided in carrying the Gospel to these northern provinces.

Near the town of Inverness is a spot called Cill Bheathain or the church of St. Baithen, and near it is Tor Bheathain or *Baithen's hill*, said to contain his sepulchre, both clearly commemorative of one of the famous Beathans or Beans of the early church (Stat. Acc. of Inverness). In the same neighbourhood is the ferry of Kessock, called after the famous St. Kessog, who miraculously escaped drowning, according to the legend, when in charge of the sons of the King of Munster, and as miraculously resuscitated the youths who had been drowned. A few miles to the west of these is Urquhart, called Urchudain Maith Dhrostan or Saint Drostan's Urquhart, after the famous saint of that name. According to the Aberdeen Breviary (Dec. 19), this saint was nephew of Columba, and thus of the royal family of Scotland. He was sent to Ireland to be educated, and became abbot of what the Breviary calls Dalquongale. The name Drostan is however manifestly Pictish, and the fact of his being described as leaving Ireland and becoming an anchorite at Glenesk, goes to shew that in all likelihood he was a Pict, but farther, that his age was later than that of Columba, from there being no mention of him by the ecclesiastical writers of the period. Drostan was however without doubt an early saint, whose name was of good repute in the north of Scotland. But it is needless to accumulate instances, which might be found throughout its borders, to shew that the ancient Scottish Church had a strong hold in the province of Moray, and that it remained unchanged from the sixth century to the twelfth.

In the reign of Alexander I., which extended from A.D. 1107 to 1124, Moray is said to have become a diocesan see. That Alexander was wishful to carry out the views and wishes of his mother and introduce the Romish Hierarchy in accordance with the English model, will appear more clearly when we come to deal with the changes introduced in St. Andrews, but there is much reason to believe that during his reign a bishop of the name of Gregory existed for the first time in Moray. There was no cathedral seat in the province (Grub's Eccl. Hist. i. 219), so that there was no Culdee College in connection with which the bishop might have been appointed, but now for the first time a bishop appears. There is no record of his consecration, nor does there appear to have been any authority establishing the diocese beyond that of the king. The authority of the pope had not as yet been recognised in Scotland. There is no record of any consecration, and the probability is that the organisation of the Church on the new model was as yet far from definite or generally understood. But the Scottish kings were becoming feudal monarchs, and as such it was needful to have a feudal nobility and an ecclesiastical hierarchy. We have said that many modern writers call this the progress of civilization, and that the object of Alexander and his brothers was to civilize the Scots. If so it was a civilization which required but four centuries to make the nation glad to get rid of it, and one that so far as the original Scots were concerned helped to sink them into a state bordering upon utter barbarism. Let the history of the Highland clans for centuries testify as to this.

The evidence existing in proof of the See of Moray having been erected by Alexander, is found in a charter given by him to the monastery of Scone, which is witnessed by Gregory, bishop of Moray, among others. (Liber de Scone, p. 4). At its first institution the diocese of Moray is said to have embraced Ross, Sutherland, and Caithness, the two latter being of King David's foundation.

To the south-east of the diocese of Moray lay that of Aberdeen. The usual account of the foundation here is, that it was planted at Mortlach, in Banffshire, most probably by Malcolm III., as already said, and was transferred to Aberdeen by his son David. The charter to Beyn of Mortlach has been referred to already, as well as the dispute respecting the Malcolm who conferred it. Keith (Bishops, note, p. 559) gives some reasons for thinking it was Malcolm II., and that the date should be 1010 and not 1070, as other writers suppose. The charter confers the church of Cloveth (Clova), with its lands, and the church of Dulmeth, that Beyn may be able to build an episcopal seat at Mortlach. It may be asked of any man who knows aught of the state of Scotland at the time, whether such a grant was within the limits of possible things in 1010. It is questionable whether even Malcolm III. had the church of Cloveth and the church of Dulmeth to grant, as this charter indicates. One thing is certain, that we hear nothing of the episcopal seat having been built. Nor can we suppose that there ever was at Mortlach anything beyond a Culdee college, and that college does not appear to have had any jurisdiction beyond Mortlach itself, and perhaps such lands as might belong to it; its jurisdiction certainly did not extend over the modern diocese of Aberdeen. The charters of the Book of Deer make no reference to any such institution. The See is said to have been transferred to Aberdeen in 1125 (Grub's Eccl. Hist., 266). The first charter to the diocese is of the thirteenth year of the reign of David I., or 1137, when Nectan is addressed as bishop, and when David grants to God, the blessed Mary and the blessed Machar, and to Nectan, Bishop of Aberdeen, the whole town of Old Aberdeen, the half waters of Ourth, Sclattie, Goule, Muirecroft, Kinmundy, Mameulach, and the church of Kirktoun, parish of Clatt; the parish of Daviot Tillienestin; the parish of Raine; the parish of Deivot, with the pertinents, &c. This charter makes no reference to Mortlach, conveys none of the lands of Mortlach, or the parishes of Cloveth and Dulmeth, to Aberdeen. Besides it is of interest to note, that while Mortlach was dedicated to St. Maluag, Aberdeen was dedicated to St. Machar. Aberdeen was, no doubt, founded early in the reign of David I., but the transference of the See from Mortlach is a mere tradition without sufficient evidence, and was probably originated, like many similar traditions, in order to give the Aberdeen foundation a claim to a higher antiquity than it could otherwise possess. The other important bishoprics originated in some older institution of the kind, and why should not this? The only difficulty was, that in St. Andrews, Dunkeld, and Brechin, older institutions of such a character did exist, and in the case of Aberdeen it was needful to go to

Mortlach to find one; and Malcolm's relation to Mortlach gave it a consequence far above that of Deer or any
other Culdee establishment in the locality. If the
tradition of the transference be true there is nothing
remarkable in David's honouring the memory of his
father so far as to convert his humble Culdee college
into a great episcopate. There was everything in such a
project to gratify his own taste, and in accordance with
the known predilections of both his father and mother. In
every view of it, however, the bishopric of Aberdeen is to
be classed among David's foundations, originating between the year 1124 and 1137, it may be as early
as 1125. It is worthy of notice that here and at
Ross the first bishops were native Celts. Their names,
Macbeth and Nectan, make this indisputable, so that
there were found among the native clergy some men
willing to accept of bishoprics. Andrew of Caithness,
and Gregory of Moray, were probably of a different
race. The Andreas and the Gregorius look like importations from some other quarter.

In all probability, in the days of David, the spoken
language of Aberdeen was Gaelic, although along the
sea shore there must have been a Teutonic population, like that which peopled the Orkneys. There
is a remarkable resemblance to this day between the
spoken language of Aberdeenshire and that of Orkney
and Shetland.

The next diocese founded to the south of Aberdeen was
that of Brechin. There is no certainty of its existence previous to the reign of Malcolm IV., when its bishop's name
appears in a charter; but the tradition is that it was founded
by David I., and there is nothing to render the tradition
improbable. This diocese was associated with the old
Culdee establishment founded by the great Kenneth II.
Nor had this establishment lost its hold on the public

2 A

mind, for David, notwithstanding his desire for the new state of things, constituted the Culdees, who were usually twelve in number, the Dean and Chapter of the diocese, an arrangement which would not have been made if the older clergy had been so corrupt as a certain class of writers has represented them. In this case the new state of things was grafted upon the old. Indeed this was David's usual policy, although in some cases, as we will see, departed from; but the change was resolved upon, and carried through at all hazards.

CHAPTER XXIV.

THE next diocese to Brechin southwards was the archdiocese of St. Andrews, regarding whose history there
has been so much controversy. The usual belief in
regard to this see is that at the earliest period in Scotland the primacy in the Church appertained to the monastery of Iona, that from thence it was transferred to
Abernethy, from thence to Dunkeld, and thence finally
to St. Andrews, during the reign of Constantine the son
of Aodh, or Hugh, when Cellach was the first bishop.
If there was a primacy in Iona to be so transferred it
was a primacy of presbyters. Writers upon the Episcopal
side allow this (Grub's Eccl. Hist., c. x.). The primacy,
as it is called, was in the hands either of the presbyter
abbot or his coadjutor presbyters in the institution. It
is but natural to ask whether such a primacy meets the
requirements of those who hold the Episcopal view ?
Are they satisfied that this was a real primacy, as they
usually understand it, and can the peculiarity of the circumstances of the ancient Scottish Church account satis-
factorily for all that is awanting in the case of these
anomalous primates ? If so, the Episcopal system has an
amount of elasticity about it which has not been hitherto
generally understood, and a presbyter, or group of presbyters, can exercise some of the most important episcopal
and arch-episcopal functions. It may also be very natu-

rally asked, of what did Iona hold the primacy. The usual way of putting it is, that Iona held the primacy of the Scottish Church. But it is very well known that the "parochia" of the Columbite system consisted of affiliated monasteries or colleges, and hence the jurisdiction of Iona must have extended to Ireland alone, for the only similar establishment said to have existed in Scotland from an early period was Abernethy, and there is not a shred of evidence to shew that it was in any way subject to the jurisdiction of Iona. As for Dunkeld, the primacy is said to have been transferred there when the church was built and the relics of Columba removed thither. But the question at once occurs, if the jurisdiction possessed by Iona was removed to Dunkeld, did Iona become thenceforth subject to Dunkeld? Of this there is no evidence whatsoever. Any supremacy that existed so far as Iona was concerned, seems to have existed in the Irish institutions of Kells and Armagh. Iona was not subjected to Dunkeld until the territorial diocese of Dunkeld was founded. The idea of primacy existing in these Columbite foundations is entirely an *ex post facto* one, and was intended to support claims of a modern growth. It has as little foundation in fact as the claims of the archbishop of York and Canterbury to the subjection of the Scottish Church, although these were at one time as earnestly maintained. The idea of primacy had never existed in the minds of these early missionaries, but grew up with the progress of events in the Church. When Scotland obtained its primate it was needful, if possible, to trace the roots of his authority into the old church, and men did so, although it finally landed their orders and jurisdiction among a group of presbyters with their presbyter chief at their head.

But the primacy of the Scottish Church is a term that

requires explanation. At all events it is a term not synonymous with the primacy of what is now called Scotland. It is not to be forgotten that although for a century after the planting of Christianity, the Pictish kingdom continued to receive its ministers from Iona, that arrangement ceased with the reign of Naitan or Nectan, who introduced the Roman Easter among his subjects. By him the Scottish ministers were expelled, and it is inconsistent with fact to maintain that from the middle of the eighth century Iona exercised any supremacy in the Pictish church. From that period the Saxon church of the south might be more justly said to possess authority among the Picts. Over the foundation at St. Andrew's Iona never possessed any jurisdiction, for its clerical founders came from among the Saxons; and by the time that the Scottish and Pictish kingdoms were united, the glory of Iona itself was passing away, and its jurisdiction could have been at most nominal, although its memory was still savoury, and its consecrated soil received the ashes of the kings for many generations.

About 820, or nearly 200 years after the Scottish clergy were expelled from the Pictish dominions, Dunkeld was founded by Constantine Mac Fergus, the Pictish king. Nothing can be more at variance with historical fact than a common impression,[1] that Dunkeld and St. Andrews arose consecutively, and that each successively received the primacy. St. Andrews existed for nearly a hundred years before Dunkeld, nor during that period was there any idea of primacy at all, although the institution seems to have been founded on the model of the Northumbrian monasteries, which were themselves originally of the Scottish type. When Dunkeld was founded there is

---

[1] It is often averred that Abernethy succeeded Iona in the primacy of Scotland. There is no evidence in support of this.

nothing in the notice we have of the event to signify that there was any primacy intended. "He built Dunkeld," is all the annalist relates of this good work of Constantine Mac Fergus. In 843, or twenty years later, Kenneth M'Alpin is said to have brought a portion of the relics of Columba to Dunkeld. From this most likely was derived the idea of primacy. This did no doubt give Dunkeld a place in the eyes of Scotsmen which it would not otherwise possess, and invested it with a new measure of consequence ; but it was of short duration, for in the reign of Constantine, the son of Aodh or Hugh, the Scoto-Pictish king, the authority is said to have been removed to St. Andrews. This is said to have been the result of the council held by Constantine at Scone, at which Cellach the bishop was present with a large assemblage of the Scots. Mr. Robertson calls this bishop Fothad, and it does require a good deal of ingenious management to synchronise the bishops and kings of this period, according to the usual chronology. The Colbertine MS. (Inn. Crit. Ess., App. p. 785) is decided as to the bishop being Cellach, and if Fordun's story be true that Fothadh was expelled by Indulf, who began his reign in 954, he could hardly have been in office in the early part of the reign of Constantine. The Colb. MS. is the best evidence on the subject we possess, and on its authority we may very well believe that Constantine, with his clergy and people, held a meeting on the Moothill of Scone about the year 906, to make arrangements regarding the Church. But that does not afford the slightest evidence to show that the transference of the primacy had anything to do with the meeting. The annalist does not say so, and short as his notice is, a matter so important was not likely to be overlooked. It is pretty manifest, from the existing evidence, and from what is known of the state of the Scottish Church at the time, that the idea of primacy was never present to men's minds, and that if there was any discussion about St. Andrews and Dunkeld at all, it would be as to which of them was the safer repository for the relics of St. Columba, seeing that the latter had recently been visited by the northmen in one of their predatory expeditions. The idea of primacy amongst these ancient colleges of presbyters is one of purely recent origin, and seems to have originated with a numerous class of writers on Scottish ecclesiastical anti-quities, who have a theory of their own to support, and who cannot conceive of anything in the past history of their country at variance with that theory, which they maintain no doubt with perfect sincerity, but with wondrous little regard to facts. Primacy in Scotland originated with the incoming of southern ideas and practices through Margaret and her sons, and was no doubt largely aided by the necessity of obtaining a suitable set-off against the diocese of York or Canter-bury, and their claims to the submission of the Scot-tish Church. The necessity for this would invest the incoming of primacy with a measure of popularity in the eye of the nation. It was a protest against English claims, and for Scottish independence.

It has been said that the removal of the primacy from Dunkeld to St. Andrews was the result of the restoration of the Church's liberties[1] in the reign of Girg, Cyrie, or Grigor, between 878 and 889. The notice in the Register of St. Andrews is—" He first gave liberty to the Scottish Church, which was in a state of servitude until that time, according to the constitution and custom of the Picts." It is difficult to see what connection this has with the primacy either of St. Andrews or Dunkeld. It has to do more probably with the condition of the Scottish Church among the

[1] Pink. Eng. ii. 269 ; Chalm. Cal. i. 429.

Picts since the days of Nectan, who expelled the Scottish clergy. That the legislation of Nectan should remain for forty years unrepealed after the days of Kenneth Macalpine, is somewhat remarkable, for it is clear by his removal of the relics of St. Columba to Dunkeld, and his bringing Scottish ministers to St. Andrews that Kenneth was friendly to the Scottish Church ; but he might be at the same time not unwilling to retain any despotic power over that church which Pictish legislation gave him, or his hands might be so full of other immediately pressing matters that the general condition of the Church could not be looked into or effectively dealt with. Grig, on the other hand, was a successful usurper, although possessing lawful rights, and it is by no means unlikely that he was willing to conciliate the clergy by giving the Church her liberty. This, and not a question of primacy, seems to have been the matter dealt with by the enfranchising act of King Grig.

From the beginning of the tenth century, it is said, that St. Andrews possessed both a bishop and an abbot. (Grub's Eccl. Hist., i. 171). On what authority this statement is made we do not learn, and in consequence it may be true or it may not. The Bishops of St. Andrews are said to have been " Episcopi Scotorum," and to have had jurisdiction over the whole nation. And yet no contemporary authority, no authority more ancient than the establishment of diocesan episcopacy, can be shown for the statement. By none such is the term Bishop of St. Andrews used, and it is a mere assumption to say that " Episcopi Scotorum " meant the Bishops of St. Andrews. In fact we know that the Bishop of St. Andrews was not " Episcopus Scotorum " down to the period of Kenneth M'Alpin, even if such an office did exist. He was more probably "Episcopus Pictorum." Yet from the reign of Kenneth downwards for two hundred

years, till that of Malcolm Ceannmor, it is impossible
to maintain that St. Andrews exercised any jurisdiction over the ancient institution at Iona, or over any portion of the territory of the northern Picts. It has been
said that St. Andrews was a See, not a diocese. It is unnecessary to show how inextricable must be the confusion
in a Church constituted on the Episcopal model, where
the jurisdiction of bishops is not confined within certain
limits. Inferences have been made on this subject entirely
unwarranted by facts. There were " Episcopi " among the
Scots, but to these the jurisdiction of the Bishop of St.
Andrews cannot be traced, in any fair sense. On this
matter the Register of St. Andrews alone is not sufficient
evidence as to events which occurred hundreds of years
before it was commenced, and under a system entirely
different from that then existing, in which the writers
were deeply interested.

Cellach is said to have been the first Bishop of St.
Andrews, although Fordun and Keith make him Fothad.
Cellach is represented as holding the office in 880, and
after. To Cellach is said to have succeeded this Fothad,
who remained in office till the reign of Indulf. By the
Four Masters he is called *Fothadh Mac Brain, Episcopus insularum Alban*, 'Bishop of the isles of Scotland,'
a very different title from that of St. Andrews. The
king is said by some historians (Fordun and Winton) to
have expelled him, for what reason is not related. It
would seem that the liberty secured to the Church by
King Grig was not acquiesced in by some of his successors. At least this was a remarkable stretch of regal
authority against the Primate, as he is called. Indulf
was a brave and vigorous king, who successfully withstood the Northmen, but we learn nothing from the
annalists of his having been unfriendly to the Church.

If, however, he expelled the bishop, it would appear that he had the power of so doing.

If the Register of St. Andrews is to be credited, and it professes in this case to copy from old Gaelic records, similar probably to the recently discovered Book of Deer, a transaction of some interest took place at this period between the bishop and the Culdees of Lochleven. It is said that "the Culdees gave the place of their cell (celluli) to the Bishop of St. Andrews, on condition that the bishop supplied them with food and clothing." The bishop is called Fothath, son of Bren, and the party making the grant is Ronan, monk and abbot. Whether Fothadh was called Bishop of St. Andrews in the original Gaelic record we have no means now of knowing, but there are several things of an interesting nature in the grant irrespective of this. For instance, Ronan of Lochleven is called "vir admirandæ sanctitatis," a remarkable statement, if the usual idea of the corruption of the Culdee Church be true. Then, in addition to the acceptance of the grant, the bishop gives his "plenary benediction to all who should observe this convention, and regard the friendship now begun (initum) between the bishop and the Culdees." Whence it is manifest that the friendship of the Culdees was viewed as a great gain by the bishop,—so great that a regard to it was held to merit his plenary benediction. These Culdees were holy men, but were manifestly hostile to the hierarchical jurisdiction which was beginning to shew itself around them, and it was of importance to have them conciliated. It is not at all unlikely, however, that this transaction is considerably antedated, and belongs to a period nearer that of Malcolm III. and his sons, than that of Indulf or his successor Duff.

Malbride (Maolbrighde) succeeded Fothadh. He is sometimes called Malise (Maoliosa), (Keith's Bishops,

p. 5.) In the Colbertine MS. (Inn. Crit. Ess., p. 278), is the entry under the reign of Culen, "Maelbrigd episcopus pausavit." There is no reference whatsoever to St. Andrews, yet he is made Bishop of St. Andrews, and introduced formally into the roll of primates. His period is given as extending from 962 to 970, but this is problematical (Grub's Eccl. Hist., i. 176). The Irish annalists mention no such bishop, but they do mention a Maelbride who died in 927, and who is in all probability the Malbride, alias Malise, who is called Bishop of St. Andrews. Malbride, son of Tornan, called St. Malbride, was successor both of Patrick and Columba, and, as already noticed, was called "the head of the piety of all Ireland and of the greater part of Europe." Can there be a doubt that this was the Malbride whom Fordun and others have attempted to enrol among the earlier primates of St. Andrews? The entry in the Colbertine MS. is so indefinite that it will perfectly well bear this interpretation. The chronology in either case is not to be depended upon within a few years. This Malbride was Abbot of Iona, and his fame might well ensure the notice given of him by the early Scottish chronicler.

The successor of Malbride is said to have been Cellach (from *Ceall,* 'a church), usually spelt Kellach. The statement is founded on one in the Colbertine MS., in which it is said, that after the death of Malbride, Cellach, son of Ferdalaig, reigned (regnavit). There was a Ceallach Mac Findguine, and a Ceallach Mac Bairedha, at this time two of the Maormors of Scotland, to whom the word "regnavit" would more properly apply than to a Celtic bishop. To be sure the bishop was the son of Ferdalaig; but granting that this Cellach was a bishop, the annalist makes no reference to St. Andrews, nor was his name attached to St. Andrews until the days of Fordun, four hundred years after. And yet it is said that he held the primacy, the period of his incumbency being stated at twenty-five years, from 970 to 995. Kenneth, son of Malcolm, the King of the Scoto-Picts, died in 994, so that it was during the supposed primacy of Cellach that the ecclesiastical establishment at Brechin was founded.

Cellach's supposed period was also that in which Cadroe, usually called St. Cadroe, flourished. This was an ecclesiastic of the Scottish school, and, through his father Faiteach, a connection of the Scottish royal family. He was trained in the great school of Armagh, an institution which arose chiefly upon the ruins of Iona, and having returned to Britain gave himself to the service of the Church, especially to the training of young ministers. After a while he left his post in Scotland, and travelling through Cumbria into England, he finally embarked for France, and being joined by an Irish coadjutor of the name of Macallin, he proceeded to Perronne, to the monastery of St. Fursey. He finally joined the order of St. Benedict, and after various changes died at Metz. His story (Colgan's edition of Vita B. Cardroc), is a remarkable instance of the connection between the Scottish and Continental Churches being continued down to the tenth century. There was a continual stream of missionaries from the Churches of Ireland and Scotland flowing towards the Continental Church, of which we have ample evidence in the numerous Gaelic MSS. belonging to these churches found in continental monasteries.

Cellach is said to have been succeeded by a second Maolbrighde or Malbride about the year 995. It is a remarkable fact that the former Malbride as well as this one is called by Fordun Malise. Are they the same man, and do they both find their representative in the great Maolbrighde of the four masters? They may not, but it is curious that in 1005 the Four masters note the death of *Maolbrighde Ua Rimhedha abbas Iae,* "Mal-

bride Ua Rimhedha abbot of Iona." There is every
probability that this is the man whom Fordun and
others have transported to the see of St. Andrews.
Nothing would be more likely than such a transference
in the days of Fordun. The Irish annalists, our best
authorities for this period, although we would fain have
better if we could, make no reference to a Malbride,
Bishop of St. Andrews, and there is no good reason for
believing that such a man ever had an existence. Maolmuire or Malmore (the servant of Mary), is the reputed
successor of Malbride, (Keith's Bishops,) (Grub's Eccl.
History.) It is said that there is difficulty in fixing the
period of his primacy, or that of his predecessor. The
Irish annals may perhaps aid in this. According to these
the head of the Columbite order was at this period a Maolmuire, a rather remarkable fact taken in connection with
those regarding the Malbrides. One Malmuire Ua h-Uch-
tain died in 1009, another of precisely the same name and
lineage in 1040. Dr. Reeves suspects that they are the
same individual, and judging by the inaccuracies in the
chronology of the time, not without reason. The second
Maolmuire is called " Coarb of Columba and Adomnan,"
(Ann. of Four Masters) identifying him fully with Scotland and Iona. The annalists make no reference to any
Maolmuire or Malmore in St. Andrews, but their reference to the other suggests very clearly the conclusion
that he, said to be of St. Andrews, was in reality the
Presbyter abbot of the ancient institution at Iona. It is
not difficult to conceive how, in after times, such men
should be called primates of the Scottish Church, and be
transferred to St. Andrews as their see.

According to Fordun and others, Alwin succeeded
Malmore, the date of his succession being variously
stated, from 1025 to 1031. He is said to have held the
See for three years. Of him we have no notice in the

Irish annals ; but it is a remarkable thing that a Saxon, for the name is a Saxon one, should at this period be Bishop of a purely Gaelic people. The name appears among the monks of Melrose in the tenth century, but it is in connection with the kingdom of Northumbria (Mon. Hist. Brit. pp. 688 n.)

Alwin's successor is said to have been Malduin,[1] called by Tighernac, Mac Gillaodran, and by the Four Masters Mac Gilleandreas. Tighernac's title for this man is *Episcopus Alban*, "Bishop of Scotland," which does by no means signify bishop of St. Andrews. The annalist further adds, that he was *gloria cleri Gaedhil*, " The glory of the Gaelic clergy." The period of this supposed Primate was that of Duncan and his successor Macbeth, his death taking place in 1055, during the reign of the latter. It is remarkable that in none of the existing authorities of the period is there any notice of this prelate, or of his fame or influence, amidst the remarkable movements that took place. It is beyond doubt that there was at the time a bishop of the old Scottish school in the Scottish Church called Malduin Mac Gillaodran, as Tighernac has it, or Mac Gilleandreas as Fordun and Winton have it, but there is nothing to fix him down at St. Andrews, save the authority of these latter writers of a much later age. No doubt the Register of St. Andrew's Priory records a grant from him as bishop, to the Culdees of Loch Leven, conveying to them the Church of Markinch with its liberties, quite in the feudal style. But it cannot be forgotten in estimating the value of such a statement, that the Priory of St. Andrews itself did not exist for a hundred years after the grant is said to have been made, and that a regular feudal charter of the period of Macbeth would be a wonder indeed. Macbeth himself is said by the same

---

[1] Probably " Maoldomhnaich " *servant of God.*

authority to have bestowed upon these Culdees the lands of Kirkness and Bolgy. This is credible enough, for the Scottish kings seem to have been liberal to these ancient schools, but a similar grant from a Bishop of St. Andrews at the same period represents a transaction so much at variance with the state of things which most writers acknowledge as existing in the Scottish Church at the time, that we may very safely count the grant for very little as evidence of the existence of a Primate of St. Andrews in 1040. The Scribe who commenced the Register had every temptation to record grants such as this on very slender proof of their existence.

It is true that many writers upon this period are prepared to base their belief in the existence of a Scottish primacy upon the fact that the Scots had but one bishop, and that he was called the bishop of the Scots, as the Irish annalists describe some of these ecclesiastics, calling them " Episcopi Alban." But what becomes of the early bishops of the rest of Scotland upon this theory ? Were there no successors of Ninian at Whithorn, or of Kentigern at Glasgow, or of the early bishops at Iona ? Were the bishops of Scotland reduced to one ? To acknowledge this would be acknowledging too much, especially in the face of such statements as we find in the early Irish annals, indicating distinctly the existence of bishops in the islands and elsewhere. The fact is, there is no evidence sufficient to shew the existence of St. Andrews as an episcopal see in the days of Malduin.

According to Fordun Malduin was succeeded by Tuchald, Tuadal, or Tuathal.[1] He is represented as granting to the same Culdees of Loch Leven the church of Sconin (Scoonie). These unfortunate denizens of Loch Leven seem to have been fattened by the incumbents of St. Andrews

---

[1] The name is probably represented by the modern Dugald.

for their own peculiar benefit at a future time, for we shall see how all these lands were reclaimed. At least these ancient bishops had a remarkable friendship for the Culdees, which was more than could be said of their successors. It is curious that the Culdees of the amous institute of St. Andrews itself came in for no share of these grants. Is there anything ungenerous in supposing that at an after period the canons of St. Andrews felt somewhat uncomfortable, from the harsh and unjust manner in which the Culdees were deprived of these lands, by David I., when transferred to them; or in further supposing, that there was a strong desire to vindicate the transaction, by endeavouring to shew that the lands were originally granted by these ancient bishops, and might, therefore, be very justly restored? It is curious that grants to Loch Leven are the only grants of Bishops on record, of the period. Tuathal is said to have filled the See for nearly four years.

The successor of Tuathal is said to have been another Fothadh, who succeeded in 1059, and was bishop during the whole reign of Malcolm Ceannmòr. The Irish annalists call him "Fothudh Archiepiscopus Alban." The title here is now known to have reference merely to the personal qualifications of the bishop (Todd's St. Patrick). Indeed even in the time of those incumbents of St. Andrews, who flourished for a long time after the period of David I., their title is simply "Bishop of St. Andrews." Fordun tells us of this Fothudh, that he was only "elect," a remarkable statement, if it be true that he held the See for thirty-four years. At the same time his name is mingled with important transactions. He is said to have married Queen Margaret to King Malcolm (Scotichron, Lib. v). He is also said to have given the church of Auchterderrane to the Culdees of Loch Leven.[1] It is at

[1] Reg. of Priory of St. Andrews. It is curious that each of three successive

the same time hard to make all the statements regarding him to hang well together. He is the second Fothadh, another of the same name appearing in the previous century, on no authority, save that Fordun saw his name on the silver cover of a book, where he was called, "primus Episcopus Scotorum," a title not unlike the "Ardescop" of the Ulster annals applied to him; then his being Bishop "elect" merely in Fordun's list is remarkable; and further, that, in the Register of St. Andrews, he is called "Modach, son of Malmykal;" and, most remarkable of all, that his name does not appear in the pages of Turgot, even as celebrating the marriage of Queen Margaret, nor does it appear in any other document of the time in which he lived, if we except the Ulster annals, and from these we can but gather that Fothadh was a bishop of the ancient Scottish church.

An interesting entry appears in the annals of Inisfallen respecting the Irish church under the year 1110. It is said that "The Synod of Rathbreasail divided Ireland into Dioceses." Now, for the first time was that church, which was so intimately associated during so many centuries with the church of Scotland, apportioned among diocesan bishops. Ireland usually took the lead of Scotland in such movements, and there is every reason to believe that she did so in that which brought the church in both countries under hierarchical rule.

One of the most important events of the period of Malcolm Ceannmor, was the foundation of the church of Dunfermline. It was designed by Queen Margaret, and erected on the spot where she was married, in commemoration of that event. It was dedicated to the Trinity (Vit. Marg. cap. vii), a new thing in the Scottish church,

bishops should have given to these Loch Leven Culdees, one church,—Malduin, Markinch; Tuathal, Scoonie; and Fothadh, Auchterderran.

2 B

whose ancient "Kils" were usually mere memorials of native worthies. Turgot does not state that a monastery was erected in the same place ; but in the reign of David a Benedictine monastery was established there, and supplied with monks from Canterbury. It is an instructive fact that Turgot, in relating the erection of this church, and in stating, at the same time, that the Queen erected, at St. Andrews, a cross of high sanctity, gives no sign that he looked upon St. Andrews as 'a place of primatial dignity. He merely speaks of it as one of many churches, which the Queen favoured, informing us, no doubt, that it was at the time a place of great resort for pilgrims.

In her measures for reforming the Scottish Church Margaret was advised and aided by Lanfranc, the archbishop of Canterbury. A letter from the archbishop exists (Scot. Eccl. Journ., vol. i., p. 120), addressed to the queen. Where was Fothadh the archbishop of St. Andrews at such a time ? How does his name never appear in connection with the great movements of the period ? Or was he disowned both by the Scottish king and the Saxon queen, notwithstanding his having joined them in wedlock ? The English archbishop, and no less the English chronicler, would have made some reference to the Scottish primate were there not some good cause to prevent them, or even had such a dignitary any existence, to bring him within the sphere of their knowledge.

And yet this is the Scottish prelate of whom it is said that he subjected the See of St. Andrews to the archdiocese of York. The English prelates, like the English kings, had long been covetous of Scottish subjection, more especially the former, who had in 1070 divided the British territory between the two metropolitan Sees of Canterbury and York, the limits of the latter extending from the Humber to the extreme north of Scotland. But it is not easy seeing what share any Scottish prelate could have in sacrificing the independence of his church. If there was no diocese of St. Andrews in the days of Fothadh, it is hard to see how he could have subjected it to the See of York. The letter of Alexander I. to Archbishop Lanfranc, in which he says that "the bishops of St. Andrews were wont to be consecrated only by the Pope himself or by the Archbishop of Canterbury" (Hailes' Ann. i. 60), is, if genuine, merely evidence of the change which Margaret and her sons were bringing on the condition of the Scottish Church, and the miserable shifts to which they were driven on the one hand to preserve their independence, while on the other they were introducing the whole Roman system into their dominions. There is something however very inexplicable in Alexander's acknowledging in this letter the authority of the English metropolitan, and yet resisting it afterwards, as will be seen, so as to endanger the very fabric of the Church he was trying to raise. Nor can it be forgotten that the recorder of that letter is Eadmer, afterwards bishop elect of St. Andrews, and a devoted servant of the See of Canterbury. Alexander's letter and Alexander's conduct are irreconcilable ; Eadmer's conduct when chosen a Scottish bishop, is perfectly reconcilable with the tone and tenor of the king's letter, and might very well be justified by its contents. This may account for its existence.

Fothadh died, according to the best authorities, in 1093 (Ann. of Ulster), the same year with King Malcolm, his incumbency and Malcolm's reign being almost contemporaneous. That during his time tendencies to very marked and decided change were appearing in the Scottish Church cannot be doubted. The interference of the queen with the practices of the Church, and her summon-

ing of councils is sufficient proof of it. How far Fothadh
or the native ministers approved of her proceedings does
not appear, nor need we wonder at Turgot's silence upon
the subject ; but it is significant that Margaret's counsellor should have been the English primate, notwithstanding the sad fate of her race in England, and that she is
made to appear as the opponent of the old Scottish Church.
And yet that she found that Church imbedded deeply in
the affections of the Scottish people, and that even to herself it had the means of commending itself, appears from
the interest she showed in Iona, where she built the chapel
referred to already, the ruins of which still exist, and from
the favour shewn by her and her husband to many of the
Culdee establishments. Her policy was to lay the foundation of changes which her sons carried out, and which
brought the Scottish Church of Columba under subjee-
tion to the See of Rome.

Fordun represents Fothadh as succeeded by Gregory,
Cathre, Edmar, and Godric, all of whom he designates as
" Elceti," as he does Fothadh himself. Where Fordun
found these men, it is impossible to say, but they appear
nowhere else. The Irish annals make no mention of
them. Nor can it be well said why he calls them " elceti"
merely. If it be owing to the absence of papal consecration, they did not differ in this from any bishops who
existed in Scotland previously, seeing there is no record
of any such ceremonial from the days of Ninian downwards. If it refers to such other canonical consecration
as was afterwards practised in the case of the Scottish
bishops, we have no evidence to show the existence of
any such. That there must have been a form of ordination in the Scottish Church is true, but the very attempt
to show, as in Alexander the First's letter, that the consecration of Scottish bishops belonged to the See of Canterbury, indicates unmistakeably that there was no Scot-

tish claim of any consequence to set up, and that couse-cration there was a different matter from what it was in England. It is remarkable that the archbishops of York and Canterbury should in the twelfth century be disput-ing in a question of consecrating bishops, of whom a suc-cession is said to have existed for eight hundred years, and that the Scottish Church could furnish no informa-tion such as could solve their difficulties. Surely the question of consecration in Scotland would have been settled by the twelfth century if any such thing, in the ordinary ecclesiastical acceptation of the term, had existed.

The four " elceti," recorded by Fordun, are said to have filled up the space between the death of Malcolm III. and 1109, the second year of Alexander I., a period of six-teen years. This was a time of much distraction in the kingdom arising from the rivalry of the Celtic and Saxon parties. Is it to be doubted that the rivalry would extend to the Church ? At least upon the establishment of the Saxon interest in the person of Edgar, and more especially of Alexander, a man of more energy of charac-ter, the Church was at once made to feel the change. During the reigns of Donald Bàn, Duncan, and even Edgar, the latter of whom filled the throne for eight years, there was no thought of getting a bishop consecrated, and whenever a bishop was in reality obtained for St. Andrews, he was chosen by the king and sent to England for consecration. It cannot be lost sight of that the early bishops of St. Andrews were all Englishmen, and that they received their consecration from England.

During the sixteen years referred to, there is little con-nected with the state of the Scottish church on record. The practice of making grants to religious institutions was extending, and foreign orders of monks began to find their way into the country. Even Donald bàn and his successor, Duncan, were the benefactors of the establishment at Loch Leven, at least so the Register of St. Andrews says. Indeed, that institution must by this time have become possessed of much wealth. Almost every monarch, for a century and a half, and several bishops, are said to have conferred lands upon it. It is at the same time worthy of notice, that in the case of this institution we have no reason to believe that the lands were held by a layman, nay, upon being gifted to the very Priory in whose Register the original grants appear, they are made over as held only by the Culdees. In the case of Loch Leven, then, the supposed corruption of the ancient church could not arise from the poverty of the inmates, owing to their lands being held by laymen. The transaction already referred to, in which the Culdees gave up their property to the bishop of St. Andrews on condition of receiving mere sustenance, is not consistent with the after history of the Institution. The relations between St. Andrews and Loch Leven, during a long period of the eleventh and twelfth centuries, is full of instruction, and well worthy of close examination. It will bring out the ingenuity and unscrupulousness of the succeeding writers of the Roman school, in misrepresent ing the real condition of the early church.

Other establishments began now to share in tokens of royal beneficence, as well as that of the nobles. Dunfermline and Loch Leven both partook of the favour of Edgar. He also resuscitated the abbey of Coldingham, in Berwickshire, which had suffered during the centuries of turmoil, to which the Lothians had been subjected, and planted it with Benedictine monks. This had originally been the seat of a nunnery, at one time presided over by the abbess Hilda. That institution had apparently long disappeared, ere Edgar had established his Benedictine monastery.[1] These Benedictines of Cold-

[1] It is worthy of notice that no nunnery appears to have existed in the

ingham were the first foreign order which found its way into Scotland.

In 1109 Alexander I. made choice of Turgot as bishop of St. Andrews. He was the first bishop who really filled the See. It is said that he succeeded after a vacancy of sixteen years; it might as well be said that he succeeded after a vacancy of one thousand. Turgot, as might be expected of one coming in with a system copied from the Saxons, was himself a Saxon. He was of a family of some consideration, spent a portion of his time in Norway, when he became a favourite with Olave, son of Harold Hardrada, the king, and after a time, owing to a shipwreck in which he lost all his property, forsaking the world and its pursuits, he devoted himself to the service of the church. He became a monk of St. Cuthbert's monastery, in Durham, which was then presided over by Alwin, a man of much zeal, and one whose fame was such, that he is in all likelihood the Alwin whom Fordun makes Bishop of St. Andrews, before Malduin. Upon the death of Alwin Turgot succeeded him, and was afterwards chosen, by Margaret of Scotland, to be her confessor. He was elevated to no ecclesiastical office in the Scottish church during the days of Margaret, and it was sixteen years after her death, when her sons were carrying out those principles which they had imbibed from her, that he was called to fill the high office of Bishop of St. Andrews. Mr Grub (Eccl. Hist. of Scot.) suggests that, as more learning and accomplishments than could be found in the Celtic church were requisite for the office, Alexander sought for a suitable bishop among the Saxons. This is not consistent with what we know of such men as Dicuil, Marianus Scotus, and Cadroe, who, though Scots, were quite abreast of the litera-

Scottish church down to this period. There is nothing to shew that there was any establishment for female recluses north of the Forth (Hailes' Ann. I. s. 3).

ture of their day ; nor does it consist with what we learn of the library at Loch Leven, in the days of David I. (Keith's Bish. App. p. 557), which could not be very much inferior to that of Durham. The selecting of an Englishman to fill the See, must have been for other causes. Eadmer (Hist. Nov.) tells us that Alexander elected Turgot with the consent of the clergy and people. This is clearly a figure of speech, used in the interest of the writer's party.

Upon the election of Turgot a controversy altogether novel in Scotland took place. The Archbishop of York claimed the right to consecrate the new Scottish Prelate. But he was unconsecrated himself, and Anselm, of Canterbury forbade his proceeding with the ceremony or authorizing others to do so. The controversy came to a close by the Archbishop of York receiving consecration, and proceeding, with the consent of Anselm to consecrate the Scottish prelate. In this proceeding the authority of both churches was saved (Simeon of Durham). Alexander and his bishop did not long accord. It is obvious that the jurisdiction of each was not very clearly defined, and that the king sat uneasy under the power which he himself had been the means of introducing. He was a man jealous of his independence, and that of his people ; and the pretensions of his Saxon bishop, who was probably too much of a devotee to the See of York, must have been distasteful to him. It is not by any means unlikely, besides, that he found the native clergy uneasy under this new rule to which they were subjected, and thus, that the new system had its troubles as well as the advantages which he expected from it.

The See of St. Andrews was no bed of roses to its first incumbent, and he soon came to feel the necessity for resigning it. It was one thing to hold the office of confessor to the zealous Margaret, the warm friend of himself and of his church; and another to be set up as ruler in a church jealous of its nationality, and accustomed hitherto to a large measure of freedom. Turgot accordingly resolved to proceed to Durham, to consult his friends, a step which shewed how utterly friendless he was in the church of which he was head, and how entirely he wanted the sympathy and support of its ministry. He left Scotland and never returned; he sickened and died at Durham in 1115, after filling the bishop's seat, with little comfort, for a period of six years.

It was now that, according to Eadmer, Alexander wrote to Ralph, Archbishop of Canterbury, soliciting his aid in procuring a new bishop for St. Andrews. His letter is that in which he is made to say that of old the Scottish bishops were in use to receive consecration from the Pope, or the Archbishop of Canterbury, although, in the case of Turgot, by an arrangement to which he and his people were no parties, the right was given up by Archbishop Lanfranc to Archbishop Thomas, of York. The latter statement is not historically true, the arrangement regarding the consecration of Turgot having been agreed to by both the English and Scottish kings (see Hailes' Ann. I. 56). It has already been stated that there is much room to believe that the letter, as it now stands, is more a composition of Eadmer's than of Alexander's, although it is quite possible that Alexander, being disappointed in York, or jealous of its pretensions, yet resolved to have a Roman bishop, did apply to the Archbishop of Canterbury. Be that as it may, the application did not succeed, and the See of St. Andrews was again vacant for five years. We do not learn that any great evils followed, nor that there were any complaints from the Scots; but Alexander was dissatisfied,

and in 1120 he made a second application to Archbishop Ralph, fixing upon Eadmer, a monk of his
diocese, as the person whom he wished as the new
bishop of the Scots. The Archbishop at this time agreed
very readily to the request of the Scottish king. Eadmer
proceeded to Scotland and, as he says himself, was
elected by the clergy and people with the assent of the
king. But he tells us that he did not receive investiture
by delivering of the pastoral staff, and ring, nor was he
asked to do homage ; that is, he did not recognise the
royal prerogative in what he held, as a high churchman
of the day, to be the prerogative of the Archbishop.

Notwithstanding the letter attributed to Alexander, in
which he acknowledges the right of the See of Canterbury to the consecration of Scottish bishops, he most
strenuously resisted the consecration of Eadmer by the
Archbishop either of Canterbury or York. Eadmer
maintained that the primacy of all Britain belonged to
Canterbury. Alexander refused to listen, but never for
once urged as a counter argument that St. Andrews
itself was a primatial See. If he could would he not
have done so ? The fact is, Alexander was constituting
a primacy, and found it no easy matter to do so.
Eadmer yielded at this time to the opposition of the
king. He received the ring from the royal hand with
some reluctance, and took the staff off the altar himself
in the presence of two bishops (Eadmer, Hist. Nov. 97),
after which he entered upon the administration of his
diocese.

Thurstan, Archbishop of York, was abroad during
these proceedings, but thinking that his rights were
violated by what was done in the case of St. Andrews,
he procured a letter from the King of England to the
Archbishop of Canterbury, prohibiting the consecration
of Eadmer, and letters from the same monarch to Alex-

ander imposing a like prohibition upon him. Eadmer was disturbed, and asked leave to return to Canterbury. Alexander, fearing the English king, became cool in his regard for the bishop, and upon Eadmer's pressing for leave to repair to Canterbury for advice, said, "Not while I live will I allow the See of St. Andrews to be subjected to that of Canterbury." Eadmer in his difficulties consulted various friends. Nicholas, an Englishman, thought by some to have been Prior of Worcester, and by others to have been an ecclesiastical agent (Hailes' Ann., i. 64), or solicitor before the ecclesiastical courts at Rome, advised him strongly to assert his independence, telling him that Scotland had furnished York with bishops but that York had never furnished any to Scotland, treating the claims of York with contempt, and maintaining that no man could be primate of another kingdom, a prerogative which the Archbishop of Canterbury now claimed. Nicholas advised him to seek consecration of the Pope. Everything in this letter shews how new the whole question of consecration of bishops was in the Scottish Church.

John, Bishop of Glasgow, who, with two monks of Canterbury, was consulted, advised Eadmer to retire, telling him that reconciliation with Alexander was altogether hopeless. These latter counsellors make one remarkable statement, for they say that Eadmer cannot accommodate himself to the usages of the Scottish Church without *dishonouring his character* and *hazarding his salvation.*[1] This statement is surely sufficient to shew, that between the Church of Rome and the Church of Scotland in the twelfth century, there was a wide distinction—a distinction so wide that an accommodation to the usages

---

[1] Eadmer, Hist. Nov. 133.

of the latter was held by the adherents of the former to be a hazarding of the soul's salvation.

Eadmer was finally suffered to retire to England. He restored the ring to the king, and laid the pastoral staff again upon the altar, and so denuded himself of his Episcopal office and prerogative. Alexander, in a communication to the Archbishop of Canterbury, threw the blame of the whole transaction upon Eadmer ; but Eadmer, in his history, appeals to the Searcher of hearts in vindication of the truth of his own account.

When he had been about a year and a-half away, Eadmer seems to have been convinced that he had been over-hasty. The reflection took hold of his mind that being "elected" to the See of St. Andrews was of more consequence than being "consecrated." Friends pressed this consideration upon him, and the penitent bishop was led to write a letter to the Scottish king, expressing regret for what he had done, and asking to be restored, adding, that his mind was changed respecting "the King of England, the Archbishop of Canterbury, and the sacerdotal benediction." The archbishop, at the same time with the convent at Canterbury, wrote to Alexander urging the recall of Eadmer. But Alexander was deaf to all these entreaties, and the bishop was never recalled to his See. Eadmer died, as is supposed, in January 1124. He was a man of literary tastes, having written a history of his time, besides the lives of several English saints.

Eadmer complains that, during the vacancy previous to his appointment, the revenues of the bishopric of St. Andrews were much dilapidated. They were under the charge of William, a monk of Edmondsbury, another English ecclesiastic introduced by the Scottish king. Yet it is hard to make Eadmer's statement agree with what Fordun relates of Alexander's bounty to this See, for it was he who granted to the bishop the territory around St. Andrews called Muckross, or the Boar's Chase. This liberality is much commended by Fordun, although it was liberality at the expense of others, and not at his own ; for this territory had belonged to the ancient college of Culdees at St. Andrews, who were deprived of it in order to endow the See. Could anything shew more clearly what a new thing a bishop and a primate at St. Andrews were, than this transaction ? It proves that there had been no adequate provision for the main-tenance of the See till then.

During a considerable portion of Eadmer's nominal incumbency the See of St. Andrews was vacant. Indeed for the greater portion of the time since its foundation it had been vacant.[1] Upon the death of Eadmer, how-ever, another election was made, when the choice fell upon Robert Prior of Scone. The Scottish clergy and people had nothing to do with the election, which was entirely a matter of Alexander the fierce himself. Truly there never was a man more fit to bring about a revolution in church and state than this king, with his impetuosity and strength of will ! The king and his wife had founded a monastery of canons regular of St. Augustine, at Scone, and had supplied it with monks from St. Oswald's, near Pontefract,—the first settlement of any foreign order north of the Forth ; and here again the ancient Celtic Church did not afford the inmates; they were drawn from England. The first Prior was the above Robert, and being again selected, though

---

[1] Mr. Grub (Eccl. Hist., vol. i., p. 217) supposes that while the Edmar introduced by Fordun into his list of bishops as preceding Turgot, is the Eadmer who succeeded him, the Godric of whom he speaks was a bishop-elect who held the office during Eadmer's absence. There seems no ground whatsoever for the supposition. Beyond doubt the Eadmers are the same, but a historian capable of converting one Edmar into two, was quite capable of producing one Godric out of nothing, or very little.

not brought immediately from England, Robert of Scone was chosen to fill the See of St. Andrews. This took place in 1124, and the election was among the last acts of Alexander's reign. It is not to be supposed that Alexander, any more than his mother, was indifferent to the memory of the great men of the Scottish Church. Being driven by a storm on Inchcolm, he found there a hermit of the Columban Church, who entertained him and his followers for three days until the storm abated. In commemoration of this event, the king founded a monastery of Premonstratensian monks there, which was dedicated to St. Columba.

It was four years after his election ere Robert was consecrated. David, Alexander's successor, was more devoted to the interests of the Papal See than his brother, but even under his government, no acknowledgment of supremacy was permitted on the part of the new bishop. The ceremony was performed in 1128, by Thurstan, Archbishop of York, and the reason given by him for dispensing with a profession of subjection, which he held to be due to his office, was, that he did it for the "love of God, and of King David." (See Wharton's Anglia Sacra, ii. 237.)

During the interval between the election and the con secration of Robert, an event occurred of some consequence to the Scottish Church. A council was held at Roxburgh by John of Crema, cardinal-legate of Pope Honorius II. The Pope had written King David requesting the presence of the bishops, and stating his willingness to interpose and decide in the question between York and St. Andrews (Hailes' Ann. i. 75 ; Chron. of Melrose, p. 68 ; Simeon of Dur.). It is not known whether David complied with the Pope's request or what was done at the council, but this was the first attempt of the Roman pontiff to hold any such meeting in Scotland, and yet a thousand years had passed since Christianity had existed in the land. Verily the power of the Church of Rome cannot boast of its antiquity among the mountains of Caledonia, and when it first shewed itself, it did not venture farther north of the Tweed than Roxburgh, a place almost within sight of the border, and which, in modern times, possesses barely a name.

Robert is said to have "co-operated with the king in every effort for the temporal improvement and spiritual benefit of the Scots" (Grub's Eccl. Hist. i. 262). In so far as establishing the Romish hierarchy might serve that purpose he certainly did. He devoted a seventh part of the offerings at the altar of the church at St. Andrews to the building of a cathedral. This was the age of church building. The crusades had made the natives of Britain acquainted with the ecclesiastical architecture of continental Europe, while they had given a marvellous impulse to the zeal of the people on behalf of the Church. This zeal took several directions—in the case of a monarch like David in establishing a hierarchy worthy as it was thought of the greatness and dignity of the Catholic Church—in the case of others, and especially churchmen, in raising structures befitting the power and grandeur to which the hierarchy was attaining. The impulse was a false and unwholesome one, and culminated in those consequences which called irresistibly for the Reformation, when its outward magnificence had become the leading characteristic of the Church of Christ. The remains of Bishop Robert's cathedral still exist in the building usually called the Church of St. Rule's. As the name implies, it was dedicated to St. Regulus in acknowledgment of the relation which the legend of both bore to have existed between him and St. Andrew. (Quar. Rev. lxxxv. 120).

As might be looked for Bishop Robert was no friend of

the Culdees. An Augustinian friar could hardly have
been so. Hence the institution of a monastery of canons
of his own order. The statement of the Register of this
monastery is, "It is not sufficient for the praise of our
God that we should collect a heap of stones unless we
procure living stones to join together as a building of
God." (Reg. Prior. St. And., p. 122). King David supported his bishop, and made over the lands of the Culdees
to the new canons, giving permission to the former if they
chose to enter the monastery, but allowing such as refused,
to enjoy their possessions while they lived. There must
have been some difficulty, however, with these refractory
Culdees, for despite of King David and Bishop Robert,
the Culdees of St. Andrews continued long to form the
chapter of the cathedral, and claimed the right of elect-
ing the Bishop. The Pope, Eugenius III., confirmed the
privileges of the canons, a farther novelty in Scotland, for
we read of no such confirmation being either sought for
or obtained in the case of Abernethy, Brechin, Dunkeld,
or the original institution at St. Andrews. It is sufficiently clear that it was under shelter of the government of Margaret's sons that the papal power found
any footing in Scotland.

The bishop, anxious to provide for his new monastery,
transferred to it the whole lands of the Culdee establishment at Loch Leven. It has been said that he did this
upon the ground of the agreement made in the previous
century between Bishop Fothadh and Ronan the Abbot.
But it must be borne in mind that most of the lands
belonging to Loch Leven had been obtained from kings
and others after that arrangement was made, and these
surely could not be claimed upon such grounds by the
bishop. The grant includes a gift of the books belonging
to the Culdees, in these terms :—"Cum Pastorali, Gradu-
ali, Missali, Origine (Origen), Sententiis Abbatis Clare

Vallensis, tribus quaternionibus de sacramentis, parte Bibliothecæ, Lectionariis, Actibus Apostolorum, Textu Evangeliorum, Prosperi tribus libris (the works of Prosper), Solomonis glossis de Canticis Canticorum, Interpretationibus dictionum, Collectione Sententiarum, Expositione super Genesim, Excerptionibus Ecclesiasticarum Regularum." (Keith Bish. App. p. 5871.) A curious catalogue, and one showing beyond a doubt that the ancient Scottish ecclesiastics were not destitute of literary culture. Along with these there would very probably be MSS. in the vernacular. David confirmed the grant of his bishop, and in terms such as to shew that the Culdees were not willing to become stripped of their property at the bidding of the latter. Like their neighbours of St. Andrews they were prepared to resist might with right. But the struggle was a hopeless one, and the king enjoined the enforcement of the grant. David's charter runs thus : "David rex Scotorum, &c. Be it known &c., that we have granted to the canons of St. Andrews the island of Loch Leven, that they may establish there a canonical order; and if the Culdees (Kaledei), who shall be found there, remain with them, living according to rule, they may continue to do so in peace ; but if any one of them resist, we order hereby that he be ejected from the island." Two things appear from this, that the Culdees were not a canonical order in the estimation of the adherents of the Papal See, and that they did not live in accordance with any fixed monastic rule; yet, according to the charter of Malduin, they were men "living in the island of Loch Leven, in the school of all the virtues, devoutly and honourably." (Keith's Bishops, p. 7.)

During a great part of the incumbency of Robert, the Scottish king was at war with England. In this war no opponent was more active or more energetic than Thur-

2 c

stan, Archbishop of York. In consequence of this there could be little intercourse between the metropolitan and the prelate, whom he claimed as a suffragan, but the relations of the two kingdoms must have shewn the inconvenience of having the ecclesiastical superiors of one kingdom subject to the civil government of another. The necessity for arbitration threw the questions of supremacy naturally into the hands of the Pope, who was now brought to exercise jurisdiction over the Scottish Church, but the power of York was in all the early appeals too much for Scotland, and for a long time the Roman Pontiff refused to liberate Scotland from its assumed supremacy.

Bishop Robert outlived King David. He died either in 1158 or 1159, during the reign of Malcolm IV. He may, in one sense, be called the first Bishop of St. Andrews, for until his day there was no regularly constituted and suitably endowed See. He was the first regularly consecrated prelate who continued to govern the diocese, and who had provided for him a maintenance suitable to his rank. The diocese did not in his day receive the pall, or attain to metropolitan rank, but the first step was taken towards it in giving it the place of a primacy, a position given to it, not in consequence of any hereditary rank, or any transference of a primacy from Iona or Dunkeld, but because of its geographical position in the kingdom of Fife, where the royal residence was fixed at the time. Had the king continued to reside at Scone, the primacy would without doubt have been fixed at Dunkeld.

CHAPTER XXV

THE Diocese of Dunkeld lay immediately to the west of those of Brechin and St. Andrews. The account of its formation given by Alexander Mylne, (Acct. of Bish. of Dunk., Bannatyne Club), at one time a canon of the see, is that a monastery of Culdees was founded there in the eighth century by Constantine, King of the Picts ; that about the year 1197, David I. changed this monastery into a Cathedral Church, expelled the Culdees, and made Gregory, their abbot, bishop of the diocese. Mylne farther states that the Culdees of Dunkeld, like those of St. Andrews, were married men. There is no doubt about the latter statement, but it is thought that the see is of older date than the reign of David. It will be re-collected that Alexander and his wife, Sybilla, founded a monastery of Augustinian monks in Scone. The foundation charter of that monastery exists, granted about the year 1115, and one of the witnesses to the document is Cormac the Bishop. King David gave his first charter to the monastery of Dunfermline, several years after, and there Cormac appears, witnessing as Bishop of Dunkeld. It is by no means improbable that the abbots of the Culdee monasteries had got into the way of calling themselves, or being called bishops, and that to these in some cases dioceses were attached, with suitable revenues, by the kings of the family of Malcolm Ceannmore. The signature of Cormac to the first of these charters does not imply that he was the diocesan bishop of Dunkeld, and the subsequent signature would seem to confirm the statement of Mylne, that the See was founded by David I. There is so much confusion in the account given of the earlier incumbents, that it is impossible to arrive at a satisfactory account of them. There are two Cormacs, one existing in 1115, another in 1180 ; two Gregories, one existing in 1127, and another in 1200 ; while one of the Gregories is said to have been the Bishop of Moray, and as such witnesses a charter of David at an early period of his reign. Were all these separate men, or does this confusion shed doubt upon these early charters ? It does look like as if some at least of these documents had been manufactured at a later time, when important purposes had to be served by them. They exist only among the records of monastic establishments ; and, with strong temptations, and amidst surrounding ignorance, it is quite conceivable that such might have been the origin of some of these early documents.

Although the limits of the Diocese of Dunkeld are not very clearly defined, there is reason to believe that it included at first the territory afterwards embraced in the dioceses of Dunblane, Argyll, and the Isles. How the incumbent of Man and the Isles settled the question of jurisdiction with the incumbent of Dunkeld we are not informed, but if much of what is said regarding the Isles be true, there must have been a measure of conflicting jurisdiction in the case of these two ecclesiastical chiefs. Be that as it may, the ancient institution at Dunkeld, formed by the great Constantine, the Pictish king, and supplied with Columba's relics by Kenneth MacAlpine, who gave it apparently a Scottish form, was converted by David into a Diocesan See. The abbot of the monastery had long been a layman, who succeeded to the possessions by hereditary succession. The family of Athole, descended from a branch of the Royal family, held the office for a long period, presenting us with the not unusual record in their case of an abbot slain on the field of battle. The ecclesiastics in the meantime carried on the duties of the monastery, and were presided over by a superior, who in this, as in similar cases, was called a prior. In the native language the abbot was the *Aba,* while the prior was the *Cealloir* or "Man of the Church." David changed all this, and substituted for a lay abbot an ecclesiastical Diocesan, putting an end indeed to the anomaly of having a layman in possession of a spiritual office, but investing the spiritual office in the hands of an ecclesiastic, with a place and a power no less dangerous to the liberties of the church and nation. It might be true as has been said, that the transferring of the property of the monastery to a layman was one of the corruptions of the Culdee church. Yet better in the hands of a. layman than in those of some ecclesiastics; and besides, it is extremely doubtful whether the corruptions of the Christian Church ever sprang from her poverty. Wealth has been a fertile source of them, poverty rarely, if ever. And farther, if this be a token of corruption, let it not be forgotten that much of the property that belonged to the Church of Scotland, is at this moment held by laymen, and that the church is not more corrupt in consequence.

To the westward of Dunkeld lies the Diocese of Dun blane, taking its name from a church dedicated to St. Blane, one of the earlier Scottish missionaries. There was anciently a Culdee monastery here, of which it is said that Blane was superior in the reign of Kenneth III., that is about the year 970, (Keith's Bish. 170), but of this we have no certainty, although it is possible. A

Bull of Pope Hadrian IV. (Vic. Hist. Lib. p. 353) who filled the papal chair from 1154 to 1159, exists, confirming the right of the See of York to the subjection of the Scottish Bishops, and addressed among others to M. Bishop of Dunblane. The authenticity of this bull has been doubted, and not without reason. The English cloister seems to have been prolific in bulls and other documents to support the claims of the English metropolitans to the subjection of the Scottish bishops. If the Bull be genuine, the M. given there as Bishop of Dunblane, may be St. Morock, who was always held, as has been said already, to have been an ecclesiastic belonging to Dunblane ; and as he was bishop in the early portion of Malcolm IV.'s reign, he might have been appointed by David I. The See is of the date either of David or Malcolm, and thus was called into existence contemporaneously with the other Scottish bishoprics, being substituted for a previously existing Culdee institution.

The next most important diocese to St. Andrews was that of Glasgow. It is usual to trace its existence back to the days of Kentigern, who is often designated the first bishop. The first bishop, however, was John, whom David I. raised to the Episcopate. Bishop Keith states with perfect candour that in the earlier writs of the cartulary of Glasgow, Kentigern is not styled a bishop, but a confessor and holy martyr. At the same time he observes that, in that most suspicious document, the *Inquisitio Davidis*, or 'Inquisition of David,' he is expressly titled a bishop. Joceline styles him a bishop in his "Life" of him, but that is no authority. But neither of these testimonies are of any value. In the case of Joceline, a writer of the twelfth century cannot be held as authority for the events of the fifth, more especially considering the bias with which he wrote ; and in the case of the "Inquisitio" there are too many reasons to believe the whole document spurious to entitle it to much weight in the settlement of such a question.[1] If any man is prepared to believe in all the possessions enumerated in that document, as belonging to the See of Glasgow, during the period of the Strathclyde Britons, and the earlier Scoto-Pictish kings, while no record, either Irish, British, or Scotch, has been retained of the name of any one of the incumbents who held them, he is entitled to much commendation for the strength of his faith. In 1107, David by disposition of his brother Edgar became Prince of Cumbria, a province extending from the Clyde to the heart of Westmoreland. Zealous as his brother Alexander, who then succeeded to the Scottish throne, was for the promotion of his mother's designs, his zeal was outrun by that of David. An English education and strong English sympathies ensured that. Alexander's throne, as has been said, was still to a large extent surrounded by the magnates of the Scottish nation, Maormors and Thanes; David's person was surrounded by a horde of Anglo-Norman nobles and knights. Not one Scottish name appears among the personal attendants of the Prince of Cumbria. David's early ambition was to improve the condition of his subjects, and among other things, to accommodate to his taste the condition of the church. A border region like Cumbria must have suffered prodigiously in the long continued conflicts between Celt and Saxon, and between the Northmen and both. It is no wonder although David should have found the condition of Church and State miserable.

---

[1] Father Innes holds this document to be genuine, (Civ. and Eccl. Hist. 135), and Mr Cosmo Innes (Pref. to Chart. of Glasg.), takes the same view of it. These are high authorities; but notwithstanding, there is much room for doubt. The whole document bears evidence of belonging to a later age than David's, and may be attributed to the zeal of medieval ecclesiastics on behalf of their own institutions.

Writers who maintain the existence of an ancient episcopacy in Scotland, allow that a generation before Prince
David's time there was no bishop of Glasgow, (Grub's
Eccl. Hist. I. 220), nor can any be discovered by ordinary
inquirers for many generations earlier. The consecration of
two bishops, Magsuen and John, by Archbishop Kinsius
of York, as related by Stubbs, is simply a part of the
case of York as got up at an after time ; while the story
of consecration by the bishops of St. Andrews and of Wales,
is very like an attempt to get up an argument of some
sort for the existence of a See ; indeed, the variety of
those who are said to have had a right to consecrate the
incumbent of Glasgow, shews that the right in reality
existed nowhere. Had any one Prelate had the right,
we would not have found it wandering for a domicile
from York to St. Andrews, and from St. Andrews to
Wales. Prince David was educated by an ecclesiastic of
British descent called John ; and as Alexander chose
Turgot his mother's confessor to fill the See of St.
Andrews, David chose his tutor John, to fill that of
Glasgow. John is said to have been a person of good
learning and great probity, who had travelled both in
France and Italy for his improvement. He is said to
have been consecrated by Pope Paschal II. in 1115.
He seems to have met with many sources of vexation
in his new office. The people over whom he was
placed were rude and intractable, perhaps were not
very willing to submit to the jurisdiction of their
bishop, which was a novelty to them. The Archbishop
of York, too, claimed the same rights in regard to
Glasgow, that he did in regard to St. Andrews, and insisted on the subjection of the bishop to his metropolitan
rule. These, with perhaps other causes, filled the newly
appointed prelate with dissatisfaction, and leaving his

post, he proceeded to Rome with an appeal to the Pope against Thurstan of York. Some say he went to the Holy Land. He was at length overtaken by an injunction of the Pope (Calixtus II.), who insisted on his return to his diocese. He obeyed the order and returned to Glasgow in the year 1123. The king richly endowed the See with grants of land, and in addition raised bishop John to the office of Chancellor of the kingdom. Among other grants we find in the Glasgow chartulary the lands of Partick. The rich endowments conferred on this see by David are not favourable to our belief in the genuineness of the "Inquisitio," for if all the lands included in the possessions of the See of Glasgow as given in that document were really enjoyed by the bishop, it is hardly probable that the king would proceed to endow it farther.

John was the original builder of the Glasgow Cathedral. It is said that a portion of the existing building is of the date of this bishop. However that may be, there is reason to believe that the first cathedral church of the diocese, was of the period of Bishop John. With the support of a Prince like David, devoted to the interest of the church, and whose zeal suffered no diminution, when he came to be king, such an enterprise as erecting a cathedral, was by no means a hopeless one. The building was probably in a style of greater simplicity than the church afterwards adopted, but the condition of the country did not preclude the idea of raising such a structure as might befit the second most important diocese in the kingdom. But one thing is beyond doubt ; the diocese and the cathedral were of nearly the same date. John who died in 1147, was succeeded by Herbert, at whose suggestion it was that Josceline of Furness wrote the life of Kentigern the reputed founder of the See. It is said that during the incumbency of this Prelate, the church of Scotland was finally released from the claims of the metropolitan of York. Herbert was himself consecrated by the Pope (Eugenius III.), at Auxerre, the same year with the decease of his predecessor. He had been formerly Abbot of Kelso. Like most of his brethren he was an Anglo-Norman, although he was chosen to preside over a diocese the inhabitants of which were chiefly Britons.

To the south-west of the diocese of Glasgow lay that of Galloway. The history of this diocese is associated with the memory of Ninian. A reference to the early chapters of the present volume will recal what has been said of him. Being long within the limits of the kingdom of Northumbria, the ancient Bernicia, this district followed the fate of the Anglo-Saxon church. Hence it shared in the organization of that church at the hand of Augustine and his successors ; and in consequence we learn of a Saxon bishop (Pecthelm) occupying the See in the days of Bede. The succeeding history of the diocese, with its candida casa, or white church, is lost in the obscurity which shrouds the eighth, ninth, and tenth centuries; and when at length it emerges into light it is at the time when Fergus was the great lord of Galloway. The Saxons had in the meantime given way to the Gaelic Celts, and they had filled the region with churches dedicated to the Finnians, Marnocks, Colmonells, and Patricks of the Scottish church. In no part of Scotland are these ancient Celtic churches more frequent than in Ayrshire and Galloway. The institution of the See of Galloway is due not to David but to Fergus, the Celtic lord of the country. An unwilling subject of David, he was his rival in liberality to the church ; and in the course of this rivalry he was led in his own province of Galloway to set up, probably with the consent of the king, the See of Candida casa, or Whithorn. Boece has said that from the days of Pecthelm downwards, Galloway had been subject to the See of Man ; an impossibility, where there was no such subjection, and no such See as Man to which to yield it. Galloway being long part of Northumbria, acquired to a large extent the character of the Augustinian church of the Anglo-Saxons ; hence, onwards until the irruption of the Gael, consequent on the inroads of the Northmen on their own country, we find occasional notices of bishops. Keith inserts the names of such as are on record in his list of bishops ; and we consequently find Frithewaldus in 764, Pectwine in 776, Ethelbert in 777, Eadwnef or Radnef in 790, all apparently consecrated in York. When the See was instituted in the twelfth century, the first bishop bore the Celtic name of Gilla Aldan. He became the occupant of the chair of the Saxon Pecthelm and Pectwine. A new race had occupied the land, but with the revived Episcopacy the claims of York to supremacy revived, without regard to races ; the bishop of Galloway, be he Celt or Saxon, must be a suffragan of York. Ancient custom gave a colour to the claim in this case which was altogether wanting in the other dioceses of Scotland, and falling in with the system which he had embraced, Gilla Aldan, in obedience to an injunction of Pope Honorius II., acknowledged the rights of York, and received consecration at the hands of the Archbishop. This was the only Scottish See from which an English metropolitan succeeded in securing obedience, and the relation continued to exist until the 14th century, or perhaps later. In 1491, when the See of Glasgow was erected into an Archbishopric, Galloway became the chief suffragan of that metropolitan See. It is, however, to be noted that, like the other Scottish Bishoprics, the date of the diocese of Galloway, as finally and fully equipped, is the beginning of the twelfth century.

The next diocese in order is that of the Isles. Here,

it might be natural to suppose, if any where, we should find the perfect organization of the early Scottish Church. Yet that organization does not appear to have been constituted on the Episcopal model. The first seat of the diocese of the Isles is found not in Iona, but in the Isle of Man. The bishop of the Sudreys (Sodor), or of the southern Hebrides and Man is his first title. Man, unlike Galloway, had never been a portion of any of the Anglo-Saxon kingdoms of England ; it had been, down to the eleventh century, a portion of the territory of the Celtic races, sometimes overrun and possessed by the Cumbri of Wales, but chiefly in the hands of a Gaelic population and Gaelic governors. It was also christianized by Gaelic missionaries, the tradition of the island itself being that the inhabitants were converted by St. Patrick. Be that as it may, the famous saints of the island are those common to it with Scotland and Ireland. Both Maughold or Machute, and Braddan or Brendan are commemorated in its churches, and these are famous names in the two neighbouring Celtic kingdoms. There is nothing then to distinguish the early history of the church in Man from that of the early Scottish or Irish church. If there were bishops in the island, they could only be bishops of the Scottish or Irish type, and what that was has been already seen.

We have observed how simultaneous was the movement in the beginning of the eleventh century in the Scottish churches towards a diocesan episcopacy. In Ireland, separate dioceses were formed for the first time, and bishops appointed to them ; in Scotland, David, following in the footsteps of his brother Alexander, covered the kingdom with them, and was imitated by his powerful subject Fergus of Galloway. In Man, Olave, son of Godred Crovan, king of the island and its dependencies, followed in the same course, and took steps to have a bishop appointed over his island territories. Celt and Teuton vied with each other during the period from 1100 to 1150, in setting up a hierarchy, till then unknown, throughout the whole of the ancient Scottish church. The fashion became an epidemic, very probably led by David, who was at the time one of the most remarkable monarchs in Europe ; but the public mind seems to have been in some measure preparing for the change during a considerable time previously. The enthusiasm that filled Europe during the early crusades seems to have carried the power of the Roman church over every barrier, into regions it had never penetrated before.

The Northmen had conquered Man about 1065, making their descent from the Irish coast ; the Hebrides be came subject to them more than thirty years later ; they then came to possess a great island kingdom, including the peninsula of Kintyre, with Man as the royal residence. Such a kingdom could not in the beginning of the 12th century be without its bishop. The first step taken by King Olave was to secure occupants for a priory which he resolved to found in Man, and he accordingly put himself in communication with Ivo, who was at the time Abbot of Furness in Lancashire. He made, as was usual, a grant of land for the purpose, and a party of brethren were sent from Furness, who occupied a priory at Rushen. Among these was Wimund, whom some writers make the first bishop of the island, and who afterwards became famous in Scottish history. Wimund seems to have been advanced to the See of the Isles, although doubts have been entertaimed of his being consecrated. Ailred makes him out an impostor, but other writers (Stubb's decem scriptores) relate his consecration by the Archbishop of York. He is called " Primus Episcopus ibi (Man) " (Matt.

Paris Hist. Ang.), which Keith explains by his being the first bishop settled by the Norwegians; but which is much more easily explicable by taking the obvious meaning of the words. Wimund's settlement in Man gave him opportunities which he could not otherwise possess of disturbing the peace of Scotland. It gave him authority in all the southern Hebrides, and secured for him the support of the Northmen in all the islands, who would be glad of any excuse for a descent upon Scotland, and above all when such a descent had the countenance and direction of a bishop. Thus, then, the See of the Isles came into existence about the year 1134.

Every diocese in Scotland was founded between 1100 and 1153 except that of Argyle, which was separated from that of Dunkeld in the beginning of the 13th century, the whole of the powerful hierarchy of Scotland having been set up by the sons of Margaret. This was a remarkable change, and as sudden as it was remarkable. Nor did it stand alone; other changes equally significant were taking place alongside of it. The ancient Culdee monasteries were fast disappearing, and great establishments in accordance with the Romish model were taking their place. Monks were introduced into every part of Scotland, covering and feeding on the land. The providing of dioceses was but a small portion of what Alexander and David did for the church, the regular clergy coming in for at least their own share in the beneficence of those kings. Of the Canons-regular of St. Augustine, Alexander I. founded an abbey at Scone in 1114. To this abbey was attached a priory in the island of Loch Tay, in the year 1122; Alexander founded another abbey of this order in Inchcolm, off the coast of Fife, in 1123; at St Andrews, Robert the bishop founded an abbey of the same order in 1140; and to this abbey was attached the priory of Loch Leven, with all its possessions. At Edinburgh, David I. founded an abbey of this order in 1128, which was dedicated to the Cross, and hence called Holyrood. The canons are said to have been brought from St Andrews (Spotswood's Rel. Houses), but it is hard to see how this could be, if St Andrews itself was not founded till 1140. They came more probably from Scone. To this abbey was attached St Mary's Isle in Galloway, as a priory. David also founded the abbey of Cambus-Kenneth, near Stirling, in 1147, and supplied it with Augustinian monks from Aroise in France. At Jedburgh the same king founded a priory about the year 1118, and converted it into an abbey towards the close of his reign. The monks of this abbey are said to have come from Beauvais in France.

Of the monks of Premontré in France, usually called the Præmonstratenses, an abbey was founded at Soulseat in Galloway by Fergus, lord of the province, in the early part of the twelfth century. At Dryburgh an abbey was founded by Hugh Moreville, constable of Scotland, and his wife, Beatrix de Bello Campo, about the same period. At Tungland in Galloway the same order had an abbey founded by Fergus, Lord of Galloway, in the reign of David, but at a date later than that of Soulseat, which supplied it with monks. These monks followed the rule of St. Augustine.

Of the order of St. Benedict or the Benedictines, an abbey was founded at Coldingham by King Edgar in 1098, who supplied it with monks from Durham. This erection was in honour of St. Cuthbert. At Dunfermline a monastery of the same order is said to have been begun by Malcolm III., but for this there is no authority. Matters were not ripe in his time for so dealing with the existing Scottish Church; but in the reign of Alexander I. there is little doubt that steps were taken for introducing Benedictine monks to Dunfermline. There was a prior of the name of Peter over the institution in Alexander's reign (Ead. Hist. v. 130). The institution began as a modest priory, although it afterwards became a famous monastery. We need not doubt that the sons of Malcolm and Margaret would pay special attention to this institution in reverence for the honoured dust of their parents which lay there. Hence David changed the priory into an abbey, and stocked it with monks from Canterbury in 1124. He attached to it at the same time the priory of Urquhart in Moray.

Of the order of the Tyronenses, or monks of Tyron, who followed the rules of St. Benedict, David I. founded an abbey at Kelso in 1128. To this abbey was attached the priory of Lesmahagow in Lanarkshire. It is questionable how far the worthy Scottish missionary Machute, after whom the place is called, would have approved of this arrangement. At Kilwinning in Ayrshire an abbey of this order was founded by Hugh Moreville, Constable of Scotland in 1140. David's Anglo-Norman followers seem to have taken example largely from their monarch in their beneficence to the church.

Of the Cluniac monks no foundation in Scotland dates so early as the reign of David, although at an after period they were the order which formed the monastic institution at Iona in the reign of William the Lion. The inmates of this later institution were drawn from Galloway, where the order had been previously established. It is strange that to form such an establishment at Iona it was needful to draw upon the inmates of a distant monastery.

Of the Cistercians an abbey was founded by David I. at Melrose in 1136. The old Culdee institution had been destroyed by Kenneth Macalpine, and it is doubtful whether it was rebuilt during the stormy period that

intervened between his time and that of David ; but the
tradition of its former fame, associated as it was with the
name of Cuthbert, would survive. Accordingly David
founded a great abbey here, and bestowed it on the Cistercians, whom he brought from the abbey of Rievaux in
Yorkshire, thus distributing his gifts impartially and
most liberally among the different existing orders of
monks, with little regard, however, to the claims of the
old clergy of a better and purer church. At Newbattle
in Mid-Lothian David founded another abbey of the
same order in 1140. The monks for this foundation
were brought from Melrose. At Dundrennan in Galloway, Fergus Lord of Galloway founded a Cistercian abbey
in 1142 ; the monks, like those of Melrose, being brought
from Rievaux. At Kinloss in Moray David founded a
great abbey of the order in 1150 (Spotswood's Rel.
Houses).

David introduced the Knights-Templar into his kingdom, their earliest foundation being at Temple in Mid-
Lothian. They afterwards extended themselves widely
over Scotland, and had numerous establishments. Considering the influence which the Crusades exerted on the
state of the church at this period, it is no wonder that
these military knights, devoted as they were specially to
the Temple, should have found a ready welcome from the
Scottish king. The knights of St. John were also welcomed by this devout and munificent king, and had
an establishment given them at Torphichen in West-
Lothian.

Prior to the twelfth century there is no evidence to
shew that there was so much as one establishment of
female recluses in Scotland proper. At an early period
we read of an establishment of nuns at Coldingham, but
we have no record of the existence of one north of the

Firth of Forth. No evidence is stronger than this for the marriage of the Culdee clergy. Celibacy has never been long confined to one of the sexes; the celibate monk has ever been accompanied in the history of the church by the celibate nun. And in the ancient Scottish Church we have no record of the existence of the latter. There were St. Bridgets and St. Kentigerns among the females of that Church, but there is no evidence to shew that these good women were nuns. With the reign of David, however, nunneries were introduced. He founded a convent of Benedictine nuns at Newcastle and another at Carlisle, and convents of Cistercian nuns at Berwick-upon-Tweed, Three fountains in the Lammermoors, and Gulane in East-Lothian, while Cospatric Earl of March, and Derder, his lady, founded a convent of the same order at Coldstream, and another at Eccles in Berwickshire.

It will thus appear that between the year 1098 and the death of David I. in 1153 there were founded in Scotland for the first time twelve bishoprics, six abbeys, and three priories of Augustinian monks; three abbeys of the Præmonstratenses; two abbeys and one priory of Benedictines; two abbeys and one priory of the Tyronenses or monks of Tyron; four abbeys of the Cistercians; several establishments of the Knights-Templars and knights of St. John; and at least five convents of nuns. And what is more remarkable is that among all these bishops, monks, and nuns, with the exception of one or two of the earlier and less prominent bishops of somewhat doubtful identity, we do not find one native Scot accepting or received into the newly-constituted offices. Bishops and monks are almost all importations from abroad; some from England, others from France. The whole Romish system was introduced into Scotland, and the men who had to organise it had to be introduced along with it. This almost entire ignoring of the ancient people and Church by David, is a very significant fact, and one that shews very distinctly the relation in which they were understood to stand to the new order of things.

CHAPTER XXVI.

THE period of sixty years from the death of Malcolm III. to that of his son David in 1153 is one of the most remarkable in the history of the Scottish Church. No other period in its history can be compared to it, save that of the Reformation. The whole organization of the Church was remodelled, so much so that it would be impossible to recognize the old Church of the reign of Malcolm and his predecessors in the great hierarchical establishment left by David. The change in the Church was not a whit less than that in the State. In the latter the Anglo-Norman influence became paramount, so much so that it began to pervade the ancient population of the soil, and feudal titles and feudal names began to be accepted by the magnates of the Celtic race. Patronymics were laid aside, and families, which had been ever known previously by their Celtic patronymics, became designated by their lands with the Anglo-Norman prefix of *de*.[1] In the Church in like manner the whole system became altered in a few years, and instead of the humble, unpretending Culdee establishment arose a powerful hierarchy, the members of which came to hold the highest offices in church and state. This change

---

[1] Of these were the family of Douglas who adopted their name from the valley of the Douglas, being in reality " de Douglas." Douglas has been said to mean *black grey;* a strange combination of words. "Glas" is in reality one of the oldest Celtic words for a stream, and appears in Fionnghlas, Conghlas, Glas, all names of streams. Douglas means simply *the black water.*

is that often referred to as the "progress of civilization;" as if civilization consisted in instituting high
offices in the Church, accompanying them with rich
endowments, and filling them with foreigners, while the
native population, who had long bravely defended
their country, and filled the offices in church and state
well, were put aside, and their liberties withheld and
appropriated to the crown. Yet this has been called
the progress of civilization; and outwardly it bore that
aspect, for there was an apparent grandeur in the church
as David left it, and a magnificence around the throne
which had never existed in the case of either before; but,
as has been said more than once, in a few centuries this
grandeur became such an intolerable burden, that the
nation refused to bear it any longer. With this aver-
ment that the changes in the Church and state in the
beginning of the twelfth century were changes in the
direction of civilization, is almost universally associated
the statement referred to frequently, that the ancient
Celtic Church was corrupted and depraved, and that in
consequence there was a loud cry for reformation. It
may not be uninteresting, ere closing this work, to take
a farther view of what the constitution of the Celtic
Church really was, and what were the influences that
served to mould it. In speaking of the ancient Scottish
Church, called by some the Culdee Church, we are not to
suppose that this was merely the Church whose founders
crossed from Ireland, and planted it in Scotland as a
branch of the Church of Ireland. It was in fact the early
Church of the British isles planted before the days of
Ninian or Palladins, and retaining its distinctive features
among the Scots for a longer time than among the other
Celtic races of the country. Hence the fact that Culdees
were not confined to Scotland and Ireland, but were
found among the Britons, their organization being to a

large extent the organization of the early Church of Britain and Ireland. Columba introduced the system among the northern Picts, but it was no new thing in the country ; for in so far as Christianity existed in what is now called Scotland, it was moulded after the same form from the beginning. Ninian and Palladius might have exercised a certain influence on behalf of Rome, but there is every reason to believe that neither of those men had successors in their ecclesiastical offices and commission. Still, before the time of Columba, an influence had crept into the Church which was largely affecting its character and development, and which in the sixth century had unquestionably produced striking changes. This was the influence of asceticism or the eremitical principle, to which reference has been made already. If we are to indicate what gave much of its peculiar character to the early Scottish Church, we would say it was this principle. The principle is a Scriptural one in so far as it simply implies that Christians are to deny themselves to worldly pleasure, and the unrestrained gratification of carnal and sensual desires. The mortifying of the flesh is a Christian duty, more so than perhaps some Christians are willing to remember. But self-denial may be carried the length of self-destruction, and the mortification of the flesh may be carried to the length of extreme carnality, so that the flesh may feed most largely and luxuriantly on what was intended for its destruction. The asceticism of the early Scottish Church did by no means attain to the height of mediæval monkery, but it reached to a development sufficient to give a very peculiar character to the religion of the period. This shewed itself mainly in the system of retirement to lone and distant islands where individual men spent months or years in devotional exercises, having little intercourse with their fellowmen, either for good or evil. From this arose the peculiar use of the words "miserus" and "miserrimus" among these early missionaries. Poverty and self-mortification became the distinguishing marks of a Christian. There was no vow to this effect, but such was the belief of the age, and a more real life of this self-denying character was attained to than in after ages, when the most solemn vows of poverty and self-humiliation covered ungovernable pride and insatiable covetousness. This tendency to asceticism was obviously the moving impulse in much that these men did as missionaries of Christ; they were soldiers and must endure hardship. As the soldiers of a Captain made perfect by sufferings, they too must willingly suffer; and they counted no journey too long or wearisome, no voyage too tedious, however stormy the sea, in the promotion of the cause to which they had devoted their lives. Self-denial and self-devotion were the moving springs of their religious life. Nor were they wrong so far; the Christian life is a warfare, implying much abnegation of self. It may be peace and joy, but it is a peace and a joy associated with a well-fought fight; for faith is a fight as well as an inlet to privilege. Rejoicing Christians are all very well, but they are a deception unless they be contending Christians too ; flowing from his conflicts and his victories through grace, the joy of the believer is one of his most precious privileges. It is true his joy is in Christ, but it is joy in Christ as one who is partaker of all things with Christ—His sufferings as well as His triumphs. It has already been said that the monastic vow of poverty, chastity, and obedience was not taken by these early missionaries, but the ascetic or eremitical spirit gave a tinge to their whole religion. Here lay much of their strength; here, too, lay the source of much of their weakness.

One thing is true, however, these missionaries held their views in perfect sincerity; they believed in truth that they could not err in acting upon those principles of self negation which so largely regulated their religious action; they thought that they could not live too far off from the world in living near to God, and never discerned that in withdrawing from the world they were withdrawing from God too, inasmuch as they were withdrawing from those practical duties to Him and their fellow-men which He was demanding of them; and that while it was clear that they were putting it out of their own power to fulfil the second table of the law, they were at the same time neglecting the more important duties embraced in the first. The early Culdees no doubt rested far on this side of mediæval monkery, but the germ of the whole lay in much of their system. It was however peculiar to the time, and was favoured by the best men who then adorned the church of Christ. It was sufficiently specious to impress them with the thought that it belonged to true religion, like many similar things of both ancient and modern growth, which though like religion and its highest and most spiritual forms, are not of it, and will one day work against it.

Such was manifestly one great influence that gave a tinge and a direction to the early Scottish church. If we look to the close of its existence we will find that another great influence lay at the root of its downfall. Towards the close of the eleventh century, the crusades with the grace and glory promised to accompany the furthering of them, were sounded trumpet-like throughout the whole of Europe. Christendom was moved by the call to arm in so great a cause. In the strength of this great movement Rome made rapid strides towards a power she never possessed before. It was the influence of the

Crusades that raised her up to the highest pinnacle of her earthly glory, a glory won at the expense of oceans of blood, shed in the most miserable of causes, and shed without the least equivalent in return, except to the Roman See ; but Rome gained much, and among other things, the tide having risen in her favour helped to break down the barrier that separated Scotland from the rest of the Christian world, bore down her ancient church, and aided by the convictions and devout ambition of her king served to plant there for the first time Rome's whole organization. Such were two of the influences which largely affected, the one the growth, and the other the downfall of the early Scottish Church.

The early church in Scotland may be said to have consisted of several societies scattered over the face of the country, as circumstances admitted of it. These societies consisted of a body of ecclesiastics, who had devoted themselves to the spread of the gospel, the ascetic in their lives being largely mingled with the practical and the useful. Their great aim was to make known the name of Christ to the ignorant and unbelieving. The president of this body was usually styled the abbot, being an adaptation of the Hebrew Abba, but in the case of the founder he was styled the " Patronus " or Patron. This Abbot was the head of the house, and governed it and all affiliated societies with the consent of his associated brethren. As already observed, one of these brethren is held by many writers to have been a bishop ; such is said to have been the case in Ireland, (Todd's Life of St. Patrick,) but there is nothing to shew that it was so at an early period among the Scottish societies. Some writers are in the habit of arguing on this question, like Innes, from what they hold to be the necessities of the case, a mode of argument very unsatisfactory to inquirers after the truth ; if the arguments of these and of other supporters of this view have any force in them, these bishops received poor treatment from Augustine of Canterbury at an early period, and from David of Scotland when instituting the Roman Hierarchy in the kingdom. That there were functionaries in the church latterly, in Scotland, who were denominated bishops is true ; and some of these were called *Ardescoip,* or as it might be translated " Archbishops," although the word means obviously bishops of more than usual sanctity, (See Dr. Todd's St. Patrick). But we gather from Adomnan and others that they were not essential to the organization of the early Scottish Church. There is not a line in existence of any author deserving of credit, to shew that the ordinary members of the Societies at Iona or elsewhere, were set apart by Episcopal ordination. Indeed, if their bishops were bishops in the modern acceptation of the term, it is impossible to see whence they derived their orders, either through one or more canonically ordained holders of the office. St. Patrick was a Presbyter, so was St. Columba, and they could not confer the orders they did not possess. But unless through the former it is inconceivable whence the Irish bishops derived their orders. That early Scottish bishops had neither diocese nor jurisdiction is now acknowledged by the most learned writers on the early Church in the country, (Dr. Todd's St. Patrick, Introd.,) but in addition to this remarkable defect, there is nothing to shew that they possessed any orders derived from a higher source than that of a Presbyter. And so much does this seem to have been felt when David I. was introducing a regular Episcopate into the kingdom, that all the new bishops of whose ordination we have authentic accounts received that ordination either from the Anglican bishops, or from Rome. No respect seems to have been shewn for the ancient Episcopacy of Scotland. So far as can be inferred from incidental notices in the Annalists, the ancient bishops, as said formerly, would seem to have been in the position of secular clergy throughout the country, without fixed charges or any very distinctly defined jurisdiction, holding office under the government of the Abbot of some one of the Ecclesiastical Societies, and gradually, in the course of years, becoming more prominent and more important, and probably acquiring more power, especially after the alliance between the Pictish Church and that of the Anglo-Saxons in the eighth century, but never acquiring the position or power of the Episcopate as it existed within the limits of the ancient Roman Empire. Judging from the organization of the Irish Church, (See Dr. Todd on St. Bridget, p. 12, St. Pat.) each Society would have had its own bishop, who conferred orders within its *parochia,* but we have no evidence of this in regard to the Scottish Church. We have in the Irish Annals, "Escop Alban" and "Escop Innsegall," but nothing to shew that bishops were bound down to the limits which circumscribed the jurisdiction of Iona or any other of the Culdee establishments. The name, "Episcopi vagantes," applied to them abroad, seems to have been sufficiently descriptive of these bishops in their labours at home.

The organization of the Culdee establishments appears to have been very complete. We have already represented its character to some extent in giving an account of the institution at Iona. These institutions, however, were by no means fixed, and admitted of very considerable changes during their existence, down to the eleventh century. It is sufficiently clear that, previous to their suppression, they had undergone alterations of a very marked kind, as compared with their earlier condition. In one respect they became exposed to peculiar influences arising from their secular relations. The grant of land in the state of society then existing, carried with it other privileges, more especially those of chieftainry, and the heads of the mission colleges, as we may call them, became not only ecclesiastical rulers, but secular chiefs. Strong temptations arose in connection with this arrangement, and it need not be wondered at if the ecclesiastical office came, in many cases, to be sought after for the sake of the secular power associated with it. Nor was the early church free from the practical influence of this temptation, for in too many cases the Abbot, like Crinan of Dunkeld, became almost the secular chief alone, and lost sight of the ecclesiastical office well nigh altogether. The word Comh-arba (Coarb), which means *an heir* or *successor*, admits of being applied to either spiritual or secular succession (see Dr Todd's St Patrick, p. 155), and the comharba of St Patrick at Armagh, or of St Columba at Hi, or of Durrow, was often more of a secular chief than an ecclesiastical office-bearer, although in the case of Iona there is not much in the way of evidence to bear out this statement. But being sufficiently clear with respect to Abernethy and Dunkeld, there is every probability that Iona was no exception to the general practice. Yet the *muinntir* "familia," or indwellers in the Culdee College, appear to have been anxious to make such arrangements as to prevent this secularizing influence. Hence the "Archinneach," or "Erenach,"* who managed the property of the monastery on behalf of the inmates. This officer, if he may be so called, was a layman, who held and managed the lands of the monastery, and received in return for his services one third of the produce. The duties attaching to the office are said (Dr Todd's St Patrick, p. 161) to have

---

* This word has been variously derived. Dr Todd favours the idea that it is formed of " Air," the preposition *on*, and " Ceann " *the head*, and that it thus signifies a *ruler* or *overseer*.

been to superintend the farmers or tenants of the church or monastery, and perhaps also to distribute amongst the poor the alms or hospitality of the co-arb and his "familia." The Erenach was a layman, probably a tenant under the head of the institute, and is understood in some cases to have held his office by hereditary succession.[1] It may be true that the appointment of such an officer was not sufficient to counteract the secularizing influence of wealth and worldly power ; but his existence shewed a desire on the part of these societies to prevent the evil effects of such an influence if possible. A third office in connection with these societies was that of the "Œconomus," or as it is called by the Ulster annalists *Feartighis.* This officer had the management of the affairs of the Society within doors, being to all intents the steward of the house (Todd's St Patrick, p. 166). From his position he wielded a large amount of influence among the brethren, and was at times brought into awkward collision with the other authorities. These three officers, the Co-arb, the Erenach, and the Œconomus, had regard to the secular affairs of the Institution ; the first to the rights of chieftainry, exercised in virtue of possessing land, although the office was usually associated with that of the Abbot or ecclesiastical president ; the second to the management of the lands, and the gathering in of the proceeds ; and the third to the management of the internal affairs of the house, providing food, fuel, clothing, and other necessaries. These offices were not originally part of the constitution of the missionary societies

---

[1] With reference to office being hereditary in the Celtic Church, it must be borne in mind that the principle of hereditary succession ran through the whole Celtic polity. The crown was hereditary, with certain modifications peculiar to the Celts themselves. The bards were hereditary, without much reference to qualification. Physicians were hereditary, it being well known that the Beatons were hereditary physicians to the Lords of the Isles for several centuries.

of the Scottish Church, but grew out of the circumstances which emerged in their history. Adomnan does refer to certain of the brethren who had charge of portions of the domestic arrangements at Iona. We read of the " Pincerna " or *butler*, as it is translated (Reeves' Vit. Col. I. 17); Laisran is called "Hortulanus" or *gardener;* then we find the " Pistor " or *baker*, the baker of the time being Genarus a Saxon (Id. III. 10); but these officers, if they may be so called, were essential in the circumstances of the brethren, and must have existed before the more important and influential offices, to which we have re-ferred, were instituted. In addition to those offices mentioned, we find reference to two others in Scotland, which do not seem to have been known in the Irish Church. These are called Fragramanach and Armanach. A charter of Donald, Lord of the Isles, dated on the 12th July 1390, confers on Lachlan Makgilleone or M'Lean, " officium Fragramanach et Armanach in insula de Hy, cum omnibus libertatibus, commoditatibus, fructibus, et pertinentiis, ad dicta officia spectantibus." *The office of Fragramanach and Armanach, with all the privileges belonging to them.* These offices do not appear in the early annals, and are apparently of a much later date. The words are thought to mean "Responsio monachorum," and " Aratio monachorum " (Reeves' Vit. Col. p. 369), and are thought to refer to certain rights to service which the monastery at Iona possessed. This may be true, for " Ar " is an obsolete Celtic term for *ploughing*, and " Freagradh " is the word still in use for *a reply;* but it would be necessary to find other instances of the use of the words before any certainty could exist with respect to their meaning. The absence of all reference to them by the Irish annalists, and the earlier Scottish authori-ties, would indicate that the offices were exceptional, and not much in use.

Within the early mission institutions at Iona and else-where, and having reference to their peculiar work, several offices are found to have existed. At the head of all stood the abbot, at first the real president of the institution, and chief of all the brethren. In the case of such men as Columba, Columbanus, Gallus, and others, these men were held in the very highest esteem by the other members and their successors. As already shewn, *Sanctus pater*, 'Holy father,' *Patronus noster*, 'our patron,' and such names, were applied to them, while a common title given to them was that of *Vir Dei*, 'man of God.'[1] For several centuries these men continued to exercise their functions as heads of these societies.[2] That the position of the abbot gradually underwent a change in those institutions is undoubted. No contrast could be greater than that between Crinan, the Abbot of Dunkeld, who fell in the field of battle, and the meek and holy Columba, who, whatever he might be in his earlier

---

[1] In attempting to shew that the term Culdee or Keledeus, is derived from *Ceile Dé*, a term which he understands to mean 'men of God,' Dr. Ebrard, in his remarkably able papers on the Culdee Church, quotes the use of the phrase "Vir Dei" by Culdee writers in support of his view. It must be observed, however, that the term "Vir Dei" is only used by those writers as applicable to their abbots or principal men, and is not applied to the Culdee brethren generally. This use of the words is perfectly intelligible without supposing them to stand for Culdee. Besides, the Gaelic word *Céile*, notwithstanding the authorities quoted by Dr. Ebrard, does not mean *man*. The fundamental idea is that of fellowship. Hence it is applied to a spouse, male or female, and is used in forming the adverb *le chéile*, "together" or with his 'fellow.' On this point Dr. Braun, who advocates *Gille Dé*, "Servum Dei," and whom Dr. Ebrard criticises, is nearer the truth than his critic, although neither of them are, in the opinion of the writer, correct. Reference has already been made to the conceits of early writers of Latin, which produced Pictones and Pictavia, and which could with equal facility produce Keledeus. "Cuiltich" is still in use among the Gael. Of "Céile Dé" or "Gille Dé" they know nothing. While making these remarks, however, on this portion of Dr. Ebrard's notices of the Culdee Church, the writer desires to add, that, so far as he can judge, Dr. E.'s general positions are well taken, and defended with remarkable learning and skill.

[2] It has already been said, that among modern Christians the closest resemblance to these early institutions will be found in the Scottish mission establishments in India. To these may be added, as perhaps in some respects having a closer resemblance, the mission institutes of the Moravian brethren.

years, was in Iona the model of a Christian missionary. Wealth had in their case its own temptations, and these were not at all times resisted, but it would be a gross perversion of truth to say that in point of purity the country gained anything by having Romish monasteries substituted for those of the Culdees. The early Benedietines were no doubt men of fervent zeal—a zeal stimulated by the great conflict going on at the time on behalf of the Holy Places in the East ; and their celibacy gave them the appearance of the greatest sanctity ; but the lapse of a few years was sufficient to shew that both liberty and purity of morals were safer in the hands of the ancient Church than in those of the more pretentious and apparently more devout monks of the Church of Rome, notwithstanding all that the writers of that Church have done to represent unfavourably the church which they supplanted. The main charge which has been brought against the Culdee Church is the secularizing of the abbots, and the consequent withdrawal of the property of the Church from ecclesiastical to secular purposes, arising mainly from the hereditary character of the abbot's office ; but it is remarkable that in the Synod held by Queen Margaret, where the faults of the old Church are brought up very fully, and stated without reserve by her biographer, little in the way of substantial charge could be made against its ministers, and this charge was not made at all. But were it true, the evil of secular heads of the ecclesiastical societies might have been remedied without altering the entire structure of the Church. How much worse was the state of things in the Church which succeeded that of the Culdees, when the principal tithes of from fifty to eighty parishes were absorbed by one monastery, while the parishes themselves were altogether neglected, or miserably served with religious ordinances. If the heads of these mission colleges became secularised, however, this arose from a perversion of the original constitution of the Church, and was in entire opposition to the nature and contemplated ends of their office. Constitutionally the abbot was an ecclesiastic, and had nothing to do with secular affairs, except as the well-being of the institution might require of him.

Besides the abbot, several offices appear to have come into existence as the Culdee system developed itself. The Annals of Ulster under 1164, as quoted above, note Mac Gilla Duib as a "Disertach;" the word "disertach" being derived, as already said, from *diseart*, in the same language, and meaning 'the man of the secluded place.' From the earliest period of the Scottish Church it has been seen that the system of retiring to a place of seclusion existed among the brethren, but by degrees it seems to have led to the institution of a distinct office. Whether this office, however, was permanent, is not very clear. It might have been held by the same individual for a long period, or the members of the brotherhood might have taken it by turns, retiring for a period of time from the duties of the monastery to the seclusion and quiet of a hermitage, where ample opportunity might have been enjoyed for prayer and meditation. In Iona, north of the ruins of the cathedral, is a small burying-ground called *Cladh an diseairt*, or the 'Burying-ground of the Hermitage,' while close to it is *Port an diseairt*, or the 'Port of the Hermitage.' Here, judging from the name, a building called a Hermitage existed, and to this, probably, the brother called the "Diseartach" retired for a time. This practice seems to have grown up in the Church, for we have no such term as "diseartach" either in Cuimean Fionn, or Adomnan. The "diseartach," like the "Culdee," is a term of later growth, but the terms in both

2 E

cases appear to have been applied to objects which had existed long before.[1] It has been thought that the Culdees possessed an eremitical order, and there are facts towards the close of their history which would seem to corroborate this. (See Mr. Jos. Robertson's Paper on the Offices in the Scottish Church, in Misc. of Spald. Club, vol. v., p. 73 *n*). But there is nothing to point to its existence in the earlier period of the Church. Scotland is said to have had both hermits and anchorites. Turgot, in his Life of Queen Margaret, tells us, that in Scotland, during her time, there were many men who, shut up in cells, although in the flesh, lived not according to the flesh, passing their lives in remarkable abstinence. That the queen often visited these men, conversing with them and seeking an interest in their prayers ; and that finding it impossible to induce them to accept any of her worldly gifts, she was glad to be asked of them to perform any duty, yielding the readiest obedience to their requests. These men Mr. Robertson seems disposed to look upon as anchorites—a more austere class of recluses than the Culdee hermits. There is not much to support this idea, but if it be true, this class must have arisen at a late period, as neither in the lives of Columba nor in the Irish annalists is there any reference to two classes of " disertaich " or hermits.

[1] Dr. Lanigan and others deny the connection of the Culdees with the Columban Church, and are followed by Dr. Braun, whose essay called forth the articles of Dr. Ebrard. They are disposed to look upon the Culdees as having been a kind of secular canons in the Church, found in Ireland, Scotland, and Wales. Writers in the interest of the Church of Rome have every reason to attempt putting these married ecclesiastics aside as representatives of the ancient Church of Columba. But the strong language of Dr. Lanigan does not serve to constitute historical truth. When he denies that the term " Culdees " is ever applied by Columba's biographers, or by Bede, to the monks of Iona, he states what is perfectly true, but it is not of the slightest value to prove that that name was not applied to them in the tenth century. All that is held on the opposite side is, that the men who came to be called Culdees at a later period, were the real representa. ives of the Columban Church. Nor is there anything opposed to this view in

In the entry for 1164 quoted from the Ulster annals appears
the name of Mac Forcellaig, who is called "cenn na Céile-n
de," *The head of the Culdees.* Let it be borne in mind that
this entry has reference to the election of an Abbot for
the monastery at Iona. Flaithbheartach or Flaherty
O'Brolachan was at the time successor of Columba in Ireland, and the leading men of the Church in the Isles of
Scotland with the consent of Somerled the Lord of Argyle
and the other magnates of the country, proceed to Ireland
to ask O'Brolachan to accept the office. The parties who
formed the deputation were " An sagart mòr" Augustin,
the great priest Augustine, no doubt the leading minister
in that part of Scotland, the " disertach" or *hermit* Mac
gilla duibh, the head of the Culdees Mac Forcellaig, &c.
It is obvious that these, along with the Fear-leighinn,
were the leading men in the church in the absence of the
abbot. There was a priest, a hermit, and the head of the
Culdees. If, as Dr. Lanigan and Dr. Reeves say, the
Culdees had no connection with the Columban order, then
the Iona brethren were not represented at all in this
election,—an arrangement altogether improbable. The
head of the Culdees in this extract can only be understood
as having been the principal man among the brethren in
the absence of the abbot. The earliest notice of the
Keledei or Culdees is in the Annals of Ulster in the year
920. Joceline of Furness, in his life of Kentigern, speaks
of them as " Clerici singulares," et vulgo " Calledei ;" and
Giraldus Cambrensis speaking of those in Bardsey off the
coast of Wales, calls them Cœlibes vel Colidei, both of

the fact, that these men were common to Ireland, Scotland, and Wales. We
could hardly expect otherwise. The Churches of Patrick, Columba, and Kentigern, were so entirely one in their original constitution, that we would naturally expect a similar development and growth among them. If the Culdees
were not the real representatives of the Columban Church, nothing has been
more unsuccessful than the attempts to prove them to have been something
different.

these writers giving us to understand that their name
originated in their celibacy, and yet at the very time they
wrote there were in existence in St. Andrews, Monymusk,
and elsewhere, numerous men who obtained the designation of Culdees, and whose claim to it never was doubted,
who were not celibates, but had wives and families.
Many of the Culdees might have practised celibacy, but
nothing is more at variance with what we know regarding them than the idea that their celibacy gave rise to
their name, when we know that in Scotland at least,
where we find them first, the majority of them did not
practise celibacy at all. As to their being secular canons,
as some writers maintain, it will be possible to give credit
to this view of them when it is shown that at the time the
name comes first into use there were canons as the name
now imports at all in the Scottish Church, or room for them
in its constitution. In the case of Loch Leven we have the
clearest insight into the real character of the ancient
Culdees. They were just the representatives of the original founders of the institution there, and held all the
property attached to it in consequence ; and we learn
sufficient from the treatment received by those Culdees
from David I. and the Bishops of St. Andrews, appointed
by him in connection with the See of Rome, to account
for very much that was written in after times respecting
the character and position of those ministers of the ancient
church. Conquerors are not usually disposed to speak
with much kindness or respect of those whom they have
overcome and dispossessed. It was so between the successful priests of the Roman Hierarchy and the ministers
of the ancient church of the Culdees, whom they had
succeeded in supplanting.

In the extract from the Ulster Annals for 1164, already
quoted, there appears, in addition to the persons mentioned above, " Dubhside am fearleighinn," *Dubhside the*

Reader. This appears to have been one of the brethren connected with the institution at Iona. We have already adverted to the scholarship of the Columban church, shewing how learning was cultivated from the outset. The knowledge of Latin among the brethren has been referred to, and Dr. Ebrard has taken pains to gather, and with considerable success, evidence of their acquaintance with Greek and Hebrew. At an early period the "Scribhneoir" or writer appears in the annals, and evidence exists to this day of the pains taken in cultivating the art of writing. Columba wrote extensively; Baithean was also a dexterous scribe, and the libraries of Oxford, Dublin, and Edinburgh, with those of some continental monasteries, have only to be visited in order to see how tastefully and skilfully both ecclesiastics and medical practitioners among the early Celts committed their thoughts to writing. Gaelic MSS. are in many cases models of caligraphic taste. Latterly the "Scribhneoir" or *writer* became the Fear-leighinn or Reader, a word implying the idea of scholarship generally. Mr. Jos. Robertson (Spald. Club Misc., vol. v., p. 76) identifies this office with that of lecturer at a more recent period, but among the early Celts themselves the word does not seem to have conveyed any idea beyond that of scholarship. In Bishop Carsewell's introduction to his Gaelic translation of John Knox's liturgy, it appears as applicable to ordinary scholars, for he tells us that the study of the Gaelic language was confined to few, including "màcaibh maith leghind," *men of good scholarship*, where the word has no reference to ecclesiastical office. In this passage the interchange of the *mac* and *fear* makes no difference in the meaning. The word is derived from Fear, *a man*, and Leighinn, *reading*, and has reference solely to the scholarship of the person to whom it was applied. Colgan (Trias Thann., pp. 631, 632) tells us that certain men, in the

Church, called *scribnidh* or scribneoir, that is, *scribes* or *writers*, till the middle of the ninth century, were charged with the duty of public reading, of elucidating the history of their own ecclesiastical society, and of writing their annals. That they came afterwards to be called *Fearleighinn*, which means *prælector* or *Scholasticus*. He tells us that in the early period of the Church these *writers* had not only to transcribe ancient monuments, but to teach, and to edit new works. In all likelihood they were originally the teachers connected with the mission societies, for these set up schools in their institutions, and had the work of the school as their special charge. Preaching the gospel and teaching the young was thus the great work to which the early Church devoted itself, and for both these great works ample provision was made.

The " sagart mòr Augustin" appears also in the deputation from Iona to Ireland, to seek an abbot for the monastery. Dr. Reeves (Vit. Col. p. 365 n) observes that such an official existed at Clonmacnois in 1109. The term indicates some distinction in the case of this Augustine, but it is clear that he was not the Abbot of the monastery, for the brethren were at the time in search of an Abbot, nor could he have been the bishop, for the Annals latterly maintain the distinction between the priest and the bishop, as in the case of Maolbrighde Ua Maelfinn, who is styled by the Ulster Annalists, " Priest, Anchorite, and Bishop," (1041). The probability is that this was the leading man among the secular ministers, and that the word " mòr " had reference to what was personal in the case of Augustine, and not to what was official. We have a *Sagart Ruadh* the "red priest," in Scottish ecclesiastical tradition. Why might there not have been a *Sagart Mòr* or " Great priest " too ? At least the term, if indicative of office, indicates merely a kind of leadership among the clergy.

It must never be forgotten that originally the Scottish church was purely a mission church. Its founders had come to preach the gospel very probably without any distinct conception of the kind of ecclesiastical organization that was to follow the adoption of the Christian faith by those whom they came to instruct. The missionaries organised themselves in the form most suitable for the work they had undertaken, leaving it to a wise and gracious providence to care for the future. Hence the missionary form of the church, and hence the extent to which it continued to retain that form in its more mature condition. But wherein did the Scottish church in its early missionary character differ from the primitive church? The very work to which these men had set themselves was that to which the Apostles had devoted their strength—the preaching of the gospel of Jesus Christ. Circumstances might have modified some of their arrangements, but the preaching of the gospel and the conversion of the heathen was the great end which they had in view. It may be said that their system led to much corruption. The same may be said of that of the apostles. Men, corrupt themselves, grafted corruptions on it, but these corruptions were not by any means so gross or so repugnant to the principles originally planted by the Apostles themselves, as were those which human ignorance and human perversity grafted on what was at one time in truth the Catholic Church. If there were corruptions in the Culdee church, Queen Margaret and her sons sought to remedy them by importing from abroad corruptions of a grosser kind which had grown up in a warmer climate, and under the influence of more powerful stimuli. The corruptions of Rome were a most inefficient remedy for the corruptions of Scotland. That the Culdee Church had been gradually adapting itself to the necessities of a national Christianity, is sufficiently obvious.   Ministers were found beyond the walls of the old mission institutes; churches were growing up in addition to the old oratories ; and many of the working clergy were men of mark and of fame.   Their lay abbots and their clanship were a source of weakness, while the marriage of the clergy in an age when an ignorant and superstitious asceticism was growing into wonderful repute, served above all things to pave the way for a system more rigid, and therefore apparently more spiritual.   With all its sources of weakness, the Culdee Church, however, was in the view of the nation superior to that which followed; and if evidence of this is sought for, it will be found in the fact that the revolution which supplanted it was the work of the king, not of the nation ; that while the foreign portion of the population aided him, he received little support from the native Scots or their ministers, and that these continued in after times to cherish the highest esteem for the memory of those men of piety and power who had distinguished their ancient national Church.

Nor has this spirit yet died away.   David might have supplanted the ancient church : he could not eradicate from the minds of the people the principles it had im planted.   It requires but little acquaintance with Scottish history to observe that these never were eradicated ; that during the reign of the Roman Church in the kingdom they continued to exist, exhibiting themselves occasionally in such outbreaks as the letter of King Robert Bruce and his nobles to Pope John, or the uprising of the Lollards of Kyle, and finally culminating in the events of the Scottish Reformation.   Those principles had regard above all things to the independence of the ancient Scottish kingdom, and church.   They exist still fresh and vigorous as ever in the Scottish mind ; nor is it easy to say for how much of what now distinguishes Scotland ecclesiastically, she is indebted to the ancient Culdee Church.

One thing is plain, that, notwithstanding the claims of the Church of Rome and its hierarchical organization to antiquity in Scotland, she can only claim 400 of the 1800 years that have elapsed since the planting of Christianity in the kingdom, viz., the period between 1150, when David established her, and 1550, when his establishment was overturned by the resuscitation of old Scottish principles at the Reformation.

THE END.

INDEX.

Books for the Library of Clergymen and Educated Laymen.

CLARK'S FOREIGN THEOLOGICAL LIBRARY.

ANNUAL SUBSCRIPTION, ONE GUINEA (PAYABLE IN ADVANCE), FOR WHICH FOUR VOLUMES, DEMY 8vo, ARE DELIVERED.

EXTRACT FROM FRASER'S MAGAZINE.

'There is clearly an awakened interest in the New Testament throughout the country : our village Chrysostoms are beginning to read Clark's translations of Olshausen ; our urban and suburban pastors are beginning to find out that there are fresher waters than Barnes can minister.' . . . 'Are you sincere and reflective? You have got the very Commentary you need in Olshausen,—the very exposition of a vital part of the Gospels which you are dimly craving for, in Rudolph Stier ; both of which are at your hands in a readable English version. You will rise from the perusal of either a wiser and a better man.'

The following are the Contents of each of the Series. Each Work may be had separately at the price within parentheses.

*** A Selection of Twelve Volumes from First Series will be supplied at the Subscription Price of Three Guineas ; or Twenty Volumes from First and Second Series at the Subscription Price of Five Guineas (or a larger number at same ratio).

FIRST SERIES.

Twenty-nine Vols. Subscription price, L.7, 12s. 6d.

Hengstenberg's Commentary on the Psalms. 3 Vols. (L.I, 13s.)

Hagenbach's Compendium of the History of Doctrines. 2 Vols. (L.I, 1s.)

Gieseler's Compendium of Ecclesiastical History. 5 Vols. (L.2, 12s. 6d.)

Neander's General Church History. 9 Vols. (L.2, 11s. 6d.)

Olshausen on the Gospels and Acts. 4 Vols. (L.2, 2s.)

Olshausen on the Romans. (10s. 6d.)

Olshausen on the Corinthians. (9s.)

Olshausen on the Galatians, Ephesians, Colossians, and Thessalonians. (10s. 6d.)

Olshausen on Philippians, Titus, and Timothy. (10s. 6d)

Olshausen and Ebrard on the Hebrews. (10s. 6d.)

Havernick's General Introduction to the Old Testament. (10s. 6d.)

SECOND SERIES.

Twenty Vols. Subscription price, L.5, 5s.

Stier on the Words of the Lord Jesus. 8 Vols. (L.4, 4s.)

Hengstenberg's Christology of the Old Testament. 4 Vols. (L 2, 2s.)

Ullmann's Reformers before the Reformation. 2 Vols. (L.1, 1s.)

Keil on Joshua. 1 Vol. (10s. 6d.)

Keil on Kings and Chronicles. 2 Vols (L.1, 1s.)

Baumgarten's Apostolic History. 3 Vols (L.1, 7s.)

THIRD SERIES.

Twenty-four Vols. (1859–60–61–62–63–64). Subscription price, L.6, 6s.

N.B.—A single Year's Books (except in the case of the current Year) cannot be supplied separately. Non-subscribers, price 10s. 6d. each Vol., with exceptions marked.

*** No Selection allowed from this Series. The following is the order of Publication but any Two Years or more can be had at Subscription price :—

1st Year (1859).
Kurtz on Old Covenant Dispensation, 3 Vols. Stier on the Risen Saviour, etc., 1 Vol.

2d Year (1860).
Hengstenberg on Ecclesiastes, 1 Vol. (9s.) Tholuck on St John, 1 Vol. (9s.) Tholuck's Sermon on the Mount, 1 Vol. Ebrard on Epistles of John, 1 Vol.

3d Year (1861).
Lange on St Matthew's Gospel, Vols. I. and II. Dorner on Person of Christ. Div. I., Vol. I. ; and Div. IL, Vol. I.

4th Year (1862).
Dorner on Person of Christ, Div. I., Vol. II Dorner on Person of Christ, Div. II., Vol. II Lange on Matthew and Mark, Vol. III. Oosterzee on St Luke. Edited by Dr Lange Vol. I. (9s.)

5th Year (1863).
Oosterzee on St Luke. Edited by Dr Lange Vol. II. (Completion.) (9s.) Dorner on Person of Christ, Div. II., Vol. III Kurtz on the Old Testament Sacrifices. Ebrard's Gospel History.

6th Year (1864).
Lange, Commentary on the Acts of the Apostles, 2 Vols.
Keil and Delitzsch, Commentary on the Pentateuch, Vols. I. and II.

Subscribers' Names received by all Booksellers.

For Lange's LIFE OF CHRIST, see separate Prospectus.

EDINBURGH : T. AND T. CLARK.

LONDON (for Non-subscribers only) : HAMILTON, ADAMS, AND Co.

JOHN ALBERT BENGEL'S

GNOMON OF THE NEW TESTAMENT

Now First Translated into English.

WITH ORIGINAL NOTES, EXPLANATORY AND ILLUSTRATIVE.

The Translation is comprised in Five Large Volumes, Demy 8vo, of (on an average) fully 550 pages each.

SUBSCRIPTION, 31s. 6d., *or free by Post* 35s.

The very large demand for Bengel's Gnomon enables the Publishers still to supply it at the Subscription Price.

The whole work is issued under the Editorship of the Rev. ANDREW R. FAUSSET, M.A., Rector of St Cuthbert's, York, late University and Queen's Scholar, and Senior Classical and Gold Medalist, T.C.D.

'There are few devout students of the Bible who have not long held Bengel in the highest estimation, nay, revered and loved him. It was not, however, without some apprehension for his reputation with English readers that we saw the announcement of a translation of his work. We feared that his sentences, terse and condensed as they are, would necessarily lose much of their pointedness and force by being clothed in another garb. But we confess, gladly, to a surprise at the success the translators have achieved in preserving so much of the spirit of the original. We are bound to say that it is executed in the most scholarlike and able manner. The translation has the merit of being faithful and perspicuous. Its publication will, we are confident, do much to bring back readers to the *devout* study of the Bible, and at the same time prove one of the most valuable of exegetical aids. The "getting up" of those volumes, combined with their marvellous cheapness, cannot fail, we should hope, to command for them a large sale.'—*Eclectic Review.*

CHEAP RE-ISSUE

OF THE WHOLE

WORKS OF DR JOHN OWEN

Edited by Rev. W. H. GOOLD, D.D., Edinburgh

WITH LIFE BY REV. ANDREW THOMSON, D.D.

In 24 Volumes, demy 8vo, handsomely bound in cloth, lettered.

With Two Portraits of Dr Owen.

Several years have now elapsed since the first publication of this Edition of the Works of the greatest of Puritan Divines. Time has tested its merits; and it is now admitted, on all hands, to be the only correct and complete edition.

At the time of publication it was considered—as it really was—a miracle of cheapness, having been issued, by Subscription, for Five Guineas.

In consequence of the abolition of the Paper Duty, the Publishers now Re-issue the Twenty-four Volumes for

FOUR GUINEAS.

As there are above Fourteen Thousand Pages in all, each Volume therefore averages *Five Hundred and Ninety Pages.*

'You will find that in John Owen the learning of Lightfoot, the strength of Charnock, the analysis of Howe, the savour of Leighton, the raciness of Heywood, the glow of Baxter, the copiousness of Barrow, the splendour of Bates, are all combined. We should quickly restore the age of great divines if our candidates were disciplined in such lore.'—*The late Dr Hamilton of Leeds.*

WORKS OF JOHN CALVIN,

IN 51 VOLUMES, DEMY 8vo.

MESSRS CLARK beg respectfully to announce that the whole STOCK and COPYRIGHTS of the WORKS OF CALVIN, published by the Calvin Translation Society, are now their property, and that this valuable Series will be issued by them on the following very favourable terms.

1. Complete Sets in 51 Volumes, Nine Guineas. (Original Subscription price about L.13.) The 'LETTERS,' edited by Dr BONNET, 2 vols., 10s. 6d. additional.
2. Complete Sets of Commentaries, 45 vols., L.7, 17s. 6d.
3. A *Selection* of Six Volumes (or more at the same proportion), for 21s., with the exception of the Institutes, 3 vols.
4. Any Separate Volume (except INSTITUTES), 6s.

THE CONTENTS OF THE SERIES ARE AS FOLLOW:—

Institutes of the Christian Religion, 3 vols.; Tracts on the Reformation, 3 vols.; Commentary on Genesis, 2 vols.; Harmony of the last Four Books of the Pentateuch, 4 vols.; Commentary on Joshua, 1 vol.; the Psalms, 5 vols.; Isaiah, 4 vols.; Jeremiah and Lamentations, 5 vols.; Ezekiel, 2 vols.; Daniel, 2 vols.; Hosea, 1 vol.; Joel, Amos, and Obadiah, 1 vol.; Jonah, Micah, and Nahum, 1 vol.; Habakkuk, Zephaniah, and Haggai, 1 vol.; Zechariah and Malachi, 1 vol.; Harmony of the Synoptical Evangelists, 3 vols.; Commentary on John's Gospel, 2 vols.; Acts of the Apostles, 2 vols.; Romans, 1 vol.; Corinthians, 2 vols.; Galatians and Ephesians, 1 vol.; Philippians, Colossians, and Thessalonians, 1 vol.; Timothy, Titus, and Philemon, 1 vol.; Hebrews, 1 vol.; Peter, John, James, and Jude, 1 vol.

In two volumes, 8vo, price 14s. (1300 pages),

THE INSTITUTES OF THE CHRISTIAN RELIGION.

By JOHN CALVIN.

Translated by HENRY BEVERIDGE.

THIS translation of Calvin's Institutes was originally executed for the 'Calvin Translation Society,' and is universally acknowledged to be the best English version of the work. The Publishers have reprinted it in an elegant form, and have, at the same time, fixed a price so low as to bring it within the reach of all.

In one volume, 8vo, price 8s. 6d.,

CALVIN:

HIS LIFE, LABOURS, AND WRITINGS.

By FELIX BUNGENER,

AUTHOR OF THE 'HISTORY OF THE COUNCIL OF TRENT,' ETC., ETC.

'M. Bungener's French vivacity has admirably combined with critical care and with admiring reverence, to furnish what we venture to think the best portrait of Calvin hitherto drawn. He tells us all that we need to know, and, instead of overlaying his work with minute details and needless disquisitions, he simply presents the disencumbered features, and preserves the true proportions of the great Reformer's character. We heartily commend the work.'—*Patriot.*

'Few will sit down to this volume without resolving to read it to the close.'—*Clerical Journal.*

In demy 8vo, price 10s. 6d.,

THE EARLY SCOTTISH CHURCH:
THE ECCLESIASTICAL HISTORY OF SCOTLAND FROM THE FIRST TO THE MIDDLE OF THE TWELFTH CENTURY.

By the Rev. THOMAS M'LAUCHLAN, M.A., F.S.A.S., Edinburgh.

THE purpose of this work is to trace the Early Planting of Christianity in Scotland, carrying it down to the period of the final establishment of Diocesan Episcopacy by David I. Sketches are given of the contemporaneous Civil History of the Kingdom, and Biographical Notices of the more distinguished of the early Missionaries, in so far as materials for such a purpose exist. The organization and practice of the early Celtic Church is made the subject of full and, it is hoped, impartial discussion. The work is intended to fill a void which has hitherto existed in the early history of Scotland.

Chapter I. The Roman Power in Scotland; II. and III. The Native Inhabitants during the Roman Occupation; IV. Religion during the Roman Period ; V. Christianity under the Roman Government; VI. The Period succeeding the Roman Occupation; VII. The Mission of Ninian; VIII. The Mission of Palladius to the Scots; IX. The Mission of St Patrick; X. Servanus, Ternan, and Kentigern; XI. The Civil History of Scotland during the Sixth Century; XII. The Mission of Columba; XIII. The Institution at Iona ; XIV. The Doctrine and Discipline of Iona; XV. The Death of Columba—His Contemporaries; XVI. Events succeeding the Death of Columba; XVII. The Mission of Aidan, etc. ; XVIII. The Controversy regarding Easter and the Tonsure; XIX. The Events of the Eighth Century ; XX. The Events of the Ninth Century ; XXI. The Events of the Tenth Century ; XXII. The Events of the Eleventh Century; XXIII. The Events of the first half of the Twelfth Century— Dioceses of Orkney, Caithness, Ross, Moray, Aberdeen, and Brechin; XXIV. The first half of the Twelfth Century—the Diocese of St Andrews; XXV. The Closing History of the Early Church.

In two volumes, demy 8vo, price 21s.,

A HISTORY OF CHRISTIAN DOCTRINE.
By WILLIAM G. J. SHEDD, D.D.,
PROFESSOR OF THEOLOGY IN UNION COLLEGE, NEW YORK.

Book I. Influence of Philosophical Systems upon the Construction of Christian Doctrine ; Book II. History of Apologies; Book III. History of Theology (Trinitarianism) and Christology; Book IV. History of Anthropology ; Book V. History of Soteriology ; Book VI. History of Eschatology ; Book VII. History of Symbols.

In demy 8vo, price 9s.,

GERMAN RATIONALISM:
IN ITS RISE, PROGRESS, AND DECLINE. A CONTRIBUTION TO THE CHURCH HISTORY OF THE 18TH AND 19TH CENTURIES.

By Dr K. HAGENBACH.

I. Characteristics of the 18th Century ; II. A Brief Survey of the Rise of Rationalism in Germany; III. Life and Manners in Germany, 1700-1750 ; IV. Pietism and its Opponents ; V. The Pioneers of Rationalism; VI. Frederick the Great and his Age ; VII. Theological Science, including Biblical Criticism, 1700-50 ; VIII. Lessing ; IX. Infidelity carried to its furthest issue; X. Thoroughgoing Protests against Infidelity ; XI. Half-way Rationalism; XII. Zinzendorf; XIII. Swedenborg, Stilling, Lavater, etc. ; XIV. Herder ; XV. Kant ; XVI. Schiller; XVII. Salzmann, Campe, Pestalozzi. Hamann, and Claudius; XVIII. Schelling ; XIX. Jacobi ; XX. Fichte ; XXI. Richter, Goethe, and Novalis; XXII. Schleiermacher ; XXIII. Hegel and his Successors ; XXIV. Rise of the Protestant Spirit in the Roman Catholic Church during the 18th and 19th Centuries.

WORKS BY THE LATE WILLIAM CUNNINGHAM, D.D.,

PRINCIPAL AND PROFESSOR OF CHURCH HISTORY, NEW COLLEGE, EDINBURGH.

In two vols. demy 8vo, price 21s., Second Edition,

HISTORICAL THEOLOGY:

A REVIEW OF THE PRINCIPAL DOCTRINAL DISCUSSIONS IN THE
CHRISTIAN CHURCH SINCE THE APOSTOLIC AGE.

Chapter 1. The Church; 2. The Council of Jerusalem; 3. The Apostles' Creed; 4. The
Apostolical Fathers; 5. Heresies of the Apostolical Age; 6. The Fathers of the
Second and Third Centuries; 7. The Church of the Second and Third Centuries;
8. The Constitution of the Church; 9. The Doctrine of the Trinity; 10. The Person
of Christ; 11. The Pelagian Controversy; 12. Worship of Saints and Images;
13. The Civil and Ecclesiastical Authorities; 14. The Scholastic Theology; 15. The
Canon Law; 16. Witnesses for the Truth during Middle Ages; 17. The Church
at the Reformation; 18. The Council of Trent; 19. The Doctrine of the Fall;
20. Doctrine of the Will; 21. Justification; 22. The Sacramental Principle; 23. The
Socinian Controversy; 24. Doctrine of the Atonement; 25. The Arminian Controversy; 26. Church Government; 27. The Erastian Controversy.

In demy 8vo (624 pages), price 10s. 6d.,

THE REFORMERS AND THE THEOLOGY OF THE REFORMATION.

Chapter 1. Leaders of the Reformation; 2. Luther; 3. The Reformers and the Doctrine
of Assurance; 4. Melancthon and the Theology of the Church of England; 5. Zwingle
and the Doctrine of the Sacraments; 6. John Calvin; 7. Calvin and Beza; 8. Calvinism and Arminianism; 9. Calvinism and the Doctrine of Philosophical Necessity;
10. Calvinism and its Practical Application; 11. The Reformers and the Lessons
from their History.

'This volume is a most magnificent vindication of the Reformation, in both its men
and its doctrines, suited to the present time and to the present state of the controversy.'
—*Witness.*

In one vol. demy 8vo, price 10s. 6d.,

DISCUSSIONS ON CHURCH PRINCIPLES:

POPISH, ERASTIAN, AND PRESBYTERIAN.

Chapter 1. The Errors of Romanism; 2. Romanist Theory of Development; 3. The
Temporal Sovereignty of the Pope; 4. The Temporal Supremacy of the Pope; 5. The
Liberties of the Gallican Church; 6. Royal Supremacy in Church of England;
Relation between Church and State; 8. The Westminster Confession on Relation
between Church and State; 9. Church Power; 10. Principles of the Free Church;
11. The Rights of the Christian People; 12. The Principle of Non-Intrusion;
13. Patronage and Popular Election.

In the Press. In demy 8vo,

INSPIRATION:

THE INFALLIBLE TRUTH, AND DIVINE AUTHORITY OF SCRIPTURE.

By JAMES BANNERMAN, D.D.,

PROFESSOR OF THEOLOGY, NEW COLLEGE, EDINBURGH.

WORKS OF PATRICK FAIRBAIRN, D.D.,

PRINCIPAL AND PROFESSOR OF THEOLOGY IN THE FREE CHURCH COLLEGE, GLASGOW.

———

In two volumes, demy 8vo, price 21s., Fourth Edition,

THE TYPOLOGY OF SCRIPTURE,

VIEWED IN CONNECTION WITH THE WHOLE SERIES OF THE DIVINE DISPENSATIONS.

' I now say, no Biblical student should be without Professor Fairbairn's Typology.'—
Dr S. Lee, in his 'Events and Times of the Visions of Daniel.'
' As the product of the labours of an original thinker, and of a sound theologian, who
has at the same time scarcely left unexamined one previous writer on the subject, ancient
or modern, this work will be a most valuable accession to the library of the theological
student. As a whole, we believe it may, with the strictest truth, be pronounced the best
work on the subject that has yet been published.'—*Record.*
' A work fresh and comprehensive, learned and sensible, and full of practical religious
feeling.'—*British and Foreign Evangelical Review.*

———

In demy octavo, price 10s. 6d., Third Edition, :

EZEKIEL, AND THE BOOK OF HIS PROPHECY,

AN EXPOSITION; WITH A NEW TRANSLATION.

———

In demy octavo, price 10s. 6d., Second Edition,

PROPHECY,

VIEWED IN ITS DISTINCTIVE NATURE; ITS SPECIAL FUNCTIONS AND PROPER INTERPRETATION.

' Its completeness, its clearness, its thorough investigation of the whole subject in a
systematic way, will render it, I think, the standard work on prophecy from this time.'—
Rev. Dr Candlish.

———

In demy octavo, price 10s. 6d.,

HERMENEUTICAL MANUAL;

OR, INTRODUCTION TO THE EXEGETICAL STUDY OF THE SCRIPTURES
OF THE NEW TESTAMENT.

PART I. Discussion of Facts and Principles bearing on the Language and Interpretation
of the New Testament.
PART II. Dissertations on particular subjects connected with the Exegesis of the New
Testament.
PART III. On the Use made of Old Testament Scripture in the Writings of the New
Testament.

' Dr Fairbairn has precisely the training which would enable him to give a fresh and
suggestive book on Hermeneutics. Without going into any tedious detail, it presents the
points that are important to a student. There is a breadth of view, a clearness and
manliness of thought, and a ripeness of learning, which make the work one of peculiar
freshness and interest. I consider it a very valuable addition to every student's library.'
—*Rev. Dr Moore, Author of the able Commentary on 'The Prophets of the Restoration.'*

Printed in Great Britain
by Amazon